MISTREATMENT IN ORGANIZATIONS

RESEARCH IN OCCUPATIONAL STRESS AND WELL BEING

Series Editors: Pamela L. Perrewé,
Jonathon R. B. Halbesleben and
Christopher C. Rosen

Recent Volumes:

RESEARCH IN OCCUPATIONAL STRESS AND
WELL BEING VOLUME 13

MISTREATMENT IN ORGANIZATIONS

EDITED BY

PAMELA L. PERREWÉ
Florida State University, USA

JONATHON R. B. HALBESLEBEN
University of Alabama, USA

CHRISTOPHER C. ROSEN
University of Arkansas, USA

United Kingdom – North America – Japan
India – Malaysia – China

Emerald Group Publishing Limited
Howard House, Wagon Lane, Bingley BD16 1WA, UK

First edition 2015

British Library Cataloguing in Publication Data
A catalogue record for this book is available from the British Library

ISBN: 978-1-78560-117-0
ISSN: 1479-3555 (Series)

CONTENTS

LIST OF CONTRIBUTORS

Contributing Editors

Pamela L. Perrewé	The Haywood and Betty Taylor Eminent Scholar of Business Administration, College of Business, Florida State University, Tallahassee, FL, USA
Jonathon R. B. Halbesleben	Department of Management, Culverhouse College of Commerce, University of Alabama, Tuscaloosa, AL, USA
Christopher C. Rosen	Department of Management, Sam M. Walton College of Business, University of Arkansas, Fayetteville, AR, USA

Contributing Authors

Maureen L. Ambrose	Management Department, University of Central Florida, Orlando, FL, USA
Caitlin E. Blackmore	Department of Psychology, Wright State University, Dayton, OH, USA
Nathan A. Bowling	Department of Psychology, Wright State University, Dayton, OH, USA
Kelly A. Camus	Department of Psychology, Wright State University, Dayton, OH, USA
Chu-Hsiang (Daisy) Chang	Department of Psychology, Michigan State University, East Lansing, MI, USA
Aurora J. Dixon	Department of Psychology, Michigan State University, East Lansing, MI, USA
Michelle K. Duffy	Carlson School of Management, University of Minnesota, Minneapolis, MN, USA

Stephanie Gumuchian Lady Davis Institute for Medical Research of the Jewish General Hospital, Montreal, Quebec, Canada

Jonathon R. B. Halbesleben Department of Management, Culverhouse College of Commerce, University of Alabama, Tuscaloosa, AL, USA

Ronald L. Hess Jr School of Business Administration, The College of William & Mary, Williamsburg, VA, USA

Russell E. Johnson Department of Management, Michigan State University, East Lansing, MI, USA

Jaclyn Koopmann Department of Management, University of Florida, Gainesville, FL, USA

Michael P. Leiter Centre for Organizational Research & Development, Acadia University, Wolfville, Nova Scotia, Canada

Matthew R. Leon Culverhouse College of Commerce, University of Alabama, Tuscaloosa, AL, USA

Yihao Liu Department of Management, University of Florida, Gainesville, FL, USA

Emily Peck Centre for Organizational Research and Development, Acadia University, Wolfville, Nova Scotia, Canada

Shani Pindek Department of Psychology, University of South Florida, Tampa, FL, USA

Kristin L. Scott College of Business and Behavioral Science, Clemson University, Clemson, SC, USA

Yifan Song Department of Management, University of Florida, Gainesville, FL, USA

Paul E. Spector Department of Psychology, University of South Florida, Tampa, FL, USA

Regina Taylor	Heider College of Business, Creighton University, Omaha, NE, USA
Mo Wang	Department of Management, University of Florida, Gainesville, FL, USA

EDITORIAL ADVISORY BOARD

OVERVIEW

In our 13th volume of *Research in Occupational Stress and Well Being*, we offer eight chapters that examine mistreatment in organizations. The first two chapters consider the role of customer mistreatment in organizations. In our lead chapter "Can I Help You? Employee Prosocial Rule Breaking as a Response to Organizational Mistreatment of Customers," Maureen L. Ambrose, Regina Taylor, and Ronald L. Hess Jr examine prosocial rule breaking in response to the organizational unfair treatment of its customers. They argue that engaging in customer-directed prosocial rule breaking may be a very likely response when employee believe their organizations' policies treat the customers unfairly. In the chapter "Customer Mistreatment: A Review of Conceptualizations and a Multilevel Theoretical Model," Jaclyn Koopmann, Mo Wang, Yihao Liu, and Yifan Song develop a conceptual and multilevel theoretical model of customer mistreatment. In their theoretical development, they consider both antecedents and outcomes as well as moderators and mediators that are specific to each level of analysis of customer mistreatment.

The next four chapters of this volume examine a variety of forms of organizational mistreatment. In the chapter "Aggression with a Conscience: A Rational and Moral Framework for Proactive Workplace Aggression," Aurora J. Dixon, Chu-Hsiang (Daisy) Chang, and Russell E. Johnson develop a model focusing on the motivations underlying proactive workplace aggression. Further, they identify situations (e.g., in-group versus out-group, status) in which perpetrators may consider their aggressive behavior as morally justifiable. In the chapter "Workplace Incivility and Its Implications for Well-Being," Michael P. Leiter, Emily Peck, and Stephanie Gumuchian, identify workplace incivility as a specific form of social mistreatment. The negative consequences of workplace incivility are examined as well as a discussion of intervention research. In the chapter "Antecedents of Workplace Ostracism: New Directions in Research and Intervention," Kristin L. Scott and Michelle K. Duffy examine workplace ostracism. Under the lens of evolutionary psychology, they argue that individuals who contribute to social and organizational goals are valued while those who threaten the group stability are shunned or ostracized.

In the final chapter of this section "Coworker Responses to Observed Mistreatment: Understanding Schadenfreude in the Response to Supervisor Abuse," Matthew R. Leon and Jonathon R. B. Halbesleben examine the construct of Schadenfreude. Using an attribution theory framework, they argue that the attribution made regarding supervisor abuse directed at a coworker may lead employees to feel that the abuse is justified, thus, the employees experience pleasure in witnessing another's pain.

The final section of this volume includes two chapters examining contextual, conceptual, and measurement issues surrounding organizational mistreatment. Shani Pindek and Paul E. Spector in their chapter "Contextual Factors in Employee Mistreatment" examine the contextual factors in employee mistreatment. They differentiate between the objective environment and perceptions of employees and develop a general framework for examining contextual factors in employee mistreatment. The final chapter "Conceptualizing and Measuring Workplace Abuse: Implications for the Study of Abuse's Predictors and Consequences," by Nathan A. Bowling, Kelly A. Camus, and Caitlin E. Blackmore, examines issues of conceptualization and measurement regarding workplace abuse. These authors suggest that problems with the conceptualization as well as the measurement of workplace abuse have slowed scientific research and inquiry.

Together, these experts in the field offer insights into the role of organizational mistreatment in occupational stress and well-being research. These chapters improve upon our current thinking and offer several exciting directions for future research. We hope you enjoy Volume 13 of *Research in Occupational Stress and Well Being*.

Pamela L. Perrewé
Jonathon R. B. Halbesleben
Christopher C. Rosen
Editors

CAN I HELP YOU? EMPLOYEE PROSOCIAL RULE BREAKING AS A RESPONSE TO ORGANIZATIONAL MISTREATMENT OF CUSTOMERS

Maureen L. Ambrose, Regina Taylor and Ronald L. Hess Jr

ABSTRACT

In this chapter, we examine employee prosocial rule breaking as a response to organizations' unfair treatment of customers. Drawing on the deontic perspective and research on third-party reactions to unfairness, we suggest employees engage in customer-directed prosocial rule breaking when they believe their organizations' policies treat customers unfairly. Additionally, we consider employee, customer, and situational characteristics that enhance or inhibit the relationship between employees' perceptions of organizational policy unfairness and customer-directed prosocial rule breaking.

Keywords: Prosocial rule breaking; customer mistreatment; organizational unfairness; justice; climate; organizational mistreatment

Mistreatment in Organizations
Research in Occupational Stress and Well Being, Volume 13, 1–31

ISSN: 1479-3555/doi:10.1108/S1479-355520150000013001

In the last decade, there has been increased interest in the antecedents and consequences of mistreatment in organizations. This research has focused primarily on employees' reactions to mistreatment by supervisors (Hoobler & Brass, 2006; Mawritz, Dust, & Resick, 2014; Mitchell & Ambrose, 2007; Tepper, 2000, 2007), peers (Duffy, Ganster, & Pagon, 2002; Milam, Spitzmueller, & Penney, 2009; Treadway, Shaughnessy, Breland, Yang, & Reeves, 2013), and customers (Shao & Skarlicki, 2014; Skarlicki, van Jaarsveld, & Walker, 2008; Sliter, Sliter, & Jex, 2012). This victim-focused research finds a broad range of negative psychological and physical effects associated with mistreatment including lower levels of job satisfaction and commitment, increased deviance behavior, decreased psychological well-being, and increased physical ailments (Hershcovis & Barling, 2010; Hershcovis et al., 2007; Yang, Caughlin, Gazica, Truxillo, & Spector, 2014).

Our focus differs from previous research in two ways. First, although the focus on the reactions of the victim has provided substantial insight about the causes and consequences of mistreatment in organizations, researchers have noted mistreatment and unfairness do not occur in dyadic isolation. Rather, other individuals may observe and be affected by the mistreatment episode. Recently, researchers have broadened their focus on mistreatment to consider observer reactions. We take this approach and focus on observer responses to mistreatment.

Second, although management research has considered the influence of customers on employee attitudes and behavior, this research has typically focused on employee responses to the demands of working with customers (e.g., emotional labor (Grandey, 2003), customer mistreatment of employees (Shao & Skarlicki, 2014; Skarlicki et al., 2008; Sliter et al., 2012)). We consider how employees might respond to the unfair treatment *of* customers. That is, we are interested in employees as "observers" of the relationship between the organization and its customers. Specifically, we explore employee customer-directed prosocial rule breaking (PSRB) as a reaction to the (un)fairness of organizational policies toward customers.

We suggest employees are not dispassionate agents of the organization. They do not always follow prescribed rules and procedures. Rather, employees may serve as unofficial arbitrators, evaluating and responding to the fairness of the organization's treatment of its customers. When faced with policies and procedures they believe treat customers unfairly, they may deliver their own form of "vigilante" justice – breaking organizational rules in an effort to assure customers are treated fairly. For example, retail employees may grant extensions to customers requesting product returns that are a few days beyond the 30-day return policy. Similarly, bank employees may waive certain bank fees they believe unfairly penalize customers. In this chapter, we apply the deontic model of justice (Cropanzano, Goldman, & Folger, 2005; Folger, 1998, 2001) and cast employees in the role of observers of injustice. We then identify factors that may influence customer-directed prosocial rule breaking when employees perceive organizational policies toward customers are unfair.

Conceptualizing customer-directed PSRB as a response to perceived unfairness can provide insights for research both on PSRB and on third-party reactions to justice. For PSRB, previous research has not considered the factors that evoke this rule-breaking behavior. Integrating previous PSRB research with research on justice provides insight not only about the causes of PSRB but also the individual and situational characteristics that enhance or inhibit the behavior. Additionally, research on third-party justice has focused primarily on third-party's motivation to punish the transgressor. Little research has considered the conditions that motivate victim-directed responses. Our model identifies both individual and situational characteristics that may foster compensatory – rather than retaliatory – reactions to observed injustice.

We begin with a review of research on PSRB and management research on employee–customer interactions. Then, we briefly review research on third-party reactions to unfairness. Finally, we develop a model of customer-directed PSRB that considers how employee, customer, and organizational characteristics may influence the relationship between employees' perceptions of unfair customer policies and customer-directed PSRB.

PROSOCIAL RULE BREAKING

Morrison (2006) introduced the construct of PSRB. Morrison notes that, while rule breaking is generally conceptualized as a negatively deviant behavior, employees may also break rules for positive, prosocial reasons. Morrison suggested employees might engage in rule breaking because they desired to perform the job in an "effective, responsible, and responsive manner" (p. 9) and they feel it is necessary to break organizational rules in order to do so. Morrison defined PSRB as "any instance where an employee intentionally violates a formal organizational policy, regulation, or prohibition with the primary intention of promoting the welfare of the organization or one of its stakeholders" (p. 6). Thus, Morrison viewed rule breaking as stemming not from a desire to harm the organization but from a desire to help.

In her initial study of PSRB, Morrison identified three forms of PSRB: rule breaking to facilitate work performance, rule breaking to help another member of the organization, and rule breaking to provide good customer service. Morrison reports three studies that utilized a mixture of methodological approaches. In the first two, Morrison focused on providing evidence of the existence of PSRB. Results from phone interviews with 24 individuals in a broad range of jobs (Study 1) and face-to-face interviews with 79 individuals (Study 2), demonstrated most individuals report engaging in PSRB. In Study 3, Morrison sought to provide greater understanding about the antecedents of PSRB. She examined six factors that might predict PSRB behavior: job meaning, job autonomy, empathy, proactive personality, risk-taking propensity, and coworker rule-breaking behavior. Morrison found employees' likelihood of engaging in PSRB was influenced by their job autonomy, the behavior of their coworkers, and their propensity for risk-taking.

Only two other studies have empirically examined PSRB. Dahling, Chau, Mayer, and Gregory (2012) suggested that research on PSRB would be advanced by the development of a generalized measure of PSRB. Thus, Dahling et al. developed and validated such a measure. In addition, in exploring the nomological network for PSRB, they examined conscientiousness, job demands, coworker behavior, and counterproductive work behavior (CWB) as correlates of PSRB. They found conscientiousness was negatively correlated with PSRB, whereas coworker behavior and CWB were positively correlated. There was no significant relationship between PSRB and job demands when correlations among the latent constructs were examined. However, for the manifest variables, job demands were significantly positively related to PSRB. Thus, these results demonstrate relationships between employee characteristics (conscientiousness) and situational characteristics (coworker behavior, job demands) and employees' PSRB.

Dahling et al. (2012) also examined the relationship between PSRB and task performance and organizational citizenship behavior directed toward individuals (OCBI). They found PSRB was negatively related to both coworker and supervisor ratings of the employee's task performance. Additionally, PSRB was not significantly related to either supervisor or coworker ratings of OCBI. Notably, their results suggest that, although actors report engaging in PSRB for positive reasons, observers – at least those within the organization – may not see positive benefits to the rule-breaking behavior.

The second study to empirically examine PSRB, explored the relationship between transformational leadership, autonomy, and PSRB (Huang, Xixi, & Xi, 2014). Huang et al. suggest transformational leaders encourage their subordinates PSRB by encouraging both prosocial behavior and innovative behavior. Transformational leaders encourage subordinates to think beyond the confines of the status quo, which could manifest itself in PSRB. In a survey study of Chinese bank employees, Huang et al. (2014) found support for this relationship. Further, job autonomy fully mediated the relationship between transformational leadership and PSRB.

One article has given the antecedents of PSRB theoretical attention. Vardaman, Gondo, and Allen (2014) conceptualize PSRB as an ethical decision. Vardaman et al. examine PSRB in the context of Victor and Cullen's (1988) ethical climate typology. Vardaman et al. suggest that in addition to the variables that have received empirical support as antecedents of PSRB (job autonomy, coworker behavior, risk-taking propensity, and conscientiousness), the components of core self-evaluation (self-esteem, generalized self-efficacy, neuroticism, and locus of control) should also predict PSRB. Further, Vardaman et al. suggest ethical climate should have both a direct effect on PSRB as well as moderate the relationship between antecedents and PSRB. Vardaman et al.'s consideration of moderating factors is notable as it reflects a theme that is consistent in the empirical work. Dahling et al. (2012) and Huang et al. (2014) both suggest that future research should explore moderators.

Although the research on PSRB is limited, the existing work suggests PSRB is a common employee behavior. Morrison (2006) reported 64% of individuals surveyed could recall an incident in which they engaged in prosocial rule-breaking behavior. Current research has considered the attributes of the individual and situation that allow rule breaking (e.g., autonomy). However, research has not considered characteristics of the situation that evoke PSRB or how individual and situational characteristics might influence the relationship between these triggers and rule-breaking behavior. We suggest PSRB can be a reaction to perceived unfairness. In particular, we suggest customer-directed PSRB can be a reaction to policies that employees – as observers of the organization–customer relationship – see as unfair to customers. That is, PSRB may be behavior that is aimed at restoring justice for the customer. Before we describe our proposed model, we review research on employee–customer relationships and on third-party reactions to fairness.

CUSTOMERS IN THE ORGANIZATIONAL LITERATURE

Most research in management on the relationship between employees and customers focuses on how interacting with customers influences employee outcomes. For example, research on emotional labor demonstrates customer interaction can be associated with less positive job attitudes and increased burnout (Gabriel, Daniels, Diefendorff, & Greguras, 2014; Grandey, 2003; Grandey, Foo, Groth, & Goodwin, 2012). Most recently, researchers have begun to examine the influence of customers' negative behavior (e.g., incivility, abuse, mistreatment) on employees' attitudes and behavior. This research demonstrates employees are negatively influenced by the unfair behavior of customers and this treatment often results in negative outcomes for the employee (e.g., cognitive strain, poor performance) and the customer (e.g., sabotage, incivility from employees).

For example, in an experimental study in which participants role-played the role of a customer-service representative in a fictional company, Rupp and Spencer (2006) found participants engaged in emotional labor and were unable to adhere to the "company" display rules when faced with interactional injustice from customers. The opposite held true when customers behaved fairly toward the "customer-service representatives." Researchers have also found that when faced with interpersonal injustice or incivility from customers, employees may engage in uncivil treatment toward customers (van Jaarsveld, Walker, & Skarlicki, 2010) or customer-directed sabotage, which is ultimately negatively related to performance ratings (Skarlicki et al., 2008; Wang, Liao, Zhan, & Shi, 2011). The relationship between customer mistreatment of employees and sabotage or poor performance has been found to be mediated by emotional labor and emotional exhaustion from employees (Sliter, Jex, Wolford, & McInnerney, 2010).

Research has also found the influence of customer mistreatment has lasting impact. Wang et al. (2013) demonstrated customer mistreatment influenced employee mood the next day. Additionally, employees can pay cognitive costs when faced with incivility from customers. Rafaeli et al. (2012) investigated the impact of verbal aggression from customers directed toward employees. Results showed aggression from customers directly impact employees' cognitive memory and indirectly influenced task performance. Finally, research has found employees respond differently to customer mistreatment depending upon the culture in which they work.

Employees in North America are more likely to have reactions like sabotage directed toward customers when faced with customer mistreatment. On the other hand, employees in East Asia are more likely to engage in more passive resistance (e.g., withdraw of organizational citizenship behaviors) in response to customer mistreatment (Shao & Skarlicki, 2014).

Although most studies examine employee responses to customer mistreatment, a few studies examine employee customer-directed prosocial behavior. Bettencourt and Brown (1997) explore employees' customer-directed prosocial behaviors. They found employees' perceptions of fairness were positively related to their customer-directed prosocial behavior. Subsequent research demonstrates customer-directed prosocial behavior is positively related to customer satisfaction ratings (Bettencourt, Gwinner, & Meuter, 2001) as well as employee performance (Grizzle, Zablah, Brown, Mowen, & Lee, 2009; Schneider, Ehrhart, Mayer, Saltz, & Niles-Jolly, 2005). Research in this area has evolved to distinguish between three different dimensions of customer OCBs (Bettencourt et al., 2001). These dimensions include (1) loyalty OCBs (i.e., representing the organization's products and services to advocates and outsiders as well as the organization's image); (2) participation OCBs (i.e., taking individual initiative to improve service delivery by the organization, coworkers, and oneself especially in communications); and (3) service delivery OCBs (i.e., behaving conscientiously during activities relating to service delivery to customers). Bettencourt et al. found job satisfaction and perceived organizational support (POS) predict loyalty OCBs. Service orientation, empathy, and trait richness were key predictors of service delivery OCBs and customer knowledge predicted participation OCBs.

Recently, Lam and Mayer (2014) investigated the antecedents and outcomes of a particular form of customer-directed OCB, customer-focused voice. The authors defined customer-focused voice as involving "upward communication of ideas, suggestions, or recommendations intended to benefit the workgroup or the organization" (p. 640). In a time lagged field study of a support service management company that delivered environmental and food services to hospitals, the authors obtained data from employees, managers and the CEO or VP of the organization receiving services. The authors found an employee's customer orientation and level of job autonomy were positively associated with customer-focused voice. The authors also found the organizational service climate moderated these relationships such that these relationships were stronger when service climate is low. This research suggests employees play an important advocacy role for customers by making suggestions and speaking up for customers and this ultimately helps organizational performance.

THIRD-PARTY JUSTICE

Some of the earliest research on observers of unfairness examined layoff "survivors" and how the fairness of the layoff procedures influenced the attitudes and behavior of employees who were not laid off (Brockner, Grover, Reed, DeWitt, & O'Malley, 1987; Brockner et al., 1994; Brockner, Wiesenfeld, & Martin, 1995). This research focused primarily on how observed unfairness affected the observer. However, the introduction of the deontic view of justice (Folger, 1998) shifted the focus of third-party justice research. In the last decade, researchers have become increasingly interested in third-party reactions to the fair/unfair treatment of others in terms of the behavior directed at the harm doer and the behavior directed at the victim.

Prior to the introduction of the deontic model of justice (Folger, 1998, 2001), justice research conceptualized individuals' concern for justice from a self-interested perspective. Individuals were concerned about fairness because fairness benefitted them in some way – either by increasing their likelihood of favorable outcomes (Thibaut & Walker, 1975) or by providing information about their standing in a group (Tyler & Blader, 2000; Tyler & Lind, 1992). The deontic model proposes that individuals can be concerned about justice for justice's sake. The deontic model suggests justice is a moral virtue and when individuals observe others being unfairly treated – even if they are not personally targeted or affected – they experience a sense of moral unease. This moral unease motivates them to react against the perpetrator and address the injustice (Cropanzano et al., 2005; Folger, 2001). Deontic behavior is the behavior motivated by this moral unease that is aimed at addressing the injustice.

Most management research on third-party reactions to mistreatment has invoked deonance as the theoretical foundation. Additionally, most of this research has focused on how third-party observers react toward the perpetrator, and specifically, third parties' willingness to take action to punish the harm doer. Turillo, Folger, Lavelle, Umphress, and Gee (2002) provide the first empirical test of the deontic model. Turillo et al. demonstrated decision-makers were willing to incur personal costs in order to punish someone who had treated another individual unfairly. Further, these self-sacrificing allocations occurred when there were no short-term or long-term benefits for doing so. Additionally, Turillo et al. demonstrated these deontic reactions occurred not only for the unfair distribution of resources but also for unfair interpersonal treatment.

Drawing on the deontic model, a number of studies have examined third-party reactions to unfairness and have focused on the observers' willingness to punish the perpetrator. For example, Umphress, Simmons, Folger, Ren, and Bobocel (2013) were interested in how the perpetrator's intentions influenced observer's reactions. They found the perpetrator intent to harm was critical to observers' intentions to punish; observers endorsed punishing perpetrators who intended to harm the victim, regardless of whether or not the victim experienced harm. Zoghbi-Manrique-de-Lara and Suárez-Acosta (2014) suggested employees respond to the unfair treatment of their peers by "punishing" the organization with increased deviant behavior and decreased OCB and that this relationship is mediated by perceptions of ethical leadership. Christian, Christian, Garza, and Ellis (2012) examined how team members reacted to the unfair treatment of a colleague. They found observers punish a supervisor who treats a valued colleague unfairly by decreasing their citizenship behaviors directed at the supervisor.

In a scenario-based study, Skarlicki and Rupp (2010) examined how the type of cognitive processing in which observers engage and the observers' moral identity influence observers' reactions toward a harm doer. Specifically, they were interested in when observers would engage in retributory behavior. Skarlicki and Rupp primed respondents toward either an expressive (i.e., relying on feelings and intuition) or rational processing (i.e., more complex, dispassionate analysis) frame. Additionally, as fairness can be viewed as a moral virtue, they considered the influence of the observer's moral identity (i.e., the extent to which morality is central to the individual's self-concept). Skarlicki and Rupp found expressive processing led to higher levels of retribution, but only for observers low in moral identity. Individuals high in moral identity responded to the injustice with high retributive responses regardless of processing frame.

Some research has also considered when observers *refrain* from punishing transgressors. As noted above, Umphress et al. (2013) found observers were less likely to seek to punish perpetrators who did not intend to harm their victims. Focusing on the role of moral motivation in deontic responses, researchers have examined when morality limits punitive responses. Rupp and Bell (2010) suggest moral regulation may lead observers to "do nothing" in response to injustice, if acting against the transgressor violates their own moral norms. Similarly, Greenbaum, Mawritz, Mayer, and Priesemuth (2013) found observers were less likely to engage in workplace deviance (a form of organizational punishment) if they were higher in moral identity. These findings are consistent with the early work of Turillo et al. (2002) who found observers were unlikely to punish the transgressor if doing so required them to behave unfairly themselves. Observers appear to be unwilling to engage in punitive behavior that violates their own moral code.

Although most research on observed injustice focuses on observers' punishment of the transgressor, some recent research has considered alternative reactions. For example, Greenbaum et al. (2013) suggest observers may respond to the unfair treatment of others by withdrawing from the situation or engaging in constructive resistance. Further, they suggest moral identity moderates this relationship. Their findings support these predictions. The relationship between unfairness and turnover intentions and the relationship between unfairness and constructive resistance was stronger for observers who were higher on moral identity. Similarly, Zoghbi-Manrique-de-Lara, Aguiar-Quintana, and Suárez-Acosta (2013) found customers were likely to withdraw from a situation when they observed unfair treatment. Specifically, they found customers are less likely to return to hotels when they feel the employees have been treated unfairly.

Researchers have also examined observers' behavior directed toward the victim. Some research has demonstrated observers may denigrate the victim and this denigration can be associated with the observer also treating the victim unfairly (Skarlicki, Ellard, & Kelln, 1998; Skarlicki & Turner, 2014). However research also suggests third parties might seek to help the victim (Kelloway, Francis, Catano, & Dupré, 2008; Priesemuth, 2013). For example, Priesemuth (2013) examined "standing up" behavior (e.g., providing help and support for the victim). She found friendship ties moderated the relationship between unfairness and standing up behavior. The relationship was more positive when friendship ties were stronger. In a study of labor strikes, Kelloway et al. (2008) also found observers may engage in victim-supporting behavior. Kelloway et al. demonstrated observers who did not hold pro-union attitudes were more likely to engage in supportive behavior toward union members when they felt the contract was unfair. And, Nadisic (2008) found supervisors may try to compensate subordinates for unfair policies or treatment by the organization.

This two-prong focus on transgressor punishment and victim support is consistent with work in social psychology on retributive and compensatory justice, which examines observers' motivation to punish the perpetrator (retributive justice) and to compensate the victim (compensatory justice; Lotz, Okimoto, Schlösser, & Fetchenhauer, 2011; Mahony & Klaas, 2008). This research typically examines these motivations in the context of criminal wrongdoing. The research demonstrates that, although the motive for retribution is typically stronger than the motive for compensation (van Prooijen, 2009), there are conditions under which compensation is the stronger motive. In the case of PSRB, we suggest there are attributes of the observer, the victim, and the situation that influence employees' propensities to respond to perceived unfairness with rule-breaking behavior aimed at "compensating" the customers. Our model is shown in Fig. 1.

ORGANIZATIONAL UNFAIRNESS AND CUSTOMER-DIRECTED PROSOCIAL RULE BREAKING

As we have discussed, we conceptualize PSRB as a deontic reaction by employees to the organization's unfair policies toward customers. Our model focuses on the conditions that affect employee reactions, influencing the likelihood that perceived unfair treatment of customers results in customer-directed PSRB. Thus, our model begins with employees' perceptions that the organizations' policies toward customers are not fair. In this chapter, we do not focus on antecedents of these fairness perceptions. Nonetheless, it is worth noting that we expect the attributes of fair policies and procedures found in previous research on employee justice perceptions and customer justice perceptions (e.g., consistency, timeliness, respect, honesty) to underlie the perceived fairness of the organizations policies. Additionally, Skarlicki and his colleagues (Skarlicki & Kulik, 2005; Skarlicki, O'Reilly, & Kulik, in press) have presented a model of third-party justice that considers attributes that influence third-party fairness perception (e.g., attribution of intent, severity of wrongdoing, transgressors

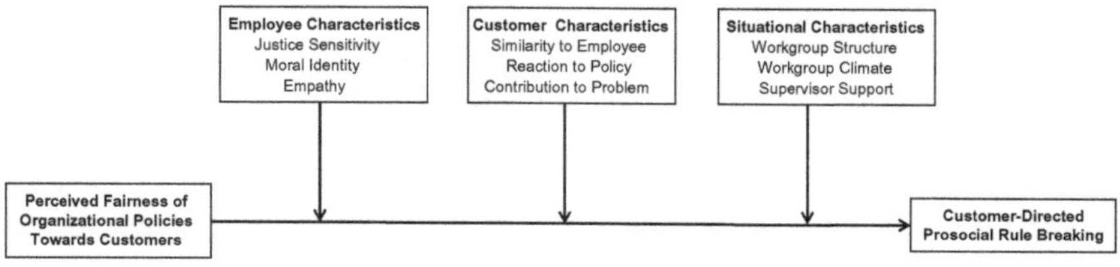

Fig. 1. Deontic Customer-Directed Prosocial Rule-Breaking Model.

history of wrongdoing) and these antecedents are applicable to the employee–organization–customer relationship as well. However, in this chapter, we focus on what happens *after* employees' judge the organization's treatment of customers to be unfair.

As can be seen in Fig. 1, we suggest "deontic" customer-directed PSRB is influenced by attributes of the employee, the customer, and the situation. Drawing on the deontic model and previous research on organizational justice and on PSRB, we identify three characteristics in each category. We begin with a discussion of employee characteristics.

EMPLOYEE CHARACTERISTICS

Morality is at the core of the deontic approach to justice. The deontic model proposes that as justice is a moral virtue, violations of fairness lead observers to experience a sense of moral unease. This moral unease motivates them to respond to the injustice (Cropanzano et al., 2005; Folger, 2001). Building from the moral foundation of deonance theory, we consider three morality-based employee characteristics that should moderate the relationship between perceived unfairness and PSRB: justice sensitivity, empathy, and moral identity.

Justice Sensitivity

Schmitt and his colleagues (Schmitt, 1996; Schmitt, Neumann, & Montada, 1995) suggest individuals differ in their sensitivity to justice. They introduced the construct of "justice sensitivity" – the stable tendency of individuals' reactions to experiences of injustice and unfairness. Schmitt (1996) originally referred to this as "sensitivity to befallen injustice." However, in subsequent work, Schmitt and his colleagues use the term "justice sensitivity" (Gollwitzer, Schmitt, Schalke, Maes, & Baer, 2005; Schmitt & Dörfel, 1999; Schmitt, Gollwitzer, Maes, & Arbach, 2005). Schmitt and his colleagues (Gollwitzer et al., 2005) describe justice sensitivity as belonging to the group of personality traits that co-determine moral behavior. Schmitt et al. identified three types of justice sensitivity that are based on three different perspectives of fairness: the victim, the observer, and the beneficiary. However, some empirical research suggests the latter two perspectives can be combined into a single construct reflecting justice sensitivity toward others ($JS_{(other)}$), which is distinct from the perspective of the victim (Fetchenhauer & Huang, 2004).

Several findings from the work on justice sensitivity are important for our discussion. First, justice sensitivity affects individuals' reactions to unfair situations and moderates the relationship between fairness and outcomes (Gollwitzer et al., 2005; Mohiyeddini & Schmitt, 1997; Schmitt & Dörfel, 1999; Schmitt et al., 2005). Second, research on justice sensitivity for observers ($JS_{(other)}$) demonstrates individuals high on this trait respond negatively to the unfair treatment of others (Fetchenhauer & Huang, 2004; Gollwitzer et al., 2005).

Individuals higher in $JS_{(other)}$ are more likely to notice justice issues surrounding them. These individuals are more likely to attend to fairness and be motivated toward action in the presence of unfairness than those lower in justice sensitivity. Thus, we expect $JS_{(other)}$ moderates the relationship between perceived organizational unfairness toward customers and customer-directed PSRB. Specifically, we propose the relationship between unfairness and customer-directed PSRB is stronger when employees are higher in justice sensitivity.

Moral Identity

Our second employee characteristic is moral identity. Being a moral person may be, but need not be, a part of a person's overall self-definition (Blasi, 1984). That is, being a good or moral person differs in its centrality in individuals' self-concepts. Moral identity refers to the extent to which an individual sees being a moral person as central to his or her self-concept (Aquino & Reed, 2002; Blasi, 1984). Thus, morality plays a more central role for individuals higher in moral identity.

Moral identity has frequently been considered in work on third-party reactions to injustice (Greenbaum et al., 2013; Rupp & Bell, 2010; Skarlicki & Rupp, 2010). Most recently, O'Reilly and Aquino (2011) suggested that in the case of third-party responses to injustice, third parties who are higher in moral identity will be more likely to experience morally motivated responses to injustice. It is important to note that research demonstrates moral identity may motivate individuals to take action but also limits the type of retributive behavior in which individuals engage. Although individuals high in moral identity are motivated to punish transgressors, they are unlikely to do so if the punishment requires them to engage in behavior they see as morally questionable (e.g., to act unfairly themselves, to behave unethically; Greenbaum et al., 2013; Turillo et al., 2002). Thus, we suggest employees higher in moral identity are particularly likely to engage in behavior that helps or compensates the victim of unfairness, rather than engage in retributive behavior aimed at harming the transgressor. PSRB reflects such compensatory behavior. Therefore, we suggest employees higher in moral identity are more likely to engage in PSRB in response to perceived organizational unfairness toward customers than employees lower in moral identity.

Empathy

Emotions play an integral role in the development of justice judgments and subsequent reactions by organizational members (Barsky, Kaplan, & Beal, 2011). Keeping our focus on the moral foundation of justice, we consider the influence of the moral emotion empathy. Moral emotions "are those emotions that are linked to the interests or welfare either of society as a whole or at least of persons other than the judge or agent" (Haidt, 2003, p. 853). Empathy has been called the foundational moral emotion because it is at the center of the human moral affective system as it elicits concerns for others in distress (Feshbach, 1975; Tangney, Stuewig, & Mashek, 2007). Empathy involves imagining another person's reaction to an event (Blader, Wiesenfeld, Fortin, & Wheeler-Smith, 2013) and then experiencing "feelings of warmth, compassion and concern for others undergoing negative experiences" (Davis, 1980, p. 6). Research has found empathy to be related to altruistic helping behavior (Batson et al., 1988) and often prompts behavior aimed at helping someone in distress (Batson, 1991; Eisenberg & Miller, 1987).

Past research has investigated the impact of empathy on PSRB. Specifically, Morrison (2006) hypothesized that empathy would be positively related to the likelihood of deciding to engage in PSRB. In a scenario study using a sample of MBA students, Morrison (2006) did not find a direct relationship between empathy and PSRB behavior. However, post hoc analyses revealed an interaction between empathy and another independent variable, job meaning (i.e., the perceived value of one's work). Specifically, Morrison found job meaning had a stronger effect for those with low rather than high empathy. This finding suggests that individuals with low empathy are more sensitive to the context in which they find themselves. However, individuals with high empathy are more likely to engage in PSRB regardless of the context because they "feel" for their customers.

Morrison's (2006) finding is consistent with research on customer-directed citizenship behaviors. This research also suggests that empathetic employees may be driven out of compassion to satisfy customer needs through superior service delivery and customer-focused citizenship behaviors (e.g., service-improvement suggestions) (Bettencourt et al., 2001). In contrast, employees that are lower in empathy may be more sensitive to the situation and thus more likely to respond based on the specific circumstances at hand. Based on this logic, we theorize that empathy moderates the relationship between perceived organizational unfairness toward customers and customer-directed PSRB such that the relationship between policy fairness and PSRB is stronger for employees lower in empathy than employees with higher empathy.

CUSTOMER CHARACTERISTICS

In addition to employee (i.e., observer) characteristics, we suggest customer (i.e., victim) characteristics influence employees' propensity to engage in deontic customer-directed PSRB. Here the research on retributive and compensatory justice is particularly relevant as it has explicitly considered how victim characteristics influence observers' motives toward punishment and compensation. Drawing on the research on retributive and compensatory justice, we consider three customer characteristics: customer similarity to the employee, customer reactions to unfairness, customer contribution.

Customer Similarity to the Employee

Research on retributive and compensatory justice has suggested that punishing an offender is a relatively straightforward method for restoring a sense of justice (Loewenstein & Small, 2007). Punishment focuses on sanctioning the offender and can be viewed as behavior designed to limit the threat the offender poses for society, other individuals, and the observer. In contrast, this research suggests the focus on victims' needs is often less salient. Further, empirical work demonstrates individuals' reactions to victims are sometimes positive and helpful (Nadisic, 2008; Priesemuth, 2013), but sometimes negative and derogative (Skarlicki et al., 1998; Skarlicki & Turner, 2014). Importantly, research demonstrates that both the relative focus on retribution and reactions to the victim are influenced by the psychological closeness between the observer and the victim (Loewenstein & Small, 2007; van Prooijen, 2010). For example, in a series of laboratory studies, van Proojen found that the relative preference for punishment occurred only when participants did not feel "an emotional proximity" to the victim. When participants were told to imagine that the victim in a scenario was someone with whom they felt a strong personal connection, they were less likely to favor an outcome that punished the offender and more likely to favor an outcome that compensated the victim.

We suggest the similarity between the employee and the customer serves a similar function. Research on similarity demonstrates individuals prefer those who are similar to themselves (Byrne, 1971; Byrne & Griffitt, 1969) and find it easier to build rapport with similar others (Bernieri, Gilles, Davis, & Grahe, 1996). Additionally, individuals are more likely to identify with a similar other (Tajfel & Turner, 1986). Identification with the victim also allows observers to more easily take the other person's perspective. This perspective-taking is associated with increased compassion and increased helping of the target (Batson, Polycarpou et al., 1997; Batson, Sager et al., 1997; Galinsky & Moskowitz, 2000; Maner et al., 2002; Myers, Laurent, & Hodges, 2014). In all, we propose the relationship between the perceived unfairness of organizational policies toward customers and customer-directed PSRB is stronger when employees perceive customers to be similar to themselves.

Customer's Response to Unfairness

The second customer characteristic we consider is the customer's reaction to the organizational policy. Only a few studies have examined the effect of the victim's response on the behavior of observers of unfairness. In the context of reactions to criminal offenders, using scenario-based studies, Gromet, Okimoto, Wenzel, and Darley (2012) found victims' satisfaction with a restorative justice process (in which offenders have the opportunity to make peace with their victim) attenuated observers' desire to punish the offender. When victims were dissatisfied with the process, observers were more likely to seek retribution. Similarly, Umphress et al. (2013) found observers responded most punitively toward transgressors when they perceived the unfairness as intentional *and* the victim expressed their unhappiness with the unfairness. Although these studies examine punishment, we expect a similar influence for customer-directed PSRB. Specifically, we propose that employees are more likely to engage in customer-directed PSRB when customers express dissatisfaction with the organizations' policies and/ or treatment.

Customer Contribution/Co-Creation

Research on compensatory and retributive justice also identifies victim contribution as an important influence on observers' reactions. In a study examining jurors and employment arbitrators, Mahony and Klaas (2008) examined how the characteristics of the offender (organizations) and of the victims (employee) influenced awards in wrongful termination lawsuit scenarios. They argue that attributes of the employee that influence perceptions that the termination was warranted (e.g., previous performance problems) influenced the recommendation for compensatory damages (while both employee attributes and organizational attributes influenced retributive choices). In other words, decision-makers were less likely to compensate individuals who appeared to have contributed to the treatment they received. That is, when the blame could be – at least in part – attributed to the victim, decision-makers were less likely to choose compensatory options.

Research in services marketing has also examined the role of customers as a key contributor during the service delivery process, although this research suggests a different perspective on contribution. Co-creation has been defined as the collective value produced from customer input and employee interaction (Etgar, 2008; Prahalad & Ramaswammy, 2004). Opportunities for customer co-creation vary by type of service. For example, significant customer involvement is required for services such as therapy, personal training, and interior home design. Research has shown that customers contribute to the service process by exerting effort and sharing important information (Chan, Yim, & Lam, 2010; Hoyer, Chandy, Dorotic, Krafft, & Singh, 2010). When service outcomes are favorable, customer co-creation leads to more service customization (Etgar, 2008) and greater satisfaction (Xie, Bagozzi, & Troye, 2008).

In many contexts, the customer's role has expanded to include activities that are ordinarily performed by service organizations (Heidenreich, Wittkowski, Handrich, & Falk, 2015). Through interaction with these customers, service employees become well aware of the level of effort and sharing that has been provided by the customer during the delivery process. When employee perceptions of customer inputs are high yet still result in unfavorable or unfair outcomes due to unfair organizational policies, we argue that employees are more likely to engage in customer-directed PSRB as a response to the perceived unfairness of the organizations' policies. Thus, we suggest that employee perceptions of the customer's contribution influences customer-directed PSRB. When the customer has not contributed to the problem, yet provided considerable inputs, we propose the relationship between perceived unfairness and customer-directed PSRB is stronger.

SITUATIONAL CHARACTERISTICS

The final set of moderators of the relationship between perceived organizational unfairness and customer-directed PSRB that we address are situational characteristics. Specifically, we consider the influence of workgroup structure, workgroup climate, and supervisor support.

Workgroup Structure

Research on workgroup structure demonstrates its influence on a broad range of individual and group-level outcomes (e.g., job satisfaction, Meadows, 1980a; Rahman & Zanzi, 1995; team innovation, Meadows, 1980b; organization-based self-esteem, Pierce, Gardner, Cummings, & Dunham, 1989; learning, Slevin & Covin, 1997). Structure has a clear influence on what individuals do in organizations and how they do it. We expect structure influences employees' customer-directed PSRB.

Research on workgroup structure typically distinguishes between two structural prototypes: mechanistic and organic (Burns & Stalker, 1961; Khandwalla, 1976/1977; Lawrence & Lorsch, 1967). Mechanistic organizations are characterized by rigid, tight, bureaucratic structures; organic organizations are characterized by flexible, loose, decentralized structures. Mechanistic and organic structures represent the ends of a continuum. Workgroups may display some characteristics of both. We suggest workgroup structure influences employees' propensity to engage in customer-directed PSRB as a response to perceived organizational unfairness because workplace structure influences situational strength and employees' behavioral flexibility.

Situational strength constrains the behavior of individuals (Mischel, 1977). In strong situations, variance in individuals' behavior is attenuated.

In weak situations, there is greater variance in behavior. Organic structures reflect weak situations, with greater behavioral "free space" (i.e., more leeway in terms of choosing one's course of action) for employees. Mechanistic structures are strong situations. They are more formalized, rigid, and bureaucratic than organic structures. Prescriptions for appropriate and normative behavior are quite clear. There are more procedures covering a wider range of situations. Additionally, those procedures are more specific and standardized. Indeed, one of the primary consequences of bureaucratic, mechanistic structures is to minimize individuals' freedom of choice (Weber, 1978) and to minimize the impact of individual preferences (March & Simon, 1958).

Meyer, Dalal, and Hermida (2010) identify formal policies and procedures as an antecedent of situational strength. Formal policies and procedures constrain behavior by "preventing employees from exercising their own *discretion* pertaining to decisions about which tasks to perform, as well as how and when to perform them" (Meyer et al., 2010, p. 126). In more mechanistic structures, employees' behavior is influenced by formal organizational rules and regulations and there is little room for employees to decide on their own course of action. In contrast, organic structures are looser and more flexible. Power is decentralized and decisions are more likely to be made and implemented at the immediate workgroup level. In organic structures employees have more leeway in terms of choosing their course of action. As employees' behavior is less constrained, they have more flexibility in how they respond to the perceived unfairness of the organization's treatment of customers *and* how they treat customers.

We suggest the greater discretion available in organic workgroups influences employees' customer-directed PSRB. Specifically, when employees believe customers have been treated unfairly, they have more opportunity to respond to this perceived unfairness when the workgroup structure is organic. Thus, we propose the relationship between perceived organizational unfairness and customer-directed PSRB is stronger in workgroups with organic structure.

Workgroup Service Climate

Workgroup climates reflect employees' shared perceptions regarding the policies, practices, and procedures that an organization rewards, supports, and expects (Schneider & Reichers, 1983). It is a reflection of the organization's values that is captured in the organization's policies and the day-to-day behavior of its members. Climate guides employee behavior as it provides employees with information about the link between behavior and outcomes (Schneider, 1975). Schneider (1975) suggests there should be a strategic focus to the climate construct. That is, it should refer to a climate for something – a climate for safety (Zohar, 2000), a climate for innovation (Jung, Chow, & Wu, 2003), a climate for service (Schneider, Parkington, & Buxton, 1980). We suggest for customer-directed PSRB, service climate is particularly relevant.

Service climate reflects employees' shared perception that organizational policies and procedures, and the employee behaviors that are expected and rewarded, emphasize service excellence (Schneider, White, & Paul, 1998). Research demonstrates service climate is positively related to customers' perceptions of service quality (Schneider et al., 1998), customer loyalty (Salanova, Agut, & Peiró, 2005), customer satisfaction (Dietz, Pugh, & Wiley, 2004; Mayer, Ehrhart, & Schneider, 2009; Schneider et al., 2005), employees' proactive customer service behavior (Raub & Liao, 2012), customer-directed OCBs (Bettencourt et al., 2001; Dimitriades, 2007; Schneider et al., 2005), and employees' voice behavior for customers (Lam & Mayer, 2014).

We suggest service climate moderates the relationship between employees' perceptions of the organization's unfair customer policies and their customer-directed PSRB behavior. In an organization with a strong service climate, employees believe a primary goal is to meet the needs of customers. When there is a strong service climate, solving customers' problem and providing quality service dominates. We suggest this focus on customers is associated with customer-directed PSRB. That is, when service climate is higher, employees are more likely to engage in customer-directed PSRB regardless of their perceptions of the fairness of the organizations' treatment of customers. If employees believe that delivering high-quality service is recognized or rewarded, customer-directed PSRB may be viewed as desirable regardless of the source of the customers' need. In contrast, when service climate is low, employees are likely to be spurred to engage in customer-directed PSRB for other reasons. That is, the unfairness of the organizations' policies or treatment drives the behavior. Much like our prediction about employee empathy, we expect employees who work in departments for which there is a strong service climate are less sensitive to the specific fairness/unfairness attributes of the customers' situations. In departments with strong service climates, customer service – and customer-directed PSRB – is the default. However, the customer-directed PSRB behavior of employees in departments with lower service climate is related to the fairness characteristics of the customers' situations. Thus, we propose the relationship between employees' perceptions of the organization's unfair treatment of customers is stronger when service climate is low than when service climate is high.

Supervisor Support

Our final situational characteristic is supervisor support. Supervisors play a critical role in the work lives of their subordinates and supervisory support is a particularly important aspect of the subordinate–supervisor relationship (Dulebohn, Bommer, Liden, Brouer, & Ferris, 2012; Eisenberger, Stinglhamber, Vandenberghe, Sucharski, & Rhoades, 2002; Liden, Sparrowe, & Wayne, 1997; Shanock & Eisenberger, 2006). Subordinates develop general views concerning the degree to which supervisors value their contributions, will "go to bat" for them, and care about their well-being. Additionally, supervisor support provides employees with both tangible and psychological resources.

In the context of customer-directed PSRB, we believe supervisor support is important because by enhancing employees resources, it allows them to engage in more costly (i.e., rule breaking) behavior. Skarlicki and Kulik (2005) argue that a third-party's decision to act in the face of observed injustice is based on a costs-benefits analysis. They suggest observers assess (among other things) the resources they have available. If they believe their actions will be supported by important others, they are more likely to take action. Similarly, O'Reilly and Aquino (2011) propose third parties who have low position power, but high resource power (e.g., subordinates with a supportive supervisor) are more likely to provide aid to the victim than to punish the transgressor. Supervisor support buffers subordinates from negative consequences associated with rule breaking. When employees feel that their supervisor supports them, we suggest they are more willing to engage in customer-directed PSRB when they feel the customer is being treated unfairly by the organization.

CONCLUSION

In this chapter, we have explored customer-directed PSRB as an employee's deontic response to the organization's mistreatment of customers. We have identified employee, customer, and situational characteristics that influence the relationship between perceptions of mistreatment and deontic PSRB. A few observations warrant attention, particularly as we consider future research in this area.

First, our model is both complex and too simple. We have proposed three categories of moderators (employee, customer, and situation) that influence the relationship between perceived unfairness and customer-directed PSRB. Further, we have identified three specific constructs for each. Empirically, sorting out the existence and relative importance of each of these moderators represents a daunting challenge. Simultaneously, there is clearly a wide variety of employee, customer, and situational moderators possible. We have only scratched the surface. We did not include a discussion of moderators explored elsewhere (e.g., coworker PSRB). We limited our consideration of employee characteristics to ones that were morally based. Research on third-party reactions to unfairness has examined only a limited number of moderators – moral identity being among the most frequent. We believe this is a reasonable place to start and investigation of these morally based moderators is likely to provide insight to both PSRB literature and third-party justice literature. Yet, justice research more broadly suggests a wide range of individual characteristics may influence individuals' reactions to their own justice experiences, and these factors are likely to influence reactions to observing others being unfairly treated as well (Kray & Lind, 2002). Further, characteristics such as employee power and efficacy are likely to play a role in deontic PSRB. Similarly, other attributes of the customer (e.g., status, length of relationship with the organization or employee) and the situation (e.g., justice climate, deviance climate) are likely to be important. Future research will undoubtedly lead to a more complex model.

Second, in an effort to keep the model manageable, we focused on the moderating effects of employee, customer, and situational characteristics. Yet, it is likely interactions between these characteristics exist. For example, the relationship between employees' perceptions of unfairness, their justice sensitivity, and customer similarity could interact to affect PSRB. Employees lower in justice sensitivity might respond most strongly when they perceive a customer who is similar to themselves is treated unfairly. Similarly, a strong fairness climate might mitigate the effect of employees' moral identity. Thus, future research considering these more complex interactions could be useful.

Third, Dahling et al. (2012) demonstrate a negative relationship between PSRB and coworkers' and supervisors' ratings of the rule-breaking employees' task performance. However, other consequences (e.g., employee attitudes, customer evaluations, workgroup performance) have not been examined. Indeed, research on third-party reactions to injustice rarely examines the longer-term consequences of deontic behavior for the observer. As such, theoretical advancements and empirical research exploring these relationships should prove fruitful. Thus, the model could clearly be expanded to include outcomes. We suspect that, just as we expect individual and situational characteristics to moderate the relationship between perceived unfairness and customer-directed PSRB, individual and situational characteristics are likely to moderate the relationship between customer-directed PSRB and outcomes.

Fourth, we have focused on customer-directed PSRB as a deontic response to perceived organizational mistreatment of customers. We acknowledge there are a variety of reasons employees may engage in customer-directed PSRB. For example, as we note in our previous discussion, the climate of the workgroup may encourage customer-directed PSRB or employee characteristic (empathy) may drive customer-directed PSRB decisions. Perceptions that organizational policies are unfair to customers are only one possible antecedent for PSRB. Although there is only limited research on PSRB, it would be useful to consider how our model might be integrated with existing research. Such a consideration might explore the relative impact of individual characteristics (such as conscientiousness, Dahling et al., 2012) and relational characteristics (leadership style, Huang et al., 2014) and fairness characteristics on employees' PSRB. Alternatively, such a consideration might focus on the moderating effects of the characteristics that have previously been conceptualized as antecedents. Much as we have argued that supervisor support moderates the relationship between perceived policy unfairness and PSRB, leadership style might play a similar role.

Finally, it is useful to consider the applicability of the deontic approach to PSRB more broadly. Our model focuses on customer-directed PSRB. However, Morrison (2006) identifies another type of "other-directed" PSRB: rule breaking aimed at benefitting coworkers (i.e., coworker-directed PSRB). Although there are clearly differences between coworker-directed PSRB and customer-directed PSRB, we believe many of the same factors are likely at play when one considers the relationship between employees' perceptions of organizational and supervisory mistreatment of their coworkers and their coworker-directed PSRB. Recent research has begun to consider third-party reactions to coworker mistreatment (Christian et al., 2012; Priesemuth, 2013), but this research is very limited. Our model may provide a framework for exploring the relationship between the observed mistreatment of coworkers and coworker-directed PSRB.

A majority of employees indicate they have engaged in PSRB. A better understanding of what drives this behavior and the consequences of the behavior can help organizations productively manage this type of employee behavior. Thus, we hope by bringing together research on employee–customer interactions, third-party justice, and PSRB, this chapter will spur interest in customer-directed PSRB and lead to research designed to help us better understand how employees respond to the perceived mistreatment of customers.

ACKNOWLEDGMENT

This research was supported by the Gordon J. Barnett Memorial Foundation.

REFERENCES

Aquino, K. F., & Reed II, A. (2002). The self-importance of moral identity. *Journal of Personality and Social Psychology*, *83*, 1423–1440.

Barsky, A., Kaplan, S. A., & Beal, D. J. (2011). Just feelings? The role of affect in the formation of organizational fairness judgments. *Journal of Management*, *37*(1), 248–279.

Batson, C. D., Polycarpou, M. P., Harmon-Jones, E., Imhoff, H. J., Mitchener, E. C., Bednar, L. L., … Highberger, L. (1997). Empathy and attitudes: Can feeling for a member of a stigmatized group improve feelings toward the group? *Journal of Personality and Social Psychology*, *72*, 105–118. doi:10.1037/0022-3514.72.1.105

Batson, C. D., Sager, K., Garst, E., Kang, M., Rubchinsky, K., & Dawson, K. (1997). Is empathy-induced helping due to self – other merging? *Journal of Personality and Social Psychology*, *73*, 495–509. doi:10.1037/0022-3514.73.3.495

Batson, D. (1991). *The altruism question*. Hillsdale, NJ: Erlbaum.

Batson, D., Dyck, J., Brandt, J., Batson, J., Powell, A., McMaster, M., & Griffitti, C. (1988). Five studies testing two new egoistic alternatives to the empathy-altruism hypothesis. *Journal of Personality and Social Psychology*, *55*, 52–77.

Bernieri, F. J., Gilles, J. S., Davis, J. M., & Grahe, J. E. (1996). Dyad rapport and the accuracy of its judgment across situations: A lens model analysis. *Journal of Personality and Social Psychology*, *71*, 110–129.

Bettencourt, L. A., & Brown, S. W. (1997). Contact employees: Relationships among workplace fairness, job satisfaction and prosocial service behaviors. *Journal of Retailing*, *73*(1), 39–61.

Bettencourt, L. A., Gwinner, K. P., & Meuter, M. L. (2001). A comparison of attitude, personality, and knowledge predictors of service-oriented organizational citizenship behaviors. *Journal of Applied Psychology*, *86*(1), 29–41.

Blader, S., Wiesenfeld, B., Fortin, M., & Wheeler-Smith, S. (2013). Fairness lies in the heart of the beholder: How the social emotions of third parties influence reactions to injustice. *Organizational Behavior and Human Decision Processes*, *121*, 62–80.

Blasi, A. (1984). Moral identity: Its role in moral functioning. In W. Kurtines & J. Gewirtz (Eds.), *Morality, moral behavior and moral development* (pp. 128–139). New York, NY: Wiley.

Brockner, J., Grover, S., Reed, T., DeWitt, R., & O'Malley, M. (1987). Survivors' reactions to layoffs: We get by with a little help for our friends. *Administrative Science Quarterly*, *32*, 526–541. doi:10.2307/2392882

Brockner, J., Konovsky, M., Cooper-Schneider, R., Folger, R., Martin, C., & Bies, R. J. (1994). Interactive effects of procedural justice and outcome negativity on victims and survivors of job loss. *Academy of Management Journal*, *37*(2), 397–409. doi:10.2307/256835

Brockner, J., Wiesenfeld, B. M., & Martin, C. L. (1995). Decision frame, procedural justice, and survivors' reactions to job layoffs. *Organizational Behavior and Human Decision Processes*, *63*, 59–68. doi:10.1006/obhd.1995.1061

Burns, T., & Stalker, G. M. (1961). *The management of innovation*. London: Tavistock.

Byrne, D. (1971). *The attraction paradigm*. New York, NY: Academic Press.

Byrne, D., & Griffitt, W. (1969). Similarity and awareness of similarity of personality characteristic determinants of attraction. *Journal of Experimental Research in Personality*, *3*, 179–186.

Chan, K. W., Yim, C. K., & Lam, S. S. K. (2010). Is customer participation in value creation a double-edged sword? Evidence from professional financial services across cultures. *Journal of Marketing*, *74*(3), 48–64.

Christian, S. J., Christian, M. S., Garza, A. S., & Ellis, A. J. (2012). Examining retaliatory responses to justice violations and recovery attempts in teams. *Journal of Applied Psychology*, *97*(6), 1218–1232. doi:10.1037/a0029450

Cropanzano, R., Goldman, B., & Folger, R. (2005). Self-interest: Defining and understanding a human motive. *Journal of Organizational Behavior*, *26*(8), 985–991. doi:10.1002/job.353

Dahling, J. J., Chau, S. L., Mayer, D. M., & Gregory, J. B. (2012). Breaking rules for the right reasons? An investigation of pro-social rule breaking. *Journal of Organizational Behavior*, *33*(1), 21–42. doi:10.1002/job.730

Davis, M. (1980). A multidimensional approach to individual differences in empathy. *JSAS Catalog of Selected Documents in Psychology*, *10*, 85–104.

Dietz, J., Pugh, S. D., & Wiley, J. W. (2004). Service climate effects on customer attitudes: An examination of boundary conditions. *Academy of Management Journal*, *47*(1), 81–92. doi:10.2307/20159561

Dimitriades, Z. S. (2007). The influence of service climate and job involvement on customer-oriented organizational citizenship behavior in Greek service organizations: A survey. *Employee Relations*, *29*(5), 469–491. doi:10.1108/01425450710776290

Duffy, M. K., Ganster, D., & Pagon, M. (2002). Social undermining in the workplace. *Academy of Management Journal*, *45*(2), 331–351. doi:10.2307/3069350

Dulebohn, J. H., Bommer, W. H., Liden, R. C., Brouer, R. L., & Ferris, G. R. (2012). A meta-analysis of antecedents and consequences of leader-member exchange: Integrating the past with an eye toward the future. *Journal of Management, 38*(6), 1715–1759. doi:10.1177/0149206311415280

Eisenberg, N., & Miller, P. A. (1987). Empathy, sympathy, and altruism: empirical and conceptual links. In N. Eisenberg & J. Strayer (Eds.), *Empathy and its development* (pp. 292–316). New York, NY: Cambridge University Press.

Eisenberger, R., Stinglhamber, F., Vandenberghe, C., Sucharski, I. L., & Rhoades, L. (2002). Perceived supervisor support: Contributions to perceived organizational support and employee retention. *Journal of Applied Psychology, 87*(3), 565–573. doi:10.1037/0021-9010.87.3.565

Etgar, M. (2008). A descriptive model of the consumer co-production process. *Journal of the Academy of Marketing Science, 36*(1), 97–108.

Feshbach, N. D. (1975). Empathy in children: Some theoretical and empirical considerations. *The Counseling Psychologist, 5*, 25–30.

Fetchenhauer, D., & Huang, X. (2004). Justice sensitivity and distributive decisions in experimental games. *Personality and Individual Differences, 36*(5), 1015–1029. doi:10.1016/S0191-8869(03)00197-1

Folger, R. (1998). Fairness as moral virtue. In M. Schminke (Ed.), *Managerial ethics: Morally managing people and processes* (pp. 13–34). Mahwah, NJ: Lawrence Erlbaum Associates.

Folger, R. (2001). Fairness as deonance. In S. W. Gilliland, D. D. Steiner, & D. P. Skarlicki (Eds.), *Research in social issues in management* (pp. 3–31). Greenwich, CT: Information Age Publishers.

Gabriel, A. S., Daniels, M. A., Diefendorff, J. M., & Greguras, G. J. (2014). Emotional labor actors: A latent profile analysis of emotional labor strategies. *Journal of Applied Psychology*. doi:10.1037/a0037408

Galinsky, A. D., & Moskowitz, G. B. (2000). Perspective-taking: Decreasing stereotype expression, stereotype accessibility, and in-group favoritism. *Journal of Personality and Social Psychology, 78*, 708–724. doi:10.1037/0022-3514.78.4.708

Gollwitzer, M., Schmitt, M., Schalke, R., Maes, J., & Baer, A. (2005). Asymmetrical effects of justice sensitivity perspectives on prosocial and antisocial behavior. *Social Justice Research, 18*(2), 183–201. doi:10.1007/s11211-005-7368-1

Grandey, A. A. (2003). When 'the show must go on': Surface acting and deep acting as determinants of emotional exhaustion and peer-rated service delivery. *Academy of Management Journal, 46*(1), 86–96. doi:10.2307/30040678

Grandey, A., Foo, S. C., Groth, M., & Goodwin, R. E. (2012). Free to be you and me: A climate of authenticity alleviates burnout from emotional labor. *Journal of Occupational Health Psychology, 17*(1), 1–14. doi:10.1037/a0025102

Greenbaum, R. L., Mawritz, M. B., Mayer, D. M., & Priesemuth, M. (2013). To act out, to withdraw, or to constructively resist? Employee reactions to supervisor abuse of customers and the moderating role of employee moral identity. *Human Relations, 66*(7), 925–950. doi:10.1177/0018726713482992

Grizzle, J. W., Zablah, A. R., Brown, T. J., Mowen, J. C., & Lee, J. M. (2009). Employee customer orientation in context: How the environment moderates the influence of customer orientation on performance outcomes. *Journal of Applied Psychology, 94*, 1227–1242.

Gromet, D. M., Okimoto, T. G., Wenzel, M., & Darley, J. M. (2012). A victim-centered approach to justice? Victim satisfaction effects on third-party punishments. *Law and Human Behavior, 36*(5), 375–389. doi:10.1037/h0093922

Haidt, J. (2003). The moral emotions. In R. J. Davidson, K. R. Scherer, & H. H. Goldsmith (Eds.), *Handbook of affective sciences* (pp. 852–870). Oxford: Oxford University Press.

Heidenreich, S., Wittkowski, K., Handrich, M., & Falk, T. (2015). The dark side of customer co-creation: Exploring the consequences of failed co-created services. *Journal of the Academy of Marketing Science, 43*, 279–296.

Hershcovis, M. S., Turner, N., Barling, J., Arnold, K. A., Dupré, K. E., Inness, M., ... Sivanathan, N. (2007). Predicting workplace aggression: A meta-analysis. *Journal of Applied Psychology, 92*(1), 228–238. doi:10.1037/0021-9010.92.1.228

Hershcovis, S. M., & Barling, J. (2010). Towards a multi-foci approach to workplace aggression: A meta-analytic review of outcomes from different perpetrators. *Journal of Organizational Behavior, 31*(1), 24–44. doi:10.1002/job.621

Hoobler, J. M., & Brass, D. J. (2006). Abusive supervision and family undermining as displaced aggression. *Journal of Applied Psychology, 91*(5), 1125–1133. doi:10.1037/0021-9010.91.5.1125

Hoyer, W. D., Chandy, R., Dorotic, M., Krafft, M., & Singh, S. S. (2010). Consumer cocreation in new product development. *Journal of Service Research, 13*(3), 283–296.

Huang, G. Y., Xixi, L. U., & Xi, W. A. N. G. (2014). The effects of transformational leadership on employee's pro-social rule breaking. *Canadian Social Science, 10*(1), 128–134.

Jung, D., Chow, C., & Wu, A. (2003). The role of transformational leadership in enhancing organizational innovation: Hypotheses and some preliminary findings. *The Leadership Quarterly, 14*, 525–544.

Kelloway, E. K., Francis, L., Catano, V. M., & Dupré, K. E. (2008). Third-party support for strike action. *Journal of Applied Psychology, 93*(4), 806–817. doi:10.1037/0021-9010.93.4.806

Khandwalla, P. N. (1976/1977). Some top management styles, their context and performance. *Organization and Administrative Sciences, 7*, 21–51.

Kray, L. J., & Lind, E. A. (2002). The injustices of others: Social reports and the integration of others' experiences in organizational justice judgments. *Organizational Behavior and Human Decision Processes, 89*(1), 906–924. doi:10.1016/S0749-5978(02)00035-3

Lam, C. F., & Mayer, D. M. (2014). When do employees speak up for their customers? A model of voice in a customer service context. *Personnel Psychology, 67*, 637–666.

Lawrence, P. R., & Lorsch, J. W. (1967). *Organization and environment*. Homewood, IL: Irwin.

Liden, R. C., Sparrowe, R. T., & Wayne, S. J. (1997). Leader-member exchange theory: The past and potential for the future. In G. R., Ferris (Ed.), *Research in personnel and human resources management* (Vol. 15, pp. 47–119). Greenwich, CT: Elsevier Science/JAI Press.

Loewenstein, G., & Small, D. A. (2007). The scarecrow and the tin man: The vicissitudes of human sympathy and caring. *Review of General Psychology, 11*(2), 112–126. doi:10.1037/1089-2680.11.2.112

Lotz, S., Okimoto, T. G., Schlösser, T., & Fetchenhauer, D. (2011). Punitive versus compensatory reactions to injustice: Emotional antecedents to third-party interventions. *Journal of Experimental Social Psychology, 47*(2), 477–480. doi:10.1016/j.jesp.2010.10.004

Mahony, D. M., & Klaas, B. S. (2008). The role of compensatory and retributive justice in determining damages in employment disputes. *Journal of Management*, *34*(2), 218–243. doi:10.1177/0149206307312504

Maner, J. K., Luce, C. L., Neuberg, S. L., Cialdini, R. B., Brown, S., & Sagarin, B. J. (2002). The effects of perspective taking on motivations for helping: Still no evidence for altruism. *Personality and Social Psychology Bulletin*, *28*, 1601–1610. doi:10.1177/014616702237586

March, J. G., & Simon, H. A. (1958). *Organizations*. Cambridge, MA: Blackwell.

Mawritz, M. B., Dust, S. B., & Resick, C. J. (2014). Hostile climate, abusive supervision, and employee coping: Does conscientiousness matter? *Journal of Applied Psychology*, *99*(4), 737–747. doi:10.1037/a0035863

Mayer, D. M., Ehrhart, M. G., & Schneider, B. (2009). Service attribute boundary conditions of the service climate-customer satisfaction link. *Academy of Management Journal*, *52*(5), 1034–1050. doi:10.5465/AMJ.2009.44635617

Meadows, I. S. G. (1980a). Organic structure and innovation in small work groups. *Human Relations*, *33*, 369–382. doi:10.1177/001872678003300602

Meadows, I. S. G. (1980b). Organic structure, satisfaction, and personality. *Human Relations*, *33*, 383–392. doi:10.1177/001872678003300603

Meyer, R. D., Dalal, R. S., & Hermida, R. (2010). A review and synthesis of situational strength in the organizational sciences. *Journal of Management*, *36*(1), 121–140. doi:10.1177/0149206309349309

Milam, A. C., Spitzmueller, C., & Penney, L. M. (2009). Investigating individual differences among targets of workplace incivility. *Journal of Occupational Health Psychology*, *14*(1), 58–69. doi:10.1037/a0012683

Mischel, W. (1977). The interaction of person and situation. In D. Magnusson & N. S. Endler (Eds.), *Personality at the crossroads: Current issues in interactional psychology*. Hillsdale, NJ: Erlbaum.

Mitchell, M. S., & Ambrose, M. L. (2007). Abusive supervision and workplace deviance and the moderating effects of negative reciprocity beliefs. *Journal of Applied Psychology*, *92*(4), 1159–1168. doi:10.1037/0021-9010.92.4.1159

Mohiyeddini, C., & Schmitt, M. J. (1997). Sensitivity to befallen injustice and reactions to unfair treatment in a laboratory situation. *Social Justice Research*, *10*(3), 333–353. doi:10.1007/BF02683307

Morrison, E. W. (2006). Doing the job well: An investigation of pro-social rule breaking. *Journal of Management*, *32*(1), 5–28. doi:10.1177/0149206305277790

Myers, M. W., Laurent, S. M., & Hodges, S. D. (2014). Perspective taking instructions and self-other overlap: Different motives for helping. *Motivation and Emotion*, *38*(2), 224–234. doi:10.1007/s11031-013-9377-y

Nadisic, T. (2008). The Robin Hood effect: Antecedents and consequences of managers using invisible remedies to correct workplace injustice. In S. W. Gilliland, D. D. Steiner, & D. P. Skarlicki (Eds.), *Justice, morality and social responsibility* (pp. 125–153). Greenwich, CT: IAP.

O'Reilly, J., & Aquino, K. (2011). A model of third parties' morally motivated responses to mistreatment in organizations. *The Academy of Management Review*, *36*(3), 526–543. doi:10.5465/AMR.2011.61031810

Pierce, J. L., Gardner, D. G., Cummings, L. L., & Dunham, R. B. (1989). Organization-based self-esteem: Construct definition, measurement, and validation. *Academy of Management Journal*, *32*(3), 622–648. doi:10.2307/256437

Prahalad, C. K., & Ramaswammy, V. (2004). Co-creation experiences: The next practice in value creation. *Journal of Interactive Marketing*, *18*(3), 5–14.

Priesemuth, M. (2013). Stand up and speak up: Employees' prosocial reactions to observed abusive supervision. *Business & Society*, *52*, 649–665.

Rafaeli, A., Erez, A., Ravid, S., Derfler-Rozin, R., Treister, D. E., & Scheyer, R. (2012). When customers exhibit verbal aggression, employees pay cognitive costs. *Journal of Applied Psychology*, *97*(5), 931–950. doi:10.1037/a0028559

Rahman, M., & Zanzi, A. (1995). A comparison of organizational structure, job stress, and satisfaction in audit and management advisory services (MAS) in CPA firms. *Journal of Managerial Issues*, *7*, 290–305.

Raub, S., & Liao, H. (2012). Doing the right thing without being told: Joint effects of initiative climate and general self-efficacy on employee proactive customer service performance. *Journal of Applied Psychology*, *97*(3), 651–667.

Rupp, D. E., & Bell, C. M. (2010). Extending the deontic model of justice: Moral self-regulation in third-party responses to injustice. *Business Ethics Quarterly*, *20*, 89–106.

Rupp, D. E., & Spencer, S. (2006). When customers lash out: The effects of customer interactional injustice on emotional labor and the mediating role of discrete emotions. *Journal of Applied Psychology*, *91*(4), 971–978. doi:10.1037/0021-9010.91.4.971

Salanova, M., Agut, S., & Peiró, J. M. (2005). Linking organizational resources and work engagement to employee performance and customer loyalty: The mediation of service climate. *Journal of Applied Psychology*, *90*(6), 1217–1227. doi:10.1037/0021-9010.90.6.1217

Schmitt, M. (1996). Individual differences in sensitivity to befallen injustice (SBI). *Personality and Individual Differences*, *21*(1), 3–20. doi:10.1016/0191-8869(96)00028-1

Schmitt, M., & Dörfel, M. (1999). Procedural injustice at work, justice sensitivity, job satisfaction and psychosomatic well-being. *European Journal of Social Psychology*, *29*(4), 443–453. doi:10.1002/(SICI)1099-0992(199906)29:4<443::AID-EJSP935>3.0.CO;2-C

Schmitt, M., Gollwitzer, M., Maes, J., & Arbach, D. (2005). Justice sensitivity: Assessment and location in the personality space. *European Journal of Psychological Assessment*, *21*(3), 202–211. doi:10.1027/1015-5759.21.3.202

Schmitt, M., Neumann, R., & Montada, L. (1995). Justice sensitivity. *Social Justice Research*, *8*, 385–401.

Schneider, B. (1975). Organizational climates: An essay. *Personnel Psychology*, *28*(4), 447–479. doi:10.1111/j.1744-6570.1975.tb01386.x

Schneider, B., Ehrhart, M. G., Mayer, D. M., Saltz, J. L., & Niles-Jolly, K. (2005). Understanding organization-customer links in service settings. *Academy of Management Journal*, *48*, 1017–1032.

Schneider, B., Parkington, J. J., & Buxton, V. M. (1980). Employee and customer perceptions of service in banks. *Administrative Science Quarterly*, *25*, 252–267.

Schneider, B., & Reichers, A. E. (1983). On the etiology of climates. *Personnel Psychology*, *36*(1), 19–39. doi:10.1111/j.1744-6570.1983.tb00500.x

Schneider, B., White, S. S., & Paul, M. C. (1998). Linking service climate and customer perceptions of service quality: Tests of a causal model. *Journal of Applied Psychology*, *83*(2), 150–163. doi:10.1037/0021-9010.83.2.150

Shanock, L. R., & Eisenberger, R. (2006). When supervisors feel supported: Relationships with subordinates' perceived supervisor support, perceived organizational support, and performance. *Journal of Applied Psychology*, *91*(3), 689–695. doi:10.1037/0021-9010.91.3.689

Shao, R., & Skarlicki, D. P. (2014). Service employees' reactions to mistreatment by customers: A comparison between North America and East Asia. *Personnel Psychology*, *67*(1), 23–59. doi:10.1111/peps.12021

Skarlicki, D. P., Ellard, J. H., & Kelln, B. C. (1998). Third-party perceptions of a layoff: Procedural, derogation, and retributive aspects of justice. *Journal of Applied Psychology*, *83*(1), 119–127. doi:10.1037/0021-9010.83.1.119

Skarlicki, D. P., & Kulik, C. T. (2005). Third-party reactions to employee (mis)treatment: A justice perspective. In B. M. Staw & R. M. Kramer (Eds.), *Research in organizational behavior: An annual series of analytical essays and critical reviews* (Vol. 26, pp. 183–229). Greenwich, CT: Elsevier Science/JAI Press.

Skarlicki, D. P., O'Reilly, J., & Kulik, C. T. (in press). The third-party perspective of (in)justice. In R. Cropanzano & M. A. Ambrose (Eds.), *Oxford handbook of justice in work organizations*. New York, NY: Oxford University Press.

Skarlicki, D. P., & Rupp, D. E. (2010). Dual processing and organizational justice: The role of rational versus experiential processing in third-party reactions to workplace mistreatment. *Journal of Applied Psychology*, *95*(5), 944–952. doi:10.1037/a0020468

Skarlicki, D. P., & Turner, R. A. (2014). Unfairness begets unfairness: Victim derogation bias in employee ratings. *Organizational Behavior and Human Decision Processes*, *124*(1), 34–46. doi:10.1016/j.obhdp.2013.11.004

Skarlicki, D. P., van Jaarsveld, D. D., & Walker, D. D. (2008). Getting even for customer mistreatment: The role of moral identity in the relationship between customer interpersonal injustice and employee sabotage. *Journal of Applied Psychology*, *93*(6), 1335–1347. doi:10.1037/a0012704

Slevin, D. P., & Covin, J. G. (1997). Strategy formation patterns, performance, and the significance of context. *Journal of Management*, *23*, 189–209.

Sliter, M., Jex, S., Wolford, K., & McInnerney, J. (2010). How rude! Emotional labor as a mediator between customer incivility and employee outcomes. *Journal of Occupational Health Psychology*, *15*(4), 468–481.

Sliter, M., Sliter, K., & Jex, S. (2012). The employee as a punching bag: The effect of multiple sources of incivility on employee withdrawal behavior and sales performance. *Journal of Organizational Behavior*, *33*(1), 121–139. doi:10.1002/job.767

Tajfel, H., & Turner, J. C. (1986). An integrative theory of intergroup conflict. In W. G. Austin & S. Worchel (Eds.), *The social psychology of intergroup relations* (pp. 33–47). Monterey, CA: Brooke-Cole.

Tangney, J. P., Stuewig, J., & Mashek, D. J. (2007). Moral emotions and moral behavior. *Annual Review of Psychology*, *58*, 345–372.

Tepper, B. J. (2000). Consequences of abusive supervision. *Academy of Management Journal*, *43*(2), 178–190. doi:10.2307/1556375

Tepper, B. J. (2007). Abusive supervision in work organizations: Review synthesis, and research agenda. *Journal of Management*, *33*(3), 261–289. doi:10.1177/0149206307300812

Thibaut, J., & Walker, L. (1975). *Procedural justice: A psychological analysis*. Hillsdale, NJ: Erlbaum.

Treadway, D. C., Shaughnessy, B. A., Breland, J. W., Yang, J., & Reeves, M. (2013). Political skill and the job performance of bullies. *Journal of Managerial Psychology*, *28*(3), 273–289. doi:10.1108/02683941311321169

Turillo, C. J., Folger, R., Lavelle, J. J., Umphress, E. E., & Gee, J. O. (2002). Is virtue its own reward? Self-sacrificial decisions for the sake of fairness. *Organizational Behavior and Human Decision Processes*, *89*(1), 839–865. doi:10.1016/S0749-5978(02)00032-8

Tyler, T. R., & Blader, S. L. (2000). *Cooperation in groups: Procedural justice, social identity, and behavioral engagement*. New York, NY: Psychology Press.

Tyler, T. R., & Lind, E. A. (1992). A relational model of authority in groups. In M. P. Zanna (Ed.), *Advances in experimental social psychology* (Vol. 25, pp. 115–191). San Diego, CA: Academic Press. doi:10.1016/S0065-2601(08)60283-X

Umphress, E. E., Simmons, A. L., Folger, R., Ren, R., & Bobocel, R. (2013). Observer reactions to interpersonal injustice: The roles of perpetrator intent and victim perception. *Journal of Organizational Behavior*, *34*(3), 327–349. doi:10.1002/job.1801

van Jaarsveld, D. D., Walker, D. D., & Skarlicki, D. P. (2010). The role of job demands and emotional exhaustion in the relationship between customer and employee incivility. *Journal of Management*, *36*(6), 1486–1504. doi:10.1177/0149206310368998

van Prooijen, J. W. (2009). Procedural justice as autonomy regulation. *Journal of Personality and Social Psychology*, *96*(6), 1166.

van Prooijen, J. W. (2010). Retributive versus compensatory justice: Observers preference for punishing in response to criminal offenses. *European Journal of Social Psychology*, *40*(1), 72–85.

Vardaman, J. M., Gondo, M. B., & Allen, D. G. (2014). Ethical climate and pro-social rule breaking in the workplace. *Human Resource Management Review*, *24*(1), 108–118. doi:10.1016/j.hrmr.2012.05.001

Victor, B., & Cullen, B. J. (1988). The organizational bases of ethical work climates. *Administrative Science Quarterly*, *33*, 101–125.

Wang, M., Liao, H., Zhan, Y., & Shi, J. (2011). Daily customer mistreatment and employee sabotage against customers: Examining emotion and resource perspectives. *Academy of Management Journal*, *54*(2), 312–334.

Wang, M., Liu, S., Liao, H., Gong, Y., Kammeyer-Mueller, J., & Shi, J. (2013). Can't get it out of my mind: Employee rumination after customer mistreatment and negative mood in the next morning. *Journal of Applied Psychology*, *98*(6), 989–1004.

Weber, M. (1978). *Economy and society: An outline of interpretive sociology*. Berkeley, CA: University of California Press. (Original work published 1922).

Xie, C., Bagozzi, R. P., & Troye, S. V. (2008). Trying to presume: toward a theory of consumers as co-creators of value. *Journal of the Academy of Marketing Science*, *36*(1), 109–122.

Yang, L., Caughlin, D. E., Gazica, M. W., Truxillo, D. M., & Spector, P. E. (2014). Workplace mistreatment climate and potential employee and organizational outcomes: A meta-analytic review from the target's perspective. *Journal of Occupational Health Psychology*, *19*(3), 315–335. doi:10.1037/a0036905

Zoghbi-Manrique-de-Lara, P., Aguiar-Quintana, T., & Suárez-Acosta, M. A. (2013). A justice framework for understanding how guests react to hotel employee (mis)treatment. *Tourism Management*, 36143–36152. doi:10.1016/j.tourman.2012.11.010

Zoghbi-Manrique-de-Lara, P., & Suárez-Acosta, M. A. (2014). Employees' reactions to peers' unfair treatment by supervisors: The role of ethical leadership. *Journal of Business Ethics*, *122*(4), 537–549. doi:10.1007/s10551-013-1778-z

Zohar, D. (2000). A group-level model of safety climate: testing the effect of group climate on microaccidents in manufacturing jobs. *Journal of Applied Psychology*, *85*(4), 587–596.

CUSTOMER MISTREATMENT: A REVIEW OF CONCEPTUALIZATIONS AND A MULTILEVEL THEORETICAL MODEL

Jaclyn Koopmann, Mo Wang, Yihao Liu and Yifan Song

ABSTRACT

In this chapter, we summarize and build on the current state of the customer mistreatment literature in an effort to further future research on this topic. First, we detail the four primary conceptualizations of customer mistreatment. Second, we present a multilevel model of customer mistreatment, which distinguishes between the unfolding processes at the individual employee level and the service encounter level. In particular, we consider the antecedents and outcomes unique to each level of analysis as well as mediators and moderators. Finally, we discuss important methodological concerns and recommendations for future research.

Keywords: Customer mistreatment; customer interactional injustice; customer incivility; customer aggression; affective work event; multilevel model

Mistreatment in Organizations
Research in Occupational Stress and Well Being, Volume 13, 33–79

ISSN: 1479-3555/doi:10.1108/S1479-355520150000013002

Customer mistreatment, which refers to the low-quality interpersonal treatment that employees receive from their customers during service interactions (Bies, 2001; Skarlicki, van Jaarsveld, & Walker, 2008; Wang, Liao, Zhan, & Shi, 2011), is a shared experience among service workers (Boyd, 2002; Grandey, Dickter, & Sin, 2004; Harris & Reynolds, 2003). Customer mistreatment may take the form of derogatory behavior, verbal aggression, or unreasonable demands (e.g., Dormann & Zapf, 2004; Skarlicki et al., 2008) and can have serious ramifications for service employee well-being, such as emotional exhaustion (e.g., Grandey et al., 2004) and physical health symptoms (e.g., Sliter, Pui, Sliter, & Jex, 2011), and work behaviors, such as service performance (e.g., Rafaeli et al., 2012; Sliter, Jex, Wolford, & McInnerney, 2010) and sabotage behavior (e.g., Wang et al., 2011).

Whereas the majority of previous studies have focused on the general tendency to experience customer mistreatment (i.e., between-person differences), new emphasis has been placed on the study of specific customer mistreatment events and employees' daily exposure to customer mistreatment. Indeed, recent experimental (e.g., Rupp & Spencer, 2006) and experience-sampling studies (e.g., Wang et al., 2013) have provided some insights into the more immediate affective and behavioral outcomes of customer mistreatment. However, customer mistreatment research would benefit from improved conceptual clarity as well as methodological rigor because these advancements are needed to more fully understand the breadth and strength of customer mistreatment's effects on service employees, customers, and organizations. Moreover, previous studies have largely treated customer mistreatment as a given component of service work without much attention paid to the employee-related, situational, or environmental causes of customer mistreatment. Therefore, we aim to contribute to the customer mistreatment literature in several ways in this chapter.

First, we synthesize the multiple conceptualizations of customer mistreatment, including customer mistreatment as interactional injustice, affective work event, signal of goal failure, and resource-depleting event, and emphasize the need for research design and research questions to align with the chosen conceptualization. Second, integrating these conceptualizations, we propose a multilevel model of customer mistreatment that summarizes previous empirical studies and provides additional avenues for future research on customer mistreatment. In particular, our multilevel perspective helps distinguish customer mistreatment as a phenomenon at the individual and service encounter levels. Specifically, we highlight that whereas individual characteristics, organizational policies, and job conditions may affect how regularly a service employee is mistreated, employee and customer states (e.g., mood and regulatory resources) may directly or indirectly (through service quality) impact the occurrence of customer mistreatment during a specific service encounter.

Furthermore, our model depicts the possible mechanisms by which customer mistreatment experiences influence short-term employee outcomes (e.g., emotional labor and stress), customer outcomes (e.g., service performance and sabotage), and potential outcomes for coworkers, family, and friends outside of the service interaction (e.g., the spill-over of aggression). Our multilevel perspective also addresses the individual-level boundary conditions that may serve as important moderators of the multilevel theoretical relations specified in the model. Finally, we consider the methodological issues present in previous research and offer concrete suggestions, such as improving construct measurement, using multisource data, incorporating longitudinal and multilevel designs, as well as including additional control variables, to improve future research.

CONCEPTUALIZING CUSTOMER MISTREATMENT

Although previous research agrees on the definition of customer mistreatment (i.e., customers' low-quality interpersonal treatment of employees), studies have used different conceptualizations to understand customer mistreatment's implications. As such, we synthesize and review the four major conceptualizations of customer mistreatment in the current section.

Customer Mistreatment as Interactional Injustice

Previous literature has identified customer mistreatment as a specific type of interactional injustice, which involves interpersonal and informational justice perceptions (Bies, 2001; Rupp, McCance, & Grandey, 2007; Rupp, McCance, Spencer, & Sonntag, 2008; Rupp & Spencer, 2006; Skarlicki et al., 2008; Spencer & Rupp, 2009), because both customer mistreatment and interactional injustice involve norm violations in workplace social interactions. Specifically, interpersonal injustice is perceived when an employee is subject to disrespectful, ignominious, or interpersonally insensitive behavior from another organizational party, such as a coworker or supervisor. Informational injustice is perceived when an employee is provided unclear, dishonest, or insufficient communication or communication that is inappropriately timed (Bies & Moag, 1986; Colquitt, 2001). These perspectives suggest that employees will feel that they have been unjustly treated when a customer talks down to them, speaks out of turn interjecting with new demands for them to handle (interpersonal forms of injustice), intentionally omits crucial information, or is reluctant and ill-natured about extending additional information when prompted (informational forms of injustice).

The general justice literature suggests that when employees perceive interpersonal or informational injustice, they give poorer appraisals of transgressors, experience lower work attitudes, and engage in withdrawal and retaliatory behaviors, such as theft and sabotage (Colquitt, Conlon, Wesson, Porter, & Ng, 2001; Skarlicki & Folger, 1997). However, in the customer service interaction, employees are often not allowed to take their frustration out on their coworkers or supervisors (Yang & Diefendorff, 2009). Moreover, general work attitudes and behaviors directed toward the organization seem less likely consequences of customer mistreatment than retaliation toward customers. Indeed, recent conceptual work on deontic justice (Cropanzano, Goldman, & Folger, 2003; Folger, 2001; Folger, Cropanzano, & Goldman, 2005) and multifoci justice (Cropanzano, Byrne, Bobocel, & Rupp, 2001; Lavelle, Rupp, & Brockner, 2007; Rupp & Cropanzano, 2002) suggests that injustice reactions are commonly directed toward offending parties.

In particular, the deontic perspective contends that for evolutionary reasons injustice will trigger judgments of moral wrongdoing, engender negative emotions, and result in retaliation against the transgressor (e.g., Folger, 2001; Folger & Skarlicki, 2008). For example, Reb, Goldman, Kray, and Cropanzano (2006) observed that terminated employees perceiving interactional injustice favored punitive treatment for the managers they held accountable. Reb et al. reasoned that terminated employees desired to punish their transgressors because doing so helps to recalibrate the moral convention and need for moral meaning. Thus, when employees are mistreated by customers, they are likely to make judgments about whether their fundamental moral right to be treated fairly has been violated (Spencer & Rupp, 2009) and are likely to "even the score" through retaliation.

Likewise, multifoci justice emphasizes that the source of injustice matters because employees assign culpability to transgressors as an inherent part of justice perceptions. In other words, the source is an important piece of injustice experiences because the source determines at whom employees direct their responses. In fact, there is a robust literature which documents that the perceived source of injustice is the target of revenge-motivated behavior by the wronged employee (Rupp & Spencer, 2006). For instance, Rupp, Shao, Jones, and Liao (2014) used meta-analysis to demonstrate that transgressor-specific justice perceptions are more strongly related to transgressor outcomes than they are to non-transgressor outcomes.

Consistent with the broader justice literature, customer mistreatment has been linked with emotional and retaliatory consequences, such as employee sabotage (Skarlicki et al., 2008), counterproductive work behavior (Yang & Diefendorff, 2009), and negative emotions (Rupp et al., 2007; Rupp et al., 2008; Rupp & Spencer, 2006; Spencer & Rupp, 2009). Given its underlying *quid pro quo* mechanism, the interactional injustice conceptualization of customer mistreatment is particularly useful for studies examining transgressor-specific (i.e., customer-directed) outcomes.

Customer Mistreatment as an Affective Work Event

Previous research has also conceptualized customer mistreatment relative to its affective consequences because such mistreatment elicits negative emotions and reduces positive emotions (Rupp & Spencer, 2006). Specifically, affective events theory contends that work events elicit affective responses which in turn drive work attitudes, motivation, and behaviors. Through primary and secondary appraisal processes, employees first acknowledge personally relevant events (e.g., events that endanger individual well-being) and then react to them with discrete emotions (Weiss & Cropanzano, 1996). Thus, affective events theory suggests that customer mistreatment may be relevant to employees' affect when customer mistreatment is personally or professionally significant to the employee. That is, if an employee feels that customer mistreatment is a hindrance to his/her work or threatens his/her self-image, the employee will subsequently experience negative emotions.

Accordingly, previous research has associated customer mistreatment with anger (e.g., Rupp et al., 2008; Spencer & Rupp, 2009) which is easily induced by moral or social norm violation (e.g., Folger, 2001; Weiss, Suckow, & Cropanzano, 1999). Anxiety has also been linked with customer mistreatment because customer mistreatment creates ambiguity about how employee performance and well-being will be affected (Wegge, Van Dick, & Von Bernstorff, 2010; Zhan, Wang, & Shi, 2013). Furthermore, an array of other negative emotions, including sadness, fear, frustration, disappointment, hurt, guilt, and shame (Groth & Grandey, 2012; Rupp et al., 2007; Volmer, Binnewies, Sonnentag, & Niessen, 2012; Wegge, Vogt, & Wecking, 2007; Yang & Diefendorff, 2009) have also been examined as affective consequences of customer mistreatment.

Affective events theory further suggests that whereas acute negative events elicit discrete and intense negative emotions, over time and with continued exposure, negative events are likely to result in low-arousal negative moods among employees (Morris, 1989; Weiss & Cropanzano, 1996). Thus, instances of customer mistreatment are more likely to result in negative emotions, such as anger, whereas accumulated customer mistreatment is more likely to result in sustainable impairment to well-being, such as depression. For example, Baranik, Wang, Gong, and Shi (2014) observed that when employees constantly experienced high levels of customer mistreatment, they tended to have lower levels of well-being.

In addition, the affective work event conceptualization aligns well with research documenting that employees and customers share similar emotions due to emotional contagion (Barger & Grandey, 2006; Elfenbein, 2014; Kim & Yoon, 2012; Tan, Der Foo, & Kwek, 2004), which can be thought of as the "tendency to automatically mimic and synchronize facial expressions, vocalizations, postures, and movements with those of another person and, consequently, to converge emotionally" (Hatfield, Cacioppo, & Rapson, 1994, p. 5). Recent conceptual work (Van Kleef, Homan, & Cheshin, 2012) also posits that emotions have interpersonal affective consequences, which in turn drive individuals' behavioral responses. Affective reactions to others' emotional displays occur when observers adopt a similar or complementary emotion based on physical or verbal cues or when observers develop positive or negative feelings about someone based on that person's emotions. Based on these mechanisms (i.e., emotional contagion and emotion-based impression), it is conceivable that customer mistreatment leads service employees to feel similar emotions such as anger; complementary emotions such as fear; or disdain toward the customer. Consequently, the employee may return the mistreatment, interacting in a discourteous manner with the customer.

In sum, an affective work event conceptualization can be valuable when studies consider customer mistreatment's impact on employee well-being because well-being is commonly linked to affective experiences (e.g., Diener, Suh, Lucas, & Smith, 1999). Additionally, this conceptualization may shed light on both the short-term emotional consequences of customer mistreatment in a service encounter (e.g., anger) and the long-term cumulative effect of customer mistreatment on employee well-being (e.g., depression) at the individual level.

Customer Mistreatment as a Signal of Goal Failure

Previous research has also conceptualized customer mistreatment as a goal failure signal. Service employees' task goals involve working with customers to address their specific problems and demands (Dormann & Zapf, 2004). In addition, service employees' personal goals entail satisfaction of affiliation and achievement needs because these needs are essential to maintaining positive self-image (DeShon & Gillespie, 2005; Dormann & Zapf, 2004; Skarlicki et al., 2008). Customer mistreatment may signal goal failure because it indicates that the customer is dissatisfied, which is incongruent with the task goal (Harris & Reynolds, 2003). Customer mistreatment may also place additional job demands on the employee, increasing the resources needed to complete the service task and reducing employee expectations of effectively meeting the service task goal (Wang et al., 2011). Likewise, customer mistreatment may signal goal failure because it limits the relatedness, accomplishment, and positive self-regard employees can experience in the service interaction (Skarlicki et al., 2008; Wang et al., 2013). Thus, customer mistreatment can be viewed as a signal to service employees that their efforts toward pursuing task and personal goals are unsuccessful.

In turn, the signal of goal failure induces a goal blockage experience (Nolen-Hoeksema, Wisco, & Lyubomirsky, 2008) and leads to cognitive and social reactions such as rumination and social sharing (Baranik et al., 2014). As one example, rumination involves recurrent thoughts that are focused on individuals' perceptions of goal failure but not how one could achieve goal success. Ruminative thoughts about goal failure occur involuntarily without provocation when individuals are not otherwise engaged in alternative activities. Goal blockage triggers rumination because it may increase the availability of the goal failure experience (e.g., customer mistreatment), facilitating the ease with which it is remembered (Martin & Tesser, 1989, 1996; Martin, Tesser, & McIntosh, 1993; Nolen-Hoeksema et al., 2008; Smith & Alloy, 2009). Unless the goal is achieved or abandoned, thoughts of the unattained goal may repeatedly interrupt individuals' lives. Consequently, individuals may re-experience the failure and its negative emotion over time, because rumination increases negatively biased thinking and pessimism while reducing efforts toward goal completion and mood-enhancing behaviors (e.g., Moberly & Watkins, 2008; Nolen-Hoeksema et al., 2008). Accordingly, previous research has conceptually or empirically linked customer mistreatment with rumination and lasting negative mood states (e.g., Rafaeli et al., 2012; Wang et al., 2013). For example, Wang et al. (2013) found that customer mistreatment was related to greater rumination up to one day later and higher negative affect up to two days later. Moreover, Volmer et al. (2012) demonstrated that civil services employees engaged in greater levels of negative work reflection on days when they experienced more customer mistreatment.

The goal failure conceptualization is consistent with Diefendorff and Gosserand's (2003) control theory of emotional labor, which suggests that service employees consider their expressed emotions in light of organizational requirements for personable service (i.e., emotional display rules). When employees perceive a discrepancy between their current emotions and the task-based emotional goal, they partake in emotion regulation, either changing the way they think to elicit authentic and compliant emotional displays or the way they are acting to fake desired emotional displays. Thus, when customer mistreatment occurs, a service employee will perceive a large discrepancy signal between their current emotions and the emotions dictated by company display rules, resulting in perceived service goal failure and emotion regulation to reduce the discrepancy. Thus, the goal failure conceptualization of customer mistreatment is particularly useful for studies examining emotional labor and other self-regulatory outcomes.

Customer Mistreatment as a Resource-Depleting Event

Previous research has also adopted a resource-based conceptualization of customer mistreatment because service employees may gain resources from cooperative customer interactions or lose resources from poor customer interactions, such as those involving customer mistreatment (e.g., Brotheridge & Lee, 2002; Dormann & Zapf, 2004; Goldberg & Grandey, 2007; Wang et al., 2011). Specifically, the conservation of resources theory (COR, Hobfoll, 1989, 2002) defines *resources* as the sum of an individual's means to achieve his or her important needs. Because individuals invest current resources in behavioral regulation, they must interact with their environment to accumulate new resources for satisfaction of valued needs (i.e., the accumulation mechanism, Hobfoll, 2002). When facing direct or primary resource loss, such as when personal possessions, self-esteem, or social relationships are threatened, individuals reinvest existing resources hoping to offset the loss (i.e., the protection mechanism). If these resources are not recouped, secondary resource loss will occur, resulting in unsuccessful loss control strategies and loss spirals (i.e., configurations of exponential resource depletion; Bacharach & Bamberger, 2007; Hobfoll, 2002) and subsequently inferior stores of resources available for regulating other work behaviors (Vohs & Heatherton, 2000).

During customer mistreatment, customers breach the norms of social interactions, placing greater claims (i.e., the interpersonal and emotional demands of the job) on employee resources while blocking employees' opportunities for resource gains. In particular, when mistreated, service employees engage in emotional and behavioral regulation to comply with organizational service rules that stipulate handling customers with professionalism, respect, and positive emotions (Goldberg & Grandey, 2007; Grandey, Kern, & Frone, 2007; Sliter et al., 2010). Therefore, in addition to causing employees to experience primary resource loss by imposing more job demands, customer mistreatment incites efforts to countervail resource loss via further resource investment (e.g., additional attentional and emotional energies directed to conforming to and fulfilling prescribed service goals). In turn, service employees may experience secondary resource loss and a loss spiral (Grandey, Foo, Groth, & Goodwin, 2012). All in all, employees are subsequently less capable of conforming to customer service rules and regulating their behavior (Wang et al., 2011).

Consistent with previous empirical studies documenting the effects of resource depletion, customer mistreatment has been linked with employee sabotage (Shao & Skarlicki, 2014; Wang et al., 2011), incivility toward customers, job demands (van Jaarsveld, Walker, & Skarlicki, 2010), withdrawal (e.g., absences, Grandey et al., 2004), reduced performance (e.g., Sliter, Sliter, & Jex, 2012), and burnout (e.g., Ben-Zur & Yagil, 2005; Dormann & Zapf, 2004; Grandey et al., 2007; Greenbaum, Quade, Mawritz, Kim, & Crosby, 2014). For example, Wang et al. (2011), using a sample of call center employees, reported that customer mistreatment was positively related to employee sabotage and this positive association was mitigated by job tenure (i.e., cognitive resource) and service rule commitment (i.e., motivational resource). Furthermore, in a series of experimental studies, Rafaeli et al. (2012) observed that customer mistreatment impaired employee task performance through the depletion of cognitive resources, namely working memory and recognition memory.

Notably, resource depletion and self-regulation impairment may be a mediating mechanism between previously discussed conceptualizations and employee outcomes because injustice perceptions, negative affective work events, and signals of goal failure are all likely to deplete service employees' resources and we more fully address this idea in a later section. From a practical standpoint, the resource-based conceptualization of customer mistreatment can be particularly impactful because studies in this paradigm often consider the individual or contextual resources that protect individuals from mistreatment's negative effects.

Concluding Comments on Conceptualizations of Customer Mistreatment

With several conceptualizations available in the existing literature, it is important to understand the appropriate use of each conceptualization in future research efforts. We suggest researchers choose their theoretical lens based on the nature of their research question. For instance, if researchers are interested in examining how customer mistreatment leads to employee retaliation toward their transgressors, then a justice-based conceptualization may be more appropriate. If researchers are interested in customer mistreatment's short-term emotional or long-term well-being consequences, then an affective work event conceptualization can be utilized. When researchers study how customer mistreatment influences self-regulatory processes, such as emotion regulation, the goal failure conceptualization is likely most suitable. The resource-based conceptualization may be applied alone to understand maladaptive behavior and coping strategies resulting from customer mistreatment or in conjunction with the other three conceptualizations to further explicate how customer mistreatment affects employees.

In addition, researchers need to be aware that to study customer mistreatment at different levels (e.g., individual level vs. service encounter level), they also have to be careful in choosing their theoretical conceptualization. Specifically, all four theoretical conceptualizations may fit, if the researchers are interested in phenomena at the service encounter level. However, if the researchers are interested in phenomena at the individual level, they need to select the theoretical conceptualization that would allow clear articulation of the emergence process of the key constructs from the service encounter level to the individual level. For example, if the affective work event conceptualization is chosen, an emotional climate-based emergence process needs to be used to connect event-based negative emotions to individual-level phenomena, such as job dissatisfaction and poor well-being. To contrast, if the goal failure conceptualization is chosen, a chronic goal blockage-based emergence process needs to be used to make a similar connection.

Based on these notions, we next develop a multilevel theoretical model to understand and differentiate the unfolding processes of customer

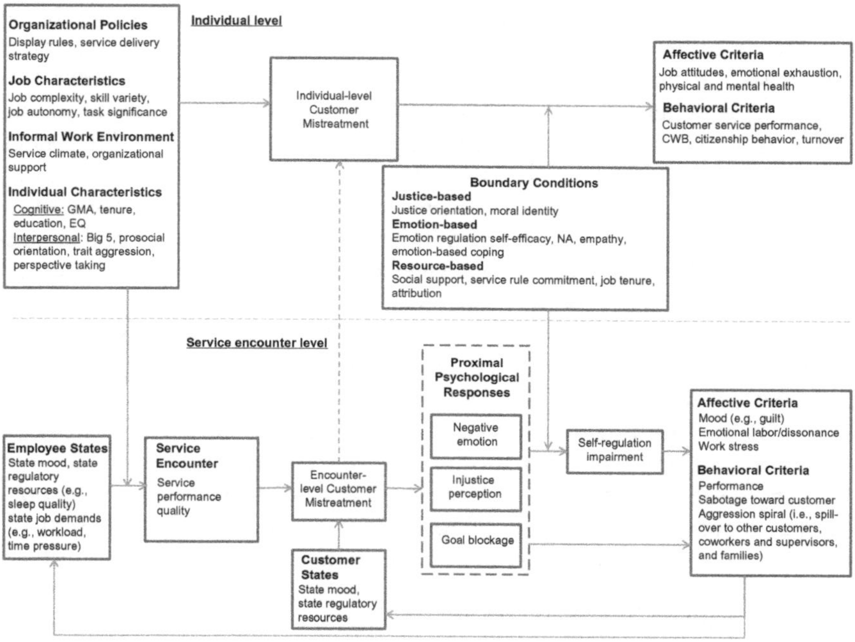

Fig. 1. A Multilevel Model of Customer Mistreatment.

mistreatment at the individual employee level and service encounter level (see Fig. 1). In this model, we also consider important boundary conditions of these unfolding processes. In the sections that follow, we first explain a multilevel view of customer mistreatment, which allows us to focus on unique antecedents and outcomes at different levels of analysis. We then provide more details regarding the specific relationships described in our theoretical model.

A MULTILEVEL MODEL OF CUSTOMER MISTREATMENT

Service Encounter-Level Customer Mistreatment versus Individual-Level Customer Mistreatment

An important intent of this chapter is to introduce a multilevel view to examine customer mistreatment at different levels, namely the service encounter level and the individual level. To study customer mistreatment from this multilevel view, it is critical to distinguish customer mistreatment experienced at the service encounter level from the average customer mistreatment experienced at the individual level. Specifically, at the service encounter level, customer mistreatment refers to the low-quality interpersonal treatment an employee receives during a particular service encounter. In other words, customer mistreatment at the service encounter level represents the fluctuations in or the within-person experience of customer mistreatment, which can vary from service encounter to service encounter. At the individual level, however, customer mistreatment refers to how frequently or commonly an employee receives low-quality interpersonal treatment when interacting with customers. In this sense, individual-level customer mistreatment emphasizes the between-person mean differences among employees in experiencing customer mistreatment.

Conceptualizing and distinguishing customer mistreatment at these two different levels are important because they provide us ways to theorize unique antecedents at corresponding levels of analysis. In particular, at the service encounter level, the nature of the specific customer service interaction, the psychological states of the service employee, and those of the customer, may all contribute to the occurrence of customer mistreatment. In contrast, at the individual level, customer mistreatment is likely to be determined by more stable individual characteristics, job conditions, and organizational policies. For example, employees are typically assigned to customers at random (to the extent that customers appear at random). Therefore, fluctuations in customer mistreatment received by the same customer service employee should even out when aggregated over multiple service encounters. However, if such aggregation reveals a general tendency for a particular employee to be mistreated across various customers, this general tendency can only be attributed to factors that are relatively stable and manifest meaningful differences between employees, such as the service ability of the employee, the quality of the product represented by the customer service employee, or the strategic importance that the company attaches to the customer experience, but not factors that change at the service encounter level. Building upon this logic, for two employees who have the same job in the same company, when one of them in general receives more customer mistreatment than the other, it is likely that the stable individual differences between these two employees drive the differences in the propensity to be mistreated, rather than factors associated with any specific service encounters.

Following this level-based distinction, we next describe a theoretical model that considers the unfolding processes of customer mistreatment at both the service encounter level and the individual level. This model summarizes previous findings but also builds upon theories that describe general principles underlying social interaction as well as service performance. This model also reflects the various theoretical mechanisms we reviewed earlier underlying the key conceptualizations of customer mistreatment.

Service Encounter-Level Customer Mistreatment – Antecedents

Employee States as Distal Antecedents

At the service encounter level, we expect that employee mood states and regulatory resources could potentially lead to customer mistreatment. Although employees' mood states may have a direct impact on perceived customer mistreatment (Dudenhöffer & Dormann, 2013), we expect that mood states and regulatory resources are more distal antecedents to service encounter-level customer mistreatment through their effects on service quality. For example, using daily objective productivity and service quality ratings and an experience-sampling design, Rothbard and Wilk (2011) showed that call center employees' start-of-day positive mood positively predicted and negative mood negatively predicted employee performance. Medler-Liraz and Kark (2012) also demonstrated that service employee hostility was negatively associated with employees' service performance, which in turn led to more customer mistreatment.

Moreover, we expect that employees' state regulatory resources could potentially lead to poor service quality and customer mistreatment in a service encounter. Specifically, when employees have fewer regulatory resources, such as when experiencing state burnout or reduced sleep quantity during the previous night, they may not be able to fully participate in the work role or exercise the self-control needed to regulate their service behaviors (Muraven & Baumeister, 2000; Muraven, Tice, & Baumeister, 1998). Additionally, employees with fewer regulatory resources may also fear further resource loss and thus are hesitant to invest their limited resources (Hobfoll, 2002). For example, in a field experiment, Chan and Wan (2012) found that employees with fewer regulatory resources were less capable of handling customer complaints. In addition, Lanaj, Johnson, and Barnes (2014) have demonstrated that when employees did not get enough sleep the previous night they felt depleted in the morning and were subsequently less engaged at work. Following these findings, it is conceivable that service employees are more likely to be mistreated if they have fewer resources available to adequately deliver customer service. Indirect evidence in the customer mistreatment literature supports this argument. According to Winstanley and Whittington (2002), state burnout may make service employees more likely targets of customer mistreatment.

Finally, we expect that job demands, which can be defined as the "physical, psychological, social, or organizational aspects of the job that require sustained physical and/or psychological (cognitive and emotional) effort and are therefore associated with certain physiological and/or psychological costs" (Bakker, Demerouti, de Boer, & Schaufeli, 2003, p. 344), may lead to service encounter-level customer mistreatment. Job demands, such as workload and time pressure, can vary on a daily basis (e.g., Teuchmann, Totterdell, & Parker, 1999) and create psychological strain on employees over time (e.g., Totterdell, Wood, & Wall, 2006). Such strain distracts employee attention away from work tasks and may drain their performance capacity (e.g., Hockey, 1993). Thus, service employees experiencing greater job demands are less likely to deliver high-quality service (van Jaarsveld et al., 2010). For instance, Wegge et al. (2007) observed that service employees under greater time pressure experienced more strain and spent less time talking to customers.

Service Encounter Quality and Customer States as Proximal Antecedents

As stated above, we expect that poor service quality could lead to customer mistreatment. Empirical and conceptual work has suggested that service failure in particular makes employees susceptible to customer mistreatment due to negative customer responses and behaviors (e.g., Groth & Grandey, 2012; Medler-Liraz & Kark, 2012; Reynolds & Harris, 2009). For instance, McColl-Kennedy, Patterson, Smith, and Brady (2009) identified customer rage-related emotions and behaviors incited by service failure; they found that retaliatory and rancorous rage were linked with verbal and physical forms of customer mistreatment. Groth and Grandey (2012) explained that customers are likely to react to dissatisfaction in negative ways, because they may feel that their service expectations have gone unmet (e.g., they may experience negative emotions or they may feel unjustly treated). When studying the service recovery experiences of airline customers, Grégoire and Fisher (2008) reported that customer-perceived justice violations resulted in feelings of betrayal and retaliation. The service recovery literature has further explained that perceived injustice may motivate customers to "teach the service provider a lesson," ensure the injustice does not happen to another customer in the future, or make the service provider understand what it feels like to be ill-treated via retaliation (Funches, Markley, & Davis, 2009). Thus, customer mistreatment is not necessarily unreasonable or unfounded and may stem from poor service quality (Harris & Reynolds, 2004).

Mirroring the effects of employee moods and regulatory resources on customer mistreatment, customer moods and regulatory resources may also lead to service encounter-level customer mistreatment. In particular, customers in negative moods may perceive their interactions with service employees as more hostile whereas customers in positive moods may experience more pleasant interactions (cf., Rothbard & Wilk, 2011). Thus, customers in negative mood states may be more likely to mistreat service employees. In addition, depleted customers, such as those lacking adequate sleep, may not possess the quantity of resources necessary to follow the social norms inherent in customer service interactions and the self-control needed to regulate uncivil or disrespectful behavior toward employees (Muraven & Baumeister, 2000). To our knowledge, research addressing customer states and their influence on customer mistreatment is very rare. However, using trained independent observers, Agasi, Decelles, and Rafaeli (2014) studied factors in the airport service environment that might impact customer negative emotions, resource depletion, and subsequent customer mistreatment at the flight level of analysis. They found that walking time to the gate, crowdedness at the gate, and temperature at the gate were all positively related to customer mistreatment intensity and the presence of babies crying at the gate was positively associated with customer mistreatment frequency. Agasi et al. suggest that these features may have drained customer resources and aroused negative emotions, making customers more likely to mistreat airline employees.

Service Encounter-Level Customer Mistreatment – Outcomes

Psychological Responses

As we reviewed earlier, extant research has conceptualized customer mistreatment from multiple perspectives, studying customer mistreatment as interactional injustice, affective work events, signals of goal failure, or resource-depleting events. Accordingly, when experiencing customer mistreatment, employees tend to have multiple immediate psychological responses, among which negative emotions, injustice perceptions, and goal blockage experiences are likely to be the three most proximal outcomes of customer mistreatment. In turn, these negative states are likely to result in resource depletion and self-regulation impairment at the service encounter level because resource depletion involves an immediate with-person comparison of available resources (e.g., within-person fluctuations in resources).

Self-regulation impairment is one of the core concepts in self-regulation theories (Baumeister, Bratslavsky, Muraven, & Tice, 1998; Baumeister & Vohs, 2003; Muraven & Baumeister, 2000). Self-regulation theories define self-regulatory resources as individuals' mental capacity to control and alter naturally occurring emotions, behaviors, and mental states (Baumeister & Vohs, 2003; Beal, Weiss, Barros, & MacDermid, 2005; Muraven & Baumeister, 2000). They propose that individuals exercise control over their attitudes and behaviors with regulatory resources and demands from the external environment impair individuals' regulatory resources. In the context of customer mistreatment, employees' experiences with rude customers are likely to create demands that consume regulatory resources (Beal et al., 2005; DeWall, Baumeister, Stillman, & Gailliot, 2007). This resource consumption devoted to regulating one's mental states following customer mistreatment is essential, because it helps employees to override aversive emotion (e.g., reduce negative emotions; Muraven & Baumeister, 2000), redirect their attention back to work (e.g., suppress injustice perceptions; Beal et al., 2005), and to refocus on meeting work-related goals (e.g., recover from goal failures; Grandey, Fisk, & Steiner, 2005); otherwise, employees would be stuck in maladaptive mental states (e.g., rumination) or lose effective regulation of their behaviors (e.g., customer sabotage). Although research has shown that regulating mental states is important for individuals to achieve desirable outcomes, individuals only have a finite amount of resources that are available for the regulation of undesirable mental states (Baumeister & Vohs, 2003; Beal et al., 2005). Therefore, employees are likely to experience resource depletion induced by demanding work events such as customer mistreatment and consequently suffer from self-regulation impairment.

Affective Criteria as Distal Outcomes

We categorize the distal outcomes of service encounter-level customer mistreatment as affective and behavioral in nature. In this section, we review affective outcomes of customer mistreatment at the service encounter level which include emotional labor and stress appraisal.

Previous studies have examined emotional labor and stress as outcomes of customer mistreatment and its negative emotions. For example,

Goldberg and Grandey (2007), Rupp and Spencer (2006), and Spencer and Rupp (2009), using call center simulations, reported causal evidence in support of the emotional labor consequences of customer mistreatment. For example, Rupp and Spencer (2006) manipulated customer mistreatment, finding that participants who were mistreated admitted to taking part in more emotional labor and were rated by others to have engaged in more emotional labor as compared to participants who were not exposed to customer mistreatment.

Some indirect evidence exists at the service encounter level for the effect of customer mistreatment on employee stress. Previous studies have conceptualized customer mistreatment as a daily hassle at work that may be stressful for employees (Sliter et al., 2010; Zhan et al., 2013). In particular, Dormann and Zapf (2004) categorized customer mistreatment as a social stressor because it may threaten service employees' self-efficacy, goal success, and resources (see also Penney & Spector, 2005). For example, Wegge et al. (2007) manipulated customer behavior toward call center employees and showed that employees serving unfriendly (vs. friendly) customers reported higher levels of psychological strain.

Behavioral Criteria as Distal Outcomes

In this section, we consider the behavioral outcomes of customer mistreatment, including service performance, employee sabotage, and aggression. Specifically, when examining the service encounter-level relationship between customer mistreatment and service performance, research has relied on self-regulation impairment as a mediating mechanism. Regulatory resources may be expended following mistreatment experiences as employees seek to assuage related discomfort and figure out why they were mistreated (Porath & Erez, 2007; Stoverink, Umphress, Gardner, & Miner, 2014). This self-regulation impairment should be particularly consequential to service performance because employees will be less able to regulate their service behavior to address customer demands in a particular service encounter. Indeed, Rafaeli et al. (2012) found that compared to participants in the neutral control condition, even one to two customer mistreatment encounters diminished participants' capacity to remember customer information and impaired their general working memory. They also found that compared to the control condition, participants handling aggressive customer requests had lower performance accuracy and this effect was mediated through working memory when high status customers were involved. Furthermore, Miron-Spektor, Efrat-Treister, Rafaeli, and Schwarz-Cohen (2011) found that participants exposed to customer anger, as compared to those who were not, had lower creative performance. Miron-Spektor et al. also showed that customer anger reduces an employees' ability to engage in complex thought processes. Finally, Goldberg and Grandey (2007) manipulated customer hostility and demonstrated that participants in the hostile customer condition (vs. the control condition) made more service performance mistakes during demanding calls, explaining that customer hostility took attentional resources away from task performance.

Self-regulation theories have also argued that resource depletion and the resultant impairment on self-regulatory capacity may make it difficult for individuals to regulate their behaviors to conform to social norms (Baumeister, 1998; Baumeister et al., 1998; Vancouver, 2000). For example, it can become difficult for individuals to inhibit their aggressive impulses and to prevent themselves from acting aggressively (Baumeister, Heatherton, & Tice, 1994; DeWall et al., 2007; Wang, Sinclair, & Deese, 2010). Thus, self-regulation impairment triggered by customer mistreatment may make employees less likely to effectively regulate and suppress their negative behavioral intentions toward rude customers. Consequently, mistreated employees may be more likely to violate their service rules by seeking revenge on those customers (i.e., customer-directed sabotage, Wang et al., 2011).

Employees whose self-regulatory capability is impaired may also take out their frustration with a particular customer on targets that are not the source of their original frustration. This phenomenon constitutes displaced aggression (Bushman, Bonacci, Pedersen, Vasquez, & Miller, 2005; Marcus-Newhall, Pedersen, Carlson, & Miller, 2000). Displaced aggression is more likely to occur when the source of initial provocation is unavailable (e.g., not present in the current environment; Bushman et al., 2005), more powerful (e.g., one's boss; Hoobler & Brass, 2006), or intangible (e.g., undesirable temperature and noise level; Baron & Bell, 1975). Although displacing one's anger onto others violates desirable social norms and expectations (e.g., the principle of reciprocity; Bordia, Restubog, & Tang, 2008) and the impulse to displace one's anger ought to be regulated and inhibited (e.g., Bushman et al., 2005), this regulation process may become less effective when employees suffer self-regulation impairment after customer mistreatment. Consequently, employees may find it difficult to regulate their aggressive impulses and may be more likely to lash out at others (i.e., exhibit more displaced aggression), including other customers, coworkers and supervisors at work, and family members at home (e.g., Liu et al., 2015). As such, displaced aggression may serve as a bridge between work life and home life. For example, it is conceivable that displaced aggression directed toward family members may have interesting implications for work–family conflict and family relationship quality. In sum, we expect that customer mistreatment in any particular encounter could lead to displaced aggression. However, to our knowledge, previous studies have not examined customer mistreatment's effects on displaced aggression.

Distal Criteria and Employee States

It is important to note that the service encounter level affective and behavioral criteria may also serve as inputs into the same or subsequent service encounters (as we illustrated in Fig. 1). For instance, a service employee's mood and work stress subsequent to a customer mistreatment encounter can influence the service employee states for ongoing or future customer encounters. In addition, the service employee's performance or sabotage toward a customer has an inherent link with service quality and may also affect the customer state (e.g., mood) in the current or future encounters (if future customers witnessed the previous customer's experience); thus, these distal criteria can subsequently impact other instances of customer mistreatment. Although a full consideration of this potentially cyclical process is beyond the scope of this chapter, we note that there are complexities to the service encounter-level process that may not be adequately captured by a simple recursive model.

Individual-Level Customer Mistreatment – Antecedents

Several aspects of the service job are likely to influence the typical customer mistreatment experienced by service employees. Specifically, we highlight formal organizational policies, job design, and informal aspects of the work environment and the reasons why we expect that they may influence customer mistreatment.

Organizational Policies

In general, we suggest that formal organizational policies, such as organizational display rules and organizational service delivery strategies, could be relevant to customer mistreatment. Organizational display rules outline the particular emotions service employees should and should not convey when interacting with customers (Diefendorff & Gosserand, 2003; Grandey, 2000). Compliance with display rules may be evaluated and rewarded because it is a part of service employees' performance requirements (e.g., Diefendorff, Richard, & Croyle, 2006). Thus, employees are more motivated to deliver appropriate emotions during service interactions when display rules exist in an organization (Diefendorff & Gosserand, 2003). Consequently, we suggest that customers will be less likely to mistreat employees operating under display rules because positive emotional displays contribute to more satisfying customer service experiences (Barger & Grandey, 2006; Pugh, 2001).

Organizations providing customer service also make important policy decisions regarding service delivery strategy, such as the extent to which service relationships are formed between customers and employees, which may influence customer mistreatment (Gutek, Groth, & Cherry, 2002). According to Gutek, Cherry, Bhappu, Schneider, and Woolf (2000), service relationships exist "when the customer expects to interact again in the future with the same service provider (and vice versa)" and "the two become interdependent" (p. 320). Whereas longer-term service relationships foster mutual investment in the relationship and cooperative behavior, the lack of service relationships provides little incentive to collaborate or develop a rapport. As such, it is conceivable that employees from organizations that emphasize building service relationships are less likely to be mistreated by customers because they face more certainty, gain more personal knowledge, and enjoy higher levels of trust with their customers (Grandey et al., 2007; Gutek et al., 2000). In fact, using three separate samples, Gutek et al. (2000) found support for higher trust in service relationship building across three service jobs (hairstylists, physicians, and auto mechanics).

Job Characteristics

We also expect that job characteristics can influence customer mistreatment due to their effects on work performance (Hackman & Oldham, 1975; Humphrey, Nahrgang, & Morgeson, 2007). For instance, job autonomy, which reflects the freedom employees have in completing their tasks, may allow service employees to cater their customer service behaviors to customer demands. Additionally, skill variety (i.e., the degree to which employees use various skills during task performance) and task significance (i.e., the influence employees have on others by completing their tasks) may provide service employees enhanced meaning, felt responsibility, and motivation to perform. In turn, employees with more autonomy, variety, and significance are likely to provide higher-quality service and be treated well by their customers (e.g., Thakor & Joshi, 2005). In contrast, job complexity concerns the intricacy of the job and how hard the job is to perform (Humphrey et al., 2007). As such, the more complex the job, the more likely an employee is to receive customer mistreatment because there are more opportunities for failures during service performance.

Informal Work Environment

The informal work environment may impact customer mistreatment as well. For instance, perceived organizational support makes employees feel respected and indebted to the organization and they are likely to reciprocate with commitment to organizational identification, positive job attitudes, and in-role and extra-role performance (Rhoades & Eisenberger, 2002). As such, in customer service jobs, employees perceiving greater levels of organizational support may go above and beyond in service interactions and display more positive emotions (Grandey, 2000), leading to more satisfying customer experiences and lower instances of customer mistreatment.

As another component of the informal work environment, service climate is defined as "employee perceptions of the practices, procedures, and behaviors that get rewarded, supported, and expected with regard to customer service and customer service quality" (Schneider, White, & Paul, 1998, p. 151). Better service climates have been suggested to enhance employee motivation and service rule compliance (Wang et al., 2011), which likely drive customer loyalty and positive appraisals of service performance (Liao & Chuang, 2004; Salanova, Agut, & Peiró, 2005). As such, it follows that employees working in organizations that emphasize high-quality customer service are less likely to be mistreated by customers. In fact, preliminary support for this argument is provided by Kao, Cheng, Kuo, and Huang (2014) who reported a negative correlation between service climate and customer-related stressors (e.g., perceptions of working with difficult customers).

Individual Characteristics

Cognitive. Certain individual attributes, such as general mental ability, job tenure, education, and emotional intelligence (EQ), are likely to create cognitive resources that enhance job knowledge, learning, and task expertise and increase employees' capacity to engage in desirable behaviors beyond those associated with the task (Kanfer & Ackerman, 1989; Tesluk & Jacobs, 1998). For instance, customer service employees with longer job tenure may have mastered the task-specific aspects of their jobs and have more resources to expend displaying the appropriate emotions and behaviors in customer service interactions (Kanfer & Ackerman, 1989; Wang et al., 2011). Similarly, employees with higher levels of EQ may be better able to detect and monitor their emotions and their customer's emotions. In turn, they can tailor their behaviors and emotional displays to meet customers' emotional needs and demands (e.g., Brackett & Mayer, 2003). Therefore, we expect that employees with beneficial levels of these cognitive attributes will be more likely to deliver satisfying service experiences and less likely to experience customer mistreatment.

Interpersonal. Furthermore, we suggest that individuals' personality traits could influence the tone of their interpersonal interactions and therefore customer mistreatment. On the one hand, personality traits, such as agreeableness, conscientiousness, extraversion, other orientation, and perspective taking, evoke a stronger desire to cooperate with others in order to achieve professional, social or relational goals, help out of concern for others' needs, and understand others' perspectives, empathizing with them (e.g., Barrick & Mount, 1991; Batson, Early, & Salvarani, 1997; De Dreu & Nauta, 2009). As such, employees possessing higher levels of these traits tend to have more positive interactions at work (e.g., Morgeson, Reider, & Campion, 2005). On the other hand, personality traits, such as neuroticism and trait aggression, have been linked with greater hostility, negative mood, stress perceptions and emotional unpredictability, leading to reduced attentiveness to others' needs, cooperation, and more negative interactions (e.g., Barrick & Mount, 1991; LePine & Van Dyne, 2001).

Based on these characterizations, we offer three explanations for why we expect these personality traits to be related to customer mistreatment. First, the norm of reciprocity (Gouldner, 1960) suggests that individuals should motivate similarly valenced treatment from their interaction partners. For instance, neurotic individuals have been shown to experience greater daily interpersonal conflict events (Bolger & Zuckerman, 1995), perhaps due to the hostile nature with which they engage with others. Alternatively and second, personality traits create biases in recall such that they influence the extent to which interpersonal events are remembered and interpreted in a positive or negative light (cf., Aquino & Thau, 2009). For instance, an employee high in perspective taking will be better able to understand how the customer feels and why they feel that way, making them less likely to ascribe negative or ambiguous customer behaviors to employee-directed mistreatment (Rafaeli et al., 2012; Rupp et al., 2008). Third, personality traits have also been associated with performance in a service context (Liao & Chuang, 2004). Indeed, Liao and Chuang found that conscientiousness and extraversion were positively related to service performance, which should contribute to respectful treatment from satisfied customers. Previous research has offered some support for the links between personality traits and customer mistreatment. In particular, Milam, Spitzmueller, and Penney (2009) showed that agreeable employees were less likely and neurotic employees were more likely to receive uncivil treatment from coworkers due to these traits' effects on inflammatory behaviors. In the customer mistreatment literature, Yang and Diefendorff (2009) observed negative correlations between customer mistreatment and both conscientiousness and agreeableness. Finally, in a cross-sectional field study of German bank tellers, Rupp et al. (2008) reported positive correlations among perspective taking and interpersonal and informational customer justice.

Individual-Level Customer Mistreatment – Outcomes

Similar to the service encounter level, we summarize previous empirical findings distinguishing between affective outcomes and behavioral outcomes of individual-level customer mistreatment. Individual-level affective outcomes may include job attitudes (e.g., job satisfaction, customer orientation) and health and well-being (e.g., emotional exhaustion, physical health complaints). Individual-level behavioral outcomes include performance (e.g., task performance, CWB, citizenship behavior) and turnover. We conclude by discussing the theoretical mechanisms that may explain individual-level customer mistreatment's effects.

Affective Criteria

Job Attitudes. Previous studies have looked at the attitudinal consequences of customer mistreatment. For example, both Holmvall and Sidhu (2007) and Walsh (2011) demonstrated that customer mistreatment was negatively related to job satisfaction. Similarly, in a sample of employed Canadian university students working in retail services or restaurants, Wilson and Holmvall (2013) also found a negative association between customer mistreatment and job satisfaction. Moreover, Harris (2013) found that customer mistreatment was negatively associated with affective commitment. These findings are also consistent with recent meta-analytical work by Hershcovis and Barling (2010) on the effects of outsider aggression on employees. Specifically, their findings revealed a negative relationship between outsider aggression and job satisfaction and affective commitment. Finally, previous studies have also examined job attitudes unique to customer service work. For example, Stock and Bednarek (2014) demonstrated that customer mistreatment negatively affected employees' customer-oriented attitude. However, most primary studies, including those involved in the meta-analysis, have relied on self-reported cross-sectional data. Thus, it is conceivable that employees unhappy with their jobs are mistreated more often or that an unmeasured variable, such as job skills or neuroticism, is causing a spurious relationship. As such, the causal relationship between customer mistreatment and job attitudes remains debatable.

Emotional Exhaustion. It has been suggested that customer mistreatment is harmful to employee physical and psychological functioning. Indeed, Harris and Reynolds (2003), using a qualitative research design, concluded that consistent customer mistreatment experiences were associated with long-term mental health consequences, such as feelings of degradation, stress, and anxiety. Empirical research has focused primarily on the relationship between customer mistreatment and emotional exhaustion, but this research has also documented the impact to self-reported health symptoms and well-being to some extent.

In regards to emotional exhaustion, Grandey et al. (2004) studied call center employees and showed that customer mistreatment was positively associated with emotional exhaustion. Moreover, using a sample of flight attendants, travel agents, and shoe sales employees, Dormann and Zapf (2004) showed that employees perceiving greater customer mistreatment reported more burnout symptoms, namely emotional exhaustion, depersonalization, and lack of personal accomplishment. Using both a convenience sample of customer-contact employees and a random sample of U.S. employees, Grandey et al. (2007) found that customer mistreatment explained incremental variance beyond coworker and supervisor mistreatment in employee emotional exhaustion. Typically, previous studies have proposed emotional labor, which includes surface acting, as one reason why customer mistreatment results in emotional exhaustion. For example, Grandey et al. (2012) observed that Australian health care workers, including nurses, speech therapists, clinical psychologists, and surgeons, who were exposed to more patient mistreatment were more likely to regulate their emotions via surface acting, which partially mediated mistreatment's effects on emotional exhaustion. However, it is critical to emphasize that most field studies have relied upon cross-sectional self-reported data, providing limited evidence that customer mistreatment causes emotional labor and subsequently emotional exhaustion.

Physical and Mental Health. Furthermore, there is mixed empirical evidence regarding the relationship between customer mistreatment and self-reported physical health, mental health, and well-being. Using a sample of nurses and a sample of public service workers, Merecz, Drabek, and Mościcka (2009) reported positive relationships between customer mistreatment and mental health problems, psychosomatic health complaints, and anxiety and insomnia. As another example, Wilson and Holmvall (2013) found that customer mistreatment was positively associated with job-related psychological strain. Yet, Sliter et al. (2011) did not find a significant relationship between customer mistreatment and physical health complaints reported three months later. Research on customer mistreatment and well-being is much less common, but one study has shown that customer mistreatment is negatively related to life satisfaction (Karatepe, 2011). In addition, using a sample of call center employees in China, Baranik et al. (2014) found that customer mistreatment was negatively associated with well-being (measured three months later) through cognitive rumination. Given the cross-sectional nature of most of the studies finding significant relationships between mistreatment and ill health and well-being, these findings could be attributed to individual differences, such as neuroticism, that affect perceptions of customer mistreatment and health and well-being. These findings may also be interpreted in the reverse causal direction (i.e., poor health results in customer mistreatment). Thus, longitudinal studies are warranted in further exploring the long-term effects of customer mistreatment on health and well-being. It would be especially enlightening if these studies controlled for previous health and well-being conditions, modeling change over time.

Behavioral Criteria

Consistent with the broader literature on workplace mistreatment (e.g., Olson-Buchanan & Boswell, 2008) and components of job performance (e.g., Rotundo & Sackett, 2002), we consider counterproductive work behaviors (CWBs), citizenship behaviors, and task performance as behavioral outcomes of customer mistreatment.

CWB. Previous research has consistently linked customer mistreatment with increased CWBs. For example, both Harris and Ogbonna (2002) and Harris and Reynolds (2003) interviewed hotel, restaurant, and bar employees across multiple hierarchical levels and identified a link between exposure to rude customers and engagement in service sabotage. From an empirical perspective, Walker, van Jaarsveld, and Skarlicki (2014) reported a statistically nonsignificant correlation between entity civility and employee civility at the individual level, indicating that insurance call center employees who did and did not feel they were typically mistreated by customers were not rated differently by independent judges in regards to their customer-directed disrespectful behavior. Additionally, using a sample of Canadian call center employees providing service in several different areas (e.g., parcel delivery, credit cards) and controlling for internal sources (i.e., supervisors, coworkers) of interpersonal justice, Skarlicki et al. (2008) found that employees who more commonly experienced customer interpersonal injustice were more likely to have sabotaged customer phone calls. Furthermore, Shao and Skarlicki (2014) conducted a field study of Chinese and Canadian hotel employees, finding that customer mistreatment elicited customer-directed sabotage behaviors. However, Canadian employees were more likely to respond with sabotage than Chinese employees. Thus, there may be important boundary conditions for the customer mistreatment-CWB relationship and we will address potential moderators in a later section.

Previous research has also explored the withdrawal forms of CWB as a result of customer mistreatment. For instance, whereas Grandey et al. (2004) observed a positive relationship between the stressfulness of customer mistreatment and absences (hours absent across the three months following measurement of customer mistreatment), they did not find a significant relationship between frequency of customer mistreatment and absences. Moreover, averaging objective withdrawal data from the three months following data collection, Sliter et al. (2012) demonstrated that mistreated employees were absent from more shifts and were more likely to show up to work more than 15 minutes late. All in all, these findings are also consistent with Hershcovis and Barling's (2010) meta-analytic correlations between outsider aggression and interpersonal and organizational deviance. Although some of these previous studies have used independent sources (e.g., raters, objective data) for the dependent variables, others have relied upon cross-sectional self-reported data for establishing the relationship between customer mistreatment and CWB.

Customer Service Performance. In the customer service context, task performance includes sales and service skills (e.g., Batt, 2002). Previous research has demonstrated a negative relationship between customer mistreatment and employee performance. According to Totterdell and Holman (2003), employees who report more customer mistreatment may not have the capacity or motivation to help their customers and could exhibit reduced performance. For example, Skarlicki et al. (2008), who showed that employees more unjustly treated by customers were more often saboteurs, found that employees engaging in higher levels of sabotage received worse performance ratings of customer service quality (courtesy, competence, decision quality, and sales skills) relative to their peers (supervisors and trained raters assessed employee performance in randomly chosen calls). Because Skarlicki et al. (2008) incorporated performance scores for the two months following the measurement of customer injustice, concern that poor performance actually caused customer injustice is somewhat alleviated. In addition, Sliter et al. (2011) reported that employees more regularly experiencing customer mistreatment were less productive (spent more unsanctioned time off computer and phone calls over the three-month period following mistreatment survey responses). Sliter et al. (2012) collected bank teller successful referrals (i.e., tellers referred customers to a bank product and customers then pursued that product) to measure sales performance and found that employees perceiving greater customer mistreatment had fewer successful referrals (averaged across the three months following data collection). Finally, Sliter et al. (2010) found that customer mistreatment negatively predicted a three-month average of customer service quality (scored based on customer reports of employee sales efforts, professionalism, transaction efficiency, and appreciation).

Citizenship Behavior. Citizenship behaviors are extra-role behaviors that can facilitate organizational functioning (Smith, Organ, & Near, 1983). Mistreated employees may be too depleted and lack the resources necessary to help out their coworkers or the larger organization (Binnewies, Sonnentag, & Mojza, 2009; Halbesleben & Wheeler, 2011). In addition, customer mistreatment may also reduce the extent to which service employees help out their coworkers or organization because it results in unfavorable job attitudes, which are one driver of citizenship behavior (e.g., Bateman & Organ, 1983). Unfortunately, previous studies have focused on customer mistreatment's relationship with citizenship behaviors directed at customers but not at coworkers or the organization (e.g., Shao & Skarlicki, 2014). However, indirect evidence suggests that customer mistreatment is negatively associated with organizational and interpersonal citizenship behaviors. For example, in a lab experiment, Porath and Erez (2007) demonstrated that compared to participants in the control condition participants in the rudeness condition displayed less helping behavior; control participants were also nine times more likely to help than participants experiencing the rudeness manipulation. In their meta-analysis, Hershcovis and Barling (2010) also found that outsider aggression was positively related to interpersonal deviance and organizational deviance.

Turnover. Using a sample of call center employees in China, Li and Zhou (2013) showed that customer mistreatment was positively related to turnover intentions. Based on a sample of over 2,000 nurses in England, Deery, Walsh, and Guest (2011) demonstrated that nurses mistreated by clients or their families were almost twice as likely to intend to leave their jobs within the next year or sooner. Finally, Wilson and Holmvall (2013) reported that working university students who were mistreated more often expressed stronger intentions to leave their jobs. Corroborating these findings, Hershcovis and Barling (2010) reported a positive association between outsider aggression and turnover intentions in their meta-analysis. Unfortunately, these studies cannot rule out the reverse temporal sequence of customer mistreatment and turnover intentions or important individual differences that may affect turnover intentions and mistreatment simultaneously. On top of these limitations, studies have yet to link customer mistreatment with actual turnover. Nonetheless, given the concern for high turnover rates and the associated costs in the customer service industry, organizations would likely benefit from taking steps (e.g., through appropriate selection processes and greater organizational support) to reduce customer mistreatment and turnover intentions in turn.

Mechanisms Linking Individual-Level Customer Mistreatment and its Outcomes

At the individual level, we contend that the effects of customer mistreatment on behavioral outcomes are distal, largely via its associations with affective outcomes. As such, it is likely that the affective outcomes serve as mediating mechanisms that transmit the effects of customer mistreatment to behavioral outcomes. Previous studies have also adopted this view. For instance, van Jaarsveld et al. (2010) demonstrated that employees subject to more customer mistreatment were more uncivil toward their customers and this relationship was partly due to employee emotional exhaustion. Moreover, Deery, Iverson, and Walsh (2002) surveyed telecommunications call center employees in Australia and found that employees perceiving customers as more disrespectful experienced greater emotional exhaustion, which positively related to absences in turn (number of one or two day absences associated with sick leave from the previous 12 months).

In addition, it is important to recognize that between-person differences in the experience of negative emotions, injustice, goal blockage, and resource availability at work may serve as more proximal mechanisms that link individual-level customer mistreatment to its outcomes. In particular, employees who experience more negative emotions, injustice perceptions, goal blockage, and have fewer available resources are more likely to exhibit affective and behavioral issues than those who have fewer such experiences. This is in contrast to the service encounter level, where the above-mentioned experiences are temporary in nature and capture the ebbs and flows within the same person, which do not immediately translate into robust between-person differences.

Individual-Level Boundary Conditions

Justice-Based Moderators

Because customer mistreatment has been linked with interactional injustice perceptions and moral outrage, it follows that individuals' traits affecting the salience of moral issues could impact how strongly employees react to customer mistreatment. For instance, moral identity involves the ease with which an individual's moral compass is activated (Aquino & Reed, 2002). Moral identity can be further delineated into internalization (i.e., the importance of morality to one's self-image) and symbolization (i.e., the extent to which individuals outwardly express their opposition to moral violations via other-observable behaviors). On the one hand, individuals high in moral identity internalization are likely to empathize and forgive wrongdoers because they consider the moral ramifications of their responses (Reed & Aquino, 2003). On the other hand, individuals high in moral identity symbolization react more strongly to mistreatment, engaging in retaliation, because they feel their identity-based moral goals have been thwarted. For example, Skarlicki et al. (2008) demonstrated that participants high (vs. low) in moral identity symbolization engaged in more customer-directed sabotage but only when moral identity internalization was also low. Thus, employees high in moral identity symbolization and low in moral identity internalization will experience stronger negative reactions (behavioral and affective) as a result of customer mistreatment.

In addition, justice orientation or sensitivity reflects the degree to which individuals espouse justice as a moral virtue and are sensitive to moral and social norm violations (Liao & Rupp, 2005). Individuals high in justice orientation are thus more likely to pick up on justice cues in the work environment and more strongly respond than individuals low in justice orientation. For instance, Liao and Rupp (2005) showed that supervisor procedural justice climates yielded more positive evaluations of commitment and satisfaction among employees high in justice orientation. Moreover, Liu, Luksyte, Wang, Zhou, and Shi (2014) found that perceived overqualification was negatively related to organization-based self-esteem and positively associated with employment-related anger only when justice sensitivity was high. Similar to moral identity, we expect justice orientation to moderate the relationships between individual-level customer mistreatment and its outcomes such that employees high in justice orientation will experience stronger negative effects to their well-being, job attitudes, and task performance and stronger positive effects to their CWB and withdrawal behavior.

Emotion-Based Moderators

Previous research has suggested that emotion-based variables may influence the strength of service employees' reactions to customer mistreatment (e.g., Baranik et al., 2014; Ho & Gupta, 2012; Walker et al., 2014; Wang et al., 2011; Yang & Diefendorff, 2009; Zhan et al., 2013). In general, it has been suggested that whereas some emotion-based traits, such as emotional regulation self-efficacy and empathy, facilitate regulation of negative emotions, other emotion-based tendencies, such as negative affectivity and maladaptive emotion-based coping (e.g., rumination or social sharing), make employees more susceptible to or prolong negative emotions and contribute to stronger negative reactions. In other words, emotion-based moderators can buffer or exacerbate employees' responses to customer mistreatment. To illustrate, for example, employees high in negative affectivity are prone to view ambiguous interpersonal treatment as more spiteful and unfair (Penney & Spector, 2005; Skarlicki, Folger, & Tesluk, 1999). Similarly, employees high in negative affectivity are more susceptible to the ill effects of such negative events at work, and thus feel greater negative emotions (e.g., Yang & Diefendorff, 2009). Further, employees high in negative affectivity utilize inadequate coping strategies to deal with heightened negative emotions (e.g., Liu, Wang, Zhan, & Shi, 2009), impairing their ability to regulate service behavior. Thus, mistreated employees who are higher in negative affectivity are more likely to respond to customer mistreatment with retaliatory behaviors. Indeed, Wang et al. (2011) found that negative affectivity moderated the positive effects of customer mistreatment on employee sabotage, such that the positive relationship was stronger when employees had higher levels of negative affectivity.

On the positive side, for example, emotional regulation self-efficacy has been defined as the extent to which individuals feel they can engage in effective emotional regulation (Wang et al., 2011). Emotional regulation self-efficacy should induce individuals to devote more attention toward their emotional display rule goals (e.g., show positive emotions to customers) even when challenges to emotion-based goals arise (cf. Bandura, 2001). Therefore, mistreated employees with higher emotional regulation self-efficacy are more likely to work through their resultant negative emotions. That is, employees exposed to customer mistreatment and higher in emotional regulation self-efficacy may be less prone to retaliate against their transgressor. Wang et al. (2011) showed that self-efficacy for emotional regulation moderated the positive effects of customer mistreatment on employee sabotage, such that the positive relationship was weaker when employees had higher levels of emotional regulation self-efficacy.

Resource-Based Moderators

Consistent with the resource-based conceptualization of customer mistreatment, it is conceivable that individuals' available cognitive (e.g., job tenure), social (e.g., support), and motivational (e.g., service rule commitment, internal attribution) resources impact employee reactions to customer mistreatment. Similar to COR theory (e.g., Hobfoll, 2002), self-regulation theory proposes that resource gain and loss in the working context could influence how effectively individuals regulate themselves in response to stressful events such as customer mistreatment (Baumeister, 1998; Baumeister et al., 1998). Specifically, we expect employees with greater resources to react less strongly than employees with fewer resources, because resource-rich employees are better able to regulate their emotions and behaviors even when mistreated (Wang et al., 2011). In particular, employees with greater access to resources may suffer less resource loss or recover resources faster when mistreated by customers. For instance, Wang et al. (2011) showed that the relationship between customer mistreatment and employee sabotage was weaker for employees high in service rule commitment, a motivational resource which focuses employees' efforts on the service task. Given the importance of these resource-based moderators for mitigating the negative consequences of customer mistreatment, continued research is needed in exploring the variety of workplace resources that may intervene in the process by which customer mistreatment influences employee and customer outcomes.

Service Encounter-Level Boundary Conditions

Moderators of the Employee States-Service Quality Relationship

Similar to the individual-level unfolding process of customer mistreatment, the service encounter-level process also has several important individual-level boundary conditions. Adopting a multilevel perspective, we posit that the service encounter-level relationship between employee states (e.g., mood, regulatory resource depletion) and service encounter quality is moderated by individual characteristics, organizational policies, and job conditions. Because we hypothesized that these individual-level variables may directly lead to the general tendency for an employee to be mistreated by customers, it is conceivable that they may also influence the extent to which employees' daily states impede service quality and thus contribute to service encounter-level customer mistreatment. First, we expect that individual characteristics associated with better interpersonal skills (e.g., agreeableness, prosocial orientation) and task competence (e.g., GMA, job tenure) should mitigate the effects of state mood and depletion on service quality. We expect these mitigating effects because the characteristics are likely to make service performance (e.g., friendly service in addition to task fulfillment) more automatic and less demanding of cognitive and attentional resources. Thus, service employees with more of these traits may have more resources available to devote to regulating behaviors associated with their depleted states or unpleasant moods (cf., Wang et al., 2011). In contrast, other individual traits (e.g., neuroticism) may exacerbate the association between employee depletion, negative mood, and service encounter quality because they make employees more prone to anxiety, stress, and irritability. Thus, neurotic individuals are likely to experience amplified negative emotions when in negative moods and react more negatively to depleted states, which results in reduced ability to provide high-quality service.

Furthermore, organizational policies and aspects of the informal work environment (e.g., display rules, service climate) that engender compliance to service quality expectations may buffer the relationship between state mood and regulatory resources and service quality, because employees will strive to meet the organizational service goals even when mistreated. As such, it is conceivable that service employees in organizations with service rules invest more attention and effort into regulating their emotions and task-related behaviors; in turn, this results in a higher likelihood that the employee will deliver high service quality. Likewise, certain organizational features (e.g., service relationships, organizational support) may buffer the relationship between employee states and service quality because these features provide employees with important social and motivational resources that can replace resources lost by employees in depleted states or foul moods. However, the customer mistreatment literature has yet to explore many of these relationships in conjunction with the proposed boundary conditions.

Moderators of the Psychological Response-Self-Regulation Impairment Relationship
In addition, we expect that the degree to which the proximal service encounter-level outcomes of customer mistreatment (e.g., negative emotions, injustice perception, goal failure) lead to self-regulation impairment is contingent upon individual-level justice-based (e.g., moral identity), emotion-based (e.g., emotion regulation self-efficacy), and resource-based (e.g., service rule commitment) moderators. As we previously discussed, certain individual traits make employees more susceptible to the negative effects of injustice (e.g., justice orientation) and negative emotions (e.g., maladaptive emotion-based coping). Thus, we expect employees with higher justice orientation and maladaptive emotion-based coping to experience even more self-regulation impairment from injustice and negative emotions, respectively, because regulating their stronger emotional, cognitive, and behavioral reactions may monopolize employee resources. Alternatively, contextual or personal resources (e.g., social support, job tenure, service rule commitment) should buffer the positive relationship between employees' mistreatment-related negative emotions, injustice perceptions, and goal failure and self-regulation impairment. We expect this protective effect because these moderators may provide employees the resource gains that allow employees to repair or counteract resource loss from these proximal negative outcomes of customer mistreatment, leading to a lower likelihood that self-regulation is compromised. In sum, justice-based moderators can alter the relationship between injustice perceptions and self-regulation impairment and emotion-based moderators are most likely to affect the relationship between negative emotions and self-regulation impairment. Resource-based moderators are unique in that they can protect against the influence of injustice, negative emotions, or goal failure on self-regulation impairment.

METHODOLOGICAL RECOMMENDATIONS

In our review of the customer mistreatment literature, we identified several methodological issues and we discuss these issues in this section. Specifically, we stress the importance of enhancing construct measurement, incorporating multisource data, using longitudinal and multilevel design, and modeling control variables.

Measurement of Constructs

We suggest that research on customer mistreatment can be strengthened by adopting certain measurement practices, including utilizing validated customer-specific measures of mistreatment, considering frequency and intensity of mistreatment, mitigating memory bias concerns, and exploring the multidimensional nature of customer mistreatment. First, previous studies of customer mistreatment seem to use a variety of measures. Because customer mistreatment has been conceptualized in numerous ways, researchers have operationalized customer mistreatment via customer aggression measures (e.g., Grandey et al., 2004), interpersonal conflict measures (e.g., Sliter et al., 2011), interactional injustice and workplace incivility measures (e.g., Kern & Grandey, 2009), among others. Whereas some studies on customer mistreatment have modified previously validated scales (e.g., interactional injustice scale, Colquitt, 2001), other studies have developed their own scales (e.g., Dormann & Zapf, 2004; Skarlicki et al., 2008). To our knowledge, research on the relationships among the various scales that measure customer mistreatment has been limited. Likewise, there have not been many studies providing comparative criterion-related validity evidence. One study of note is Wilson and Holmvall (2013), which provided discriminant validity evidence of a developed customer incivility scale, customer psychological aggression, and customer interpersonal injustice. Moreover, Wilson and Holmvall demonstrated that their developed customer incivility scale predicted employee outcomes above and beyond a workplace incivility scale adapted to the customer context. However, it is still unclear whether one overall construct (customer mistreatment) has been tapped by these various measures and whether the various measures have incremental predictive value. As such, meta-analytic efforts to summarize the current literature and advance future theory and research may be limited without greater understanding of the relationships among the different measures of customer mistreatment.

Second, current research has asked employees how often customer mistreatment has occurred to them (i.e., frequency) or the extent to which customers have mistreated them (i.e., intensity). For example, Grandey et al. (2004) demonstrated that customer mistreatment frequency and perceived stressfulness of customer mistreatment were positively associated with emotional exhaustion. However, only the stress associated with customer mistreatment influenced employee absences through emotional exhaustion. Moreover, although more frequent than supervisor or coworker mistreatment (Grandey et al., 2007), customer mistreatment has a low base rate (Grandey et al., 2012) and researchers may limit the variance they can capture when using a frequency response scale. For example, Grandey et al. (2007) reported that on average participants were verbally abused by customers less than once a month in their first study and less than one to three days a month in their second study. Thus, the intensity of customer mistreatment might have stronger ramifications than the frequency of customer mistreatment for employee outcomes. We suggest that researchers consider whether frequency or intensity matches their theorizing and research questions and the extent to which their sample context will exhibit meaningful variation in customer mistreatment frequency and intensity.

Finally, most previous studies have measured and operationalized customer mistreatment as a unidimensional construct (e.g., Skarlicki et al., 2008; Wang et al., 2011). Since customer mistreatment ranges in intention and severity, it is possible that customer mistreatment can be represented by several types or sets of behaviors (Zhan et al., 2013). For example, Dormann and Zapf (2004) conceptualized customer interactions as social stressors and distinguished between four kinds of customer-related social stressors (CSS). Drawing from the CSS framework, Zhan et al. (2013) conceptualized customer mistreatment as either aggressive (e.g., verbal attacks on the employee) or demanding (e.g., making unreasonable requests of the service employee). Zhan et al. argued that this distinction is important because whereas aggressive mistreatment might more strongly impact employees' emotions, demanding mistreatment might more strongly deplete employees' cognitive resources. Thus, examining the multidimensional nature of customer mistreatment could further clarify the relationships within customer mistreatment's nomological network.

Multisource Data

We also recommend that researchers collect data from service employees as well as other sources, such as coworkers, customers, and independent raters. First, multisource data that comes from first-hand observers other than the focal employee can be useful for assessing congruence in judgments of customer mistreatment. For example, one can assess the similarity between employees' perceptions of customer mistreatment and the independent coding of objective customer service call recordings. In doing so, multiple ratings of customer mistreatment can provide validity evidence for self-reported customer mistreatment. In addition, obtaining data from multiple sources can pinpoint more objective measures of customer mistreatment, enabling the examination of how much focal service employee tendencies (e.g., interpersonal characteristics) or states (e.g., mood) influence their perceptions of the extent to which their customers have mistreated them. Second, the congruence (i.e., interaction) between employee ratings and others' ratings of mistreatment could have important downstream effects on workplace outcomes. For example, if an employee perceives greater customer mistreatment than his or her coworker observed as a third party, the employee may behave in more conflictual ways with that coworker or experience amplified negative emotions because his or her mistreatment has gone unrecognized.

Second, multisource data may also facilitate the examination of third-party effects. Specifically, coworkers or other customers may observe customer mistreatment of a service employee and behaviorally or emotionally react (Groth & Grandey, 2012). Additionally, third parties may influence whether or not the employee perceives customer mistreatment. For instance, an employee may not have interpreted a curt exchange with a customer as mistreatment, but upon discussing the situation with other coworkers, conclude that the customer mistreated them. Similarly, because employees may engage in social sharing of their customer mistreatment to assuage their negative emotions (Zhan et al., 2013), employees' family members or friends may be pertinent third parties. In addition to their potential influence on employees' mistreatment perceptions, family and friends may also suffer ill effects as listeners in the social sharing interaction. For instance, family members may subsequently experience negative emotions and have difficulty sleeping that evening. Finally, although focal employees' reactions to customer mistreatment might be more selfish in nature, third parties' reactions might be more evolutionary in nature. In particular, whereas mistreated employees may retaliate because a customer violated *their* right to be treated respectfully, third parties may retaliate because the moral order of society has been violated. Thus, the unfolding process for third-party reactions to customer mistreatment may be phenomenologically different and thus requires further inquiry (Skarlicki & Kulik, 2004).

Third, multisource data is important because it may facilitate the direct operationalization of the underlying mechanisms specified in conceptualizations of customer mistreatment. For example, to operationalize goal blockage, customer service records could be utilized to assess the degree to which the customer service employee met productivity goals (e.g., time on call) when exposed to customer mistreatment. As another example, self-regulation impairment may be operationalized via objective measures, such as blood glucose levels (e.g., Gailliot & Baumeister, 2007). Finally, customers may be a useful source for operationalizing service employees' emotional displays as complementary or supplementary.

Longitudinal and Multilevel Design

Previous research has suggested that the customer mistreatment literature should move beyond cross-sectional research designs and incorporate longitudinal and multilevel data (e.g., Goldberg & Grandey, 2007; Walker et al., 2014; Zhan et al., 2013). We further contend that a longitudinal, multilevel research design is the only way to directly test the comprehensive theoretical model presented in this chapter because the cross-sectional design that has been typical practice in previous research on customer mistreatment does not match the research questions suggested by this model. Therefore, cross-sectional data cannot be used to meaningfully evaluate our multilevel model. That is, to accurately represent this model, data that captures multiple service encounters over time must be collected. In particular, only a multilevel, longitudinal approach can disentangle the unique antecedents, mechanisms, and consequences across the individual and service encounter levels; facilitate a comparison of the unique processes at the individual and service encounter levels; and allow for examination of higher-level boundary conditions that strengthen or weaken the effects of service encounter-level customer mistreatment (e.g., Walker et al., 2014; Wang et al., 2011; Wang et al., 2013). However, we recognize that while it would be a commendable research effort it may not be realistic or feasible for the entire multilevel model to be tested simultaneously.

Furthermore, longitudinal multilevel designs, such as experience-sampling methodology, can provide unique insight into how long the negative effects of customer mistreatment persist over time. For instance, experience-sampling data can be used to examine whether and how customer mistreatment at an initial time point (Day t) influences employee rumination and negative mood in the following days (Wang et al., 2013). In addition, other important research questions that have yet to be explored in the customer mistreatment literature necessitate longitudinal, multilevel data. For example, based on COR theory's description of resource loss and loss spirals, the consequences of customer mistreatment at one point in time and changes in customer mistreatment might not be the same. Specifically, employees' reactions to customer mistreatment could depend upon the rate of exposure. For example, Taylor, Bedeian, Cole, and Zhang (2014) found that changes in workplace incivility were positively associated with changes in burnout one week later, controlling for current and prior levels of incivility. By analyzing longitudinal data via latent change score modeling, researchers can separate the effects of customer mistreatment levels and trajectories in customer mistreatment and their implications for employee outcomes, such as performance, turnover intentions, and well-being, over time.

CONCLUSIONS

Customer mistreatment is a well-documented phenomenon that can harm customer service employee performance and well-being. Our chapter summarized the four major conceptualizations of customer mistreatment. Drawing on these conceptualizations, we developed a multilevel model that specifies the unique antecedents and outcomes of customer mistreatment at the service encounter and individual levels. Further, we presented mediators of the effects of service encounter-level customer mistreatment and boundary conditions that may impact the unfolding process of customer mistreatment at both the service encounter and individual levels. Finally, we discussed ways to enhance the methodological rigor of future customer mistreatment research.

REFERENCES

Agasi, S., Decelles, K. A., & Rafaeli, A. (2014, August). Relating aversive organizational context to customer aggression. In D. X. H. Wo (Chair). Antecedents and consequences of customers' misbehaviors: Opening the black blox. Symposium conducted at the 75th annual meeting of the academy of management, Philadelphia, PA.

Aquino, K., & Reed, A. (2002). The self-importance of moral identity. *Journal of Personality and Social Psychology*, *83*, 1423–1440.

Aquino, K., & Thau, S. (2009). Workplace victimization: Aggression from the target's perspective. *Annual Review of Psychology*, *60*, 717–741.

Bacharach, S. B., & Bamberger, P. A. (2007). 9/11 and New York City firefighters' post hoc unit support and control climates: A context theory of the consequences of involvement in traumatic work-related events. *Academy of Management Journal*, *50*, 849–868.

Bakker, A. B., Demerouti, E., de Boer, E., & Schaufeli, W. B. (2003). Job demands and job resources as predictors of absence duration and frequency. *Journal of Vocational Behavior*, *62*, 341–356.

Bandura, A. (2001). Social cognitive theory: An agentic perspective. In S. T. Fiske, D. L. Schacter, & C. Zahn-Waxler (Eds.), *Annual review of psychology* (Vol. 52, pp. 1–26). Palo Alto, CA: Annual Reviews.

Baranik, L. E., Wang, M., Gong, Y., & Shi, J. (2014). Customer mistreatment, employee health, and job performance: Cognitive rumination and social sharing as mediating mechanisms. *Journal of Management*. Advance online publication.

Barger, P. B., & Grandey, A. A. (2006). Service with a smile and encounter satisfaction: Emotional contagion and appraisal mechanisms. *Academy of Management Journal, 49*, 1229–1238.

Baron, R. A., & Bell, P. A. (1975). Aggression and heat: Mediating effects of prior provocation and exposure to an aggressive model. *Journal of Personality and Social Psychology, 31*, 825–832.

Barrick, M. R., & Mount, M. K. (1991). The big five personality dimensions and job performance: A meta-analysis. *Personnel Psychology, 44*, 1–26.

Bateman, T. S., & Organ, D. W. (1983). Job satisfaction and the good soldier: The relationship between affect and employee "citizenship". *Academy of Management Journal, 26*, 587–595.

Batson, C. D., Early, S., & Salvarani, G. (1997). Perspective taking: Imagining how another feels versus imaging how you would feel. *Personality and Social Psychology Bulletin, 23*, 751–758.

Batt, R. (2002). Managing customer services: Human resource practices, quit rates, and sales growth. *Academy of Management Journal, 45*, 587–597.

Baumeister, R. F. (1998). The self. In D. T. Gilbert, S. T. Fiske, & G. Lindzey (Eds.), *Handbook of social psychology* (4th ed., pp. 680–740). New York, NY: McGraw-Hill.

Baumeister, R. F., Bratslavsky, E., Muraven, M., & Tice, D. M. (1998). Ego depletion: Is the active self a limited resource? *Journal of Personality and Social Psychology, 74*, 1252–1265.

Baumeister, R. F., Heatherton, T. F., & Tice, D. M. (1994). *Losing control: How and why people fail at self-regulation*. San Diego, CA: Academic Press.

Baumeister, R. F., & Vohs, K. D. (2003). Willpower, choice, and self-control. In G. Loewenstein, D. Read, & R. F. Baumeister (Eds.), *Time and decision: Economic and psychological perspectives on intertemporal choice* (pp. 201–216). New York, NY: Russell Sage Foundation.

Beal, D. J., Weiss, H. M., Barros, E., & MacDermid, S. M. (2005). An episodic process model f affective influences on performance. *Journal of Applied Psychology, 90*, 1054–1068.

Ben-Zur, H., & Yagil, D. (2005). The relationship between empowerment, aggressive behaviours of customers, coping, and burnout. *European Journal of Work and Organizational Psychology, 14*, 81–99.

Bies, R. J. (2001). Interactional (in)justice: The sacred and the profane. In J. Greenberg & R. Cropanzano (Eds.), *Advances in organizational justice* (pp. 89–118). Stanford, CA: Stanford University Press.

Bies, R. J., & Moag, J. S. (1986). Interactional justice: Communication criteria for fairness. In B. Sheppard (Ed.), *Research on negotiation in organizations* (Vol. 1, pp. 43–55). Greenwich, CT: JAI Press.

Binnewies, C., Sonnentag, S., & Mojza, E. J. (2009). Daily performance at work: Feeling recovered in the morning as a predictor of day-level job performance. *Journal of Organizational Behavior, 30*, 67–93.

Bolger, N., & Zuckerman, A. (1995). A framework for studying personality in the stress process. *Journal of Personality and Social Psychology*, *69*, 890–902.

Bordia, P., Restubog, S. L. D., & Tang, R. L. (2008). When employees strike back: Investigating mediating mechanisms between psychological contract breach and workplace deviance. *Journal of Applied Psychology*, *93*, 1104–1117.

Boyd, C. (2002). Customer violence and employee health and safety. *Work, Employment & Society*, *16*, 151–169.

Brackett, M. A., & Mayer, J. D. (2003). Convergent, discriminant, and incremental validity of competing measures of emotional intelligence. *Personality and Social Psychology Bulletin*, *29*, 1147–1158.

Brotheridge, C. M., & Lee, R. T. (2002). Testing a conservation of resources model of the dynamics of emotional labor. *Journal of Occupational Health Psychology*, *7*, 57–67.

Bushman, B. J., Bonacci, A. M., Pedersen, W. C., Vasquez, E. A., & Miller, N. (2005). Chewing on it can chew you up: Effects of rumination on triggered displaced aggression. *Journal of Personality and Social Psychology*, *88*, 969–983.

Chan, K. W., & Wan, E. W. (2012). How can stressed employees deliver better customer service? The underlying self-regulation depletion mechanism. *Journal of Marketing*, *76*, 119–137.

Colquitt, J. A. (2001). On the dimensionality of organizational justice: A construct validation of a measure. *Journal of Applied Psychology*, *86*, 386–400.

Colquitt, J. A., Conlon, D. E., Wesson, M. J., Porter, C. O., & Ng, K. Y. (2001). Justice at the millennium: A meta-analytic review of 25 years of organizational justice research. *Journal of Applied Psychology*, *86*, 425–445.

Cropanzano, R., Byrne, Z. S., Bobocel, D. R., & Rupp, D. E. (2001). Moral virtues, fairness heuristics, social entities, and other denizens of organizational justice. *Journal of Vocational Behavior*, *58*, 164–209.

Cropanzano, R., Goldman, B., & Folger, R. (2003). Deontic justice: The role of moral principles in workplace fairness. *Journal of Organizational Behavior*, *24*, 1019–1024.

Deery, S., Iverson, R., & Walsh, J. (2002). Work relationships in telephone call centres: Understanding emotional exhaustion and employee withdrawal. *Journal of Management Studies*, *39*, 471–496.

Deery, S., Walsh, J., & Guest, D. (2011). Workplace aggression: The effects of harassment on job burnout and turnover intentions. *Work, Employment & Society*, *25*, 742–759.

De Dreu, C. K., & Nauta, A. (2009). Self-interest and other-orientation in organizational behavior: Implications for job performance, prosocial behavior, and personal initiative. *Journal of Applied Psychology*, *94*, 913–926.

DeShon, R. P., & Gillespie, J. Z. (2005). A motivated action theory account of goal orientation. *Journal of Applied Psychology*, *90*, 1096–1127.

DeWall, C. N., Baumeister, R. F., Stillman, T. F., & Gailliot, M. T. (2007). Violence restrained: Effects of self-regulation and its depletion on aggression. *Journal of Experimental Social Psychology*, *43*, 62–76.

Diefendorff, J. M., & Gosserand, R. H. (2003). Understanding the emotional labor process: A control theory perspective. *Journal of Organizational Behavior*, *24*, 945–959.

Diefendorff, J. M., Richard, E. M., & Croyle, M. H. (2006). Are emotional display rules formal job requirements? Examination of employee and supervisor perceptions. *Journal of Occupational and Organizational Psychology*, *79*, 273–298.

Diener, E., Suh, E. M., Lucas, R. E., & Smith, H. L. (1999). Subjective well-being: Three decades of progress. *Psychological Bulletin*, *125*, 276–302.

Dormann, C., & Zapf, D. (2004). Customer-related social stressors and burnout. *Journal of Occupational Health Psychology*, *9*, 61–82.

Dudenhöffer, S., & Dormann, C. (2013). Customer-related social stressors and service providers' affective reactions. *Journal of Organizational Behavior*, *34*, 520–539.

Elfenbein, H. A. (2014). The many faces of emotional contagion An affective process theory of affective linkage. *Organizational Psychology Review*, *4*, 326–362.

Folger, R. (2001). Fairness as deonance. In S. W. Gilliland, D. D. Steiner, & D. P. Skarlicki (Eds.), *Research in social issues in management* (pp. 3–31). Greenwich, CT: Information Age.

Folger, R., Cropanzano, R., & Goldman, B. (2005). What is the relationship between justice and morality? In J. Greenberg & J. A. Colquitt (Eds.), *Handbook of organizational justice* (pp. 215–245). Mahwah, NJ: Lawrence Erlbaum Associates Publishers.

Folger, R., & Skarlicki, D. P. (2008). The evolutionary bases of deontic justice. In S. W. Gilliland, D. D. Steiner, & D. P. Skarlicki (Eds.), *Justice, morality, and social responsibility* (pp. 29–62). Charlotte, NC: Information Age.

Funches, V., Markley, M., & Davis, L. (2009). Reprisal, retribution and requital: Investigating customer retaliation. *Journal of Business Research*, *62*, 231–238.

Gailliot, M. T., & Baumeister, R. F. (2007). The physiology of willpower: Linking blood glucose to self-control. *Personality and Social Psychology Review*, *11*, 303–327.

Goldberg, L. S., & Grandey, A. A. (2007). Display rules versus display autonomy: Emotion regulation, emotional exhaustion, and task performance in a call center simulation. *Journal of Occupational Health Psychology*, *12*, 301–318.

Gouldner, A. W. (1960). The norm of reciprocity: A preliminary statement. *American Sociological Review*, *25*, 161–178.

Grandey, A., Foo, S. C., Groth, M., & Goodwin, R. E. (2012). Free to be you and me: A climate of authenticity alleviates burnout from emotional labor. *Journal of Occupational Health Psychology*, *17*, 1–14.

Grandey, A. A. (2000). Emotional regulation in the workplace: A new way to conceptualize emotional labor. *Journal of Occupational Health Psychology*, *5*, 95–110.

Grandey, A. A., Dickter, D. N., & Sin, H. P. (2004). The customer is not always right: Customer aggression and emotion regulation of service employees. *Journal of Organizational Behavior*, *25*, 397–418.

Grandey, A. A., Fisk, G. M., & Steiner, D. D. (2005). Must "service with a smile" be stressful? The moderating role of personal control for American and French employees. *Journal of Applied Psychology*, *90*, 893–904.

Grandey, A. A., Kern, J. H., & Frone, M. R. (2007). Verbal abuse from outsiders versus insiders: Comparing frequency, impact on emotional exhaustion, and the role of emotional labor. *Journal of Occupational Health Psychology*, *12*, 63–79.

Greenbaum, R. L., Quade, M. J., Mawritz, M. B., Kim, J., & Crosby, D. (2014). When the customer is unethical: The explanatory role of employee emotional exhaustion onto work–family conflict, relationship conflict with coworkers, and job neglect. *Journal of Applied Psychology*, *99*, 1188–1203.

Grégoire, Y., & Fisher, R. J. (2008). Customer betrayal and retaliation: When your best customers become your worst enemies. *Journal of the Academy of Marketing Science*, *36*, 247–261.

Groth, M., & Grandey, A. (2012). From bad to worse: Negative exchange spirals in employee–customer service interactions. *Organizational Psychology Review*, *2*, 208–233.

Gutek, B. A., Cherry, B., Bhappu, A. D., Schneider, S., & Woolf, L. (2000). Features of service relationships and encounters. *Work and Occupations*, *27*, 319–352.

Gutek, B. A., Groth, M., & Cherry, B. (2002). Achieving service success through relationships and enhanced encounters. *Academy of Management Perspectives*, *16*, 132–144.

Hackman, J. R., & Oldham, G. R. (1975). Development of the job diagnostic survey. *Journal of Applied Psychology*, *60*, 159–170.

Halbesleben, J. R., & Wheeler, A. R. (2011). I owe you one: Coworker reciprocity as a moderator of the day-level exhaustion–performance relationship. *Journal of Organizational Behavior*, *32*, 608–626.

Harris, L. C. (2013). Service employees and customer phone rage: An empirical analysis. *European Journal of Marketing*, *47*, 463–484.

Harris, L. C., & Ogbonna, E. (2002). Exploring service sabotage: The antecedents, types and consequences of frontline, deviant, antiservice behaviors. *Journal of Service Research*, *4*, 163–183.

Harris, L. C., & Reynolds, K. L. (2003). The consequences of dysfunctional customer behavior. *Journal of Service Research*, *6*, 144–161.

Harris, L. C., & Reynolds, K. L. (2004). Jaycustomer behavior: An exploration of types and motives in the hospitality industry. *Journal of Services Marketing*, *18*, 339–357.

Hatfield, E., Cacioppo, J. T., & Rapson, R. L. (1994). *Emotional contagion*. New York, NY: Cambridge University Press.

Hershcovis, M. S., & Barling, J. (2010). Towards a multi-foci approach to workplace aggression: A meta-analytic review of outcomes from different perpetrators. *Journal of Organizational Behavior*, *31*, 24–44.

Ho, V. T., & Gupta, N. (2012). Testing an empathy model of guest-directed citizenship and counterproductive behaviours in the hospitality industry: Findings from three hotels. *Journal of Occupational and Organizational Psychology*, *85*, 433–453.

Hobfoll, S. E. (1989). Conservation of resources: A new attempt at conceptualizing stress. *American Psychologist*, *44*, 513–524.

Hobfoll, S. E. (2002). Social and psychological resources and adaptation. *Review of General Psychology*, *6*, 307–324.

Hockey, G. R. J. (1993). Cognitive–energetical control mechanisms in the management of work demands and psychological health. In A. Baddely & L. Weiskrantz (Eds.), *Attention: Selection, awareness, and control* (pp. 328–345). Oxford: Clarendon Press.

Holmvall, C. M., & Sidhu, J. (2007). Predicting customer service employees' job satisfaction and turnover intentions: The roles of customer interactional injustice and interdependent self-construal. *Social Justice Research*, *20*, 479–496.

Hoobler, J. M., & Brass, D. J. (2006). Abusive supervision and family undermining as displaced aggression. *Journal of Applied Psychology*, *91*, 1125–1133.

Humphrey, S. E., Nahrgang, J. D., & Morgeson, F. P. (2007). Integrating motivational, social, and contextual work design features: A meta-analytic summary and theoretical extension of the work design literature. *Journal of Applied Psychology*, *92*, 1332–1356.

Kanfer, R., & Ackerman, P. L. (1989). Motivation and cognitive abilities: An integrative/aptitude-treatment interaction approach to skill acquisition. *Journal of Applied Psychology*, *74*, 657–690.

Kao, F. H., Cheng, B. S., Kuo, C. C., & Huang, M. P. (2014). Stressors, withdrawal, and sabotage in frontline employees: The moderating effects of caring and service climates. *Journal of Occupational and Organizational Psychology*, *87*, 755–780.

Karatepe, O. M. (2011). Customer aggression, emotional exhaustion, and hotel employee outcomes: A study in the United Arab Emirates. *Journal of Travel & Tourism Marketing*, *28*, 279–295.

Kern, J. H., & Grandey, A. A. (2009). Customer incivility as a social stressor: The role of race and racial identity for service employees. *Journal of Occupational Health Psychology*, *14*, 46–57.

Kim, E., & Yoon, D. J. (2012). Why does service with a smile make employees happy? A social interaction model. *Journal of Applied Psychology*, *97*, 1059–1067.

Lanaj, K., Johnson, R. E., & Barnes, C. M. (2014). Beginning the workday yet already depleted? Consequences of late-night smartphone use and sleep. *Organizational Behavior and Human Decision Processes*, *124*, 11–23.

Lavelle, J. J., Rupp, D. E., & Brockner, J. (2007). Taking a multifoci approach to the study of justice, social exchange, and citizenship behavior: The target similarity model. *Journal of Management*, *33*, 841–866.

LePine, J. A., & Van Dyne, L. (2001). Voice and cooperative behavior as contrasting forms of contextual performance: Evidence of differential relationships with big five personality characteristics and cognitive ability. *Journal of Applied Psychology*, *86*, 326–336.

Li, X., & Zhou, E. (2013). Influence of customer verbal aggression on employee turnover intention. *Management Decision*, *51*, 890–912.

Liao, H., & Chuang, A. (2004). A multilevel investigation of factors influencing employee service performance and customer outcomes. *Academy of Management Journal*, *47*, 41–58.

Liao, H., & Rupp, D. E. (2005). The impact of justice climate and justice orientation on work outcomes: A cross-level multifoci framework. *Journal of Applied Psychology*, *90*, 242–256.

Liu, S., Luksyte, A., Wang, M., Zhou, L., & Shi, J. (2014). Overqualification and counterproductive work behaviors: Examining a moderated mediation model. *Journal of Organizational Behavior*. Advance online publication.

Liu, S., Wang, M., Zhan, Y., & Shi, J. (2009). Daily work stress and alcohol use: Testing the cross-level moderation effects of neuroticism and job involvement. *Personnel Psychology*, *62*, 575–597.

Liu, Y., Wang, M., Chang, C.-H., Shi, J., Zhou, L., & Shao, R. (2015). Work-family conflict, emotional exhaustion, and aggression toward others: The moderating roles of workplace interpersonal conflict and perceived managerial family support. *Journal of Applied Psychology*, *100*, 793–808.

Marcus-Newhall, A., Pedersen, W. C., Carlson, M., & Miller, N. (2000). Displaced aggression is alive and well: A meta-analytic review. *Journal of Personality and Social Psychology*, *78*, 670–689.

Martin, L. L., & Tesser, A. (1989). Toward a motivational and structural theory of ruminative thought. In J. S. Uleman & J. A. Barg (Eds.), *Unintended thought* (pp. 306–326). New York, NY: Guilford Press.

Martin, L. L., & Tesser, A. (1996). Some ruminative thoughts. In R. R. Wyer (Ed.), *Advances in social cognition* (Vol. 9, pp. 1–47). Ruminative Thoughts. Hillsdale, NJ: Lawrence Erlbaum Associates, Inc.

Martin, L. L., Tesser, A., & McIntosh, W. D. (1993). Wanting by not having: The effects of unattained goals on thoughts and feelings. In W. D. Wegner & C. Papageoriou (Eds.), *Handbook of mental control* (pp. 552–572). Englewood Cliffs, NJ: Prentice Hall.

McColl-Kennedy, J. R., Patterson, P. G., Smith, A. K., & Brady, M. K. (2009). Customer rage episodes: Emotions, expressions and behaviors. *Journal of Retailing*, *85*, 222–237.

Medler-Liraz, H., & Kark, R. (2012). It takes three to tango: Leadership and hostility in the service encounter. *The Leadership Quarterly*, *23*, 81–93.

Merecz, D., Drabek, M., & Mościcka, A. (2009). Aggression at the workplace: Psychological consequences of abusive encounter with coworkers and clients. *International Journal of Occupational Medicine and Environmental Health*, *22*, 243–260.

Milam, A. C., Spitzmueller, C., & Penney, L. M. (2009). Investigating individual differences among targets of workplace incivility. *Journal of Occupational Health Psychology*, *14*, 58–69.

Miron-Spektor, E., Efrat-Treister, D., Rafaeli, A., & Schwarz-Cohen, O. (2011). Others' anger makes people work harder not smarter: The effect of observing anger and sarcasm on creative and analytic thinking. *Journal of Applied Psychology*, *96*, 1065–1075.

Moberly, N. J., & Watkins, E. R. (2008). Ruminative self-focus and negative affect: An experience sampling study. *Journal of Abnormal Psychology*, *117*, 314–323.

Morgeson, F. P., Reider, M. H., & Campion, M. A. (2005). Selecting individuals in team settings: The importance of social skills, personality characteristics, and teamwork knowledge. *Personnel Psychology*, *58*, 583–611.

Morris, W. N. (1989). *Mood: The frame of mind.* New York, NY: Springer-Verlag.

Muraven, M., & Baumeister, R. F. (2000). Self-regulation and depletion of limited resources: Does self-control resemble a muscle? *Psychological Bulletin*, *126*, 247–259.

Muraven, M., Tice, D. M., & Baumeister, R. F. (1998). Self-control as a limited resource: Regulatory depletion patterns. *Journal of Personality and Social Psychology*, *74*, 774–789.

Nolen-Hoeksema, S., Wisco, B., & Lyubomirsky, S. (2008). Rethinking rumination. *Perspectives on Psychological Science*, *3*, 400–424.

Olson-Buchanan, J. B., & Boswell, W. R. (2008). An integrative model of experiencing and responding to mistreatment at work. *Academy of Management Review*, *33*, 76–96.

Penney, L. M., & Spector, P. E. (2005). Job stress, incivility, and counterproductive work behavior (CWB): The moderating role of negative affectivity. *Journal of Organizational Behavior*, *26*, 777–796.

Porath, C. L., & Erez, A. (2007). Does rudeness really matter? The effects of rudeness on task performance and helpfulness. *Academy of Management Journal*, *50*, 1181–1197.

Pugh, S. D. (2001). Service with a smile: Emotional contagion in the service encounter. *Academy of Management Journal*, *44*, 1018–1027.

Rafaeli, A., Erez, A., Ravid, S., Derfler-Rozin, R., Efrat-Treister, D. E., & Scheyer, R. (2012). When customers exhibit verbal aggression, employees pay cognitive costs. *Journal of Applied Psychology*, *97*, 931–950.

Reb, J., Goldman, B. M., Kray, L. J., & Cropanzano, R. (2006). Different wrongs, different remedies? Reactions to organizational remedies after procedural and interactional injustice. *Personnel Psychology*, *59*, 31–64.

Reed, A., & Aquino, K. F. (2003). Moral identity and the expanding circle of moral regard toward out-groups. *Journal of Personality and Social Psychology*, *84*, 1270–1286.

Reynolds, K. L., & Harris, L. C. (2009). Dysfunctional customer behavior severity: An empirical examination. *Journal of Retailing*, *85*, 321–335.

Rhoades, L., & Eisenberger, R. (2002). Perceived organizational support: A review of the literature. *Journal of Applied Psychology*, *87*, 698–714.

Rothbard, N. P., & Wilk, S. L. (2011). Waking up on the right or wrong side of the bed: Start-of-workday mood, work events, employee affect, and performance. *Academy of Management Journal*, *54*, 959–980.

Rotundo, M., & Sackett, P. R. (2002). The relative importance of task, citizenship, and counterproductive performance to global ratings of job performance: A policy-capturing approach. *Journal of Applied Psychology*, *87*, 66–80.

Rupp, D. E., & Cropanzano, R. (2002). The mediating effects of social exchange relationships in predicting workplace outcomes from multifoci organizational justice. *Organizational Behavior and Human Decision Processes*, *89*, 925–946.

Rupp, D. E., McCance, A. S., & Grandey, A. A. (2007). A cognitive–emotional theory of customer injustice and emotional labor: Implications for customer service, fairness theory, and the multifoci perspective. In D. De Cremer (Ed.), *Advances in the psychology of justice and affect*, (pp. 205–232). Charlotte, NC: Information Age.

Rupp, D. E., McCance, A. S., Spencer, S., & Sonntag, K. (2008). Customer (in)justice and emotional labor: The role of perspective taking, anger, and emotional regulation. *Journal of Management*, *34*, 903–924.

Rupp, D. E., Shao, R., Jones, K. S., & Liao, H. (2014). The utility of a multifoci approach to the study of organizational justice: A meta-analytic investigation into the consideration of normative rules, moral accountability, bandwidth-fidelity, and social exchange. *Organizational Behavior and Human Decision Processes*, *123*, 159–185.

Rupp, D. E., & Spencer, S. (2006). When customers lash out: The effects of customer interactional injustice on emotional labor and the mediating role of discrete emotions. *Journal of Applied Psychology*, *91*, 971–978.

Salanova, M., Agut, S., & Peiró, J. M. (2005). Linking organizational resources and work engagement to employee performance and customer loyalty: The mediation of service climate. *Journal of Applied Psychology*, *90*, 1217–1227.

Schneider, B., White, S. S., & Paul, M. C. (1998). Linking service climate and customer perceptions of service quality: Tests of a causal model. *Journal of Applied Psychology*, *83*, 150–163.

Shao, R., & Skarlicki, D. P. (2014). Service employees' reactions to mistreatment by customers: A comparison between North America and East Asia. *Personnel Psychology*, *67*, 23–59.

Skarlicki, D. P., & Folger, R. (1997). Retaliation in the workplace: The roles of distributive, procedural, and interactional justice. *Journal of Applied Psychology*, *82*, 434–443.

Skarlicki, D. P., Folger, R., & Tesluk, P. (1999). Personality as a moderator in the relationship between fairness and retaliation. *Academy of Management Journal*, *42*, 100–108.

Skarlicki, D. P., & Kulik, C. T. (2004). Third-party reactions to employee (mis) treatment: A justice perspective. *Research in Organizational Behavior*, *26*, 183–229.

Skarlicki, D. P., van Jaarsveld, D. D., & Walker, D. D. (2008). Getting even for customer mistreatment: The role of moral identity in the relationship between customer interpersonal injustice and employee sabotage. *Journal of Applied Psychology*, *93*, 1335–1347.

Sliter, M., Jex, S., Wolford, K., & McInnerney, J. (2010). How rude! Emotional labor as a mediator between customer incivility and employee outcomes. *Journal of Occupational Health Psychology*, *15*, 468–481.

Sliter, M., Sliter, K., & Jex, S. (2012). The employee as a punching bag: The effect of multiple sources of incivility on employee withdrawal behavior and sales performance. *Journal of Organizational Behavior*, *33*, 121–139.

Sliter, M. T., Pui, S. Y., Sliter, K. A., & Jex, S. M. (2011). The differential effects of interpersonal conflict from customers and coworkers: Trait anger as a moderator. *Journal of Occupational Health Psychology*, *16*, 424–440.

Smith, C. A., Organ, D. W., & Near, J. P. (1983). Organizational citizenship behavior: Its nature and antecedents. *Journal of Applied Psychology*, *68*, 653–663.

Smith, J. M., & Alloy, L. B. (2009). A roadmap to rumination: A review of the definition, assessment, and conceptualization of this multifaceted construct. *Clinical Psychology Review*, *29*, 116–128.

Spencer, S., & Rupp, D. E. (2009). Angry, guilty, and conflicted: Injustice toward coworkers heightens emotional labor through cognitive and emotional mechanisms. *Journal of Applied Psychology*, *94*, 429–444.

Stock, R. M., & Bednarek, M. (2014). As they sow, so shall they reap: Customers' influence on customer satisfaction at the customer interface. *Journal of the Academy of Marketing Science*, *42*, 400–414.

Stoverink, A. C., Umphress, E. E., Gardner, R. G., & Miner, K. N. (2014). Misery loves company: Team dissonance and the influence of supervisor-focused interpersonal justice climate on team cohesiveness. *Journal of Applied Psychology*. Advance online publication.

Tan, H. H., Der Foo, M., & Kwek, M. H. (2004). The effects of customer personality traits on the display of positive emotions. *Academy of Management Journal*, *47*, 287–296.

Taylor, S. G., Bedeian, A. G., Cole, M. S., & Zhang, Z. (2014). Developing and testing a dynamic model of workplace incivility change. *Journal of Management*. Advance online publication.

Tesluk, P. E., & Jacobs, R. R. (1998). Toward an integrated model of work experience. *Personnel Psychology*, *51*, 321–355.

Teuchmann, K., Totterdell, P., & Parker, S. K. (1999). Rushed, unhappy, and drained: An experience sampling study of relations between time pressure, perceived control, mood, and emotional exhaustion in a group of accountants. *Journal of Occupational Health Psychology*, *4*, 37–54.

Thakor, M. V., & Joshi, A. W. (2005). Motivating salesperson customer orientation: Insights from the job characteristics model. *Journal of Business Research*, *58*, 584–592.

Totterdell, P., & Holman, D. (2003). Emotion regulation in customer service roles: Testing a model of emotional labor. *Journal of Occupational Health Psychology*, *8*, 55–73.

Totterdell, P., Wood, S., & Wall, T. (2006). An intra-individual test of the demands-control model: A weekly diary study of psychological strain in portfolio workers. *Journal of Occupational and Organizational Psychology*, *79*, 63–84.

Vancouver, J. B. (2000). Self-regulation in organizational settings: A tale of two paradigms. In M. Boekaerts, P. R. Pintrich, & M. Zeidner (Eds.), *Handbook of self-regulation* (pp. 303–341). San Diego, CA: Academic Press.

van Jaarsveld, D. D., Walker, D. D., & Skarlicki, D. P. (2010). The role of job demands and emotional exhaustion in the relationship between customer and employee incivility. *Journal of Management*, *36*, 1486–1504.

Van Kleef, G. A., Homan, A. C., & Cheshin, A. (2012). Emotional influence at work: Take it EASI. *Organizational Psychology Review*, *2*, 311–339.

Vohs, K. D., & Heatherton, T. F. (2000). Self-regulatory failure: A resource-depletion approach. *Psychological Science*, *11*, 249–254.

Volmer, J., Binnewies, C., Sonnentag, S., & Niessen, C. (2012). Do social conflicts with customers at work encroach upon our private lives? A diary study. *Journal of Occupational Health Psychology*, *17*, 304–315.

Walker, D. D., van Jaarsveld, D. D., & Skarlicki, D. P. (2014). Exploring the effects of individual customer incivility encounters on employee incivility: The moderating roles of entity (in) civility and negative affectivity. *Journal of Applied Psychology*, *99*, 151–161.

Walsh, G. (2011). Unfriendly customers as a social stressor: An indirect antecedent of service employees' quitting intention. *European Management Journal*, *29*, 67–78.

Wang, M., Liao, H., Zhan, Y., & Shi, J. (2011). Daily customer mistreatment and employee sabotage against customers: Examining emotion and resource perspectives. *Academy of Management Journal*, *54*, 312–334.

Wang, M., Liu, S., Liao, H., Gong, Y., Kammeyer-Mueller, J., & Shi, J. (2013). Can't get it out of my mind: Employee rumination after customer mistreatment and negative mood in the next morning. *Journal of Applied Psychology*, *98*, 989–1004.

Wang, M., Sinclair, R., & Deese, M. N. (2010). Understanding the causes of destructive leadership behavior: A dual-process model. In B. Schyns & T. Hansbrough (Eds.), *When leadership goes wrong: Destructive leadership, mistakes, and ethical failures* (pp. 73–97). Charlotte, NC: Information Age Publishing.

Wegge, J., Van Dick, R., & Von Bernstorff, C. (2010). Emotional dissonance in call centre work. *Journal of Managerial Psychology*, *25*, 596–619.

Wegge, J., Vogt, J., & Wecking, C. (2007). Customer-induced stress in call centre work: A comparison of audio-and videoconference. *Journal of Occupational and Organizational Psychology*, *80*, 693–712.

Weiss, H. M., & Cropanzano, R. (1996). Affective events theory: A theoretical discussion of the structure, causes and consequences of affective experiences at work. In B. M. Staw & L. L. Cummings (Eds.), *Research in organizational behavior* (Vol. 18, pp. 1–74). San Francisco, CA: JAI Press.

Weiss, H. M., Suckow, K., & Cropanzano, R. (1999). Effects of justice conditions on discrete emotions. *Journal of Applied Psychology*, *84*, 786–794.

Wilson, N. L., & Holmvall, C. M. (2013). The development and validation of the incivility from customers scale. *Journal of Occupational Health Psychology*, *18*, 310–326.

Winstanley, S., & Whittington, R. (2002). Anxiety, burnout and coping styles in general hospital staff exposed to workplace aggression: A cyclical model of burnout and vulnerability to aggression. *Work & Stress*, *16*, 302–315.

Yang, J., & Diefendorff, J. M. (2009). The relations of daily counterproductive workplace behavior with emotions, situational antecedents, and personality moderators: A diary study in Hong Kong. *Personnel Psychology*, *62*, 259–295.

Zhan, Y., Wang, M., & Shi, J. (2013). Lagged influences of customer mistreatment on employee mood: Moderating roles of maladaptive emotion regulation strategies. *Research on Emotion in Organizations*, *9*, 203–224.

AGGRESSION WITH A CONSCIENCE: A RATIONAL AND MORAL FRAMEWORK FOR PROACTIVE WORKPLACE AGGRESSION

Aurora J. Dixon, Chu-Hsiang (Daisy) Chang and Russell E. Johnson

ABSTRACT

A number of theoretical frameworks exist to explain perpetrators' motivation for workplace aggression. Most of them consider these behaviors as retaliatory actions from individuals who experience triggering events in their workplaces. The current chapter describes a model that focuses on the motivations underlying proactive workplace aggression, and identifies situations where perpetrators consider their aggressive behaviors as morally justifiable. In particular, we argue that depending on the targets' in- versus out-group membership and higher- versus lower-status in the hierarchy, aggressive behaviors may be viewed as acceptable to achieve perpetrators' goals of forcing compliance or managing identity. The model extends the current literature by considering non-retaliatory

Mistreatment in Organizations
Research in Occupational Stress and Well Being, Volume 13, 81–106

ISSN: 1479-3555/doi:10.1108/S1479-355520150000013003

workplace aggression, and by identifying potential avenues for future research and intervention to reduce proactive workplace aggression.

Keywords: Workplace aggression; in-groups and out-groups; compliance; identity; motivation; non-retaliatory

Much of the research on motivation underlying workplace aggression has focused on how aggression occurs in response to provocation (Felson, 2004). Historically, the understanding of motives underlying aggressive behaviors is through the lens of the frustration–aggression hypothesis (Berkowitz, 1989). This hypothesis suggests that various events in life cause emotions such as anger and frustration. Individuals alleviate these negative emotions through aggression as a means of catharsis. Indeed, research has shown that frustration, along with other negative emotions such as anger and agitation, is a predictor of individuals' aggressive behaviors toward the actor of the mistreatment (e.g., Berkowitz, 1989). In addition to negative emotions, there is an abundance of research on the motivations of aggressors who have been harmed in some way. These aggressors are considered to be vigilantes or protectors of justice (e.g., Skarlicki & Folger, 1997), lacking in self-control (e.g., DeWall, Baumeister, Stillman, & Gaillot, 2007), or victims of the environment (e.g., Andersson & Pearson, 1999).

The perspective of viewing aggressors as reactors has provided us with a great deal of understanding regarding the motivations and causes of workplace aggression, but there is a lack of attention to cases where perpetrators are "proactive" with their aggression (Felson, 2004). Acts of proactive aggression are commonly observed in the workplace, but the motivation underlying their perpetrators has received little attention. For example, abusive supervision is defined as "subordinates' perceptions of the extent to which supervisors engage in the sustained display of hostile verbal and nonverbal behaviors, excluding physical contact" (Tepper, 2000, p. 178), and is estimated to affect 13.6% of the U.S. workers (Schat, Frone, & Kelloway, 2006). Although not included in the original definition, the intentional nature of abusive supervision was emphasized in a recent review, such that "supervisors perpetrate abusive behavior for a purpose" (Tepper, 2007, p. 265), and this purpose may include, but are not limited to, harming subordinates. Similarly, bullying is another form of aggression that commonly occurs in the workplace, and may be viewed as a proactive form of aggression. Bullying is defined as repeated, unprovoked aggression intended to cause some sort of harm to another individual (Bartlett & Bartlett, 2011). Defined as "inactions to socially engage another" (Robinson, O'Reilly, & Wang, 2013, p. 207), workplace ostracism can be viewed as proactive aggression, as it can serve multiple purposes for the aggressor, such as establishing the power hierarchy or reinforcing the social norms. Finally, sexual harassment, especially in the quid-pro-quo form, is another example of proactive aggression against a target (e.g., Berdahl, 2007). In this case, perpetrators utilize aggression in order to gain sexual advances.

By ignoring the proactive forms of workplace aggression, our understanding of the full range of motivations underlying such behaviors is limited. This chapter aims to capture the motivations behind proactive, unprovoked aggressive behaviors, and why perpetrators may sometimes judge these behaviors justified. Specifically, we propose a framework of workplace aggression that captures different perpetrator motivations underlying proactive aggressive acts. This framework clarifies why people are motivated to instantiate aggression, as well as why such acts are justifiable to perpetrators. To understand why people would commit aggression in the absence of a triggering event, we detail a framework of "moral aggression." In our framework, we draw from both Felson's (1993) rational choice model and Rai and Fiske's (2011) moral motives underlying morality judgment. Our framework contributes to the workplace aggression literature by focusing on a subset of aggressive behaviors that are not only unprovoked, but also viewed as acceptable means to accomplish specific goals in the eyes of the perpetrators.

We first review the major theoretical models in the workplace aggression research that focuses on perpetrator motives and identify unifying themes across these frameworks. We then discuss the rational choice model of aggression proposed by Felson (1993) and the moral motives framework proposed by Rai and Fiske (2011). We integrate the two perspectives to propose our model of moral aggression in the workplace. Finally, we highlight the theoretical and practical implications of our framework.

PERPETRATOR MOTIVES: A LITERATURE REVIEW

Extant research has identified a number of motives underlying the perpetration of aggression in the workplace. In particular, research tends to revolve around three main themes concerning perpetrator motives: (a) aggression as vigilantism (e.g., Tripp, Bies, & Aquino, 2007); (b) the role of negative emotion, self-control, or both for precipitating aggressive behavior (e.g., Martinko, Gundlach, & Douglas, 2002), and (c) the impact of the environment as a main driver for aggressive behavior (e.g., Andersson & Pearson, 1999). Each of these has been helpful in understanding the motivation of the perpetrators of workplace aggression, and a single model or theory often incorporates multiple themes (e.g., Douglas et al., 2008). Below we discuss these themes in more detail and draw on specific models and theories of workplace aggression to illustrate their application.

Aggression as Vigilantism

The first theme of the existing workplace aggression research considers the aggressor to be motivated by justice. From this perspective, aggression is used as a means for alleviating wrongs that have been done against either the aggressor or another person in the environment. In this case, aggression is considered as a retaliatory behavior, enacted in response to an offense of some form. Several prominent models that focus on retributive justice as the primary motive of workplace aggressors are described below.

Skarlicki and Folger's (1997) retaliation framework considers aggression as a justice-based reaction. This model of workplace aggression focuses specifically on workplace retaliatory behaviors, which are behaviors directed toward harming the organization. These retaliatory behaviors include various forms of workplace aggression, such as negative gossip, spreading harmful rumors, and talking back to people. Skarlicki and Folger attribute these behaviors to perceived injustices within the organization. Their model predicts that when employees experience injustice in the form of unfair procedures, unfair interpersonal treatment, or unfair communication, they are likely to retaliate by engaging in workplace aggression. Empirical findings (e.g., Hershcovis et al., 2007; Skarlicki & Folger, 1997) support a significant relationship between justice perceptions and aggressive behavior at work. These findings indicate that aggressors are in part motivated by retributive justice concerns.

Another example of justice-motivated aggression is highlighted in the vigilante model of aggression proposed by Tripp et al. (2007). According to this perspective, workplace aggression is a means for restoring justice when other responses to the original transgression of injustice do not suffice. In particular, when a transgression occurs, organizations can restore justice for victims through punishing the original perpetrator, which in turn can circumvent retaliatory aggression. In addition, if perpetrators of the original transgression show repentance and apologize, this repentance may fulfill victims' wishes for retribution. In both cases, justice is restored and forgiveness is likely to occur, which reduces victims' motivation to engage in retaliatory aggression. However, when proper vindication is not fulfilled in the eyes of victims, they may use aggression to balance the relationship between themselves and the people who have wronged them, or avoid any further interactions with the original perpetrators to minimize future harm.

According to Tripp et al.'s (2007) model, a number of situational and individual factors can influence victims' beliefs about the likelihood of institutional punishment for the perpetrator or the occurrence of perpetrator repentance, which in turn influence the decision to aggress against a wrongdoer. For example, organizations with a high procedural justice climate are more likely to properly redress the unfair incidents that occur between organizational members. Victims of the original transgression, in this case, are more likely to believe that justice will be restored through institutional channels. Retaliatory aggression at the individual level will likely not be necessary, and victims are less likely to act as vigilantes. Power can also influence the decision to aggress against a wrongdoer. For example, if the victim of the transgression has more organizational power than the perpetrator, then the victim will likely have more freedom to restore justice through various paths. A powerful victim may opt for alternative means to quickly restore justice (i.e., aggressing against the original perpetrator), rather than waiting for the system to formally respond. As such, retaliatory aggression is more likely to occur when victims of the initial transgression have more power and options to restore justice.

Aggression as a Result of Negative Emotions and Lapses in Self-Control

The second theme of current workplace aggression literature is that aggression is treated as the result of negative emotions, the failure to exercise self-control, or both. In this case, while there are numerous events that may prompt aggression, aggression only occurs when individuals experience a high level of negative emotions, and/or cannot control their aggressive impulses. Based on this theme, perpetrators of workplace aggression are considered as individuals who fail to suppress their negative emotions or impulsive reactions. These models and theories can be traced back to the frustration–aggression hypothesis (Berkowitz, 1989). Based on this hypothesis and subsequent extensions to this idea, aggression is a means through which catharsis can occur to alleviate negative emotions. When individuals do not have the necessary self-control, aggression becomes a more likely strategy to cope with the negative emotions.

Martinko et al. (2002) proposed a model that focuses primarily on the emotional component of workplace aggression. They provide a causal reasoning theory for motivation underlying counterproductive work behaviors (CWB), which include verbal aggression against coworkers and other behaviors aimed at harming other organizational members or damaging organizational property (e.g., sabotage). Within the model, emotional reactions are key to workplace aggression. Martinko et al. (2002) argue that retaliatory CWBs occur as a result of cognitive processing leading to an attributional judgment regarding a triggering event. After a triggering event occurs at work, individuals cognitively process whether the event is (a) internally attributable to themselves or externally attributable to some entity or source in the environment, and (b) stable or unstable. When the attribution is external and stable, employees experience frustration and anger that is targeted toward an organizationally related entity. This frustration and anger, according to Martinko et al., will directly lead to an organizationally directed CWB. When people experience these intense emotions, they react in a way that releases these emotions in a cathartic way, aligning with the frustration–aggression hypothesis (e.g., Berkowitz, 1989).

In addition to negative emotions, differences in self-control between and within individuals can help account for aggression as a response (e.g., DeWall et al., 2007). The original basis for the consideration of self-control, or lack thereof, as an antecedent for aggression can be linked to the field of social psychology (e.g., DeWall et al., 2007). Within the study of self-regulation depletion, self-control is considered to be a finite resource that can be exhausted as individuals try to control and regulate their daily behaviors. Depletion in self-regulatory resources makes the control of undesirable behaviors increasingly difficult (e.g., Baumeister, Bratslavsky, Muraven, & Tice, 1998). The inability to control one's behavior in the face of tempting events applies to the inability to control aggressive behaviors (DeWall et al., 2007). In this case, individuals who have depleted self-regulation resources are unable to sufficiently control aggressive impulses, which readily translate into aggressive behavior. This happens despite the fact that aggression is considered a socially undesirable behavior and should be suppressed. Empirical research findings have shown that when people have reduced self-regulation capacity as indicated by greater effort in controlling their behavior, and difficulty in maintaining attention toward difficult tasks, they are more likely to behave in aggressive ways (DeWall et al., 2007). These results are supportive of the overall consideration of self-regulation as one contributor to the expression of workplace aggression, a theme that becomes apparent in many models of workplace aggression (e.g., Douglas et al., 2008).

Douglas et al. (2008) present the Elaboration Likelihood Model of aggression that includes both self-regulatory concerns and affectivity concerns in the decision-making process. In their model, a triggering event leads to a number of different processing mechanisms: cognitive, attitudinal, and affective. A triggering event initiates the three processing mechanisms that result in a causal attribution for why the triggering event occurred, in a similar manner as Martinko et al.'s (2002) model. Each of these processing mechanisms varies on the speed at which they occur, with cognitive-initiated requiring the most time and resources, and affective-initiated requiring the least. Once the causal attribution has been made via one or more processing routes, factors such as mood, self-control, and attitudes impact the behavior that is ultimately expressed as a response to the triggering event. Within this model, Douglas et al. (2008) highlight a number of propositions relating emotionality and self-control with retaliatory aggression. Douglas et al. posit that if a person is struck by intense anger as a result of the triggering event, their processing mechanisms will default to the affective-initiated route, circumventing cognitive attributions of causation, which would result in a greater likelihood of retaliation through aggression. They additionally posit that negative attitudes toward perceived causes of triggering events will result in event-blurred reactions, which have a greater association with aggression. These propositions pinpoint the importance of affect and affectively related variables in the understanding of retaliatory aggression. In these cases, reactions are not logically determined choices, rather more reflexive impulses brought on by harm. However, Douglas and colleagues recognize the role of self-control, or lack thereof, in the ultimate result of aggression. Key to this model is the moderating relationship of self-control between the processes and the resulting behavior. If people are able to exert self-control over their negative emotions, they will likely not react to triggering events in an aggressive way.

Aggression as a Product of the Environment

The third perspective of workplace aggression that has received attention in the current literature is one in which aggressors' behaviors can be attributed, at least in part, to the perceived social norms of their environment. Within these models, aggression is considered to be a norm or an expected way to act in the work context, and therefore is inescapable. In these environments, aggressive behaviors become the way in which people feel they must operate in order to succeed or fit in with other individuals in their groups or the organization. Within these frameworks, justice, negative emotions, and self-regulation often play a role, but the main antecedent behind aggression is its prevalence.

Many, if not all, of the theories discussed above include some aspect of environmental inputs on aggressive behaviors beyond the existence of a provoking incident (e.g., Douglas et al., 2008). For example, the Elaboration Likelihood Model of aggression as defined by Douglas et al. (2008) includes organizational policies as an antecedent to the processing aspect of decision-making in aggression. In Tripp et al.'s (2007) vigilante model, the presence of a procedural justice climate impacts whether or not people engage in retaliatory aggression. These examples highlight the fact that people make use of cues of normative behavior from their surroundings, and these cues indicate whether aggressive behavior is encouraged or discouraged (e.g., Tripp et al., 2007). However, other theories exist in which environmental factors play the central role in guiding people's aggressive behaviors at work (e.g., Andersson & Pearson, 1999).

Andersson and Pearson (1999) describe a theory of aggressive behavior as the outcome of incivility within the workplace. They describe workplace environments as places in which behavioral norms are either maintained or violated. In their theory, polite and civil behavior maintains a positive environment in which people show respect for one another. Andersson and Pearson highlight the importance of a context in which people treat one another in polite, considerate ways as being critical in preventing behavioral deterioration. Polite and considerate behaviors serve as cues to individuals on the proper ways to treat one another, thereby creating norms of respect among organizational members. Unfortunately, these norms are not always established or upheld, allowing incivility to proliferate in the workplace. Acts of incivility are low-grade aggressive behaviors, and consist of subtly disrespectful behaviors and impoliteness (Andersson & Pearson, 1999). When incivility becomes a norm in organizations, such norms can gradually increase organizational members' acceptance of aggression. This spiral eventually leads to more serious forms of aggression, as a response to a trigger point (e.g., a provoking incident such as unfair treatment). Andersson and Pearson (1999) therefore highlight the development and reinforcement of a social norm for respectful treatment between members as the primary way to prevent incivility and aggression in the workplace.

Extending beyond incivility, Robinson and O'Leary-Kelly (1998) proposed a model that focuses on organizational culture that supports antisocial behavior. Antisocial behavior refers to behaviors that are against the organization's wishes, and includes incidents of workplace aggression. In their model, Robinson and O'Leary-Kelly highlight the importance of social learning within workgroups as well as organizational culture for punishment of antisocial behavior as predictors of these behaviors. When workgroup members commit more antisocial behaviors, individuals will be more likely to act in the same way. These behaviors become normative for workgroup members. Coworkers not only expect these behaviors to occur, but they also feel positively toward those behaviors such that turnover intentions are negatively related to antisocial behavior in workgroups where this behavior is common. Robinson and O'Leary-Kelly's empirical study supported that individuals who worked in groups with more antisocial behavior were more likely to commit those behaviors. This tendency is presumably due to the establishment of a norm for accepting and even promoting antisocial behavior in groups where such behavior is prevalent. As such, individuals conform to the group norm and engage in these aggressive and rule-bending behaviors.

Summary

Three major themes have arisen in the theoretical development of workplace aggression concerning perpetrator motives. First, aggression is viewed as vigilantism, such that perpetrators engage in aggressive behaviors in order to pursue justice. Second, aggression is a response attributed to negative emotions, a lack of self-control, or both. Depleted perpetrators cannot regulate their aggressive impulses elicited by negative emotions, and seek catharsis through engaging in aggressive behaviors. Finally, aggression is seen as a product of the environments in which it occurs. Perpetrators engage in aggressive behaviors in order to conform to the social norms that accept or even encourage these behaviors.

While the abovementioned theoretical perspectives have been fruitful in directing research concerning workplace aggression, they have largely focused on aggressive behaviors as reactive acts to either situational forces (e.g., aggressive norms), events (e.g., unfair treatment), or other individuals (e.g., provoking coworker or customers). Very little is known about the motivation underlying the non-retaliatory workplace aggression. In the following section, we will present a model that combines the rational choice model of violence (Felson, 1993) and a moral motives model of behavior (Rai & Fiske, 2011) to explain the motives underlying the proactive forms of workplace aggression.

RATIONAL CHOICE MODEL OF AGGRESSION

The rational choice model of aggression was proposed by Felson (1993), and highlights the instrumental values of aggression and violence. He adopts the position of a social interactionist, and argues that violence is motivated by how people will react to that violence, and should be viewed as a social event between two people. He proposes that aggression and violence are ways through which individuals can get something valuable from others. In particular, aggressive or violent acts can be used instrumentally to gain a resource, to force behavior, or to influence perceptions. Thus, when people engage in aggression and violence, they are not doing it out of blind passion or lack of judgment. Rather, such engagement is based on rational calculation with the intention to maximize their potential benefits. Perpetrators are concerned with one or more desires, which they believe can be achieved through aggression and violence.

Felson (1993) outlines three motivations behind aggression as well as the two forms of aggression that can occur. As we expand on below, the three motivations underlying aggression are justice, compliance, and social identity. These motivations are manifested in two possible forms of aggression: dispute-related and predatory aggression. Dispute-related aggression can be linked to an ongoing disagreement between individuals or groups who aggress against one another. In these cases, there is a history of perceived wrongdoing or conflict between the individuals or groups that drives the aggressive acts between them. This kind of aggression is akin to the retaliatory aggression approach, which is an important and valuable perspective, but well covered in the current literature. As such, we will focus on the predatory aggression, which refers to aggressive acts that are not prompted, but are initiated to meet one of the three needs – justice, compliance, or social identity – of the perpetrators (Felson, 1993).

Justice

According to Felson (1993), justice as a motivation is the drive to get "pay back" from someone who wronged the aggressor. Retributive justice is not necessarily a direct "pay back;" a person might retaliate in a violent or aggressive way to some perceived slight that was not violent at all. It is a way in which balance can be restored, but does not need to be exactly equal. The motive of dispute-related justice is consistent with the current understanding of workplace aggression (e.g., Skarlicki & Folger, 1997), such that when individuals retaliate against the original perpetrators of the unfair or negative treatment in order to restore the balance, they are acting in accordance with the motive of justice. For example, Aquino, Lewis, and Bradfield (1999) conducted research on the relationship between workplace deviance, including workplace aggression against other organization members, and justice perceptions. Their results support that justice perceptions were negatively related to organizational and interpersonal deviance. This indicates a plausible relationship between overall justice perceptions and aggressive behaviors. Similarly, Aquino, Tripp, and Bies (2001) investigated the relationships between original offenders and their victims, blame attributions, and the likelihood of revenge behaviors. They found a positive relationship between blame attributions and revenge-taking, supporting justice as a motive underlying retaliatory aggression.

Given that this motive is well captured by the current literature concerning retaliatory aggression (e.g., Skarlicki & Folger, 1997; Tripp et al., 2007), it is not the key focus in our proposed model. Interestingly, Felson (1993) describes predatory aggression motivated by justice as a sort of "Robin Hood" type of behavior: aggressing against someone who has an unfair amount of resources, but who has not directly wronged anyone, in order to redistribute resources. According to Felson (1993), this kind of aggression is highly uncommon, in part because individuals can usually assign the blame to a specific target, making their aggressive behaviors dispute-related or retaliatory rather than predatory in nature. As such, we consider justice-motivated aggression as mainly dispute-related aggression, and focus our model on the predatory aggression motivated by the next two types of motives.

Compliance

Aggression motivated by compliance is instrumental aggression. Compliance refers to the forcing of people's behavior to match someone else's expectations or desires for how they should behave (Felson, 1993). That is, when aggression is motivated by compliance, it is purposefully used to result in some sort of behavior that a person would not necessarily do otherwise. Felson (1993) suggests armed robbery as an example of predatory aggression motivated by compliance. Perpetrators of robbery use it as a tool in order to force victims' behavior. By using violence, they are able to compel victims to give them money or goods, something that likely would not have occurred otherwise. Another example of aggression motivated that may be motivated by compliance is abusive supervision. Tepper (2007, p. 273) states "some supervisors abuse their subordinates because they find them provocative and difficult to deal with." These supervisors are motivated to "rein in" the behavior of their subordinates with aggression, compelling them behave in ways that they would not normally behave otherwise. This is different from justice-related aggression in that the driver of compliance is based on forcing a specific behavior from the victim, rather than getting even.

There is some initial support for the compliance motive as a driver for workplace aggression. Lian, Ferris, Morrison, and Brown (2014) examined the reciprocal relationship between abusive supervision and subordinate deviance. They hypothesized that abusive supervision may trigger subordinate deviance as retaliatory aggression against the initial transgression (i.e., abuse from the supervisor). On the other hand, subordinate deviation may also lead to subsequent abusive supervision. Supervisors, in this case, engage in abusive behaviors in order to alter their subordinates' unwanted behaviors. Their results indicated that over a 6-month period of time, abusive supervision and subordinate deviance were reciprocally related. However, with a 20-month lag, only subordinate deviance led to abusive supervision, and not vice versa. This result highlights the role of compliance as a motive underlying abusive supervision, such that supervisors engaged in abusive supervision in response to subordinates' deviance behavior in an effort to reduce these undesirable behaviors from their subordinates.

Predatory compliance-driven aggression is intended to result in a desired behavior from the victim (Felson, 1993). In these cases, perpetrators act aggressively not necessarily because the target is behaving in an unwanted way, but because they want to direct the target's behavior. Although not typically studied, it is possible to posit that aggression is engaged to motivate productive behaviors from perpetrators' coworkers, subordinates, and even leaders. For example, perpetrators may yell at their coworkers in order to prompt them to produce a technical report on time.

Social Identity

Maintaining social identity through aggression can be related to concerns for relationships or how you are socially perceived (Felson, 1993). Identity-motivated aggression is intended as a way of presenting oneself in a certain light. An example of workplace aggression motivated by identity management would be giving a coworker the silent treatment in order to portray a more powerful status within a workgroup. This motive is different from both justice and compliance in a number of ways. Instead of focusing on changing the distribution of resources (justice motives) or others' behaviors (compliance motives), identity-motivated aggression is aimed at changing perceptions (Felson, 1993). When people are concerned about how other people see them, they may use aggression to project a desired image.

Like the other motives of aggression, social identity can motivate dispute-related aggression. For example, Aquino and Douglas (2003) found that hierarchical status, individual attitudes toward revenge, and aggressive modeling moderated the relationship between identity threat and antisocial workplace behaviors. In particular, identity threat was positively related to perpetrators' likelihood to engage in antisocial behavior when they were of lower status in their hierarchy. This suggests that identity threat motivates lower-status employees to engage in reactive aggression.

Social identity can also motivate predatory aggression because the perpetrators want to present themselves in a particular way (Felson, 1993). Felson (1993) suggests bullying as a way to enforce a self-image of power and assertiveness. Interestingly, research on bullying in the workplace tends to focus on the victims' experiences or outcomes (e.g., Bartlett & Bartlett, 2011; Hershcovis, 2011), rather than identifying the motives underlying the bullying behaviors. We argue that social identity motives may help explain the bullying behaviors in the workplace.

Not only do we focus on predatory aggression motivated by different concerns as described by Felson (1993), we also identify scenarios where these predatory aggressive acts are viewed as morally justifiable from the perpetrators' perspective. We next discuss the moral motives model (Rai & Fiske, 2011) to provide a basis for our argument.

MORAL MOTIVES

Rai and Fiske (2011) present a framework of moral motives. This framework is intended to explain differences in morality judgments across cultures and individuals, such as the diverse perceptions of when it is appropriate to use capital punishment. This framework is an expansion on Fiske's (1992) elementary forms of sociality. According to Fiske, cultural social behavior is driven by a combination of four drivers, called relational models. These relational models are different ways of considering relationships and include communal sharing, authority ranking, equality matching, and market pricing. Communal sharing is based on the idea that everyone in a person's in-group deserves his or her respect and kindness by nature of their membership in the group. Authority ranking defines relationships based on where one stands in a hierarchy within a group, with different people deserving different treatment. In these cases, individuals who are more highly ranked in their hierarchies are expected to be treated with more respect compared to those who are of lower ranking. Equality matching in relationships emphasizes a total balance of exchange relationships among individuals regardless of their in-group membership or status. Finally, market pricing relationships are proportional, such that people should balance their relationship with regards to the proportionality of their input. Different combinations of these four models are what lead differences in behavior from culture to culture, and even individual to individual. They are not necessarily mutually exclusive, but may clash at times.

This perspective, though societal at its conceptualization, has been applied to more individual relationship analyses. Giessner and van Quaquebeke (2010) adapted Fiske's (1992) framework as a way to map out how and why leaders behave in ethical ways. In particular, differences in leader behavior can be explained by considering the relational models. Leader ethicality can be explained as a way of maintaining relationships with regard to one or more relational models, and as such, different leaders may behave differently. In addition to providing explanation for why leaders behave ethically and in different ways, Giessner and van Quaquebeke (2010) discuss how the framework is useful in understanding how and why leaders and followers vary in their ethicality judgments of the same behavior. Specifically, different ethicality judgments may occur when there is a mismatch between the relational model held by the leader versus the follower. For instance, if leaders use the authority ranking model in their ethicality judgments, they may believe that it is justifiable for them to severely punish followers for insubordination. However, if their followers use the equality matching model instead, they may consider the punishment unwarranted and unethical.

Rai and Fiske (2011) expanded on Fiske's (1992) original theory to further identify four moral motives that are used to better understand various opinions and judgments concerning morally ambiguous situations. The four moral motives serve as the driving force behind social behaviors that are considered to be moral or immoral in some way. The motives are unity, hierarchy, equality, and proportionality. These motives define what is moral and immoral with relation to social situations, but each with their own unique conceptualization of what morality is and why. Arguably, these moral motives can be divided into reactive motives and proactive motives. The reactive moral motives, which are intended to restore moral balance or justice in relationships, include equality and proportionality (Rai & Fiske, 2011). Proactive moral motives, which drive behavior to maintain an established environment of morality (Rai & Fiske, 2011), include unity and hierarchy. The various moral motives need not be mutually exclusive. People may take each into consideration with different weights or in different situations (Rai & Fiske, 2011). Because of the different motives, different people may consider the same behavior as morally acceptable versus unacceptable. These differences in morality judgments can help us to understand why perpetrators engage in aggression in the workplace, and how they believe that their behaviors are morally justifiable. With this framework, aggression is not necessarily an antisocial act, but is instead a way in which to maintain moral balance. The interplay between these moral motives and the aggression driven by different rational choices is the key to our model of moral workplace aggression.

MORAL AGGRESSION MODEL AND REACTIVE MORAL MOTIVES

Two moral motives – equality and proportionality – are particularly relevant when it comes to reactive aggression. According to Rai and Fiske (2011), equality considers reciprocity to be the basis for morality judgment. This is an "eye-for-an-eye" way of approaching behaviors. When equality is the main motive in morality issues, behaviors that are both immoral and moral are reciprocated in an equivalent way. That is, when people do favors for others, those favors should be returned in essentially the same exact way. On the other hand, this value stipulates that when people behave immorally against victims, it is justifiable for the victims to engage in the same immoral act against the perpetrators. In this case, retaliatory behaviors are considered to be the right thing to do in order to re-establish balance. For example, if a coworker works extra hours to assist you with a task, you should repay the favor by working extra hours to assist him or her in the future. However, if the coworker spreads rumors to damage your reputation, it is morally justifiable to spread vicious rumors against him or her as payback.

The second reactive moral motive is proportionality (Rai & Fiske, 2011). This motive is similar to equality in that behaviors between individuals are supposed to be reciprocated. However, the degree of reciprocation is different. In proportionality judgments of morality, moral and immoral behaviors should be addressed with behaviors that proportionally match the severity of the first act. The behaviors do not have to be the same; only the moral "weight" of the actions should be the same. For example, if a coworker spreads rumors to damage your reputation, instead of spreading rumors against your coworker, you may engage in other forms of aggressive acts against him/her (e.g., giving him/her the silent treatment). These aggressive behaviors are morally justifiable provided that they cause your coworker a similar amount of loss compared to your loss.

Both of these motives provide a moral reasoning behind Felson's (1993) justice motivation for aggression. Justice as a motive for aggression is closely related to the concepts of unity and proportionality. When perpetrators of aggression are driven by justice, they attempt to restore the fair exchange between the two parties of a relationship. These retaliatory aggressions are morally justifiable if they meet the equality or proportionality principles. In other words, if the retaliatory aggression causes similar damage to the perpetrator of the original transgression, such aggression is considered morally justifiable based on Rai and Fiske's (2011) model. Although these motives provide for an understanding of the morality judgments involved in retaliatory aggression, they do not play a role in the model of aggression being presented here. As such, we will move on to the moral motives of aggression that relate to proactive aggression.

MORAL AGGRESSION MODEL AND PROACTIVE MORAL MOTIVES

The main focus for our model of workplace aggression is the understanding of proactive aggression as a moral or morally justifiable behavior from the perpetrators' perspective. This understanding is dependent on the proactive moral motives outlined by Rai and Fiske (2011). The first proactive moral motive is unity. Unity is based on the judgment of in- versus out-group status of the behavioral target, and such status is the key to evaluating the appropriateness of any behavior. Behaviors are considered moral if they benefit individuals' in-group as a whole or other individual in-group members. The in-group status of another individual indicates that he/she deserves fair, if not preferential treatment. On the other hand, if someone threatens the in-group, behaviors that may otherwise be considered immoral can be justified as moral if they serve to protect the group. For example, based on this moral motive, it would be acceptable to give an in-group member a bonus even though an out-group member is more deserving of the reward. Similarly, allowing in-group members to have the first choice in the project assignment, or bending the rules for in-group members are other examples where unfair behaviors may be considered justifiable when evaluated through the lens of unity moral motive. From an aggression perspective, behavior will also be driven by group membership; a person might consider stealing from an out-group member to be acceptable if it benefits his or her in-group, but would not feel the same way about stealing from an in-group member. Maintaining safety and moral balance is considered at the group level (Rai & Fiske, 2011). When unity is the primary moral motive, people take in- and out-group membership into account when determining what behaviors would be appropriate or inappropriate (Rai & Fiske, 2011). Thus, unity as a moral value highlights the importance of considering the targets' in- versus out-group status when perpetrators determine whether to engage in aggression.

The second proactive moral motive is hierarchy (Rai & Fiske, 2011). This moral motive is based on the maintenance of a tiered system that individuals use to define the relative status of themselves compared to the behavioral target. Compared to others, individuals may be of higher, equal, or lower status, and their behavior is driven by the desire to maintain this hierarchy (Rai & Fiske, 2011). In these relationships, lower-ranked individuals are expected to respect and serve those of higher ranks. On the other hand, higher-ranked individuals are expected to behave in ways that assist and protect those of lower ranks. Within the designations of this motive, higher-ranked individuals are justified to behave in aggressive ways toward lower-ranked individuals if the latter have been disrespectful or challenging the existing hierarchy. On the other hand, lower-ranked individuals are entitled to act in an aggressive manner if high-ranked individuals do not fulfill their roles and responsibilities of protecting and leading the lower-ranked members of the group. Hierarchy motive suggests that those of different status in the hierarchy have different responsibilities in order to maintain the relationship. In this case, hierarchy as a moral motive highlights power distance as a primary concern in determining the appropriateness of behaviors. The relative status difference between perpetrators and targets of aggression is a salient point for judging whether aggression is justified.

Rai and Fiske (2011) consider these motives to be unrelated, suggesting that individuals may hold strong beliefs about both, about one, or about neither. The interaction between these two proactive moral motives is the foundation for understanding both why proactive aggression occurs in the workplace, and why perpetrators of these behaviors view them as justifiable. Specifically, our model examines the intersection between in- versus out-group membership of the target with higher- or equal-status, versus lower-status of the target relative to the perpetrators, and identifies situations where proactive aggressions are morally justifiable. We also relate these moral motives with Felson's (1993) motives for aggression. In particular, we argue that in the case when targets of aggression are of higher or equal status compared to the perpetrators, moral aggression is concerned with identity management. However, when the targets of aggression are of lower status compared to the perpetrators, moral aggression is driven by compliance concerns (Felson, 1993).

Specifically, an organization reflects a system of hierarchies (e.g., leaders and subordinates, managers and employees) that can be divided into various in- and out-groups (e.g., workgroups, departments; Tajfel & Turner, 1979). Hierarchical position is crucial in the determination of whether identity management or compliance concerns (Felson, 1993) will drive proactive behavior when interacting with different groups of people. When individuals interact with others who are of lower hierarchical status (e.g., a manager interacting with a subordinate), aggression will be motivated by compliance for instrumental reasons. First, individuals with higher status may possess different sources of power (e.g., legitimate power, reward power) that can be applied to influence subordinates' behaviors. Next, consistent with the hierarchy moral motive, those occupying the higher-status positions have the responsibility to direct the behavior of subordinates in order to maintain the status quo (Rai & Fiske, 2011). In this case, aggression can be considered as one of the tactics through which managers can use to influence subordinates' behaviors.

Alternatively, proactive aggression against others of higher rank is likely to be driven by identity concerns. Occupying a lower status in a hierarchy means that individuals must defer respect to those with higher status so long as those higher-status members fulfill their duties as leaders and protectors of the group interest (Rai & Fiske, 2011). In addition, individuals of lower status may infer their self-worth from the treatment they receive from the high-status individuals, particularly with regards to their identity (e.g., Tyler & Blader, 2003). Because of their lower status, subordinates within hierarchies may be especially concerned with how they are being perceived by others, and may be motivated to behave aggressively in order to project a self-image that is desirable to both themselves and those of higher status (Felson, 1993). Because of this, lower-ranked individuals may consider proactive aggression motivated by identity management as moral. For example, lower-ranked employees might perceive an insult toward a manager justified as it asserts themselves as valued group members with some degree of power. In these cases, lower-status individuals are ensuring that the hierarchical system does not become corrupt, that higher-ranked members value the subordinates, and that the interests of themselves and their hierarchies are maintained.

The interaction between hierarchical concerns and unity concerns is critical in understanding the various proactive aggressions that can occur in organizations. In the same way that hierarchical concerns direct individuals' behaviors in organizations, in- and out-group membership status also direct behaviors. Unity concerns, as explained by Rai and Fiske (2011), define the desires and needs of the in-group and its members as the ultimate goal of member behaviors. As such, aggression directed toward protecting the sanctity of the in-group, or benefitting the interests of the in-group, will be considered to be morally justifiable. This concern interacts with hierarchical concerns in such a way that different aggressive behaviors are morally justifiable under different scenarios. This interaction is the crux of our model of moral aggression in the workplace. Our model is summarized in Table 1.

Each of the four cells in our model defines the circumstances in which aggressive behaviors are morally justified from perpetrators' perspective. The first two cells of interest highlight situations in which targets of aggression are individuals of higher or equal status as compared to the perpetrator and for which the concern is identity management. The first cell represents situations in which these targets are members of the perpetrators' in-group. When these individuals are being considered as targets of aggression, the concern at hand is maintenance of the interests of the in-group while asserting the aggressors' roles as valued members of the in-group (Rai & Fiske, 2011). In these cases, perpetrators are concerned with

Table 1. Model of Moral Aggression.

Target Group Membership	Target Hierarchy Level	
	Higher or equal (identity)	Lower (instrumental)
In-group	Value establishment	Compliance
Out-group	Preservation	Exploitation

presenting themselves in a way that ensures that they are perceived as valuable members of the group. Such images may be accomplished through aggression if the aggressive behaviors are used to maintain the interests of the in-group and the sanctity of the hierarchy (Rai & Fiske, 2011). For example, individuals may see yelling at their supervisors to advocate for their departmental benefit as morally justifiable, as it projects their image as valuable in-group members advancing the in-group interests. Similarly, aggressing against a coworker may be viewed as an acceptable way to portray an assertive image as someone who is deserving of respect. Finally, a perpetrator may ostracize a fellow group member in order to portray the image of "enforcer of group norm." Based on these assertions, we propose the following proposition.

> **Proposition 1.** When the target is of higher or equal status and an in-group member, proactive aggression to project the image as valuable group members will be viewed as morally justifiable.

The second cell accounts for aggression that occurs when the target is an out-group member of higher or equal status compared to the perpetrator. In these cases, concerns for in-group welfare and respect for hierarchy are manifested in different ways. The benefit of the in-group is always of concern for the perpetrator, and in this case, they do not have to consider treating their target in a way that ensures fairness of in-group dynamics. Instead, these behaviors are driven by a desire to provide something for the in-group that is of a protective nature against the out-group (Rai & Fiske, 2011). Although group membership concerns become unimportant in consideration of fairness, respect for hierarchy is still maintained, and members who are more hierarchically powerful, or equally powerful, are deserving of respect (Rai & Fiske, 2011). As such, aggression against these individuals will continue to be concerned with identity management, but will be focused on asserting identity as a way of preserving in-group interests. In these cases, the identity being projected through aggression is that the perpetrators belong to a powerful group, and are representative of a group that deserves respect. For instance, a team leader may give another team's leader the silent treatment in order to present his or her team as superior. In order to establish that even lower-level employees of one group are more dominant than a rival group's leaders, an employee of one department may give the silent treatment to another department's manager. Based on the interaction between these two organizational levels, the following proposition is made.

Proposition 2. When the target is of higher or equal status and an out-group member, proactive aggression to ensure preservation of the in-group's high status will be viewed as morally justifiable.

The third and fourth cells focus on situations in which the targets of aggression are of lower hierarchical status than the perpetrators. The third cell focuses on lower status in-group members as targets. In these cases, the hierarchical distance between perpetrator and victim impacts relationships in such a way that the perpetrator has more power in their shared group, while also having a responsibility to lead and guide subordinates in ways that benefit the group as a whole (Rai & Fiske, 2011). Because of this, there must be a balance that ensures that any aggression committed toward the subordinate is for the good of the in-group (Rai & Fiske, 2011). In these cases, aggression can be used proactively such that it ensures that lower-status group members conform to the group norms or act in a way that will benefit the group. For example, threatening subordinates when they first arrive at their new jobs can be used as a way to ensure their compliance with organizational norms and future directions from leaders. Removing subordinates' cubicle decorations without consulting them is one way for leaders to ensure a professional and orderly physical work environment. Finally, engaging in abusive acts against the subordinates may be one way that the leaders can correct their subordinates' counterproductive work behavior (e.g., Lian et al., 2014). Based on the interaction between in-group membership and lower hierarchical position, we propose the following:

Proposition 3. When the target is of lower status and an in-group member, proactive aggression to ensure compliance will be viewed as morally justifiable.

The fourth and final cell captures the last possible combination of the two person characteristics, lower in status and out-group membership. In these cases, concern for hierarchy does not play a major role in determining morality judgment about the behavior. Because the target of aggression is of lower status than the perpetrator, there is no concern for deferring respect to that person (Rai & Fiske, 2011). In these cases, perpetrators are mainly concerned with the welfare of the in-group (Rai & Fiske, 2011). To the extent that aggression can lead to advantageous outcomes for their in-group, they are likely to view these behaviors as morally defensible. Aggression is used as a way to exploit other people for the good of the in-group. For instance, stealing supplies from a lower-ranked out-group member so that the in-group members' work rhythm is maintained is acceptable. A team leader may threaten members of a competing team in order to get information about their proposal for a competitive contract. Thus, we propose the following:

Proposition 4. When the target is of lower status and an out-group member, proactive aggression to exploit that individual will be viewed as morally justifiable.

In addition to the justifiability, our model also provides insights for the severity of the aggression. In particular, we argue that the depending on the targets' group membership and hierarchical status, perpetrators may consider aggression of varying severity (e.g., low-grade aggression such as incivility versus high intensity aggression of threatening physical violence) to accomplish their identity management or compliance motives. Because in-group membership is a major motive for morality judgment (Rai & Fiske, 2011), people will behave in less severe ways toward in- and out-group members in different scenarios. In considerations of aggression against in-group members, there is a great deal of concern for the maintenance of the internal strength of the in-group (Rai & Fiske, 2011). Additionally, based on the hierarchy motive, more vulnerable members of the group (i.e., low-status members) deserve more protection than other, more powerful members of the group (Rai & Fiske, 2011). As such, aggression against lower-status in-group members is likely to be less severe compared to aggression against high- or equal-status in-group members, as individuals are protective of their lower-status in-group members. This leads to the following proposition.

Proposition 5. Aggression against in-group members for ensuring value will be more severe than aggression for compliance.

Alternatively, when targets of aggression are out-group members, there will be limited concern with their protection based on their rank. In-group concerns drive behavior in such a way that the ultimate goal is to maximize the benefits of in-group members (Rai & Fiske, 2011). As such, out-group members' welfare is of minimum consideration. There is, however, a concern for respecting the hierarchical systems of out-groups due to the respect that various members deserve (Rai & Fiske, 2011). Because of the concern for hierarchy, people who are more highly ranked than others in their group will be considered more deserving of respect (Rai & Fiske, 2011). Based on this concern for respect, more highly ranked out-group members will be treated less severely than lower-ranked members, leading to the following proposition.

Proposition 6. Aggression against out-group members that is used for exploitation will be more severe than aggression for preservation.

DISCUSSION

Theoretical Implications

The implications of this model of proactive workplace aggression point to a number of future research directions. First, the motives of compliance and identity management as presented by Felson (1993) should be considered when studying non-retaliatory workplace aggression. The motive of justice (Felson, 1993) has been focused on widely throughout the literature (e.g., Hershcovis et al., 2007). However, there is little research on the other two motives in the workplace context, and these are promising directives toward understanding proactive aggression.

Second, our model highlights the importance of relationships between aggressors and their victims. The relational model of aggression (Hershcovis & Barling, 2007) has highlighted the relative power difference and the frequency of interaction between perpetrators and victims as predictors of the *outcomes* of aggression. Our model expands Hershcovis and Barling's perspective, and suggests that these relationship characteristics, along with in- versus out-group status (Rai & Fiske, 2011), may influence perpetrators' motives and moral justification for aggression.

A third direction for future research is to focus on the rational motives and moral values of aggressors as a means for identifying the situations in which they would feel their behaviors are morally justifiable. By better understanding the motives that drive people's aggressive behaviors, there can be greater promise of prediction, and further development of the proposed model. Finally, this model highlights the importance of collecting multi-source data from multiple time sources in order to better understand aggression and its motivators. Specifically, longitudinal data from multiple parties involved in acts of aggression can help develop a more comprehensive understanding of the reciprocal relationships and various situations in which aggression occurs.

Practical Implications

In addition to providing future directions for empirical research on proactive workplace aggression, this model highlights possible intervention opportunities. Workplace aggression may be prevented through at least three means: (a) through the reduction of incentives for identity management and compliance via aggression and (b) by highlighting equality as a moral motive so that aggression is not morally justifiable. Organizations may institute greater punishment initiatives in order to reduce the attractiveness of aggression as a means for compliance or identity management. This would make the costs of aggression outweigh the benefits, eliminating the desirability of achieving the goals motivating the aggressive behavior (Felson, 1993). Organizations may also direct employees to adopt the moral motive of equality (Rai & Fiske, 2011). Based on this motive, individuals would be driven to treat others as they want to be treated, and as such, they would be motivated to act in non-aggressive ways toward other people regardless of their group membership (Rai & Fiske, 2011).

Limitations and Conclusion

Although our model expands the current understanding of motives underlying perpetrators of workplace aggression, it has limitations. The model is based on the assumption that people committing predatory aggression are making their choice rationally and cognitively. However, people may be limited information processors and don't always act rationally (Simon, 1979). People act in impulsive ways, and in many cases involving aggression; they may not be making a value judgment (e.g., Martinko et al., 2002). Future research should be focused on understanding when individuals are motivated to engage in these rational decision-making processes for aggression. In addition, our model assumes that people take consideration of unity and hierarchy motives (Rai & Fiske, 2011) in equal ways, and in all of their interactions and relationships. However, as highlighted by Rai and Fiske (2011), people vary on what moral motives they consider to be important, and in what situations. Future expansions on this model should take into account individuals' differences in their considerations of the various moral motives, and how that impacts what motivates any proactive aggression they might commit.

In sum, our model expands the current understanding of workplace aggression to include proactive aggression that is not reactive toward an incendiary event or injustice. It provides an explanation of what drives these behaviors, and why people feel that they are justified in conducting themselves in aggressive ways. This model also provides directions for interventions for preventing proactive workplace aggression.

REFERENCES

Andersson, L. M., & Pearson, C. M. (1999). Tit for tat? The spiraling effect of incivility in the workplace. *Academy of Management Review*, *24*, 452–471. doi:10.2307/259136

Aquino, K., & Douglas, S. (2003). Identity threat and antisocial behavior in organizations: The moderating effects of individual differences, aggressive modeling, and hierarchical status. *Organizational Behavior and Human Decision Processes*, *90*, 195–208. doi:10.1016/S0749-5978(02)00517-4

Aquino, K., Lewis, M. U., & Bradfield, M. (1999). Justice constructs, negative affectivity, and employee deviance: A proposed model and empirical test. *Journal of Organizational Behavior*, *20*, 1073–1091. doi:10.1002/(SICI)1099-1379(199912)20:7 < 1073::AID-JOB943 > 3.0.CO;2-7

Aquino, K., Tripp, T. M., & Bies, R. J. (2001). How employees respond to personal offense: The effects of blame attribution, victim status, and offender status on revenge and reconciliation in the workplace. *Journal of Applied Psychology*, *86*, 52–59. doi:10.1037/0023-9010.86.1.52

Bartlett, J. E., & Bartlett, M. E. (2011). Workplace bullying: An integrative literature review. *Advances in Developing Human Resources*, *13*, 69–84. doi:10.1177/1523422311410651

Baumeister, R. F., Bratslavsky, E., Muraven, M., & Tice, D. M. (1998). Ego depletion: Is the active self a limited resource? *Journal of Personality and Social Psychology*, *74*, 1252–1265. doi:10.1037//0022-3514.74.5.1252

Berdahl, J. L. (2007). Harassment based on sex: Protecting social status in the context of gender hierarchy. *Academy of Management Review*, *32*, 641–658. doi:10.5465/AMR.2007.24351879

Berkowitz, L. (1989). Frustration-aggression hypothesis: Examination and reformulation. *Psychological Bulletin*, *106*, 59–73. doi:10.1037//0033-2909.106.1.59

DeWall, C. N., Baumeister, R. F., Stillman, T. F., & Gailliot, M. T. (2007). Violence restrained: Effects of self-regulation and its depletion on aggression. *Journal of Experimental Social Psychology*, *43*, 62–76. doi:10.1016/j.jesp.2005.12.005

Douglas, S. C., Kiewitz, C., Martinko, M. J., Harvey, P., Kim, Y., & Chun, J. U. (2008). Cognitions, emotions, and evaluations: An elaboration likelihood model for workplace aggression. *Academy of Management Review*, *33*, 425–451. doi:10.5465/AMR.2008.31193490

Felson, R. B. (1993). Predatory and dispute-related violence: A social-interactionist approach. In R. V. Clark & M. Felson (Eds.), *Routine activity and rational choice*. (Vol. 5, pp. 103–125). Advances in Criminological Theory. New Brunswick, NJ: Transaction Publishers.

Felson, R. B. (2004). Violence as instrumental behavior. In E. K. Kelloway, J. Barling, & J. J. Hurrell, Jr. (Eds.), *Handbook of workplace violence* (pp. 7–28). London, UK: Sage.

Fiske, A. P. (1992). The four elementary forms of sociality: Framework for a unified theory of social relations. *Psychological Review*, *99*, 689–723. doi:10.1037//0033-295X.99.4.689

Giessner, S., & van Quaquebeke, N. (2010). Using a relational models perspective to understand normatively appropriate conduct in ethical leadership. *Journal of Business Ethics*, *95*, 43–55. doi:10.1007/s10551-011-0790-4

Hershcovis, M. S. (2011). "Incivility, social undermining, bullying … oh my!": A call to reconcile constructs within workplace aggression research. *Journal of Organizational Behavior*, *32*, 499–519. doi:10.1002/job.689

Hershcovis, M. S., & Barling, J. (2007). Towards a relational model of workplace aggression. In J. Langan-Fox, C. L. Cooper, & R. J. Klimoski (Eds.), *Research companion to the dysfunctional workplace: Management challenges and symptoms* (pp. 268–284). Cheltenham, UK: Edward Elgar Publishing Limited. doi:10.4337/9781847207081

Hershcovis, M. S., Turner, N., Barling, J., Arnold, K. A., Dupré, K. E., Inness, M., ... Sivanathan, N. (2007). Predicting workplace aggression: A meta-analysis. *Journal of Applied Psychology*, *92*, 228–238. doi:10.1037/0021-9010.92.1.228

Lian, H., Ferris, D. L., Morrison, R., & Brown, D. J. (2014). Blame it on the supervisor or the subordinate? Reciprocal relations between abusive supervision and organizational deviance. *Journal of Applied Psychology*, *99*, 651–664, doi:10.1037/a0035498

Martinko, M. J., Gundlach, M. J., & Douglas, S. C. (2002). Toward an integrative theory of counterproductive workplace behavior: A causal reasoning perspective. *International Journal of Selection and Assessment*, *10*(1–2), 36–50. doi:10.1111/1468-2389.00192

Rai, T. S., & Fiske, A. P. (2011). Moral psychology is relationship regulation: Moral motives for unity, hierarchy, equality, and proportionality. *Psychological Review*, *118*, 57–75. doi:10.1037/a0021867

Robinson, S. L., & O'Leary-Kelly, A. M. (1998). Monkey see, monkey do: The influence of work groups on the antisocial behavior of employees. *The Academy of Management Journal*, *41*, 656–672. doi:10.2307/256963

Robinson, S. L., O'Reilly, J., & Wang, W. (2013). Invisible at work an integrated model of workplace ostracism. *Journal of Management*, *39*, 203–231. doi:10.1177/0149206312466141

Schat, A. C. H., Frone, M. R., & Kelloway, E. K. (2006). Prevalence of workplace aggression in the US workforce: Findings from a national study. In E. K. Kelloway, J. Barling, & J. J. Hurrell (Eds.), *Handbook of workplace violence* (pp. 47–91). Thousand Oaks, CA: Sage.

Simon, H. A. (1979). Information processing models of cognition. *Annual Review of Psychology*, *30*, 363–396. doi:10.1146/annurev.ps.30.020179.002051

Skarlicki, D. P., & Folger, R. (1997). Retaliation in the workplace: The roles of distributive, procedural, and interactional justice. *Journal of Applied Psychology*, *82*, 434–443. doi:10.1037//0021-9010.82.3.434

Tajfel, H., & Turner, J. C. (1979). An integrative theory of intergroup conflict. In W. G. Austin & S. Worchel (Eds.), *The social psychology of intergroup relations* (pp. 33–47). Monterey, CA: Brooks/Cole.

Tepper, B. J. (2000). Consequences of abusive supervision. *Academy of Management Journal*, *43*, 178–190. doi:10.2307/1556375

Tepper, B. J. (2007). Abusive supervision in work organizations: Review, synthesis, and research agenda. *Journal of Management*, *33*, 261–289. doi:10.1177/0149206307300812

Tripp, T. M., Bies, R. J., & Aquino, K. (2007). A vigilante model of justice: Revenge, reconciliation, forgiveness, and avoidance. *Social Justice Research*, *20*, 10–34. doi:10.1007/s11211-007-0030-3

Tyler, T. R., & Blader, S. L. (2003). The group engagement model: Procedural justice, social identity, and cooperative behavior. *Personality and Social Psychology Review*, *7*, 349–361. doi:10.1207/S15327957PSPR0704_07

WORKPLACE INCIVILITY AND ITS IMPLICATIONS FOR WELL-BEING

Michael P. Leiter, Emily Peck and Stephanie Gumuchian

ABSTRACT

Workplace incivility has been identified as a specific form of social mistreatment causing distress despite its low intensity. Research on workplace incivility has touched on a variety of personal and contextual factors associated with incivility's prevalence including research on both antecedents and outcomes. The research has been especially concerned with identifying a wide range of negative consequences of incivility, including various occupational, interpersonal, and health-related implications. Theoretical explorations have considered links of incivility to sexism and racism, and its reflection of attachment styles, as well as its inherent connection with the stressor-emotion model of counterproductive work behavior (Spector & Fox, 2005). The power of incivility to elicit distress has been attributed to its capacity to signal riskiness of social situations that thwart core social motives

Mistreatment in Organizations
Research in Occupational Stress and Well Being, Volume 13, 107–135

ISSN: 1479-3555/doi:10.1108/S1479-355520150000013004

(i.e., self-control). Intervention research has been relatively rare, but progress is evident.

Keywords: Workplace incivility; civility; intervention; worklife; occupational health; social mistreatment

WORKPLACE MISTREATMENT

Workplace mistreatment has become a focus of applied organizational research over the last decade (Gallus, Bunk, Matthews, Barnes-Farrell, & Magley, 2014). Mistreating others at work can occur in a variety of ways such as bullying (Leymann, 1996; McAvoy & Murtagh, 2003), emotional abuse (Keashly, 1998), abusive supervision (Tepper, 2000, 2007), counterproductive work behaviors (Ones, 2002), and social undermining (Duffy, Ganster, & Pagon, 2002). When any form of workplace mistreatment occurs within an organization a series of occupational problems often ensue (Andersson & Pearson, 1999). This chapter will explore incivility, a less intense and more ambiguous form of workplace mistreatment (Leiter, Day, Oore, & Spence Laschinger, 2012). The defining characteristics of incivility, its antecedents and consequences, as well as outlining methods to reduce its presence will be reviewed within this chapter.

Incivility provides a distinct focus within the realm of mistreatment in two ways. First, the greater frequency of incivility, due in part to its low intensity, makes it a relevant and important aspect of a workplace setting. Its greater importance is derived from the ability of even low-intensity actions in large quantities to have strong implications on work environments. Second, incivility, among other forms of workplace mistreatment, reflects the social culture of a work unit, not only the shortcomings of individuals. Yet, this social culture is less apparent than one that is ridden with high intensity forms of workplace mistreatment and can often go undetected. Both of these qualities allow a focus on incivility to advance knowledge regarding employees' experience of work environments.

INCIVILITY

The frequently cited definition of Incivility is that of Andersson and Pearson (1999) as "low-intensity deviant behavior with ambiguous intent to harm the target, in violation of workplace norms for mutual respect. Uncivil behaviors are characteristically rude and discourteous, displaying a lack of regard for others" (p. 457). This definition identifies three key characteristics of incivility: norm violation, ambiguous intent, and low intensity. The two characteristics of ambiguous intent and low intensity differentiate incivility from other forms of workplace mistreatment (Lim, Cortina, & Magley, 2008; Pearson, Andersson, & Wegner, 2001). The aspect of norm violation is not exclusive to incivility, as other forms of workplace mistreatment violate norms in a more direct and powerful way, for example, bullying or aggression. However, norm violation is an important aspect of incivility because it is the key feature of mistreatment. Behaviors that are low intensity and have ambiguous intent, but do not violate workplace norms are not considered forms of workplace mistreatment. Therefore, the violation of workplace norms is the key feature that makes incivility a form of workplace mistreatment. Within this section, elaborations on the three key components of incivility will be made and comparisons to other forms of workplace mistreatment will be explored.

The quality of ambiguous intent allows for situations in which the person behaving may not have intended the behavior to offend anyone. Employees whose work is disrupted by a colleague talking loudly about his weekend legitimately consider that behavior to be rude and inconsiderate regardless of whether the talker had any intention of behaving badly toward these colleagues. The perceived lack of consideration inherent in the behavior is sufficient for it to be designated as uncivil.

Adding to the uncertainty arising from ambiguous intent is the variability in what individuals or workgroups consider to be rude behavior. Some people may consider an off-color joke to be a welcomed diversion in their workday while others consider it offensive if not threatening. This ambiguity in the definition arises from the quality of incivility being "in violation of workplace norms for mutual respect" (Andersson & Pearson, 1999, p. 457). Workgroups vary in the specifics of those norms and individuals within workgroups vary in their interpretation of such norms. In today's changing and diverse workplaces, it may be difficult to find clearly articulated norms of civil behavior. People from a variety of cultural or religious backgrounds or from different generations may differ greatly in their definition of civil behavior. In the context of such uncertainty, measures of incivility are generally left to the recipient to define what behaviors constitute incivility rather than exhaustively listing every nuance of rude behavior. It is important to note that some of the above-mentioned actions are found within various forms of workplace mistreatment. For example, the silent treatment is a type of ostracism (Williams, 2007) but being ignored or excluded is also a form of incivility (Cortina, Magley, Williams, & Langhout, 2001). The differentiating features between incivility and other forms of mistreatment, as seen in this example, is both the low intensity and ambiguous intent to harm that accompany these actions.

In contrast, a misuse of power defines bullying (Einarsen, Aasland, & Skogstad, 2007). The recipient of the behavior in question is not necessarily the ultimate authority on whether specific actions constitute bullying. For example, employees may feel intimidated by their boss who threatens their job security to require them to work unpaid overtime but employees may also feel intimidated by a boss giving them a well-deserved poor performance review. The former situation reflects bullying while the latter reflects legitimate uses of supervisory authority. This definition of bullying allows for a clearer assessment of whether a behavior constitutes bullying.

From this perspective incivility has a distinct quality within the realm of mistreatment. It goes beyond the narrative of a person purposely inflicting bad behavior on colleagues. At times people may engage in uncivil behavior with conscious intent to harm or at least a conscious awareness that this behavior will be poorly received. Much of what is considered uncivil reflects a lack of social graces or disagreement among colleagues on the norms of proper workplace behavior. As such, incivility calls for action on the workgroup level. By developing a consensus on a clearly articulated code of proper workplace conduct and explicitly labeling behaviors – such as off-color jokes – that at least some individuals find offensive, the workgroup reduces ambiguity. When members behave in conflict with these explicit norms, they can no longer claim that the offense is unintended. Deliberate conversations about workplace social behavior can thereby provide a basis for improving the quality of social behavior among members of workgroups.

Sulea, Filipescu, Horga, Orţan, and Fischmann (2012) identified five main types of nonphysical forms of workplace mistreatment: abusive supervision, ostracism, undermining, unwanted sexual attention, and incivility. Unlike incivility, abusive supervision, ostracism, undermining, and unwanted sexual attention are often unambiguously intentional as the perpetrators act with the intent to aggravate or exclude the victim (Britton, Sliter, & Jex, 2012; Duffy et al., 2002; Kim, 2014; Lim & Cortina, 2005; Schneider, Swan, & Fitzgerald, 1997; Tepper, 2000, 2007; Williams, 2007). Further, many perpetrators of incivility may not realize that their actions are negatively affecting other people in their work environments.

Incivility also differs from other forms of workplace mistreatment because of its low intensity (Kim, 2014; Lim & Cortina, 2005; Schneider et al., 1997; Tepper, 2000, 2007; Williams, 2007). Sulea et al.'s (2012) other forms of nonphysical workplace mistreatment are described as being "hostile" (p. 557) and as a means to "sever a sense of belonging and connection with others" (p. 558). While incivility is often much less intense, and often described as being more of a "daily hassle" (Sulea et al., 2012, p. 558).

The effortless nature of incivility as well as its ambiguity may contribute to its costly effects within an organization. The impact of incivility seems inconsistent with its key characteristics, of low intensity and ambiguous intent. It has been proposed that the disproportionate impact of incivility arises from the meaning that recipients assign to subtle behaviors (Leiter, 2013). Incivility and disrespect from coworkers imply that colleagues are challenging the legitimacy of the recipients' membership within the workgroup. The implicit rejection undermines the recipients' sense of belonging that serves as a fundamental motivation in worklife (Deci & Ryan, 1991). Without a sense of belonging, employees cannot develop confidence in their autonomy or efficacy through their work. In light of the importance of these motivations, people have an acute sensitivity to subtle signs of their social standing within their workgroups. Any behavior from others that challenges their standing within the group is distressing.

Incivility in the Workplace

Acts of workplace incivility are multifaceted, occurring in various ways among all individuals within a work environment. Lim et al. (2008) suggested that the most typical forms of incivility manifest in "sarcasm, disparaging tones and remarks, hostile stares, and the 'silent treatment.'" (p. 95). Incivility can also include ignoring or making demeaning and rude comments about someone. A common measure of workplace incivility, the Workplace Incivility Scale (WIS; Cortina et al., 2001), describes incivility as taking the form of condescending behaviors, unprofessional and demeaning remarks made both privately and publicly, unwanted personal discussions, and doubting the abilities of capable employees.

The ambiguous intent of incivility does not absolve actors of responsibility for showing disregard for others. For example, speaking loudly outside of a coworker's office while the coworker attempts to work or bumping into someone without acknowledging the accidental encounter are both forms of incivility (Leiter, 2013). These unintentional instances represent the effortless nature of incivility in that they reflect a simple lack of awareness of others. Reading emails on one's cell phone while in a meeting or walking through a group of coworkers rudely interrupting their conversation requires little extraneous effort yet may cause frustration and irritability among coworkers. In contrast, being civil and aware of others within one's workgroup requires more effort. For example, when encountering a group of employees having a conversation in the hallway, a civil behavior would be to politely excuse oneself through the group, or even take a different route. These respectful actions require more effort and conscious attention that some individuals do not wish to expend, often resulting in acts of incivility. While the offensive impact of thoughtless, inconsiderate behavior may be unintended, the behavior also indicates that the actor neglected to make the necessary effort to consider the broader impact of his or her behavior.

Civility in the contemporary workplace represents not only respect and regard for others, but also a lack of intentional and deliberate acts of workplace mistreatment. Calculated acts of mistreatment, stemming from sexism or racism for example, are not acceptable in modern workplaces (Cortina, 2008). Formal complaints about these types of behaviors are widely encouraged and accepted, which helps reduce sexism and racism in the workplace. However, some argue that these deliberate forms of abuse continue today; simply masked as ambiguous, low-intensity acts of incivility (Cortina, 2008). Although acts of incivility may lack explicit racial or sexist content, recipients of incivility are disproportionately women or members of visible minorities. This pattern suggests that incivility reflects a persistent bias.

Predictors and Outcomes of Incivility

During the initial phase of incivility as a research focus, researchers have focused on addressing how and why incivility occurs while also identifying the wide range of negative implications it may have within a workplace. Acts of incivility occur frequently yet often go unremarked due to their subtle and ambiguous nature.

Pearson, Andersson, and Porath (2000) believe that "incivilities do not only permeate our social lives; they also taint the office and the factory" (p. 1). The negative implications of incivility may extend beyond the recipient of such behavior, infiltrating entire organizations (Lim et al., 2008). The effects of incivility on a workplace can be long-lasting, detrimental to an organization, and difficult to reverse. Lim et al. (2008) believe it is crucial for organizations to address the outcomes and consequences of uncivil behavior in hopes of ultimately reducing workplace incivility.

Within the following sections, various predictors of incivility including stressful organizational environments, personality characteristics, attachment style, and other personal characteristics will be explored. Additionally, the implications incivility can have on employees' occupational, interpersonal, psychological and physical health will be outlined.

Predictors of Incivility

Researchers have explored individual and workplace characteristics associated with receiving and instigating workplace incivility. On a fundamental level, experiencing negative emotions at work appears to be a key factor in predicting incivility within the workplace. Ogungbamila (2013) reported that individuals with negative feelings toward their jobs were more likely to act uncivilly. Ghosh, Dierkes, and Falletta (2011) also found that subordinates with negative emotions toward their supervisors or mentors were more likely to act uncivilly. Within the organization as a whole, an employee's awareness of organizational politics predicted an increased likelihood of engaging in workplace incivility (Ogungbamila, 2013; Reio & Ghosh, 2009). In general, these studies found that experiencing negative emotions was associated with both receiving and instigating incivility.

One explanation for the relationship between experiencing negative emotions and acting uncivilly is the idea that negative emotions are at the core of the stress experience (Lazarus, 1993). When employees hold negative emotions and then experience a stressor at work, this stressor may act as the trigger for their engagement in uncivil acts. The stressor-emotion model of counterproductive work behavior elaborates on this experience (Spector & Fox, 2005). Specifically, it states that when an individual experiences stressful job conditions, these conditions are likely to induce negative emotions within that employee (Spector & Fox, 2005). These negative emotions may manifest into the individual committing acts of incivility or may be the root of appraising all environmental events as ones that are stressful and negative. This potential causality may proceed in various directions, as one's negative state may affect the interpretation of incoming behaviors or stressful triggers. Additionally, one's negative state may induce uncivil actions, therefore altering the overall state of the work environment into one that is predominately negative.

The research of Spector and Fox (2005) also directs us toward two specific emotions that when experienced, may lead an employee to act in an uncivil manner. Both anger and frustration arise when an employee experiences an emotionally arousing or stressful situation, stimulating the possibility of committing a counterproductive work behavior (Spector & Fox, 2005). The same theory can be applied to incivility. When experiencing a stressor that is perceived as unfair, or inequitable, an employee will attempt to restore justice within their work environment. More than likely, if the stressor is causing feelings of anger and frustration within the employee their attempt to restore this justice will manifest into uncivil acts (whether intentional or not).

Further speculation arises within the work of Baumeister, Vohs, and Tice (2007) whose research focuses primarily on the function of self-control within the workplace. As previously mentioned one of the primary characteristics differentiating incivility from other forms of workplace mistreatment is the potential for an uncivil act to occur unintentionally. One of the explanations for this mechanistic process may arise when observing an employee's depletion of self-control (Baumeister et al., 2007). When experiencing a stressful event an employee expends their emotional resources in a variety of ways such as through coping with negative feelings, with the adverse events, and even through event appraisal. Self-control within the workplace is crucial yet this function depends on limited resources within the individual (Baumeister et al., 2007). These resources are necessary for an individual to exercise self-control over their behaviors and impulses, but after repeated exposure to stressful events, one may lose the ability to avoid impulsive behaviors (i.e., unconscious acts of incivility). The research of Baumeister et al. (2007) provides further explanations for the presence of incivility and the mechanisms behind its unintended presence.

A personal characteristic that has received increased attention recently is attachment style. The construct's potential rests on its focus on social perception and social behavior. Rather than a general personality characteristic, attachment styles are established ways of experiencing oneself in relation to other people.

The background theory proposes attachment styles as persistent frameworks through which people experience themselves and others (Bowlby, 1969). Secure attachment styles reflect confidence in one's capacity to participate constructively in social encounters. The theory proposes two directions in which attachment becomes problematic. First, attachment anxiety reflects fear of harsh judgments, humiliation, and abuse from others. Second, attachment avoidance reflects mistrust of others. Based on dubious views of other people, people with attachment avoidance reduce their contact with others and limit their emotional involvement in social interactions when they cannot be avoided (Mikulincer & Florian, 1995). The two dimensions may occur simultaneously producing an inconsistent approach characterized by both avoidance and anxiety.

The relatively few studies that have applied attachment styles to work relationships have shown a potential for explaining some of the personal characteristics related to workplace incivility. Researchers have found that employees with secure attachment styles are more likely to have increased energy at work, resulting in more citizenship behaviors and fewer workplace deviance behaviors than employees with other attachment styles (Little, Nelson, Wallace, & Johnson, 2011). They argue that securely attached employees are able to devote most of their mental and physical energy to completing their tasks at work and staying focused, while employees with insecure attachment styles for example, spend excessive energy coping with their interpersonal relationship issues and fears (Little et al., 2011). In relation specifically to incivility it has been documented that employees with secure attachment styles report less supervisor, coworker, and instigated incivility than employees with preoccupied, fearful, or dismissive attachment styles (Leiter, Day, & Price, 2014). Individuals who report low levels of civility within their workgroup have been found to report more supervisor incivility and coworker incivility, and research shows that this relationship becomes strengthened among individuals with anxious attachment styles (Leiter, Magley, Shapiro, & Tennen, 2014).

Other personal factors have been examined as predictors of incivility. Both marital status and number of children parented have been found to predict the presence of incivility (Miner, Pesonen, Smittick, Seigel, & Clark, 2014; Ogungbamila, 2013). Specifically, Ogungbamila (2013) found that single employees were less likely to engage in acts of civility than employees who were married. Further, Miner et al. (2014) found that being a mother was not associated with the likelihood of acting uncivil, but that mothers with three or more children were often treated more uncivilly than those without children or with fewer children. While gender was not found to be a significant predictor of incivility in this study, Reio and Ghosh (2009) reported that young men were more likely to engage in both interpersonal and organizational incivility than young women. It appears, therefore, that there is a gender difference in instigated incivility among young adults.

There are still gaps within the research addressing how and why incivility occurs within some organizations and not others. It has been proposed that a growing presence of incivility within contemporary workplaces may result from an increased use of technology at work (Giumetti et al., 2013; Pearson et al., 2000). Recent research has confirmed that acts of incivility may spread rapidly through online mediums (e.g., Giumetti et al., 2013) but others have found higher levels of hostility in interactions via electronic devices (e.g., Chapman, Sheehy, Heywood, Dooley, & Collins, 1995). Others suggest that to better understand how and why incivility occurs, researchers should employ more detailed approaches; exploring incivility at the day-level between and within employees, for example (Hershcovis, 2011; Leiter et al., 2012; Leiter, Magley et al., 2014).

Occupational Outcomes

Incivility impacts various occupational processes ranging from engagement levels and work capacity to turnover intentions and absenteeism. Changes in these constructs impact the employee individually, their workgroup, and the organization. Although identifying predictors of incivility has received some attention in the literature, majority of the research focuses on identifying the consequences of incivility. One reason for slower progress in identifying personal factors associated with experiencing incivility is concern that such a perspective could encourage victim blaming (Gentry & Whitley, 2014). Surveys that have identified consequences of incivility have made a compelling case for addressing the problem. Overall, the evidence indicates that experiencing incivility is associated with a wide range of negative consequences for individuals, workgroups, and organizational productivity.

A central construct in incivility research is that not only are acts of incivility damaging for the victim, they are contagious as well; they can spread throughout organizations, affecting both targets and non-targets (Lim et al., 2008). Research has found that incivility has a negative relationship with productivity (Ghosh, Jacobs, & Reio, 2011; Giumetti et al., 2013; Pearson et al., 2000). Incivility disrupts employee work routines and reduces the effective work capacity of its recipients (Pearson et al., 2000). It is clear that incivility can limit the effectiveness of employees while at work. In fact, Giumetti et al. (2013) discovered that when placed in an uncivil work condition, participants were more likely to perform poorly on a simulated math task than participants who were not in the uncivil work condition. Additionally, when employees feel that they are not respected in their work environments, they are more likely to develop feelings of low organizational productivity and commitment (Ghosh, Dierkes et al., 2011).

Disrespect within the workplace can come from customers as well as coworkers and management. Within the service industry, for example, high levels of customer incivility have been associated with a decreased quality of service given to customers (Sliter, Jex, Wolford, & McInnerney, 2010). The occupational consequences of incivility are similar despite differences in the people who instigate the incivility.

Incivility appears to prompt psychological and physical withdrawal. For example, uncivil work environments are responsible for the development of lower job engagement among employees (Giumetti et al., 2013). Associated with lower engagement, many employees physically withdraw through absenteeism and even develop turnover intentions as potential ways to escape the incivility (Ghosh, Jacobs et al., 2011; Ghosh, Reio, & Bang, 2013; Giumetti, McKibben, Hatfield, Schroeder, & Kowalski, 2012; Laschinger, Leiter, Day, & Gilin, 2009; Miner-Rubino & Reed, 2010; Pearson et al., 2000). Researchers have also explored the occupational consequences of incivility from supervisors and coworkers within the workgroup separately and the effects were found to be equally detrimental. Ghosh et al. (2013) and Giumetti et al. (2012) reported that supervisor incivility (both cyber and direct) was related to the development of turnover intentions among staff. While Miner-Rubino and Reed (2010) found that incivility present within a workgroup correlated positively with the development of turnover intentions among group members. Regardless of the source of incivility, it was associated with withdrawal intentions.

Ultimately, whether through increased levels of absenteeism, reduced organizational commitment, the development of turnover intentions, or a reduction in productivity, employees' reactions to incivility can be detrimental to an organization (Ghosh, Dierkes et al., 2011; Laschinger et al., 2009; Miner-Rubino & Reed, 2010; Pearson et al., 2000). On a broader level, incivility can have a financial impact on organizations; through lower productivity or greater psychological distress among staff (Ghosh, Dierkes et al., 2011; Miner-Rubino & Reed, 2010; Pearson et al., 2000). In more severe cases, acts of incivility may even develop into violence or other harsher forms of workplace mistreatment.

Employee and Relationship Outcomes

In the immediate sense, incivility is problematic for the employees participating in uncivil encounters. Individuals experiencing consistent incivility at work often feel emotionally exhausted, increasing their risk of developing burnout syndrome (Giumetti et al., 2012; Miner-Rubino & Reed, 2010). Sliter et al. (2010) found that individuals experiencing ongoing customer incivility may also develop increased levels of emotional exhaustion.

Not only is incivility associated with negative implications for its recipients, but the consequences can extend to all employees within the organization, including the witnesses (Ghosh, Jacobs et al., 2011; Lim et al., 2008). For bystanders, witnessing incivility among colleagues indicates that the workplace culture carries risks of disrespect and poor collegial support. The fact that a group member can be treated badly suggests that anyone, including the witness, can be treated badly. Bystanders contend with the question of intervention. Intervening directly carries risks of becoming the focus of social mistreatment; intervening indirectly through a supervisor reduces that immediate risk, but reporting such incidents may not be well received by the supervisor. Regardless of the specific dynamic, witnessing incivility has distressing implications for bystanders as well as for participants in the exchange (Ferguson & Barry, 2011).

The relationship between incivility and employees' attitudes about various aspects of their workplace has also been explored. When individuals participate in an uncivil workplace culture, they are likely to develop strong feelings of dissatisfaction toward every aspect of their jobs. Specifically, uncivil work environments have been associated with lower job satisfaction, lower supervisor satisfaction, and decreased coworker satisfaction (Ghosh, Jacobs et al., 2011; Laschinger et al., 2009; Lim et al., 2008; Lim & Lee, 2011; Miner et al., 2014; Miner-Rubino & Reed, 2010; Reio & Ghosh, 2009). Researchers have also found that not only is coworker initiated incivility associated with decreased coworker satisfaction, but it has also been shown to increase employee perceptions of unfair treatment and inequity at work (Lim & Lee, 2011).

Psychological and Physiological Health Outcomes

Incivility has also been associated with a variety of negative psychological and physiological health outcomes among employees. Miner et al. (2014) found that women experiencing high levels of incivility were at an increased likelihood of experiencing symptoms of depression. Similar results were found by Lim and Lee (2011) who found that coworker initiated incivility was associated with increased depression as well as an increase in the amount of psychological distress experienced by the victim. Both work-group and individual employee incivility have also been found to be associated with an employee's mental health (Lim et al., 2008). Employees subjected to high levels of incivility may feel increased distress, discomfort, and overall unhappiness (Lim et al., 2008). Giumetti et al. (2013) discovered that individuals placed in a high incivility condition were likely to report decreased mental, emotional, and social energy, as well as increased levels of negative emotions. Experiencing incivility has an emotional impact.

There is an abundance of research exploring the physiological correlates of workplace mistreatment, however the type of workplace mistreatment often examined in this literature is bullying (see Glendinning, 2001; Salin, 2003). Researchers who have explored the relationships between incivility and employees' physical health have found that incivility is associated with both direct and indirect tolls on an individual's physiological health (Ghosh, Jacobs et al., 2011). In fact, Reio and Ghosh (2009) discovered that employees who work in environments laden with incivility were likely to perceive their physical health as being poorer than it actually is. Current research regarding the negative relationship between incivility and an employees' physiological health has remained at the general level, as self-reports are predominately used to measure physiological symptoms. More research is needed in this area to provide a detailed evaluation of the processes that lead to physical consequences. The direction of the influence may be complex. It may be that being physically ill increases employees' likelihood of behaving uncivilly.

As seen, incivility is associated with a range of problematic conditions for organizations, associated with both occupational and interpersonal outcomes. Frequent acts of incivility may manifest into other forms of workplace mistreatment leading to serious implications for the victims and others involved. As Pearson, Andersson, and Porath (2005) pointed out, incivility has the potential to prompt a spiral of reciprocal and accelerating mistreatment. Uncivil behavior both defines incivility as part of the work-group culture and motivates recipients to exact revenge or reciprocity through instigating incivility in response. Many organizations are struggling to reduce the amount of incivility within their workplaces. To this date, successful grand scale intervention measures that can adequately tackle the intervention conundrum have not yet been demonstrated, but there are encouraging signs of progress.

REDUCING INCIVILITY

With increased awareness of incivility in work environments comes the implementation of programs designed to reduce its harmful outcomes. As outlined earlier, incivility is associated with a variety of negative precursors and a wide range of negative outcomes for individual employees and organizations (Ghosh, Jacobs et al., 2011; Ghosh et al., 2013; Giumetti et al., 2013; Lim et al., 2008; Miner et al., 2014; Miner-Rubino & Reed, 2010; Pearson et al., 2000). High frequencies of incivility within workgroups have been associated with decreased employee productivity (Ghosh, Jacobs et al., 2011; Pearson et al., 2000), increased absenteeism and turnover intentions (Giumetti et al., 2012; Miner-Rubino & Reed, 2010; Pearson et al., 2000), increased burnout (Giumetti et al., 2012; Miner-Rubino & Reed, 2010), a series of psychological correlates such as depression, and negative feelings and emotions (Giumetti et al., 2013; Lim et al., 2008; Miner et al., 2014). Finding an intervention method capable of mitigating the harmful effects of incivility is crucial for the well-being of employees and organizations.

The effortless nature of incivility emphasizes the challenges in implementing interventions capable of alleviating acts of incivility that occur so unconsciously. The following section will review basic programs that have attempted to reduce the amount of workplace mistreatment as well as highlight the most effective and contemporary incivility intervention programs.

Psychological Detachment

Some approaches to workplace stress concentrate on moderating employees' reaction to events rather than changing the sources of distress. One strategy within this approach is assuring that employees have a real break from work on weekends, days off, and vacations to reduce the stress caused by their work environments (Binnewies, Sonnentag, & Mojza, 2010; de Bloom et al., 2010, 2011; Sonnentag, 2012; Sonnentag, Mojza, Binnewies, & Scholl, 2008).

Both weekends and vacations have been found to help employees combat the negative effects of incivility and other workplace stressors (Binnewies et al., 2010; de Bloom et al., 2010, 2011). When on a vacation or away for a weekend, employees are given an opportunity to psychologically detach themselves from the stress found within their work environments and their job tasks (Binnewies et al., 2010; de Bloom et al., 2010, 2011). Psychological detachment has been defined as withdrawing oneself from one's workplace both physically and mentally, allowing the body and mind a break from the stressors found within their work environments (Sonnentag, 2012; Sonnentag et al., 2008). The idea of psychologically detaching oneself from work poses the logical concern that employee engagement levels may be reduced after time away from their jobs (Sonnentag, 2012; Sonnentag et al., 2008).

The notion of allowing employees psychological detachment from their workplaces follows Spector and Fox's (2005) stressor-emotional model, in that a vacation or holiday may provide an employee with an opportunity to reduce anger and frustration and other negative emotions that stem from stressful workplace events. A vacation or holiday provides employees with opportunities to recuperate and reduce negative emotions. Returning to their workplace with an increase in positivity may result in employees appraising stressful events in a less adverse light.

Time away from work arising from vacations and weekends has been associated with a variety of positive workplace and employee outcomes (Binnewies et al., 2010; de Bloom et al., 2010, 2011). Binnewies et al. (2010) conducted a longitudinal, qualitative study to determine the effects of having time off work among German employees. Employees who had constant access to the internet and who were not shift workers (i.e., mainly administrative employees) were surveyed at the beginning and end of the work week for four consecutive working weeks. They found that the health and well-being of employees increased after a vacation or weekend away from work (de Bloom et al., 2010). de Bloom et al. (2010) also used longitudinal methods to explore the concept of taking time off work, specifically for a winter sports vacation. Dutch employees working at travel agencies or winter sport stores were surveyed two weeks prior to the vacation, during the vacation, and at one, two, and four weeks after the vacation. It was found that following the vacation, many employees reported higher levels of satisfaction, increased positive moods, as well as increased energy (de Bloom et al., 2010). Ultimately, these employees felt less psychological stress, tension, and even had overall better health statuses (de Bloom et al., 2010, 2011).

Vacations and weekends away are associated with employee work outcomes. In their exploration of Dutch employees who took a winter sports vacation, Binnewies et al. (2010) found that employees showed increased task performance, initiative, and an increased number of citizenship behaviors upon returning to work from their vacation.

The results supporting vacations and weekends as a means to reduce workplace and psychological stress and increase citizenship, energy, initiative and task performance are encouraging. The two projects outlined above, of Dutch and German employees, both used detailed methods, namely week-level diary methods, to qualitatively examine their participants (Binnewies et al., 2010; de Bloom et al., 2010). These methods reduce the retrospective bias of single-panel surveys and therefore increase the accuracy of participant reports. However, important limitations exist within each project. For example, in the exploration of German employees over four working weeks, no blue collar employees or shift workers were surveyed, limiting the generalizability to employees in sectors other than administrative and office work sectors. Additionally, ratings for the weekend were collected on Monday morning, and as a result the requirement of participants to think retroactively may lead to decreases in the accuracy of their reported weekend experiences. In this case, although the detailed week-level diary method was used, an even more detailed method, such as a daily diary may increase the accuracy of the results (Binnewies et al., 2010). In the exploration of Dutch employees one major constraint on the generalizability of the results is the homogenous sample that was used. All participants came from similar work sectors and all participated in a winter sports vacation. The results are therefore less generalizable to employees who take vacations other than winter sports vacations (de Bloom et al., 2010).

Although weekends and vacations may provide employees with temporary relief from their stressful work environments, they do not provide a comprehensive solution to the detrimental effects of incivility. Given the limitations found within the two main explorations of psychological detachment from work in the form of weekends and vacations, it is important to consider other types of interventions aimed at reducing incivility and increasing the number of positive work experiences.

Although a unique form of workplace mistreatment, theories regarding the antecedents of other forms of workplace mistreatment such as harassment may apply to incivility. Bowling and Beehr (2006) identified three main categories of causes for antecedents of workplace harassment: the perpetrator, the victim, and characteristics of the work environment. Both environmental and individual difference factors were found to influence the presence of harassment (Bowling & Beehr, 2006). Areas such as the human resource systems within organizations and changing or negative organizational cultures and climates were indicative of workplace harassment. A negative workplace climate can easily add to the number of stressful events experienced by employees within an organization.

Various personality characteristics of both the perpetrator and the victim may influence the presence of workplace harassment. Perpetrators who are impulsive, emotionally reactive, and rebellious are at a greater likelihood of actively participating in workplace harassment (Bowling & Beehr, 2006). Victims who commonly experience conflict at work may be experiencing conflict within other interpersonal relationships, suggesting that there is a part of the victims' personality acting as an antecedent for experiencing harassment. Additionally, victims who are submissive in their actions may be more likely to experience workplace harassment (Bowling & Beehr, 2006). Although there are some characteristics that have been identified as being antecedents of workplace harassment both on the side of the victim as well as with the perpetrator, the research in this area is far from concrete.

Reframing Reactions to Incivility

Some employers and organizations are constantly looking for ways to improve the work conditions and environments for their employees. Due to the detrimental effects of incivility within work environments, researchers have started to design strategies to help reduce the amount of incivility present within workplaces. Kirk, Schutte, and Hine (2011) implemented an expressive-writing intervention program to help reduce incivility at work and to promote the presence of positive workplace outcomes among Australian employees. After completing a pre-intervention survey, all participants were required to write for 20 minutes at the end of their work day for the following three days. Those in the intervention group were given specific instructions on what to write about (i.e., their "deepest thoughts and feelings") (Kirk et al., 2011, p. 186) with respect to their work day and to further determine whether this conscious reflection is associated with their sense of efficacy. Those in the control group were simply asked to write about anything with respect to their non-workday. All participants completed a post-intervention survey two weeks after completing the writing task.

They found that employees within the writing intervention condition showed increased levels of emotional self-efficacy, emotional intelligence, as well as positive affect (Kirk et al., 2011). The authors argued that these outcomes are important because emotional intelligence is a key precursor of civil behavior. They proposed that individuals exercising emotional intelligence have a greater capacity to understand and manage their emotions while considering others around them. As a result they are more likely to respect their coworkers and treat them in a civil manner (Kirk et al., 2011). However, the study did not report any actual decreases in incivility or increases in civility for those participating in the intervention.

Educating Employees about Uncivil Behavior

Gedro and Wang (2013) implemented a workplace strategy based on employee education as a means to help reduce the amount of incivility in work environments. Gedro and Wang (2013) sought to determine whether providing individuals with detailed information about workplace incivility through a three-step training program would help reduce its presence within an organization.

The first step of the program was to introduce the common terms and expressions used to describe acts of incivility or bullying within a work environment. The trainers taught participants about workplace mistreatment and workplace civility in a classroom lesson style to introduce the academic terminology used in organizational research to describe various constructs, for example, incivility. The instruction noted described a range of actions that could be interpreted subjectively as lacking civility. The presentation advised participants about the ambiguous intent inherent in uncivil behavior. Participants were asked to rate, on a scale from one to ten, how much a given series of actions at work would affect them.

Lastly, individuals were given opportunities to employ their new knowledge of workplace mistreatment and civility by using it to carefully evaluate case studies. Participants were divided into small groups and asked to explore the case studies together. Then, in a discussion format, they responded to series of questions about the case study. After completing the three stages of the program, the trainers offered participants various strategies that they could implement to help create a positive social work environment composed of civility and mutual respect. The trainers also identified the effects this type of work environment can have on an organization. Based on participant feedback and organization wide surveys containing civility measures, researchers argued that the enhanced knowledge and awareness gained from this training program could help employees, human resources specialists, as well as management foster a civil and healthy work environment (Gedro & Wang, 2013). However, the study did not report actual changes in incivility or civility nor did it include a control group.

The outcome of this study may have differed had the intervention focused on targeting supervisors or other employees in positions with more responsibility than just participants from various organizations. Perhaps, this intervention may be more effective when targeting management as primary change agents in the incivility reduction process. To increase the methodological quality of this study, perhaps it should be re-run as a randomized controlled trial to show whether changes were apparent among the group level as opposed to solely collecting information from participant self-reports.

In contrast to the previous intervention model, Bowen, Privitera, and Bowie (2011) argued that educating individuals about workplace violence and incivility was not enough to actually reduce its presence. They proposed an intervention strategy that incorporates more elaborate illustrations of how incivility and violence arise from a combination of internal and external stressors (Bowen et al., 2011). They speculated on implementing a holistic framework of prevention focusing on the public health model. This model incorporates aspects of neurobiological, behavioral, organizational, mental health, and educational theory (Bowen et al., 2011).

The model they proposed would occur in three stages. First, they suggest creating a positive social environment through education on appropriate workplace behaviors and the organization's policies and procedures with the goal of preventing any issues of workplace mistreatment. Next they suggest a stage where employees are taught about their emotions through several domains, including social and neurological approaches. This stage is used to address any issues of workplace mistreatment as they occur. Finally, they proposed a third stage when workplace mistreatment becomes a crisis within an organization. This stage would include a swift action in response events using various methods with involvement of the organization's human resources department. They review case studies pertaining to this framework but do not present evidence supporting its efficacy.

Reio and Ghosh (2009) conducted a cross-sectional study on 402 volunteer training participants and discovered high levels of both interpersonal and organizational incivility. Although the study did not directly test an intervention method, Reio and Ghosh (2009) discussed various intervention strategies. They proposed that the presence of positive socialization programs and a focus on enhancing employees' understanding of affective reactions and interactions may prove to be beneficial at reducing the frequency of incivility (Reio & Ghosh, 2009). They conclude that encouraging positive interactions among all staff may help reduce the amount of negative perceptions and negative affect surrounding certain acts of incivility (Reio & Ghosh, 2009).

None of the intervention programs reviewed to this point reported a discernible difference in the frequency of incivility or the negative effects of incivility within a work environment. The correlational data and longitudinal surveys reviewed here point to potential targets for intervention, but there has been few instances evaluating their implementation, comparing their impact to control groups, and evaluating the extent to which gains sustain after the intervention phase is complete.

Civility, Respect, and Engagement at Work (CREW)

One program that has been found to have positive work outcomes on an immediate organizational level is the Civility, Respect and Engagement at Work Intervention (CREW). CREW was created and first initiated by the Veterans Health Administration (VHA) in an attempt to increase the amount of workplace civility found within organizations nationwide (Osatuke et al., 2009). CREW focuses primarily on social relationships, with the intention of fixing and promoting positive employee interactions and affect in an attempt to foster a cohesive and civil work environment (Leiter et al., 2012; Leiter, Laschinger, Day, & Oore, 2011; Osatuke et al., 2009).

CREW is a behavioral intervention program that leads an intact workgroup through a process of reflection on its workgroup culture. On the basis of discussions, supplemented by profiles derived from employee surveys, participants are required to consider how they define civility, respect, incivility, and disrespect in their workgroup. The process encourages participants to be explicit about the workplace norms for social behavior that they expect their workplaces to meet, in addition to identifying instances in which those norms are violated. The process reflects an assumption that employees most often discuss instances of incivility when complaining to their friends. They rarely approach incivility as a workplace problem that requires analysis leading to an action plan. CREW introduces that format by putting working relationships on the agenda for discussion.

CREW groups are led by employees of the participating organization who receive training and mentoring throughout the six-month CREW process. The advantages of using local facilitators rather than outside consultants is that the local facilitators have a deep knowledge of the organization and that after completion of CREW, the organization retains the experience and expertise developed during facilitation.

CREW sessions include both conversation and behavioral practice. For example, a group may talk about how group members rarely express appreciation with one another. They would not only identify this problem but proceed to identify the kind of appreciation that they would find meaningful in their work. The facilitator would then lead the group through role playing the expression of appreciation to not only clarify the issue but to initiate momentum toward enacting such behavior. This behavioral practice would proceed to practicing the targeted behavior in the actual work setting and reporting back to the group on that experience.

The process continues for six months of regular meetings. The meeting agendas do not follow a set schedule. Instead, facilitators draw from a CREW Toolkit of exercises and discussion topics that pertain to the group's challenges that are identified in the survey profile and the group's discussions in previous CREW meetings. The CREW Companions working with the consulting or research team actively mentor the facilitators as they plan and reflect upon their CREW sessions. The process is shaped by the assumption that social behavior does not change easily. To implement effective change requires a structured process with behavioral practice elements that encourage participants to try new ways of interacting. The group format provides opportunities for employees to help one another in their efforts to establish a more civil workplace culture. The ongoing process provides opportunities for reflection and consolidation of new ways of behaving.

To this date, two major studies have implemented CREW in an attempt to promote positive workplace interactions, and to create civil and healthy work environments (Leiter et al., 2011, 2012; Osatuke et al., 2009). Osatuke et al. (2009) collected pre-intervention and post-intervention data from 38 workgroups from 20 VHA facilities. Significant differences within the intervention groups were found, as levels of perceived workplace civility increased from pre-intervention to post-intervention (Osatuke et al., 2009). The control units remained constant on civility over the study interval. This study established that the CREW process resulted in an improvement in civility. The study did not investigate the extent to which improvements in civility were associated with changes in other aspects of worklife.

Leiter et al. (2011) replicated the improvement in civility for CREW in contrast to no changes for control groups in their exploration of the efficacy of the CREW intervention. They further examined the extent to which improved civility was associated with changes in other constructs, including supervisor incivility, respect, cynicism, job satisfaction, management trust, and absences. The survey was administered before the six-month CREW intervention and after CREW was completed. Findings indicated that within the eight intervention units, positive improvements were made in almost all areas measured in the survey (Leiter et al., 2011). These improvements were significantly better than those made in the comparison groups. The analysis also demonstrated that improvements in civility mediated improvements in most of the other constructs.

Leiter et al. (2012) presented a one-year follow-up of the CREW intervention reported in Leiter et al. (2011). Within this study, three surveys were completed: before the intervention; immediately after the intervention; and then one year later. A total of 957 healthcare workers within Nova Scotia and Ontario participated in this study with 262 in the intervention units, and 695 in the comparison units. This three part survey allowed researchers to observe whether the positive impact of CREW was sustained after the intervention was complete. The findings indicated encouraging results as a one-year follow-up survey found continued improvements in workplace civility, experienced supervisor incivility, as well as burnout and physical stress symptoms (Leiter et al., 2012). A CREW participant in this study commented about the positive changes they began to see in their workplace:

> I have observed an increase of civility among peers and co-workers. I find my co-workers on average are respecting each other and trying to recognize positives, rather than focusing on the negatives all the time! Co-workers that used to talk negatively about new concepts or practices at (*participant's workplace*) now catch themselves and try to think about the benefits or the potential improvements that new concepts/practices might bring to the work environment. (Survey Respondent; *Leading Workplace Communities*, Nova Scotia, 2012)

The follow-up results suggest that CREW was associated with a self-sustaining change in the workgroup dynamics. That is, after groups managed to increase civility in their day-to-day interactions, these more positive exchanges encouraged positive responses from others, initiating a positive civility spiral that could sustain gains after the intervention was complete.

CREW is a unique workplace intervention as it focuses on identifying problematic workplace areas, and providing resources and solutions specific to the problems experienced in those units. Although this method has proven to be beneficial for some organizations, many of these improvements demand extensive resources that organizations may not have access too. Some organizations may also have difficulty with CREW if employees are not committed to the intervention process. The issue of commitment to the CREW intervention process of meetings and surveys is captured by another participant of a CREW intervention study,

> I have been impressed with the CREW interventions when these interventions were taking place. I enthusiastically took part in CREW discussions and proudly presented results of our work at a Quality Week event. We found, broadly, that CREW interventions worked when we carried them out and didn't work when we didn't carry them out. (Survey Respondent; *Leading Workplace Communities*, Nova Scotia, 2012)

As previously mentioned, awareness of incivility within organizations is growing, and its presence is partially due to the effortless nature with which it occurs. Interventions aimed at reducing incivility within organizations are facing uphill battles as significant resources, time, and commitments are required to even slightly improve rates of civility at an individual level. Unfortunately, many organizations give sufficient priority to addressing workplace incivility and many employees do not prioritize the time necessary to implement the process. As a result, both researchers and organizations are faced with an intervention conundrum, as the growing presence of incivility is effortless, yet actively reducing its presence requires extreme efforts and resources.

Many of these interventions, including CREW, work with deliberate action. They identify problematic areas, employ strategies to address these problems, and then hopefully produce positive outcomes. The problem with employing these strategies to reduce incivility is that individuals acting in an uncivil manner may be unaware that they are doing so, and are likely resistant toward participating in these intervention programs. Acting uncivil may occur naturally for many employees, therefore limiting the applicability of intervention methods such as CREW. Employees may feel as though they are acting normally when uncivil, and attempting to alter their behavior may feel awkward, unnatural, and ultimately discomforting for individuals participating in the interventions.

Although the CREW intervention has been found to have a series of positive implications on organizations, the question of whether it can truly combat the overriding presence of incivility within organizations arises. Researchers and organizations are faced with the difficult task of developing interventions that are both grand-scheme and can occur as a process requiring much less intentional effort.

CONCLUSION

Although people get along with one another at work most of the time, they behave badly to one another more often than they should. Social mistreatment can take a variety of forms. Incivility differs from other forms of workplace mistreatment in its ambiguous intent, challenge to workplace norms, and low intensity. Although less severe than other forms of workplace mistreatment, it has a detrimental impact on organizations.

Incivility has been found to impact employees' health and well-being (Lim et al., 2008; Lim & Lee, 2011), reduce productivity levels (Ghosh, Jacobs et al., 2011; Giumetti et al., 2013; Pearson et al., 2000), increase turnover intentions and absenteeism (Ghosh, Dierkes et al., 2011; Ghosh et al., 2013; Giumetti et al., 2012), and ultimately lead to burnout among staff (Giumetti et al., 2012; Miner-Rubino & Reed, 2010). These are only some of the occupational and individual consequences that a work environment with relatively high levels of incivility can have on its employees. Incivility infiltrates workplaces through its effortless nature. When an individual acts discourteous or inconsiderate toward the organization, a coworker, or even a supervisor, they are damaging the social environment of their workplace. One of the main components of incivility, ambiguous intent, allows individuals to sidestep responsibility for their behavior. It is easy for employees to act without awareness, but to act in a deliberate manner, aware of the impact of each action, requires attention, time, and effort. This contrast between the effortless nature of incivility, and the effort demanding aspects of civility, presents researchers with an intervention conundrum.

Researchers are continuously trying to define a comprehensive intervention that can address the effortless nature of incivility. To this date, the CREW intervention has been found to be effective, but only in a limited capacity. CREW is an intervention that aims to reduce incivility by identifying both weaknesses and strengths within struggling work units. It provides education, resources, and support to the individuals working within those units. CREW implements a behavioral process designed to encourage participants to reflect on their social behavior and to practice more civil, respectful, and supporting actions. Although there is convincing evidence of CREW's efficacy, it is a resource-intense intervention requiring active and sustained commitment from participants. These qualities limit its applicability.

Workplace incivility has become a lively research focus over the past 15 years. Part of the appeal as a research focus lies with its irrational quality.

On the surface, workplaces call for some level of proper behavior if not decorum. Most occupations have a preference for employees who enact a level of self-management in their behavior at work. At work, employees are expected to act as adults. Beyond these externally imposed expectations, individuals are intrinsically motivated to seek a sense of belonging that would seem to be more available through civil, respectful social encounters. For the most part people do behave civilly. For example, Leiter et al. (2011) reported the average score on coworker incivility as 0.78 on a seven-point scale on which 0 indicated never and 1 indicated once or twice over the previous month. The challenge is not that employees are running roughshod through the workplace. The challenge is that people occasionally lapse into incivility and that rare instances of incivility appear to have a powerful emotional impact on recipients and observers of such behavior.

Workplace incivility has interest as a group-level phenomenon. Rather than an extreme behavior exhibited only by seriously disturbed or ill-intentioned people, incivility encompasses low intensity, annoying behaviors that fall within the repertoire and experience of most people. The interesting issue is not so much discovering that people are capable of behaving rudely to one another, but that workgroups can settle into a persistent pattern of incivility and disrespect. The objective for intervention becomes establishing a new workplace culture characterized by mutually supportive dialogue.

REFERENCES

Andersson, L. M., & Pearson, C. M. (1999). Tit for tat? The spiraling effect of incivility in the workplace. *Academy of Management Review*, *24*, 452–471. doi:10.1016/S0090-2616(00)00019-X

Baumeister, R. F., Vohs, K. D., & Tice, D. M. (2007). The strength model of self-control. *Current Directions in Psychological Science*, *16*, 351–355.

Binnewies, C., Sonnentag, S., & Mojza, E. J. (2010). Recovery during the weekend and fluctuations in weekly job performance: A week-level study examining intra-individual relationships. *Journal of Occupational & Organizational Psychology*, *83*, 419–441. doi:10.1348/096317909X418049

Bowen, B., Privitera, M. R., & Bowie, V. (2011). Reducing workplace violence by creating healthy workplace environments. *Journal of Aggression, Conflict and Peace Research*, *3*, 185–198. doi:10.1108/17596591111187710

Bowlby, J. (1969). *Attachment: Attachment and loss* (Vol. 1), New York, NY: Basic Books.

Bowling, N. A., & Beehr, T. A. (2006). Workplace harassment from the victim's perspective: A theoretical model and meta-analysis. *Journal of Applied Psychology*, *91*(5), 998.

Britton, A. R., Sliter, M. T., & Jex, S. M. (2012). Is the glass really half-full? The reverse-buffering effect of optimism on undermining behavior. *Personality & Individual Differences*, *52*, 712–717. doi:10.1016/j.paid.2011.12.038

Chapman, A. J., Sheehy, N. P., Heywood, S., Dooley, B., & Collins, S. C. (1995). The organizational implications of teleworking. *International Review of Industrial and Organizational Psychology*, *10*, 229–248.

Cortina, L. M. (2008). Unseen injustice: Incivility as modern discrimination in organizations. *Academy of Management Review*, *33*, 55–75. doi:10.5465/AMR.2008.27745097

Cortina, L. M., Magley, V. J., Williams, J. H., & Langhout, R. D. (2001). Incivility in the workplace: Incidence and impact. *Journal of Occupational Health Psychology*, *6*, 64–80. doi:10.1037/1076-8998.6.1.64

de Bloom, J., Geurts, S. E., Sonnentag, S., Taris, T., de Weerth, C., & Kompier, M. J. (2011). How does a vacation from work affect employee health and well-being? *Psychology & Health*, *26*, 1606–1622. doi:10.1080/08870446.2010.546860

de Bloom, J., Geurts, S. E., Taris, T. W., Sonnentag, S., de Weerth, C., & Kompier, M. J. (2010). Effects of vacation from work on health and well-being: Lots of fun, quickly gone. *Work & Stress*, *24*, 196–216. doi:10.1080/02678373.2010.493385

Deci, E. L., & Ryan, R. M. (1991). A motivational approach to self: Integration in personality. *Nebraska Symposium on Motivation*, *38*, 237–288. doi:10.1037/0003-066X.55.1.68

Duffy, M. K., Ganster, D. C., & Pagon, M. (2002). Social undermining in the workplace. *Academy of Management Journal*, *45*, 331–351. doi:10.2307/3069350

Einarsen, S., Aasland, M. S., & Skogstad, A. (2007). Destructive leadership behaviour: A definition and conceptual model. *The Leadership Quarterly*, *18*, 207–216. doi:10.1016/j.leaqua.2007.03.002

Ferguson, M., & Barry, B. (2011). I know what you did: The effects of interpersonal deviance on bystanders. *Journal of Occupational Health Psychology*, *16*(1), 80. doi:10.1037/a0021708

Gallus, J. A., Bunk, J. A., Matthews, R. A., Barnes-Farrell, J. L., & Magley, V. J. (2014). An eye for an eye? Exploring the relationship between workplace incivility experiences and perpetration. *Journal of Occupational Health Psychology*, *19*, 143–154. doi:10.1037/a0035931

Gedro, J., & Wang, J. (2013). Creating civil and respectful organizations through the scholar-practitioner bridge. *Advances in Developing Human Resources*, *15*, 284–295. doi:10.1177/1523422313488062

Gentry, R. H., & Whitley, B. E., Jr. (2014). Bulling in graduate school: Its nature and effects. *The Qualitative Report*, *19*(71), 1–18. Retrieved from http://www.nova.edu/ssss/QR/QR19/gentry71.pdf

Ghosh, R., Dierkes, S., & Falletta, S. (2011). Incivility spiral in mentoring relationships: Reconceptualizing negative mentoring as deviant workplace behavior. *Advances in Developing Human Resources*, *13*, 22–39. doi:10.1177/1523422311410639

Ghosh, R., Jacobs, J. L., & Reio, T. G. (2011). The toxic continuum from incivility to violence: What can HRD do? *Advances in Developing Human Resources*, *13*, 3–9. Retrieved from http://adh.sagepub.com/

Ghosh, R., Reio, T. G., Jr., & Bang, H. (2013). Reducing turnover intent: Supervisor and co-worker incivility and socialization-related learning. *Human Resource Development International*, *16*, 169–185. doi:10.1080/13678868.2012.756199

Giumetti, G. W., Hatfield, A. L., Scisco, J. L., Schroeder, A. N., Muth, E. R., & Kowalski, R. M. (2013). What a rude e-mail! Examining the differential effects of incivility versus support on mood, energy, engagement, and performance in an online context. *Journal of Occupational Health Psychology, 18*, 297–309. doi:10.1037/a0032851

Giumetti, G. W., McKibben, E. S., Hatfield, A. L., Schroeder, A. N., & Kowalski, R. M. (2012). Cyber incivility @ work: The new age of interpersonal deviance. *Cyberpsychology, Behavior, and Social Networking, 15*, 148–154. doi:10.1089/cyber.2011.0336

Glendinning, P. M. (2001). Workplace bullying: Curing the cancer of the American workplace. *Public Personnel Management, 30*, 269–286. doi:10.1177/009102600103000301

Hershcovis, M. S. (2011). "Incivility, social undermining, bullying ... oh my!": A call to reconcile constructs within workplace aggression research. *Journal of Organizational Behavior, 32*, 499–519. doi:10.1002/job.689

Keashly, L. (1998). Emotional abuse in the workplace: Conceptual and empirical issues. *Journal of Emotional Abuse, 1*, 85–117. doi:10.1300/J135v01n01_05

Kim, P. (2014). A simple model of ostracism formation. *Plos ONE, 9*, 1–6. doi:10.1371/journal.pone.0094333

Kirk, B. A., Schutte, N. S., & Hine, D. W. (2011). The effect of an expressive-writing intervention for employees on emotional self-efficacy, emotional intelligence, affect, and workplace incivility. *Journal of Applied Social Psychology, 41*, 179–195. doi:10.1111/j.1559-1816.2010.00708.x

Laschinger, H., Leiter, M., Day, A., & Gilin, D. (2009). Workplace empowerment, incivility, and burnout: Impact on staff nurse recruitment and retention outcomes. *Journal of Nursing Management, 17*, 302–311. doi:10.1111/j.1365-2834.2009.00999.x

Lazarus, R. S. (1993). Why we should think of stress as a subset of emotion. In L. Goldberger & S. Breznitz (Eds.), *Handbook of stress: Theoretical and clinical aspects* (2nd ed., pp. 21–39). New York, NY: The Free Press.

Leiter, M. P. (2013). *Analyzing and theorizing the dynamics of the workplace incivility crisis*. Amsterdam: Springer.

Leiter, M. P., Day, A., Oore, D. G., & Spence Laschinger, H. K. (2012). Getting better and staying better: Assessing civility, incivility, distress, and job attitudes one year after a civility intervention. *Journal of Occupational Health Psychology, 17*, 425–434. doi:10.1037/a0029540

Leiter, M. P., Day, A., & Price, L. (2014, May). Attachment styles at work: Measurement, collegial relationships, and burnout. In M. G. González-Morales (Chair), *Novel approaches to the study of workplace incivility and victimization*. Symposium in the Annual Convention of SIOP, Honolulu, HI.

Leiter, M. P., Laschinger, H. K. S., Day, A., & Oore, D. G. (2011, April). The impact of civility interventions on employee social behavior, distress, and attitudes. *Journal of Applied Psychology, 96*, 1258. doi:10.1037/a0024442

Leiter, M. P., Magley, V. G., Shapiro, J. C., & Tennen, H. (2014, April). Affect and exhaustion before and after incivility: A daily diary perspective. In A. Day (Chair), *Workplace mistreatment: Examining antecedents and outcomes of incivility and aggression*. Symposium at the 11th European Association of Occupational Health Psychology conference, London, UK.

Leymann, H. (1996). The content and development of mobbing at work. *European Journal of Work and Organizational Psychology, 5*, 165–184. doi:10.1080/13594329608414853

Lim, S., & Cortina, L. M. (2005). Interpersonal mistreatment in the workplace: The interface and impact of general incivility and sexual harassment. *Journal of Applied Psychology*, *90*, 483–496. doi:0.1037/0021-9010.90.3.483

Lim, S., Cortina, L. M., & Magley, V. J. (2008). Personal and workgroup incivility: Impact on work and health outcomes. *Journal of Applied Psychology*, *93*, 95–107. doi:10.1037/0021-9010.93.1.95

Lim, S., & Lee, A. (2011). Work and nonwork outcomes of workplace incivility: Does family support help? *Journal of Occupational Health Psychology*, *16*, 95–111. doi:10.1037/a0021726

Little, L. M., Nelson, D. L., Wallace, J. C., & Johnson, P. D. (2011). Integrating attachment style, vigor at work, and extra-role performance. *Journal of Organizational Behavior*, *32*, 464–484. doi:10.1002/job.709

McAvoy, B. R., & Murtagh, J. (2003). Workplace bullying: The silent epidemic. *BMJ: British Medical Journal*, *117*(1204), 1–3. Retrieved from http://www.nzma.org.nz/journal/117-1204/1125/

Mikulincer, M., & Florian, V. (1995). Appraisal and coping with a real-life stressful situation: The contribution of attachment styles. *Personality and Social Psychology Bulletin*, *21*, 408–416. doi:10.1177/0146167295214011

Miner, K. N., Pesonen, A. D., Smittick, A. L., Seigel, M. L., & Clark, E. K. (2014). Does being a mom help or hurt? Workplace incivility as a function of motherhood status. *Journal of Occupational Health Psychology*, *19*, 60–73. doi:10.1037/a0034936

Miner-Rubino, K., & Reed, W. D. (2010). Testing a moderated mediational model of work-group incivility: The roles of organizational trust and group regard. *Journal of Applied Social Psychology*, *40*, 3148–3168. doi:10.1111/j.1559-1816.2010.00695.x

Ogungbamila, B. (2013). Perception of organizational politics and job-related negative emotions as predictors of workplace incivility among employees of distressed banks. *European Scientific Journal*, *9*, 125–138. Retrieved from http://www.eujournal.org/index.php/esj

Ones, D. S. (2002). Introduction to the special issue on counterproductive behaviors at work. *International Journal of Selection & Assessment*, *10*, 1–4. doi:10.1111/1468-2389.00188

Osatuke, K., Mohr, D., Ward, C., Moore, S. C., Dyrenforth, S., & Belton, L. (2009). Civility, respect, engagement in the workforce (CREW): Nationwide organization development intervention at Veterans Health Administration. *Journal of Applied Behavioral Science*, *45*, 384–410. doi:10.1177/0021886309335067

Pearson, C., Andersson, L., & Porath, C. (2005). Workplace incivility. In S. Fox & P. E. Spector (Eds.), *Counterproductive work behavior: Investigations of actors and targets* (pp. 177–200). Washington, DC: American Psychological Association. doi:10.1037/10893-008

Pearson, C. M., Andersson, L. M., & Porath, C. L. (2000). Assessing and attacking workplace incivility. *Organizational Dynamics*, *29*, 123–137. doi:10.1016/S0090-2616(00)00019-X

Pearson, C. M., Andersson, L. M., & Wegner, J. W. (2001). When workers flout convention: A study of workplace incivility. *Human Relations*, *54*, 1387–1419. doi:10.1177/00187267015411001

Reio, T. G., & Ghosh, R. (2009). Antecedents and outcomes of workplace incivility: Implications for human resource development research and practice. *Human Resource Development Quarterly*, *20*, 237–264. doi:10.1002/hrdq.20020

Salin, D. (2003). Ways of explaining workplace bullying: A review of enabling, motivating and precipitating structures and processes in the work environment. *Human Relations*, *56*, 1213–1232. doi:10.1177/00187267035610003

Schneider, K. T., Swan, S., & Fitzgerald, L. F. (1997). Job-related and psychological effects of sexual harassment in the workplace: Empirical evidence from two organizations. *Journal of Applied Psychology*, *82*, 401–415. Retrieved from http://www.apa.org/pubs/journals/apl/

Sliter, M., Jex, S., Wolford, K., & McInnerney, J. (2010). How rude! Emotional labor as a mediator between customer incivility and employee outcomes. *Journal of Occupational Health Psychology*, *15*, 468–481. doi:10.1037/a0020723

Sonnentag, S. (2012). Psychological detachment from work during leisure time: The benefits of mentally disengaging from work. *Current Directions in Psychological Science*, *21*, 114–118. doi:10.1177/0963721411434979

Sonnentag, S., Mojza, E. J., Binnewies, C., & Scholl, A. (2008). Being engaged at work and detached at home: A week-level study on work engagement, psychological detachment, and affect. *Work & Stress*, *22*, 257–276. doi:10.1080/02678370802379440

Spector, P. E., & Fox, S. (2005). The stressor-emotion model of counterproductive work behavior. In S. Fox & P. E. Spector (Eds.), *Counterproductive work behavior* (pp. 151–174). Washington, DC: APA.

Sulea, C., Filipescu, R., Horga, A., Orţan, C., & Fischmann, G. (2012). Interpersonal mistreatment at work and burnout among teachers. *Cognitie, Creier, Comportament* [*Cognition, Brain, Behavior*], *16*, 553–570. Retrieved from http://www.cbbjournal.ro/

Tepper, B. J. (2000). Consequences of abusive supervision. *Academy of Management Journal*, *43*, 178–190. doi:10.2307/1556375

Tepper, B. J. (2007). Abusive supervision in work organizations: Review, synthesis, and research agenda. *Journal of Management*, *33*, 261–289. doi:10.1177/0149206307300812

Williams, K. D. (2007). Ostracism. *Annual Review of Psychology*, *58*, 425–452. doi:10.1146/annurev.psych.58.110405.085641

ANTECEDENTS OF WORKPLACE OSTRACISM: NEW DIRECTIONS IN RESEARCH AND INTERVENTION

Kristin L. Scott and Michelle K. Duffy

ABSTRACT

We explore the antecedents of workplace ostracism and delineate possible organizational interventions to deter ostracism. Under the lens of evolutionary psychology we argue that individuals deemed capable of contributing to social and organizational goals become valued group members while those who threaten group stability and viability risk being shunned or ostracized. Specifically, we review empirical evidence and present the results of a pilot study suggesting that those who are perceived to violate injunctive and descriptive norms, as well as threaten one's self-concept are at increased risk for ostracism. In terms of intervention, we propose mindfulness techniques and organizational support as a route to deter employees' inclinations to ostracize coworkers. Thus, a primary goal of this chapter is to explicate a framework for identifying the predictors and deterrents of workplace ostracism in order to generate additional research on this important topic.

Keywords: Workplace ostracism; mindfulness; organizational norms; organizational interventions; organizational goals; social goals

---

Mistreatment in Organizations
Research in Occupational Stress and Well Being, Volume 13, 137–165

ISSN: 1479-3555/doi:10.1108/S1479-355520150000013005

Anthropological records indicate that human beings adopted elements of social organization as long as 750,000 years ago, began interacting cooperatively in groups around 400,000 years ago and initiated multi-group trade roughly 40,000 years ago (c.f., Petersen, 2012). Historically socialized groups offered many benefits that included access to improved safety or security, shared resource accumulation and social support. Human beings have long worked together to achieve these ends and over time common patterns of thoughts, behaviors, and emotions developed across individuals to facilitate and protect group life thus enabling the social system to thrive and succeed (Buss, 2005). Evolutionary theorists argue that many of the shared traits and behaviors required for group living became uniquely innate to human beings so that they could successfully navigate complex social environments (Cosmides, Tooby, & Barkow, 1992). Among these commonalities are norms concerning social interaction patterns intended to support and enhance group efficiency. More specifically, evolutionary theory informs us that individuals deemed capable of contributing to these goals become valued group members while those who threaten group stability and viability risk being shunned or ostracized (Kurzban & Leary, 2001).

Acknowledging the biological basis of exclusion and ostracism, Baumeister and Leary (1995) initiated much of the research in this area with their seminal publication describing the tenets of belongingness theory. They held that individuals possess an innate need to belong and gain acceptance from others so they can enjoy the advantages and protection that group life has to offer. They further argued that being ostracized by others thwarts this biologically driven need to belong and, therefore, is very devastating to the targets of such actions. Indeed, scholarly work exploring individuals' reactions to being socially ostracized has garnered increasing research attention since the articulation of belongingness theory (see Blackhart, Baumeister, & Twenge, 2006; Robinson, O'Reilly, & Wang, 2013, Williams, 2001, 2007 for reviews). Some initial studies were fueled by the desire to explain mass shootings in schools and organizations and sought to predict why or how individuals might respond aggressively or violently to peer ostracism (e.g., Leary, Kowalski, Smith, & Phillips, 2003; Twenge, Baumeister, Tice, & Stucke, 2001; Twenge & Campbell, 2003). In a similar vein, an onslaught of laboratory-based research ensued that demonstrated a link between social exclusion and a range of negative outcomes such as aggression (e.g., Bourgeois & Leary, 2001; Twenge et al., 2001), self-defeating behaviors (Twenge, Catanese, & Baumeister, 2003), lowered performance on complex tasks (Baumeister, Twenge, & Nuss,

2002), and impaired self-regulatory control (Baumeister, DeWall, Ciarocco, & Twenge, 2005).

A small but growing body of research demonstrates similar patterns within organizational settings (c.f., Robinson et al., 2013 for a review). Workplace ostracism, defined as being ignored or excluded by one or more fellow employees (Ferris, Brown, Berry, & Lian, 2008), is part of a larger family of related workplace aggression constructs (e.g., bullying, incivility, social undermining) that are "conceptually distinct, but operationally similar" (Aquino & Thau, 2009; Hershcovis, Reich, Parker, & Bozeman, 2012, p. 2). Coworker ostracism, much like workplace incivility (e.g., rude discourteous behavior; Andersson & Pearson, 1999) is a low intensity, nonviolent form of aggression that may or may not be used with the intent to harm others. While this behavior may be viewed as more "acceptable" than harassment among employees, research suggests that this less conspicuous form of aggression is more damaging to worker self-esteem, a sense of belonging, well-being, and turnover compared workplace harassment (O'Reilly, Robinson, Berdahl, & Banki, 2014). Not surprisingly, workplace ostracism is linked to a number of negative employee and organizational outcomes, including lower levels of work-related self-worth (e.g., Penhaligon, Louis, & Restubog, 2009; Scott, Zagenczyk, Schippers, Purvis, & Cruz, 2014; Williams & Zadro, 2005), less self-control and higher turnover intentions (Renn, Allen, & Huning, 2013; Scott, Tams, Schippers, & Lee, 2015), higher levels of job-related tension or distress (e.g., Hitlan, Cliffton, & DeSoto, 2006; Scott et al., 2015; Wu, Yim, Kwan, & Zhang, 2012) and lower performance (e.g., DeWall, Baumeister, & Vohs, 2008; Ferris et al., 2008). Some recent studies suggest that extenuating factors such as high levels of organizational support, perceiving that one is ostracized because he or she is the object of colleagues' envy or believing that one's chances for reinclusion are attainable can mitigate some of these reactions by improving cooperation, citizenship behavior, worker self-esteem, and task performance (e.g., Scott et al., 2015; Scott et al., 2014).

The cumulative body of research presents a clearer picture of why, when, and how individuals respond to being ostracized and we know that, for the most part, reactions are not positive. With that said, the extant literature is lacking a cogent theoretical framework that addresses the following questions: (1) why do people ostracize others and (2) what might individuals or organizations do to deter this type of behavior and mitigate the undesirable outcomes so often linked to being the target of ostracism? The goal of this chapter is to explore these two questions. We investigate these issues under the lens of evolutionary psychology theory as an overarching framework for our research model and shed light on who is most at risk for becoming ostracized in the workplace by integrating theory and research from the social norms and identity literatures.

In terms of our first question, evolutionary theorists contend that normative human thought and behavioral patterns are innate tendencies that manifest in response to recurrent environmental problems (Cosmides et al., 1992). One particularly important facet of evolutionary theory concerns the mechanisms (i.e., social norms) by which human beings attain social goals and support organized social structures (Kendrick et al., 2002). Social norms and guidelines are functional, or adaptive, in the sense that they facilitate shared goals and outcomes and help individuals understand what is required to maintain a valued role within the social system (Cialdini & Trost, 1998). We adopt this model as a framework for discussing why and how workplace ostracism develops at the group (e.g., normative expectations and guidelines) and individual (e.g., self-worth protection) levels.

We bolster our arguments by offering some preliminary qualitative and correlational findings from a two-part pilot study of 275 working adults employed across a variety of industries and positions. Subjects were recruited using Study Response (an academic-based resource that obtains survey participants through an online recruitment procedure). At time 1, we collected general demographic (e.g., age, race, sex, education) and employee information centered on personality and beliefs (e.g., positive and negative affect, self-esteem, beliefs about human equality, job satisfaction). Respondents were further asked to provide a vignette of a time that they avoided, ignored, or ostracized someone at work. Specifically they were asked "In the space below, describe a time when you wanted to avoid interacting, socializing or working with another person and how you behaved when doing so." We emphasized that there were no right or wrong answers and to just be as specific as possible about why they wished to exclude this particular individual. Following the vignette, subjects responded to a series of research-based survey items that reflected a range of descriptive information about the ostracized target such as the degree to which the target was uncivil, emotionally unstable, antisocial, or a positive contributor to the workplace. At time 2, subjects responded to questions about their job, coworker, and supervisor satisfaction along with self-reported exclusionary behavior. We used non-narrative data, in part, to evaluate the relationship between perpetrator characteristics and self-reported exclusion at a later point in time. Throughout the chapter, we include quotes from the participants along with correlational data that we believe sheds further light on this under-explored workplace phenomenon.

With respect to our second question, though we believe evolutionary theory provides a compelling rationale as to why ostracism develops in the workplace, we further argue that ostracism utilized in a biologically protective sense is likely to have dysfunctional consequences within the modern workplace. In primitive hunter and gatherer societies where group interdependence was critical to navigating life or death situations ostracism was likely effective, if not necessary. But in day-to-day organizational life ignoring and shunning other colleagues is unlikely to resolve tension and other problems that arise, thus making ostracism problematic in this setting. Evolutionary theorists have acknowledged that inhibition of maladaptive emotions, attitudes and behaviors are also essential to survival (c.f., Nicholson, 2012). We, therefore, argue that individual and organizational interventions should be aimed at deterring ostracism by helping employees to recognize the latent tendency to avoid or ostracize others and instead deal professionally with social infractions or conflict. One potential employee-focused (i.e., individual) technique that we believe holds much promise in this regard lies within the stress management literature and is known as mindfulness, or the process of paying attention to what is happening in the moment – to both internal (thoughts, bodily sensations) and external stimuli (physical and social environment) – and observing those stimuli without judgment or evaluation and without assigning meaning to them (Glomb, Duffy, Bono, & Yang, 2011). Recent studies reveal that mindfulness techniques can enhance individual self-control through improved emotional, attentional and impulse regulation (e.g., Baer, 2003; Hofmann, Sawyer, Witt, & Oh, 2010). Building on these findings, we argue that mindfulness practices can deter ostracism in the workplace by helping employees to better recognize these automatic thoughts and subsequent behaviors that often compel exclusionary behavior and instead adopt professional and effective means for dealing with conflict.

The tenets of evolutionary theory rest firmly in the notion that people tend to adopt behaviors that help them to successfully navigate their circumstances, thus underscoring the critical role that environmental conditions play in shaping innate human behavioral tendencies. Accordingly, we acknowledge the vital role that the organization plays in the further shaping employee responses to mindfulness training. Specifically, we assert that employee success with mindfulness training is contingent upon the degree to which organizations offer support for such initiatives. The functionality of our ancestral groups hinged on having clear goals (e.g., survival), cooperation, productivity, and accountability and, while not formalized in primitive groups, these practices remain the pillars of successful organizations today (Nicholson, 2012). Thus, we round out our chapter by outlining a framework for implementing mindfulness training drawing on organizational support theory to guide our recommendations. Below, we begin with a discussion of our proposed framework for describing how ostracism emerges in an organizational setting below, followed by an account of suggested intervention strategies (see Fig. 1 for an illustrative overview).

EVOLUTIONARY THEORY OF SOCIAL NORMS AND WORKPLACE OSTRACISM

We acknowledge that there are various perspectives that may explain why individuals choose to engage in workplace ostracism though it is not possible to address them all in this chapter. In our review of the extant literature, a common theme was that the practice of ostracism, historically, emerged as a means of social control to stabilize or protect a group or society. Indeed, ostracism as a nonviolent form of social sanction against those who fail to adhere to commonly held norms and expectations and threaten social stability is not a new phenomenon: our primitive ancestors used it to signal their disapproval or to eliminate the weakest members of their group in order to protect their safety and long-term prosperity (Axelrod, 1986). In ancient Greece, members of society were periodically banished from the community in an effort to minimize interpersonal conflict and maintain social order. The modern equivalent of such actions, at a societal level, is the reliance upon and enforcement of legal norms (i.e., laws), the violation of which may result in exclusion from society through incarceration (e.g., Posner & Rasmusen, 1999).

Just as organized society requires stability and social order, so too does the modern workplace. An organizational context provides an ideal setting in which to explore this phenomenon given that workers are generally dependent on one another to accomplish joint tasks and attain expected goals (Bowles, 1985; Lindenberg, 1997). In addition, social stability and adherence to expected behavioral patterns are critical to organizational efficiency and success (Fulmer, Gerhart, & Scott, 2003). To develop a framework that explicates why employees are likely to utilize ostracism in the workplace we integrate social norms theory with the evolutionary perspective.

Antecedents of Workplace Ostracism		**Target and Perpetrator Characteristics**	**Propositions**
Group Level Injunctive Norms Discourage harmful behavior to promote social stability, effective functioning and prosperity	→	▪ Perceived as dangerous ▪ Threatens social stability or functioning ▪ Perceived as a liability or unstable ▪ Has little to offer the group	Proposition 1 : Employees perceived as a threat to employee or work group functioning is positively related to perpetrator exclusion. Proposition 2 : Employee unreliability is positively related to perpetrator exclusion. Proposition 3 : Employee lack of contribution is positively related to perpetrator exclusion.
Group Level Descriptive Norms Dictate preferred beliefs, attitudes, behaviors commonly held by the group. Promotes peer pressure, conformity and group efficiency.	→	▪ Nonconformist ▪ Perceived as a threat to group efficiency ▪ Threatens collective solidarity ▪ Perceived as incapable of learning and adopting group values or behaviors	Proposition 4 : Group exclusionary behavior moderates the relationship between target employee characteristics and perpetrator exclusion such that the more coworkers who exclude the target the more likely the perpetrator is to exclude the target.
Individual Level Self-Concept Maintenance Strive to maintain a positive self-image within a valued group or context.	→	Negative Deviates ▪ Those who threaten goals of self - enhancement or uncertainty reduction (elicit anger, fear, anxiety, etc.) Positive Deviates ▪ Envied outperformers Ingroup/Outgroup bias ▪ Those with different beliefs or values ▪ (e.g., Sexism, racism, social dominance)	Proposition 5 : Employee emotional negativity is positively related to perpetrator exclusion. Proposition 6 : Employee arrogance is positively related to perpetrator exclusion. Proposition 7 : Employee antisocial behavior is positively related to perpetrator exclusion. Proposition 8 : Envy of the target employee is positively related to perpetrator exclusion. Proposition 9 : Perpetrator social dominance orientation is positively related to perpetrator exclusion. Proposition 10 : Perpetrator modern racism beliefs are positively related to perpetrator exclusion.

⇧

Organizational Intervention

Mindfulness Training
Organizational Support

Fig. 1. A Model of the Antecedents of Workplace Ostracism.

Under the umbrella of evolutionary theory, scholars have noted that because humans evolved in groups many traits, attitudes, and behaviors exist to facilitate the survival of social systems and therefore form the basis of collectively held social processes, goals and motives (Buunk & Dijkstra, 2012). One branch of this study is known as social influence which is broad and includes theories related to attitude change, conformity, identification, and persuasion among others (see Cialdini & Goldstein, 2004; Smith, 1982; Turner, 1991; Wood, 2000 for reviews). Of critical importance to this body of work is the study and documentation of normative group behavior – that can include ostracism. While social norms may perpetuate cultural traditions (e.g., celebrations, religious customs, rites of passage; Solomon, Greenberg, & Pyszczynski, 1991), a large volume of research documents the necessity of social norms for ensuring group functionality, prosperity, and the attainment of shared goals (e.g., Katz & Kahn, 1978; Shaw, 1936). Thus, social norms play a critical role in group survival as they minimize interpersonal discord and facilitate efficiency (Feldman, 1984).

To understand how social norms can influence ostracism in the workplace, we draw on the seminal work of Cialdini and Trost (1998) which identified three primary goals that normative behavior serves within socially interdependent settings. Following an exhaustive review of relevant literature and conducting their own observational and empirical research on social behavioral action patterns, these scholars concluded, "we were continually struck by the extent to which these behaviors could be interpreted as purposive (but not necessarily conscious) attempts to achieve a relatively small set of goals: to behave effectively, to build and maintain relationships, and to manage self-concept" (Cialdini & Trost, 1998, p. 151). These findings formed the basis of their theoretical framework that describes the processes by which social norms emerge and potentially fulfill the above-mentioned goals. Specifically, Cialdini and Trost (1998) termed these goal directed processes: (1) injunctive norms (i.e., informal or prescriptive guidelines about how to behave within the group); (2) personal norms (i.e., perceptions of group norms and standards as they pertain to protecting one's self-concept and the group's image); and (3) descriptive (i.e., the popular or most strongly held norms that tend to influence the group's behavior as a whole). This framework provides a fruitful starting point for discussing why and how social norms guide expectations and behaviors in socially organized settings – from both an aggregate and individual perspective. We elaborate on each goal in the section that follows, integrating relevant theories on stigmatization, identity, and social learning as related to evolutionary theory to further develop our proposed model.

Injunctive Norms

We begin with a discussion of injunctive norms described by Cialdini and Trost (1998) as behaviors that are informally prescribed by group members for the purpose of building and maintaining relationships. These types of norms reflect collectively shared standards and expectations regarding what is considered both appropriate and inappropriate behavior in terms of facilitating strong interpersonal bonds. At the heart of these social actions lies the goal of creating trust and communality among members that is facilitated largely through the guiding principles of social exchange. Exchange-based relationships are characterized by regular or frequent contact as well as the presence of an on-going social bond – both of which serve to create an implicit obligation between individuals to assist one another and foster the expectation that favorable treatment will be maintained over time (Blau, 1964). Of considerable importance to social exchange relationships is the norm of reciprocity, a generalized moral norm that requires individuals to help (and not harm) individuals who help them (Gouldner, 1960). There is widespread agreement that the norm of reciprocity is a universal principle and is shared to varying degrees by all world cultures (see Cropanzano & Mitchell, 2005 for a review). Accordingly, Cialdini and Trost (1998) note that reciprocally altruistic behavior is essential to establishing strong interpersonal relationships and this may explain the pervasiveness of this form of social behavior.

Another important goal of injunctive norms is to assist individuals and groups with meeting material needs and resources that are necessary for group prosperity and success. As a result, individuals are encouraged to meaningfully contribute skills, knowledge, expertise, or material goods that promote group viability and longevity. This facet of collective behavior also aids in the development of group hierarchal roles by conferring popularity and status among members. Thus, injunctive norms not only prescribe that individuals treat others with kindness, mutual respect, and benevolence but also set the expectation that group members add value to the social system.

Injunctive norms are utilized in these ways among employees to establish trust and foster mutual dependence. These norms also help employees understand what is expected of them, prescribe roles, and facilitate work flow. Employees are also encouraged to participate and behave in ways that promote group or organizational success. Therefore, just as injunctive norms helped our ancestral groups survive and prosper, workplace social norms are also integral to operational functioning and efficiency that are key drivers of firm performance.

Norms against Harmful Behavior

Injunctive norms further address those actions that are detrimental to group or organizational viability. Here we integrate the work of Kurzban and Leary (2001) whom offer an evolutionary-based account of why individuals become stigmatized in socially organized settings as a basis for explicating what may constitute harmful behavior and, consequently, drive workplace ostracism. First, they contend that individuals who fail to reciprocate altruistic actions or, even worse, take advantage of other individuals are likely to be avoided or ostracized because they are deemed a threat to social order and stability. Indeed, social exchange researchers have suggested that individuals who are unwilling to engage in reciprocity are likely to become targets of corrective actions, such as ostracism (Gouldner, 1960; Helm, Bonoma, & Tedeschi, 1972). Some workplace examples include employees who: routinely require help, demand others' time and attention, are not trustworthy or are unwilling to assist others (especially after being helped by others). Qualitative feedback from our pilot research appears to corroborate our contention as one worker noted,

> I worked with a woman who was very untrustworthy. She would report another employee for things that were not actual problems. I avoided her by spending most of my time out of the office. I requested the ability to work from home and had very little face to face contact with her.

Second, Kurzban and Leary (2001) further suggest that individuals who have little to offer or contribute to the larger whole are also likely to be shunned or excluded. Employees such as these may lack adequate skills or knowledge and are unwilling or unable to add value to the work environment. We argue that workers who are not adept at developing social relationships or viewed as unpopular may also be perceived as weak exchange partners and therefore ostracized by other employees. One employee in our pilot sample noted,

> I wanted to avoid working with a co-worker because they are not dedicated and often lazy. I wanted to avoid working with them because I did not feel they did their share of work or cared about our work place. I feel that by not associating with this person I was more respected because this person did not have anyone's respect.

Another worker commented,

> I worked with a person who over reacted to a situation. They were not completely honest about the situation. I did not trust that person. I had little faith in their intelligence and ability. Therefore, I did not allow myself to rely on their performance. I avoided them. When help was needed, I got help elsewhere.

In addition, a recurring theme was that workers who were viewed as needy and wanting to talk too much therefore wasting time were often the targets of ostracism. As one employee stated, "An employee here where I work tends to talk a lot socially and waste time. I try not to make eye contact with him to avoid getting in a long conversation about nothing."

Third, in addition to prescribing appropriate behavior injunctive norms also dictate expectations concerning behaviors that are directly harmful or detrimental to the group and its members. In particular, actions that are threatening, hostile, deviant or unpredictable are generally considered inappropriate if not unacceptable and subject to social sanction. Kurzban and Leary (2001) describe these actions as "dangerous" to the viability of the group. We assert that employees exhibiting aggressive behavior such as social undermining (e.g., withholding important information, slander, work sabotage; Duffy, Ganster, & Pagon, 2002), incivility (e.g., rude, discourteous, self-righteous; Pearson, Andersson, & Wegner, 2001) openly hostile or potentially violent behaviors are considered a threat to the work group and, therefore, likely to invoke ostracism. Furthermore, Kurzban and Leary (2001) suggest that individuals who are perceived as deviant (e.g., lie or steal), psychologically unstable or behaviorally unpredictable are likely viewed as a liability to the group because they threaten social constancy. Consequently, they are at risk of being ostracized. Employees offered several anecdotal examples of wanting to exclude colleagues who exhibited these types of harmful or volatile behaviors:

> In grad school I had to do a project with an unstable person. I focused on the project and getting it finished quickly with minimal group contact-each person worked separately. We worked via email rather than face to face contact. She was unstable emotionally and I saw her lash out at another student before–very irrational. Minimal contact worked out because the unstable person focused on her part of the project without harming the group.

Another commented:

> I had a female friend/co-worker who was very difficult to work with because she was moody and her attitude was unpredictable. I just ignored her completely.

Researchers have acknowledged that ostracism among employees, particularly as a subtle and not overtly harmful form of social control is pervasive (e.g., O'Reilly et al., 2014; Williams, 2007). Despite this, only one study of which we are aware has explored the antecedent conditions of workplace ostracism. In a field study of employee-dyads across two organizations researchers adopted a social exchange perspective and argued that employees who display workplace incivility are more likely to be distrusted by their colleagues and therefore become the targets of workplace ostracism (Scott, Restubog, & Zagenczyk, 2013). They found support for their proposed model. Furthermore, and in accordance with Feldman's (1984) assertion that the group is more likely to reject the person who violates group norms when the deviant has not been a "good" group member previously, these scholars found that this mediated relationship is strengthened when the target employee is perceived to be a weak exchange partner but attenuated when he or she is viewed as a valuable exchange partner. These findings suggest that some degree of deviance or incivility may be tolerated if the target is viewed as an employee with something to offer in terms of value, social capital, etc.

In sum, injunctive norms reflect the collectively established behavior considered acceptable among group or organizational members. These are shared ideals and expectations concerning appropriate actions that should be demonstrated so that the social system can remain stable and successful. Employees who are perceived as threatening, unreliable or having little to offer are most at risk for being shunned or ostracized.

Proposition 1. Employees perceived as a threat to employee or work group functioning is positively related to perpetrator exclusion.

Proposition 2. Employee unreliability is positively related to perpetrator exclusion.

Proposition 3. Employee lack of contribution is positively related to perpetrator exclusion.

Descriptive Norms

To sustain group life, members must work efficiently together with some degree of synchronized and planned behavior. Behaviors proven popular or successful tend to be widely adopted throughout the group via observational learning or, at times, due to collective pressure. Cialdini and Trost (1998) termed these shared behavior patterns "descriptive norms" that enable group efficiency by signaling what actions are deemed most useful or valued by the collective whole. From an evolutionary perspective, descriptive norms historically have helped individuals survive or prosper because they prompt imitation or copycat behavior of successful others via social learning (Boyd & Richerson, 1988). These types of norms establish what the group collectively respects in terms of attitudes, beliefs and behaviors and, therefore give rise to popular rituals, fads or trends that support notoriety, status, and operational proficiency. Within an organizational setting, descriptive norms may dictate a range of outcomes such as the number of hours employees are expected to work, how to treat customers, and performance expectations – among others. Scholars sometimes refer to this phenomenon as "herd mentality" – or the general wisdom of the group (Surowiecki, 2004). Having descriptive norms in place make it easier for newcomers to learn what is expected or signal what members need to do to be successful and, as a result, facilitate group functioning.

However, we also note that sometimes herd behavior can reinforce antisocial behavior. There are a number of studies that have shown that "group think" and peer pressure can hinder performance (e.g., Esser, 1998), encourage unethical behavior (e.g., Sims, 1992; Treviño, Weaver, & Reynolds, 2006) or even prompt widespread mistreatment or bullying (sometimes known as mobbing) behaviors in the workplace (e.g., Robinson & O'Leary-Kelly, 1998; Vardi & Wiener, 1996; Zapf & Einarsen, 2005). Accordingly, we argue that descriptive norms could allow ostracism to become popularized across a work group or organization. For example, an employee might occasionally avoid or ignore a coworker. However, if the focal employee learns that other colleagues have also ignored the target coworker, then he or she may ostracize that worker to a greater degree because he or she feels that it is more acceptable to do so. In other words, the effect of peer pressure and normative influence has the potential to exacerbate the extent to which certain employees are ostracized in the workplace if it is viewed as a suitable form of social control. We contend that descriptive norms likely exert a moderating influence on the relationship between various antecedent factors and workplace ostracism and encourage future research in this area.

Proposition 4. Group exclusionary behavior moderates the relationship between target employee characteristics and perpetrator exclusion such that the more coworkers who exclude the target the more likely the perpetrator is to exclude the target.

Managing Self-Concept

Individuals not only want their groups to thrive and prosper, but they also want to flourish within their social network a well. This desire is biologically manifested as a strong need for belonging and status that influences how people connect themselves to their social environment – especially in their work lives (Baumeister & Leary, 1995; Buunk & Dijkstra, 2012). This is largely because group life affords individuals many personal benefits that include opportunities to enhance their self-worth (Crocker & Wolfe, 2001), receive social support (Beehr, Jex, Stacy, & Murray, 2000), and establish a shared worldview (Seashore, 1977). For these reasons, individuals seek to become members of groups that reinforce their attitudes, values, and beliefs and develop a sense of "oneness to some human aggregate" (Ashforth & Mael, 1989, p. 21). With that said, many hours of adult life are spent at work and, subsequently, this domain exerts a strong influence on an employee's personal identity and self-image (Dutton, Roberts, & Bednar, 2010). Thus, as Cialdini and Trost (1998) note, managing and protecting the self-concept is an important goal for individuals within a socially interdependent setting such as the workplace. If their meaningful connection with the group, or the group itself is threatened, individuals are quick to defend themselves and their group members (Abrams & Hogg, 2006).

To further clarify how this process unfolds, we expound upon Cialdini and Trost's (1998) reasoning by integrating belongingness theory with social identity theory (SIT) defined as the degree to which individuals find meaning in and derive a positive self-image from group membership (Turner, 1982). SIT theorists note that group membership helps people answer the question "who am I" and the more vested one is in a group, the more positively they will view the group and themselves as part of it (Tajfel & Turner, 1985). In other words, SIT represents the level of belongingness an employee shares with his or her colleagues. As a result, they are motivated to protect themselves and their status within their valued ingroup and reject or shun those who are viewed as outsiders (Castano, Yzerbyt, Paladino, & Sacchi, 2002); known formally as ingroup and outgroup bias (Turner, 1975). We draw on this theory and related research to argue that employees are likely to avoid or ostracize those who: (1) threaten them or (2) endanger their status in the group and; (3) jeopardize the unity or success of their valued work group or organization. We adopt Hogg, Fielding, and Darley's (2005) labeling of individuals who commit these acts as negative or positive deviates and expound on our rationale below.

Negative Deviates

Hogg et al. (2005) offer an identity-based perspective that describes the conditions under which group members are likely to be marginalized or rejected by other members of the group. They assert that individuals have two primary goals within a group setting: self-enhancement and uncertainty reduction. If the group member or the group's status is threatened or if self-certainty is threatened "then the people and the groups they belong to will take action to respond to the threat" (p. 199). As such, "negative deviates" as they refer to them are generally ostracized because they threaten the employee's identity and relative standing within the organization. For example, colleagues who endanger, demean, belittle, or mistreat them are likely to be avoided or ostracized. As one employee noted,

> There is an assistant coach whom I do not like. If I see her in the hall I look in the opposite direction to find someone else to say hi to or become involved with what I am doing to avoid interacting with her without appearing mean. I do not care for her arrogant attitude, she is immature and inappropriate with students and I do not want to associate with that type of person.

Another worker said of her boss,

> During the last months/year of my previous job I had, over time, developed a strong dislike for my boss for various reasons. It became apparent to her that I didn't agree w/ the way she was operating the business. I avoided her at all costs even though I was in a position of authority and had to report directly to her.

In short, colleagues who are seen as a liability or jeopardizing others' reputations and success are likely to be ostracized as are those are who are perceived as mean, emotionally needy, aggressive, or dangerous. Our pilot work offers preliminary evidence to support this assertion. The results revealed that self-reported ostracism of coworkers was positively correlated with target emotional negativity ($r = .53$, $p < .001$), arrogance ($r = .58$, $p < .001$), social awkwardness ($r = .55$, $p < .001$), displayed incivility ($r = .57$, $p < .001$), undermining behavior ($r = .56$, $p < .001$), or social loafing ($r = .41$, $p < .001$). Ostracism was also positively correlated with the target being perceived as a weak exchange partner (e.g., having little to offer, taking more than they were willing to give) ($r = .45$, $p < .001$). Clearly, a finer grained analysis of these relationships is warranted but we are encouraged by these initial findings and hope they spur additional research in this domain.

Proposition 5. Employee emotional negativity is positively related to perpetrator exclusion.

Proposition 6. Employee arrogance is positively related to perpetrator exclusion.

Proposition 7. Employee antisocial behavior is positively related to perpetrator exclusion.

Positive Deviates

While we often think of protecting ourselves from negative, threatening, or demeaning colleague workers whom Hogg and colleagues term "positive deviates" may become targets of ostracism as well. These individuals are seen as a threat because they are perceived as the "out performers" of the group. Hogg et al. (2005) note that positive deviates may or may not become ostracized depending on how they attribute their performance. If they give accolades to the group for their performance (i.e., are humble) they potentially elevate group status and are no longer a threat. If, however, high performers do not recognize the group or, worse yet, they are boastful or egotistical about their perceived superiority they threaten group members' sense of self and their status and therefore are likely to become targets of ostracism. As an example, one worker noted,

> I wanted to avoid a colleague at work. Colleague is a know-it-all and many days I don't want to interact with him because I don't want him to learn what projects I am working on and give me his opinions on how I need to proceed with project. Generally I try to avoid him by not walking by his office or directly calling him on the phone.

Along these lines, one of the stronger correlations we found in our pilot work was between feelings of envy and coworker ostracism. Specifically, employees experiencing coworker-directed envy reported engaging in higher levels of ostracism. Evolutionary theorists note that social comparisons (as reflected by envy) are of adaptive value so that individuals can "size up" their competitors and better prepare themselves for success (Smith, 2008). Opportunities for outperformance abound in organizational life (Duffy, Shaw, & Schaubroeck, 2008). Our pilot work suggests that envy could be a key driver of workplace ostracism as employees struggle with this type of self-concept threat. Being envious of colleagues was highly correlated with self-reported coworker ostracism ($r = .47$, $p < .001$). We think this is an interesting and potentially fruitful avenue for future research.

Proposition 8. Envy of the target employee is positively related to perpetrator exclusion.

Perceived Ingroup versus Outgroup Status

Under the umbrella of social identity research is a sizeable body of work that has explored how members of different groups react to and treat one another. This subset of research argues that individuals seek membership in groups that reinforce their self-concept (e.g., shared values, attitudes, beliefs). The process by which they identify those groups due to self-perceived similarities is known as social categorization (Turner, 1985). The resulting body of work from this perspective has consistently demonstrated that individuals favor members of their own group over those in out groups (i.e., ingroup bias) and, thus, are potentially untrusting, hostile or aggressive toward those viewed as threatening (see Abrams & Hogg, 2006; Brewer, 1979; Hogg & Terry, 2000 for reviews). Accordingly, we contend that ingroup bias likely plays a role in determining who becomes an ostracized target.

Our pilot study research provides some indication that self-favoring attitudes and beliefs that form the backbone of shared identity or ingroup bias behavior exist in the workplace and could, indeed, trigger ostracism. In a telling comment, one employee stated, "I did not agree with someone's beliefs and they offended me. I ignored them by trying to avoid all types of contact with them." We surmise that employees' beliefs or values likely play a role in which colleagues they accept or reject. As such, we explored whether employees' beliefs concerning sexism, racism or social dominance (the belief that all individuals are not created equal) are related to self-reported ostracism. Of these, sexism and social dominance were positively correlated with coworkers-directed avoidance and exclusion. ($r = .17$, $p < .05$; $r = .21$, $p < .01$, respectively). We think it is also important to note that general feelings of "dislike" were strongly and positively related to ostracism. We acknowledge, however, that dislike could represent a wide range of factors and encourage scholars to pursue a finer grained analysis of the role that employee values, beliefs or attitudes play in determining their propensity to engage in exclusion and the degree to which these values are shared (or not) by colleagues could moderate these relationships. Establishing a meaningful role within a valued group offers individuals numerous advantageous – especially in the workplace where work-related identities form the basis of self-worth, security and fulfillment for many people. For these reasons, employees are likely to ostracize those who jeopardize their reputation at work – whether that is because they exhibit negative behaviors such as loafing or undermining or they are perceived to be an outperformance threat.

Proposition 9. Perpetrator social dominance orientation is positively related to perpetrator exclusion.

Proposition 10. Perpetrator modern racism beliefs are positively related to perpetrator exclusion.

Summary

In sum, changing environmental conditions and problems have posed challenges for human beings for thousands of centuries. Individuals responded by working collectively to share resources, enhance safety and promote viability. Norms concerning socially acceptable behavior were adopted to improve within group functioning and became engrained as automatic behavioral tendencies that carry over into the workplace today. Given the biologically enduring characteristics of ostracism it should come as little surprise that this type of behavior persists in today's workplace. Indeed, our primitive instincts do not turn off when we go to work and strive to satiate our needs for safety, stability and self-preservation. As our theoretical framework and related pilot work suggests, employees are likely to ostracize those who threaten individual, group, or organizational well-being. We hope our discussion provides insight into myriad antecedents of workplace ostracism and stimulates additional research on this important topic.

INTERVENTION

> I have a consultant who argued with my client over something I considered unnecessary and that offended the client. I had to contact the consultant's manager and I have no interest in having this person work for my project again. I told the manager I did not need him again. He made me and my company look bitter and ridiculous. I am still bothered, this occurred almost 2 months ago. I took the right steps in addressing, but still upset with the consultant, so when he is involved in conversations, I ignore him. I have gone out of my way to utilize other resources so I don't have to deal with him.

The employee in this situation was so troubled that he or she ruminated about the incident for almost two months and stopped working with him to protect himself and the company. While social ostracism may have yielded lifesaving benefits among our ancestors, today this type of coping behavior is not conducive to efficient organizational functioning. Although incidents of workplace violence attract considerable media attention, non-violent forms of organizational aggression such as workplace ostracism are far more prevalent and cost organizations an estimated $2–$200 billion US dollars annually (Barling, Dupre, & Kelloway, 2009; Bennett & Robinson, 2000; Lawrence & Robinson, 2007). The pervasiveness of ostracism is likely because these are subtle behaviors that are difficult to detect and generally go unpunished within an organizational context (Williams, 2001). While attempting to deter ostracism among employees may be difficult for organizations, given the range of negative outcomes associated with such behavior, ostracism should not be ignored. However, the literature is generally silent on how to deter employees from ignoring or excluding one another.

Because the work environment dictates the success of human resources practices, we argue that organizational involvement and support are crucial to curtailing ostracism (Galinsky & Stein, 1990). Specifically, we propose that mindfulness training and organizational support interventions offer promise in this realm. We elaborate on these efforts below.

Mindfulness and Workplace Ostracism

Mindfulness is defined as "a state of consciousness characterized by receptive attention to and awareness of present events and experiences, without evaluation, judgment, and cognitive filters," mindfulness is linked to improved self-regulatory functioning as well as a range of employee outcomes including concentration, coping, decision making, learning, and self-confidence (Glomb et al., 2011, p. 119). Though some individuals possess a natural aptitude for being mindful (i.e., trait mindfulness) a body of research also shows that mindfulness is a process that can be learned over time with training and practice (Kabat-Zinn, 1990). Mindfulness interventions outside the workplace have yielded positive effects on individuals' management of chronic pain, handling of mental and emotional stressors, creativity, and athletic performance (Baer, 2003). Within organizational settings, initial evidence suggests mindfulness training helps employees experience less emotional exhaustion and burnout as well as improved job satisfaction and overall task performance (Glomb et al., 2011; Hülsheger, Alberts, Feinholdt, & Langer, 2013). Preliminary, recent evidence suggests mindfulness training may also help employees deal with interpersonal challenges at work (Duffy, Glomb, Bono, & Yang, 2014; Molet, Macquet, Lefebvre, & Williams, 2013; Ramsey & Jones, 2015).

How might mindfulness deter ostracism within the workplace? We suggest here that mindfulness practices trigger a cycle of responses to others and the external environment that promote more functional workplace interactions and decrease the likelihood of negative interactions including ostracism (Duffy et al., 2014). Overall, we propose that mindfulness training can interrupt some of our built in evolutionarily driven responses. Specifically, we propose four key ways in which mindfulness reduces our innate proclivity (see above) to ostracize others. We outline these below.

During mindfulness practice, individuals acknowledge their internal and external states with a nonjudgmental and nonreactive focus on thoughts and feelings by utilizing word labeling techniques that help them experience these events objectively rather than reflexively (Baer, Smith, Hopkins, Krietemeyer, & Toney, 2006). As such, mindfulness *decreases the tendency to respond reactively* to potentially noxious people and stimuli in the workplace. Decreasing one's internal reactivity can provide an emotional as well as physiological "pause" when facing stressful events at work. As Glomb et al. (2011) note, reactivity and automaticity have "the unfortunate consequence of restricting individuals' perceptions and experiences of the present moment" (p. 126).

Specifically, mindfulness techniques give workers the mental tools needed to overcome innate automaticity tendencies, by disrupting automatic mental processes and physiological responses as well as helping them to separate their emotions or experiences from the self (Glomb et al., 2011). While under dire circumstances, automaticity allows individuals to react quickly to threats and improve chances for survival, reactions such as these are not as useful in the modern workplace as they were in primitive, life-threatening contexts. Though it may be natural to want to defend ourselves against threats to personal or group wellbeing such feelings do not have to consume us or direct our behavior. Mindfulness provides a mechanism for derailing such reactions by helping workers to recognize what is happening, label their thoughts or feelings and see their circumstances more objectively (Brown & Ryan, 2003).

In the case of our research participant above, the employee may not have reacted to the consultant's behavior with such heightened physiological arousal and subsequent rumination had a mindfulness practice been in play. As noted earlier, others' behavior that is perceived as deviant or as violating group norms can be perceived as threatening to the group thus triggering exclusionary behaviors designed to help or save the group at large. To the extent that mindfulness can help individuals be less reactive emotionally and physiologically to perceived threats such as the consultant's behavior the likelihood of ostracism should be reduced because the chain of reactivity is broken.

Second, mindfulness reduces "ego involvement," promoting a healthy detachment from events and others (Duffy et al., 2014). When people are highly "ego-involved," they become motivated to protect and enhance self-esteem in all interactions (Heppner et al., 2008). While at times functional, such ego involvement can trigger interpersonally aggressive behavior as well. Indeed, as we postulate above, protecting and enhancing one's self-image, may be a key driver of ostracism. Social and psychological research suggests that mindfulness may reduce ego involvement in two ways. First, mindfulness practices enhance one's ability to allow negative thoughts regarding people and situations to "stream by without being imbued with heightened self-relevant implications" (Heppner et al., 2008, p. 487). Second, negative interpersonal events are not "attached to the self" (Heppner et al., 2008). As a result of this increased space, there is less enmeshment between the self and others. Others and events are not personalized in a way that evokes hostile cognitions, rumination, and desire to defend. Individuals are able to maintain a positive sense of self in the face of adversity. Recall that negative events can make people feel that their self-worth is under attack. Decoupling the self from events weakens this trigger because the mindfulness process allows individuals to reflect neutrally on the stimuli therefore reducing the impact on their self-concept. As Heppner and colleagues note, when individuals become highly ego involved, negative interactions are interpreted as increasingly self-relevant with exaggerated self-relevant implications that can prompt aggressiveness.

With respect to our participant's reaction above, the months of rumination regarding the consultant and subsequent ostracism may not have occurred had a mindfulness practice been in place. Instead, the present moment awareness characteristic of mindfulness allows one to experience "the passing drama of feelings, social pressures, desires, and even of being esteemed or disparaged by others without getting 'hooked' or attached" (Ryan & Brown, 2006, p. 129). In addition to these benefits, mindfulness should increase *compassion and empathy* for others (Duffy et al., 2014). Empirical evidence suggests that mindfulness is linked to social connectedness and pro-social behavior (Ramsey & Jones, 2015). Reframing how one sees others, an ability to imagine others' pain and suffering, coupled with a concern and desire to help are key aspects of empathy and compassion. In the case of our research subject, a mindfulness practice may have led him to see the consultant in a different and more compassionate light. Rather than viewing the consultant as a threatening problem, he may have been able to step back in a more tolerant and connected manner, decreasing the desire to ostracize and, instead, determine ways to improve his performance.

Thus, in addition to cultivating a reduced tendency toward automatic reactivity, less ego involvement, and increased empathy, mindfulness enables employees to give pause to stressful interpersonal situations and allows them opportunities for flexible responding (Glomb et al., 2011). Response flexibility is the ability to "pause before taking verbal or physical action" (Siegel, 2007). The ability to pause before responding to a person or event, (i.e., strategic nonreactive responding), allows greater response flexibility to people and situations. Rather than reacting to workplace situations in a habitual manner, response flexibility allows one the power to act in alignment with one's goals, needs, and values (Glomb et al., 2011). While mostly conducted outside the workplace, research suggests mindfulness contributes to response flexibility in a number of contexts but particularly within interpersonal communication (Bishop et al., 2004). Building on this, we propose that increased response flexibility would decrease instances of relational aggression in response to perceived threats and disagreements. In the case of our participant, we would predict that mindfulness would have promoted a more thoughtful consideration of how to respond to the consultant's behavior – with exclusion being simply one option of many.

In sum, mindfulness brings awareness to the primal tendency to ostracize others who threaten individual and group viability by offering techniques that help employees to be less emotionally and physiologically reactive, separate the self from stressful situations thereby feeling less attacked or threatened, increase empathy, and not act on automatic emotion (e.g., anger, envy) or cognitions (e.g., social dominance), In addition, mindfulness training can make them aware that ostracizing is not an effective problem resolution strategy. Mindfulness builds flexibility, empathy, emotional regulation, and control as well as decreases angry rumination and the tendency to give in to automatic impulses. Researchers are noting a wide range of positive outcomes associated with this technique and we believe it holds much promise in reducing workplace ostracism.

Organizational Support

While attempting to deter exclusionary behavior may be challenging for organizations, we think that this issue should not be ignored given the myriad of negative outcomes associated with workplace ostracism. Because the work environment dictates the success of human resources practices – including mindfulness interventions and other initiatives that build a culture of inclusiveness – organizational involvement and support are crucial to curtailing ostracism (Galinsky & Stein, 1990). The evolutionary perspective offers insight to help guide organizational leaders in this regard. The functionality of our ancestral groups hinged on having clear goals (e.g., survival), cooperation, productivity, and accountability and, while not formalized in primitive groups, these practices remain the pillars of successful organizations today (Nicholson, 2012). Employees need to understand what is expected of them, be given the tools and resources to meet those standards and be held accountable for their actions. Mindfulness is an important tool that can likely deter workplace ostracism; however, company leaders must ensure that organizational norms, standards, evaluation systems, and reward tools accompany this training to truly optimize efforts to reduce this type of behavior.

Ancillary theory and evidence within the organizational support literature (OST; Eisenberger, Huntington, Hutchison, & Sowa, 1986) offers specific strategies that modern organizations can adopt to ensure the success of mindfulness training and related employee outcomes. The general premise of OST is that employees perceive their value to the company based on how they are treated by the organization and its agents. A body of evidence in this research domain has shown that fair treatment, supervisor support, meaningful rewards, and favorable job conditions are powerful signals that employees are cared for and valued by the company. In turn, these factors positively impact a range of outcomes including worker job satisfaction, commitment, performance, and cooperation (see Rhoades & Eisenberger, 2002 for a review). With this in mind, we contend that organizational leaders must not only express the desire to eradicate ostracism from the workplace but also be willing to take visible steps, such as those noted above, to ensure the success of these initiatives.

As a first step, organizations should offer mindfulness training to all employees during working hours with clear communication as to why it is being conducted (i.e., to improve worker interactions and relationships) as this sends a strong message to employees about the organization's desire for an inclusive, tolerant culture that values its employees and their well-being. Second, supervisors must support this initiative by not only allowing workers to attend the training but also attending it themselves and encouraging everyone to practice learned techniques throughout the work day. If employees are going to take this process seriously they need to see their manager doing so as well. Third, organizational performance appraisals should evaluate workers on their ability to handle interpersonal conflict, refrain from avoidance behavior, and utilize mindfulness techniques as this will help establish accountability for these goals throughout the company. For those employees who successfully do so, a forth step should be to link organizational reward and recognition programs with performance appraisals outcomes as this will further reinforce desired behaviors. Further, "catching" workers in the act of utilizing mindfulness or dealing effectively with a coworker with whom they've had trouble in the past is another meaningful way of acknowledging and rewarding them for positive behavioral displays. In short, we contend that human resources practices (e.g., training, supervisor support, performance management, reward systems) ought to be designed and implemented with the goal of improving employee relations through focused self-control and thoughtful communication. The systematic coordination of these practices is key to ensuring that mindfulness training is effective and to garner widespread organizational support for diminishing workplace ostracism.

SUMMARY

In this chapter, we adapted an evolutionary psychology model as a framework for delineating why and how workplace ostracism develops at the group (e.g., normative expectations and guidelines) and individual (e.g., self-worth protection) levels. We report a cross-disciplinary set of findings regarding the origins of ostracism and bolster our arguments by offering some preliminary qualitative and correlational findings from a pilot study of 275 working adults employed across a variety of industries and positions. Building on these findings, we offer two potential interventions that may decrease incidence of ostracism at work. The antecedent conditions that give rise to workplace ostracism remain virtually unexplored and we further note that the evolutionary perspective and related theory on social norms heavily emphasizes the target characteristics that give rise to being a victim of ostracism. In this chapter, we acknowledge some perpetrator-related factors that precipitate exclusionary behavior (e.g., self-favoring attitudes and beliefs); however, we encourage researchers to substantively explore the additional reasons that perpetrators engage in acts of exclusion. We also acknowledge that our data were largely exploratory and therefore subject to alternative explanations thus offering latitude for future studies. We hope that our research model provides a platform for additional work in this important area.

REFERENCES

Abrams, D., & Hogg, M. A. (2006). *Social identifications: A social psychology of intergroup relations and group processes*. London: Routledge.

Andersson, L. M., & Pearson, C. M. (1999). Tit for tat? The spiraling effect of incivility in the workplace. *Academy of Management Review*, *24*(3), 452–471.

Aquino, K., & Thau, S. (2009). Workplace victimization: Aggression from the target's perspective. *Annual Review of Psychology*, *60*, 717–741.

Ashforth, B. E., & Mael, F. (1989). Social identity theory and the organization. *Academy of Management Review*, *14*(1), 20–39.

Axelrod, R. (1986). An evolutionary approach to norms. *American Political Science Review*, *80*, 1095–1111.

Baer, R. A. (2003). Mindfulness training as a clinical intervention: A conceptual and empirical review. *Clinical Psychology: Science and Practice*, *10*(2), 125–143.

Baer, R. A., Smith, G. T., Hopkins, J., Krietemeyer, J., & Toney, L. (2006). Using self-report assessment methods to explore facets of mindfulness. *Assessment*, *13*(1), 27–45.

Barling, J., Dupré, K. E., & Kelloway, E. K. (2009). Predicting workplace aggression and violence. *Annual Review of Psychology*, *60*, 671–692.

Baumeister, R. F., DeWall, C. N., Ciarocco, N. J., & Twenge, J. M. (2005). Social exclusion impairs self-regulation. *Journal of Personality and Social Psychology*, *88*(4), 589.

Baumeister, R. F., & Leary, M. R. (1995). The need to belong: Desire for interpersonal attachments as a fundamental human motivation. *Psychological Bulletin*, *11*, 497–529.

Baumeister, R. F., Twenge, J. M., & Nuss, C. K. (2002). Effects of social exclusion on cognitive processes: Anticipated aloneness reduces intelligent thought. *Journal of Personality and Social Psychology*, *83*, 817–827.

Beehr, T. A., Jex, S. M., Stacy, B. A., & Murray, M. A. (2000). Work stressors and coworker support as predictors of individual strain and job performance. *Journal of Organizational Behavior*, *21*, 391–405.

Bennett, R. J., & Robinson, S. L. (2000). Development of a measure of workplace deviance. *Journal of Applied Psychology*, *85*(3), 349.

Bishop, S. R., Lau, M., Shapiro, S., Carlson, L., Anderson, N. D., Carmody, J., … Devins, G. (2004). Mindfulness: A proposed operational definition. *Clinical Psychology: Science and Practice*, *11*, 230–241.

Blackhart, G. C., Baumeister, R. F., & Twenge, J. M. (2006). Rejection's impact on self-defeating, prosocial, antisocial, and self-regulatory behaviors. In K. D. Vohs & E. J. Finkel (Eds.), *Self and relationships: Connecting interpersonal and intrapersonal processes* (pp. 237–253). New York, NY: Guilford.

Blau, P. M. (1964). *Exchange and power in social life*. New York, NY: Wiley.

Bourgeois, K. S., & Leary, M. R. (2001). Coping with rejection: Derogating those who choose us last. *Motivation and Emotion*, *25*(2), 101–111.

Boyd, R., & Richerson, P. J. (1988). The evolution of reciprocity in sizable groups. *Journal of Theoretical Biology*, *132*(3), 337–356.

Bowles, S. (1985). The production process in a competitive economy: Walrasian, Neo-Hobbesian, and Marxian models. *American Economic Review*, *75*, 16–36.

Brewer, M. B. (1979). The psychology of prejudice: Ingroup love and outgroup hate? *Journal of Social Issues*, *55*(3), 429–444.

Brown, K. W., & Ryan, R. M. (2003). The benefits of being present: Mindfulness and its role in psychological well-being. *Journal of Personality and Social Psychology*, *84*(4), 822.

Buunk, A. P., & Dijkstra, P. (2012). The social animal within organizations. In S. C. Roberts (Ed.), *Applied evolutionary psychology* (pp. 36–51). New York, NY: Oxford University Press Inc.

Castano, E., Yzerbyt, V., Paladino, M. P., & Sacchi, S. (2002). I belong, therefore, I exist: Ingroup identification, ingroup entitativity, and ingroup bias. *Personality and Social Psychology Bulletin*, *28*(2), 135–143.

Cialdini, R. B., & Goldstein, N. J. (2004). Social influence: Compliance and conformity. *Annual Review of Psychology*, *55*, 591–621.

Cialdini, R. B., & Trost, M. R. (1998). Social influence: Social norms, conformity, and compliance. In D. T. Gilbert, S. T. Fiske, & G. Lindzey (Eds.), *The handbook of social psychology* (4th ed., Vol. 2, pp. 151–192). Boston, MA: McGraw-Hill.

Cosmides, L., Tooby, J., & Barkow, J. H. (1992). Introduction: Evolutionary psychology and conceptual integration. In J. H. Barkow, L. Cosmides, & J. Tooby (Eds.), *The adapted mind* (pp. 3–15). New York, NY: Oxford University Press.

Crocker, J., & Wolfe, C. T. (2001). Contingencies of self-worth. *Psychological Review*, *108*(3), 593–623.

Cropanzano, R., & Mitchell, M. S. (2005). Social exchange theory: An interdisciplinary review. *Journal of Management*, *31*(6), 874–900.

DeWall, C. N., Baumeister, R. F., & Vohs, K. D. (2008). Satiated with belongingness? Effects of acceptance, rejection, and task framing on self-regulatory performance. *Journal of Personality and Social Psychology*, *95*(6), 1367.

Duffy, M. K., Ganster, D. C., & Pagon, M. (2002). Social undermining in the workplace. *Academy of Management Journal*, *45*(2), 331–351.

Duffy, M. K., Glomb, T. M., Bono, J. B., & Yang, T. (2014). Mindfulness meditation and social relationships at work. *Academy of management meeting*, Philadelphia.

Duffy, M. K., Shaw, J. D., & Schaubroeck, J. M. (2008). Envy in organizational life. In R. Smith (Ed.), *Envy: Theory and research* (pp. 167–189). Oxford, UK: Oxford Press.

Dutton, J. E., Roberts, L. M., & Bednar, J. (2010). Pathways for positive identity construction at work: Four types of positive identity and the building of social resources. *Academy of Management Review*, *35*(2), 265–293.

Eisenberger, R. L., Huntington, R., Hutchison, S., & Sowa, D. (1986). Perceived organizational support. *Journal of Applied Psychology*, *71*, 500–507.

Esser, J. K. (1998). Alive and well after 25 years: A review of groupthink research. *Organizational Behavior and Human Decision Processes*, *73*(2), 116–141.

Feldman, D. C. (1984). The development and enforcement of group norms. *Academy of Management Review*, *9*(1), 47–53.

Ferris, D. L., Brown, D. J., Berry, J., & Lian, H. (2008). The development and validation of the workplace ostracism scale. *Journal of Applied Psychology*, *93*, 1348–1366.

Fulmer, I. S., Gerhart, B., & Scott, K. S. (2003). Are the 100 best better? An empirical investigation of the relationship between being a "great place to work" and firm performance. *Personnel Psychology*, *56*(4), 965–993.

Galinsky, E., & Stein, P. J. (1990). The impact of human resource policies on employees balancing work/family life. *Journal of Family Issues*, *11*(4), 368–383.

Glomb, T. M., Duffy, M. K., Bono, J. E., & Yang, T. (2011). Mindfulness at work. *Research in Personnel and Human Resources Management*, *30*, 115–157.

Gouldner, A. W. (1960). The norm of reciprocity: A preliminary statement. *American Sociological Review*, *25*, 161–178.

Helm, B., Bonoma, T. V., & Tedeschi, J. T. (1972). Reciprocity for harm done. *The Journal of Social Psychology*, *87*(1), 89–98.

Heppner, W. L., Kernis, M. H., Lakey, C. E., Campbell, W. K., Goldman, B. M., Davis, P. J., & Cascio, E. V. (2008). Mindfulness as a means of reducing aggressive behavior: Dispositional and situational evidence. *Aggressive Behavior*, *34*(5), 486–496.

Hershcovis, M. S., Reich, T. C., Parker, S. K., & Bozeman, J. (2012). The relationship between workplace aggression and target deviant behaviour: The moderating roles of power and task interdependence. *Work & Stress*, *26*(1), 1–20.

Hitlan, R. T., Cliffton, R. J., & DeSoto, M. C. (2006). Perceived exclusion in the workplace: The moderating effects of gender on work-related attitudes and psychological health. *North American Journal of Psychology*, *8*, 217–236.

Hofmann, S. G., Sawyer, A. T., Witt, A. A., & Oh, D. (2010). The effect of mindfulness-based therapy on anxiety and depression: A meta-analytic review. *Journal of Consulting and Clinical Psychology*, *78*(2), 169.

Hogg, M. A., Fielding, K. S., & Darley, J. (2005). Fringe dwellers: Processes of deviance and marginalization in groups. In D. Abrams, M. A. Hogg, & J. M. Marques (Eds.), *The social psychology of inclusion and exclusion* (pp. 191–210). New York, NY: Psychology Press.

Hogg, M. A., & Terry, D. I. (2000). Social identity and self-categorization processes in organizational contexts. *Academy of Management Review*, *25*(1), 121–140.

Hülsheger, U. R., Alberts, H. J. E. M., Feinholdt, A., & Langer, J. W. B. (2013). Benefits of mindfulness at work: The role of mindfulness in emotion regulation, emotional exhaustion, and job satisfaction. *Journal of Applied Psychology*, *98*(2), 310–325. doi:10.1037/a0031313

Kabat-Zinn, J. (1990). *Full catastrophe living: The program of the stress reduction clinic at the University of Massachusetts Medical Center*. New York, NY: Delta.

Katz, D., & Kahn, R. L. (1978). *The social psychology of organizations* (2nd ed.). New York, NY: Wiley.

Kendrick, D. T., Maner, J. K., Butner, J., Li, N. P., Becker, D. V., & Schaller, M. (2002). Dynamical evolutionary psychology: Mapping the domains of the new interactionist paradigm. *Personality and Social Psychology Review*, *6*, 347–356.

Kurzban, R., & Leary, M. R. (2001). Evolutionary origins of stigmatization: The function of social exclusion. *Psychological Bulletin*, *127*(2), 187–208.

Lawrence, T. B., & Robinson, S. L. (2007). Ain't misbehavin: Workplace deviance as organizational resistance. *Journal of Management*, *33*(3), 378–394.

Leary, M. R., Kowalski, R. M., Smith, L., & Phillips, S. (2003). Teasing, rejection, and violence: Case studies of the school shootings. *Aggressive Behavior*, *29*, 202–214.

Lindenberg, S. (1997). Grounding groups in theory: Functional, cognitive, and structural interdependencies. *Advances in Group Processes*, *14*, 281–331.

Molet, M., Macquet, B., Lefebvre, O., & Williams, K. D. (2013). A focused attention intervention for coping with ostracism. *Consciousness and Cognition*, *22*(4), 1262–1270.

Nicholson, N. (2012). The evolution of business management. In S. C. Roberts (Ed.), *Applied evolutionary psychology* (pp. 16–35). New York, NY: Oxford University Press Inc.

O'Reilly, J., Robinson, S. L., Berdahl, J. L., & Banki, S. (2014). Is negative attention better than no attention? The comparative effects of ostracism and harassment at work. *Organization Science*. Retrieved from http://dx.doi.org/10.1287/orsc.2014.0900

Pearson, C. M., Andersson, L. M., & Wegner, J. W. (2001). When workers flout convention: A study of workplace incivility. *Human Relations*, *54*(11), 1387–1419.

Penhaligon, N. L., Louis, W. R., & Restubog, S. L. D. (2009). Emotional anguish at work: The mediating role of perceived rejection on workgroup mistreatment and affective outcomes. *Journal of Occupational Health Psychology*, *14*(1), 34.

Petersen, M. B. (2012). The evolutionary psychology of mass politics. In S. C. Roberts (Ed.), *Applied evolutionary psychology* (pp. 115–130). New York, NY: Oxford University Press Inc.

Posner, R. A., & Rasmusen, E. B. (1999). Creating and enforcing norms, with special reference to sanctions. *International Review of Law and Economics*, *19*, 369–382.

Ramsey, A. T., & Jones, E. E. (2015). Minding the interpersonal gap: Mindfulness-based interventions in the prevention of ostracism. *Consciousness and Cognition*, *31*, 24–34.

Renn, R., Allen, D., & Huning, T. (2013). The relationship of social exclusion at work with self-defeating behavior and turnover. *The Journal of Social Psychology*, *153*(2), 229–249.

Rhoades, L., & Eisenberger, R. (2002). Perceived organizational support: A review of the literature. *Journal of Applied Psychology*, *87*(4), 698.

Robinson, S. L., & O'Leary-Kelly, A. M. (1998). Monkey see, monkey do: The influence of work groups on the antisocial behavior of employees. *Academy of Management Journal*, *41*(6), 658–672.

Robinson, S. L., O'Reilly, J., & Wang, W. (2013). Invisible at work: An integrated model of workplace ostracism. *Journal of Management*, *39*(1), 203–231.

Ryan, R. M., & Brown, K. W. (2006). What is optimal self-esteem? The cultivation and consequences of contingent vs. true self-esteem as viewed from the self-determination theory perspective. In M. H. Kernis (Ed.), *Self-esteem issues and answers: A sourcebook of current perspectives*. New York, NY: Psychology Press.

Scott, K. L., Restubog, S. L. D., & Zagenczyk, T. J. (2013). A social exchange-based model of the antecedents of workplace exclusion. *Journal of Applied Psychology*, *98*(1), 37–48.

Scott, K. L., Tams, S., Schippers, M., & Lee, K. Y. (2015). Opening the blackbox: Exploring the link between workplace exclusion, perceptions of envy and worker helping behavior, health and turnover. *European Journal of Work and Organizational Psychology*, *24*(2), 239–255.

Scott, K. L., Zagenczyk, T. J., Schippers, M., Purvis, R. L., & Cruz, K. S. (2014). Coworker exclusion and employee outcomes: An investigation of the moderating roles of perceived organizational and social support. *Journal of Management Studies*, *51*(8), 1235–1256.

Seashore, S. E. (1977). *Group cohesiveness in the industrial work group*. New York, NY: Arno.

Shaw, M. (1936). *Group dynamics* (3rd ed.). New York, NY: Harper.

Siegel, D. (2007). *Mindsight: The new science of personal transformation*. New York, NY: Bantam.

Sims, R. R. (1992). Linking groupthink to unethical behavior in organizations. *Journal of Business Ethics*, *11*(9), 651–662.

Smith, M. J. (1982). *Persuasion and human action: A review and critique of social influence theories*. Belmont, CA: Wadsworth Publishing Company.

Smith, R. H. (2008). *Envy: Theory and research*. New York, NY: Oxford University Press.

Solomon, S., Greenberg, J., & Pyszczynski, T. (1991). A terror management theory of social behavior: The psychological functions of self-esteem and cultural worldviews. *Advances in Experimental Social Psychology*, *24*, 93–159.

Surowiecki, J. (2004). *The wisdom of crowds: Why the many are smarter than the few and how collective wisdom shapes business, economies, societies, and nations*. New York, NY: Doubleday.

Tajfel, H., & Turner, J. C. (1985). The social identity theory of intergroup behavior. In S. Worchel & W. G. Austin (Eds.), *Psychology of intergroup relations* (2nd ed., pp. 7–24). Chicago, IL: Nelson-Hall.

Treviño, L. K., Weaver, G. R., & Reynolds, S. J. (2006). Behavioral ethics in organizations: A review. *Journal of Management*, *32*(6), 951–990.

Turner, J. C. (1975). Social comparison and social identity: Some prospects for intergroup behaviour. *European Journal of Social Psychology*, *5*(1), 1–34.

Turner, J. C. (1982). Towards a cognitive redefinition of the social group. *Social identity and intergroup relations* (pp. 15–40). Cambridge: Cambridge University Press.

Turner, J. C. (1985). Social categorization and the self-concept: A social cognitive theory of group behavior. *Advances in Group Processes*, *2*, 77–122.

Turner, J. C. (1991). *Social influence*. Pacific Grove, CA: Thomson Brooks/Cole Publishing Co.

Twenge, J. M., Baumeister, R. F., Tice, D. M., & Stucke, T. S. (2001). If you can't join them, beat them: Effects of social exclusion on aggressive behavior. *Journal of Personality and Social Psychology*, *81*, 1058–1069.

Twenge, J. M., & Campbell, W. K. (2003). "Isn't it fun to get the respect that we're going to deserve?" Narcissism, social rejection, and aggression. *Personality and Social Psychology Bulletin*, *29*, 261–272.

Twenge, J. M., Catanese, K. R., & Baumeister, R. F. (2003). Social exclusion and the deconstructed state: Time perception, meaninglessness, lethargy, lack of emotion, and self-awareness. *Journal of Personality and Social Psychology*, *85*(3), 409.

Vardi, Y., & Wiener, Y. (1996). Misbehavior in organizations: A motivational framework. *Organization Science*, *7*(2), 151–165.

Williams, K. D. (2001). *Ostracism: The power of silence*. New York, NY: Guilford Press.

Williams, K. D. (2007). Ostracism. *Annual Review of Psychology*, *58*, 425–452.

Williams, K. D., & Zadro, L. (2005). Ostracism: The indiscriminate early detection system. In K. D. Williams, J. P. Forgas, & W. von Hippel (Eds.), *The social outcast: Ostracism, social exclusion, rejection, and bullying* (pp. 19–34). New York, NY: Psychology Press.

Wood, W. (2000). Attitude change: Persuasion and social influence. *Annual Review of Psychology*, *51*(1), 539–570.

Wu, L. Z., Yim, F. H.-K., Kwan, H. K., & Zhang, X. (2012). Coping with workplace ostracism: The roles of ingratiation and political skill in employee psychological distress. *Journal of Management Studies*, *49*, 178–199.

Zapf, D., & Einarsen, S. (2005). Mobbing at work: Escalated conflicts in organizations. In S. Fox & P. E. Spector (Eds.), *Counterproductive work behavior: Investigations of actors and targets* (pp. 237–270). Washington, DC: American Psychological Association. vii, 329. Retrieved from http://dx.doi.org/10.1037/10893-010

COWORKER RESPONSES TO OBSERVED MISTREATMENT: UNDERSTANDING SCHADENFREUDE IN THE RESPONSE TO SUPERVISOR ABUSE

Matthew R. Leon and Jonathon R. B. Halbesleben

ABSTRACT

One particular egregious type of workplace mistreatment is supervisor abuse, which has received extensive attention due to its heavy cost to organizations including up to 23 billion dollars in annual loss resulting from increases in absenteeism, health care costs, and productivity loss. Employees attribute causes to abusive supervision, and these attributions impact subsequent reactions. In some cases, employees may feel that abusive supervision is justified, leading to the reaction of Schadenfreude, or pleasure in another's pain. In this chapter, we discuss antecedents to Schadenfreude, its role in observed mistreatment, and propose a conceptual model based on attribution theory.

Keywords: Abusive supervision; attributions; attribution theory; workplace mistreatment; Schadenfreude

Mistreatment in Organizations
Research in Occupational Stress and Well Being, Volume 13, 167–192

ISSN: 1479-3555/doi:10.1108/S1479-355520150000013006

INTRODUCTION

Observing workplace mistreatment negatively impacts employee affect, productivity, and quality of life (Miner & Eischeid, 2012; Tepper, 2007). Further, observing mistreatment can have a ripple effect across employees, with research suggesting that the impact of observed mistreatment grows as more employees observe the mistreatment (Miner-Rubino & Cortina, 2004). In general, mistreatment is action that violates conventional workplace norms for mutual respect, displays a lack of regard for others, and is considered destructive (Cortina, Magley, Williams, & Langhout, 2001; Lazarus & Folkman, 1984). Mistreatment encompasses many behaviors, including incivility, petty tyranny, and aggression (Ashforth, 1997; Miner & Eischeid, 2012; Miner-Rubino & Cortina, 2004; Schat, Desmarais, & Kelloway, 2006).

One particular egregious type of mistreatment is supervisor abuse, which has received extensive attention due to its heavy cost to organizations including up to 23 billion dollars in annual loss from increases in absenteeism, health care costs, and productivity loss (Martinko, Harvey, Sikora, & Douglas, 2011; Tepper, Duffy, Henle, & Lambert, 2006). Abusive supervision is defined as "subordinates' perceptions of the extent to which supervisors engage in the sustained display of hostile verbal and nonverbal behaviors, excluding physical contact" (Tepper, 2000, p. 178). Abusive supervision is a subjective assessment that is determined by the perceptions of the subordinates; as such, it is possible that two employees could view a supervisor's behavior differently (Martinko et al., 2011; Tepper, 2007).

When observing abusive supervision, there are at least three focal employees. First is the supervisor, who must engage in the act of abuse against another employee. This employee is the target: he or she is the recipient of the abuse. Finally, the observer acts as a third-party witness to the abuse. Clearly, not all abusive supervision is witnessed. Here, we are referring to instances in which a third-party (i.e., a coworker) witnesses the abusive supervision and then attributes causes to it, resulting in behavioral and affective reactions. For clarity throughout this chapter, these parties will be referred to as the supervisor, the target, and the observer, respectively. Additionally, the terms supervisor mistreatment, abusive supervision, and supervisor abuse will be used interchangeably.

While abusive supervision clearly impacts the targeted employee, it can also impact the target's relationship with coworkers that observe the mistreatment. Almost exclusively, abusive supervision is perceived as a negative event that is detrimental to the workplace environment (Tepper, 2007).

It directly impacts organizational culture, employee attitudes, and diminishes relationships between leaders and subordinates (e.g., Harvey, Harris, Gillis, & Martinko, 2014; Pelham & Hetts, 2001; Rotundo, Nguyen, & Sackett, 2001). Recent research indicates that perceptions of abusive supervision are influenced by individual differences in the observer's attribution styles (i.e., the pre-existing biases one has when making causal explanations; Martinko et al., 2011). This suggests that, under certain circumstances, observed mistreatment may be viewed as justifiable, or even positively, by some employees.

The varying reactions, an observer experiences underscores the role of attributions in observed abusive supervision. Specifically, the attribution process can be used to predict employee behaviors and affect following the event (Harvey et al., 2014; Tepper, 2007). This is particularly true if the observer has pre-existing notions about either the supervisor or the target of abuse (Mitchell, Vogel, & Folger, 2014). As such, it is possible that some observers may not experience the traditionally negative emotional states resulting from observing supervisor mistreatment. In other words, they may take pleasure from witnessing another person's misfortune instead of feeling stress or anxiety.

These negative feelings are manifest through the emotion of Schadenfreude, which is malicious pleasure at another's misfortune (Leach, Spears, Branscombe, & Doosje, 2003). Not only is Schadenfreude a threat to organizational relationships, it can exacerbate the costly outcomes of supervisor mistreatment toward employees that have existing relationships with the target of abuse (e.g., friends, peers, or other group members). For example, the witnessed abuse of a target can trigger feelings of anger in observers that have a positive relationship with the target. As such, it is important to understand how Schadenfreude manifests itself following observed mistreatment, especially within the target's immediate network.

Although theoretical accounts of Schadenfreude are plentiful and date back decades (e.g., Heider, 1958), empirical research on the construct did not begin until the late 1990s (Van Dijk, Goslinga, & Ouwerkerk, 2008). As such, due to the relatively small amount of empirical investigation, the causes and effects of Schadenfreude remain somewhat controversial (Van Dijk, Goslinga, & Ouwerkerk, 2008). For example, previous research has generated contradictory results regarding the role of perceived responsibility on the exhibition of Schadenfreude. Van Dijk, Ouwerkerk, Goslinga, and Nieweg (2005) found that targets who were perceived as responsible for their misfortune induced higher levels of Schadenfreude in observers than targets who were not perceived as responsible for their misfortune. On the other hand, similar research suggests that only sympathy, not Schadenfreude, is elicited when a target is perceived as responsible for their misfortune (Brigham, Kelso, Jackson, & Smith, 1997; Feather & Sherman, 2002). In this case, the attributions about the target may play a major role in determining whether the observer experiences Schadenfreude over other reactions.

According to attribution theory, employees observe their coworkers' behaviors and attribute causes to it in order to make sense of the workplace (Kelley, 1967, 1973; Weiner, 1985, 1986). Witnessing observed mistreatment can strongly impact coworker relationships, particularly if the observer already harbors negative feelings toward the mistreated coworker (Leach et al., 2003; Tepper, 2007). By integrating attribution theory, we can extend the workplace mistreatment literature by developing a model for the manifestation of Schadenfreude following observation of supervisor mistreatment that addresses inconsistencies in the literature. In this chapter, we discuss antecedents to Schadenfreude, its role in observed mistreatment, and propose a new model of Schadenfreude based on attribution theory.

In the following sections, we propose a conceptual model of employee reactions to observed mistreatment. Based on social attribution theory work by Weiner (1985), we outline a process whereby an observer witnesses abusive supervision of another employee, which triggers the attribution process. During this process, the observer determines locus of control, controllability, and stability associated with the abusive supervision. This process results in the level of Schadenfreude the observer feels toward the subject. In turn, Schadenfreude influences relationship quality and future interactions. We briefly discuss the implications of this attribution model of Schadenfreude for future research and practice related to mistreatment at work (Fig. 1).

ATTRIBUTION THEORY

Employees interpret behavior in terms of its causes and these interpretations play an important role in determining reactions to the behavior. Weiner (1985) posited that people perceive causes for past successes and failures in an effort to discern expectations for future success and failure. This is an automatic process that is triggered without any external signals (Wong & Weiner, 1981). For example, if an employee is promoted, that event should trigger an attribution process where the employee attempts to

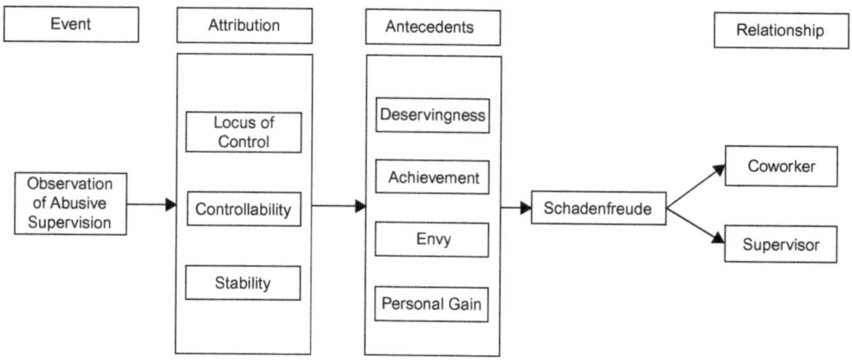

Fig. 1. Attribution-based Model of Observer Reaction to Abusive Supervision.

determine the cause of the promotion in order to manage expectations about the effects of work behaviors on future promotions. Similarly, employees try to assign causes to abusive supervision. Often, this occurs through the observer's attempts to understand target behaviors and how those behaviors may have caused the abuse. After the attribution process is triggered, individuals select a causal dimension to determine the reasons for behavioral outcomes (Miles, 2012; Weiner, 1985, 1986). These dimensions include locus of control, stability, and controllability.

Locus of control is the process of determining whether the cause of a behavior or outcome is external or internal to the person (Weiner, 1985). Internal factors include individual characteristics and behaviors like the person's effort, ability, and skill; conversely, external factors include environmental variables such as luck, chance, or task difficulty (Heider, 1958; Rotter, 1966). In the case of abusive supervision or other mistreatment, the observer would have to decide whether the abuse was generated from the target (e.g., through poor or unethical behavior, lack of ability) or if it was a product of the environment or other employees (e.g., a bad supervisor, a hostile work environment, organizational policy). So, an employee may feel different emotions based on whether they perceive the abuse as arising from an internal cause or an external cause.

Attribution research focusing on locus of control has found that observers are more likely to attribute a target's failures or other negative outcomes to an internal locus (Hewstone, 1989). In other words, observers will blame targets for their misfortune. For example, if an observer witnesses a target get punished, the observer is more likely to think that the target brought the punishment on him or her rather than the abuse being due to bad luck or the environment. When an observer emphasizes internal causes for others' behaviors and outcomes, even in light of external factors, it is called the fundamental attribution error (Ross, 1977). Although the fundamental attribution error has been shown to decrease over time, it never fully disappears (Burger, 1991; Truchot, Maure, & Patte, 2003). In fact, it is a common occurrence that highlights the observer's lack of ability to properly attribute causes to target's behaviors due to existing biases.

Observer biases are especially pronounced if the observer has preexisting feelings or experiences to affirm the bias (Truchot et al., 2003). This effect is especially prominent if the target's behaviors are relevant to the observer (Hewstone, 1989; Miller, 1984; Truchot et al., 2003). Social psychology explains this process at multiple levels: cognitive and social. On a cognitive level, the behavior of others is often more salient than the situation itself (Heider, 1958; Truchot et al., 2003). That is, behaviors are more likely to stand out than the environment. Heider (1958) noted that observers will focus on target behaviors over the environment because the observer tends to bundle the target and the behaviors as a causal unit that is responsible for an outcome. This process generally assigns little role to the environment as a cause and further encourages a focus on the target (Burger & Pavelich, 1994; Forgas, 1998; Hofmann & Stetzer, 1998). Socially, internal responsibility for an outcome is generally more valued in Western individualistic societies (Bond, 1988; Schwartz & Bardi, 2001; West & Altink, 1996). As such, observers are more likely to attribute the outcome of a situation to internal causes rather than external ones (Harman, 1999; Jellison & Green, 1981; Tetlock, 1985). This norm of internality is shared across individuals where observers receive more social approval and generate more positive responses from peers when assigning internal attributions to perceived outcomes (Jellison & Green, 1981).

From the locus of control literature, we can infer that if an observer attributes supervisor abuse to properties of the target Schadenfreude is more likely to occur. This is explicated more clearly in work by Feather and Sherman (2002) who found that Schadenfreude is tied to deservingness. That is, an observer was more likely to report high levels of Schadenfreude if he or she felt that the target deserved the punishment they received. This parallels more general work regarding observer bias and may show why Schadenfreude, rather than other emotion, occurs following the observation of abusive supervision. This is discussed in more detail below, in the "Antecedents to Schadenfreude" section of the chapter.

In summary, several areas of research suggest that an observer is more likely to attribute an internal locus of control to outcomes associated with an observed target. This may be due to a pre-existing relationship with the target, fundamental attribution error, cognitive cues, or social norms. In the case of perceived abusive supervision, an observer should be inclined to assign the cause of the abusive supervision to the target. That is, the target will be blamed for being abused. If a contentious relationship is present between the observer and the target, it is likely that the observer will experience Schadenfreude. In addition to the observer and target's relationship status, the determination of locus of control may result in other antecedents to Schadenfreude such as perceptions of deservingness or perceptions of the target's achievements and performance. Along with locus of control, levels of stability and controllability are estimated during the attribution process and may add to levels of Schadenfreude experienced by the observer.

The Role of Causal Dimensions in the Attribution Process

Stability refers to whether the cause of a behavior or outcome tends to be consistent and enduring or changing and transient over time (Weiner, 1985). So, if an outcome is attributed to a stable cause, then that same outcome should be anticipated in the future if the cause reoccurs (Weiner, 2000). As such, stability affects one's expectations of a behavior (Martinko et al., 2011). For example, if a supervisor yells at an employee every time the employee is late for work, then the cause of the abusive supervision (i.e., being late for work) will be considered stable. Here, an observer may feel Schadenfreude if they perceive that stable behavior led to supervisor's abuse; this is because stable behaviors that lead to a similar outcome imply that the outcome is predictable, and therefore avoidable. So, if being late for work always leads to supervisor abuse, then the abuse should cease to be an unexpected outcome and should be considered avoidable by coming to work on time.

Regarding the role of stability, research suggests that self-serving, hostile, and pessimistic attribution styles are all characterized by stable attributions (Martinko et al., 2011). With respect to supervisor abuse, if an observer perceives that the abuse is due to a stable cause such as the target's poor job performance, then the observer will perceive that the abuse is a deserved outcome of the target's behavior (Weiner, 1985). On the other hand, observers may be less likely to perceive abusive supervision as deserved if they attribute it to an external factor such as the supervisor having a bad day. Research suggests that there is a positive relationship between observer's perceptions of supervisor abuse and perceptions of failure in the workplace if the abuse is perceived as stable (Martinko et al., 2011). That is, an observer will expect supervisor abuse to occur following a target's failure if supervisor abuse is perceived as stable.

If behavior is not stable across situations, there is a higher likelihood of error in determining its cause (Harvey, Town, & Yarkin, 1981). In this case, if the perceived abusive supervision is considered to be unstable (i.e., no discernible cause) or if the target's behavior is not determined as the cause of the abuse, then stability may be perceived to be low. Additionally, if the traits of the target or supervisor (e.g., personality) are perceived to be unstable, it will be more difficult to assign causes to behaviors.

Finally, controllability is the perception that a person controls his or her own behaviors or outcomes (Weiner, 1985). This is different from locus of control in the sense that locus of control refers to whether the cause resides within (i.e., internal) or outside (i.e., external) the person, whereas controllability refers to whether the cause of a behavior or outcome is controlled by a person's own will (Weiner, 2000). For example, some causes such as laziness or tolerance, although internal to the person, are also controlled by the person's own will. On the other hand, artistic aptitude or physical coordination – again, an internal locus – are not necessarily under optional control; that is, one either has artistic aptitude or not regardless of will (Weiner, 1985). In the case of abusive supervision, an observer must decide how much of the abuse is due to the target's voluntary behaviors or choices (e.g., laziness) in addition to the target's abilities (e.g., intelligence).

Attribution theory focuses on why an outcome occurred, whether it will happen again, and who or what, if anything, should be blamed (Weiner, 2000). To answer these questions, an observer uses causal ascriptions (i.e., locus of control, stability, and controllability; Weiner, 1985). These perceptions determine one's emotional reaction to an event through causal ascriptions that impact subsequent emotional experiences – in this case, Schadenfreude (Weiner, 1985). Moreover, these causal ascriptions are attributed based on the observer's knowledge of the target and the observed event (Weiner, 1985). As such, the observer's previous beliefs about the target of abuse will play a major role in the determination of locus of control, stability, and controllability of witnessed abuse. In the next section, we discuss the attribution process in relation to observing abusive supervision. Further, we detail how this process may lead to the reaction of Schadenfreude.

ABUSIVE SUPERVISION AND THE ATTRIBUTION PROCESS

Abusive supervision is a salient and relevant event that employees use to make sense of their work environment (Tepper, 2007). Employees experience strong emotional reactions to witnessing abusive supervision which impact existing relationships. For instance, abusive supervision directly and negatively impacts the relationship between the supervisor and the victim due to the victim's suffering (Mitchell et al., 2014). Consequences include heightened psychological distress, burnout, stress, and turnover (Martinko, Harvey, Brees, & Mackey, 2013).

In addition to the direct impact of supervisor abuse on targets, perceptions of supervisor abuse can lead to negative outcomes such as emotional exhaustion, coworker abuse (i.e., an observer or target abusing the target after witnessing the target being abused by the supervisor), and other improper behavior (Aryee, Chen, Sun, & Debrah, 2007; Liu, Kwong Kwan, Wu, & Wu, 2010; Tepper, Henle, Lambert, Giacalone, & Duffy, 2008; Wheeler, Halbesleben, & Whitman, 2013). Moreover, research suggests that abusive supervision can impact coworker interactions such that an observer or target may display aggressive behaviors toward coworkers, particularly if an employee already has an impaired ability to self-regulate (Harris, Harvey, Harris, & Cast, 2013; Thau & Mitchell, 2010; Wheeler et al., 2013).

Perceived abusive supervision acts as a trigger that begins an attribution process due to its salience as a negative event that adversely impacts employee affect, behaviors, and relationships (Douglas & Martinko, 2001; Martinko et al., 2011; Tepper et al., 2006). If the proper antecedents are in place (i.e., perceptions of deserved misfortune, potential personal gain, feelings of inferiority, the target is a high achiever), the observer will experience Schadenfreude as a result of witnessing the abusive supervision. This creates a social threat to the relationship between the observer and subject that can impact relationship quality and future interactions. Additionally, witnessing abusive supervision can alter the relationship between the observer and the supervisor.

In a positive work environment with healthy existing coworker relationships, abusive supervision has been shown to create solidarity among peers

(Tepper, 2007). Research suggests that, if positive coworker relationships exist, then abusive supervision should lead to emotions of anger in observers (Mitchell et al., 2014). This anger is not targeted toward the victim of abuse, rather it is targeted toward the supervisor (LePine & Van Dyne, 2001). On the other hand, perceiving the abusive supervision of a target that holds a bad relationship with the observer, then the abuse may elicit a positive response from the observer that strengthens the supervisor–observer relationship. This may be based on whether the observer views the target as either an in-group or out-group member.

Here, attribution theory can identify how employees perceive the environment and the employees within it. This can explain how an employee feels about witnessing abuse, define relationships between employees (e.g., in-group and out-group status), and describe what actions are engaged in based on the observer's emotions. In a general sense, attribution theory provides the foundation for a predictive model of Schadenfreude and its effects on work relationships beyond our current understanding. More specifically, attribution theory can be used to create empirical tests that can be used to explain the role of observer perceptions and emotions following observed supervisor abuse in a multitude of work environments.

Measuring attributions allows scholars to accurately identify the context of the work environment, perceptions of supervisor behavior, judgments of coworkers, and the emotions of the observer. These measures provide information on in-groups and out-groups within an organization, pre-existing employee beliefs, and subsequent behaviors following observed supervisor abuse. As such, an attribution approach delivers a strong theoretical platform for exploring the occurrence of Schadenfreude across a wide range of work settings and structures.

As mentioned above, an important factor in the relationship between the observer and the supervisor is whether the observer is part of the supervisor's in-group. Employees can feel emotions such as Schadenfreude as a result of group identity and their in-group's relation to out-groups (e.g., social identity theory; Hewstone, Rubin, & Willis, 2002; Pettigrew & Tropp, 2006; Stets & Burke, 2000; Tajfel & Turner, 1985). While some research suggests that frequent contact between in-group and out-group members can reduce bias, these results are controversial (Amir, 1969, 1976; Cook, 1984; Harrington & Miller, 1992; Jackson, 1993; Patchen, 1999; Pettigrew, 1971, 1986, 1998). As such, feelings of identification as part of the supervisor's in-group may increase following perceived abusive supervision of an out-group member.

People classify themselves and others into various social categories based on prototypical characteristics assigned to members of various social groups (Tajfel & Turner, 1985; Turner, 1985). This is a heuristic process that allows individuals to quickly and easily (although sometimes unreliably) assign group identifications to themselves and others. Identifying with a group includes perceiving oneself as psychologically intertwined with the group, personally experiencing success and failures of the group, identifying with group values and norms, and defining oneself based on group-relevant social referents (Ashforth & Mael, 1989). These ideas have been applied in a broad range of organizational literature to study how an individual adapts his or her identity to the workplace, fits into an organization, and assigns values to him/herself and others (Ashforth, Harrison, & Corley, 2008; Ashforth & Mael, 1989; Dutton, Roberts, & Bednar, 2010; Hogg & Terry, 2000).

When employees classify themselves as part of a different group than a coworker, it can create tension between both parties (Schaubroeck & Lam, 2004). While perceived abusive supervision of an out-group target may strengthen the relationship between the observer and supervisor, the opposite effect may occur between the observer and target. While Schadenfreude may play a positive role in the observer-supervisor relationship, it could lead to issues between the target and observer.

Employees often react strongly to specific events that occur in the workplace; this is particularly true if the event is salient and relevant to the well-being of the employee (Schaubroeck & Lam, 2004; Weiss & Cropanzano, 1996). These emotional reactions can lead to interpersonal dynamics that affect existing relationships and employee morale (Exline & Lobel, 1999; Weiss & Cropanzano, 1996). Schadenfreude is such a reaction. Schadenfreude can negatively impact coworker relationships by increasing antagonistic feelings between an observer and a target, acting as reinforcement for enjoying the misfortune of coworkers, and increase feelings of separation between coworkers (Mitchell et al., 2014; Schaubroeck & Lam, 2004; Waldron, 2009).

Due to the strong negative effects of Schadenfreude, perceived supervisor abuse may pull a group further apart instead of bringing them together as traditionally thought. At this time, the social implications of Schadenfreude are not well understood and merit further research. Empirical data exploring an attribution framework should prove valuable for scholars and managers alike. In the following sections, we explore currently known antecedents to Schadenfreude as well as the methodological implications of testing attribution-based models of the relationship between abusive supervision and Schadenfreude.

ANTECEDENTS TO SCHADENFREUDE

Schadenfreude is opportunistic in that it relies on external circumstances that cause other's misfortune and make it legitimate to enjoy the opportunity (Brigham et al., 1997; Smith, 1991). Early empirical work identified several circumstances that can increase the likelihood of Schadenfreude. Specifically, Schadenfreude is more likely to occur when the target is perceived to deserve the misfortune, misfortune occurs to a target that is a high achiever, the target is envied by the observer, or the observer stands to personally gain from the target's misfortune (Feather, 1993, 1994; Mitchell, Vogel, & Folger, 2012; Mitchell et al., 2014; Portmann, 2000; Van Dijk, Ouwerkerk, Goslinga, Nieweg, & Gallucci, 2006). Regardless of the reason for Schadenfreude, each requires the observer to make attributions regarding the target. In the following sections, we review current knowledge of known antecedents of Schadenfreude while integrating tenets and assumptions of attribution theory.

Schadenfreude may occur when a third-party observer reacts to the misfortune of another (Feather & Sherman, 2002). Despite its malicious nature, it is considered a positive emotion because it involves the positive feeling of pleasure (Ben-Ze'ev, 2000; Feather, 1999; Heider, 1958). Additionally, Schadenfreude is often conceptualized as the opposite of sympathy because sympathy implies a caring and empathic relationship toward the target (Brigham et al., 1997; Feather & Sherman, 2002).

Schadenfreude is dependent on external circumstances to cause another person's misfortune (Brigham et al., 1997; Smith, 1991). More specifically, unlike feelings of pride or gloating that arise from direct competition or defeat of another, Schadenfreude can only occur when a third party or circumstance (e.g., a supervisor) causes another's misfortune (Leach et al., 2003). As such, Schadenfreude suggests an antagonistic relationship with the subject of distress because the pleasure is derived from observing the subject's misfortune, not by directly causing it (Heider, 1958).

Schadenfreude and Deserved Misfortune

One of the most powerful predictors of Schadenfreude is the observer's belief that the target deserves the misfortune (Feather & Sherman, 2002). In their experiment, they found that Schadenfreude was most closely related to deservingness, but also tied to resentment. The belief of deservingness can arise from the observer's perceptions of fairness, past history with the target, or the observer's perception of the target's effort (Feather, 2008). Additionally, perceptions of deservingness can be impacted by the causal dimensions of the attribution process (Weiner, 1985).

Attribution serves a primary function in the emotion of Schadenfreude in the sense that it is more likely to occur if the observer perceives that the subject deserved the misfortune (Van Dijk et al., 2008). In the workplace, an observer is more likely to feel Schadenfreude if he or she attributes fault to the subject for the misfortune (Heider, 1958). As such, perceptions of deservingness have a strong impact on subsequent emotions following observation of abusive supervision (Feather & Sherman, 2002; Smith, Powell, Combs, & Schurtz, 2009; Van Dijk et al., 2005). Perceptions of deservingness can enhance antagonistic relationships, particularly if the observer already has negative feelings toward the subject of abuse.

In a traditional attribution model, deservingness is clearly tied to the causal dimension of locus of control where an observer will judge whether the target was abused due to the target's own actions or to external circumstances. For example, one may feel that observed abuse is not justified toward a coworker if the coworker put in high effort (i.e., internal locus of control), but was still punished because of the supervisor's erratic disciplinary policies (i.e., unstable cause of punishment). On the other hand, if the coworker puts in low effort (i.e., internal locus of control) or if the observer has pre-existing negative biases toward the coworker, then the observer may not feel that the abuse is unwarranted.

Schadenfreude and High Achievers

Schadenfreude is more likely to occur when the target is a high achiever (Feather, 1993, 1994). In this case, achievement can include any personal or work-related reward, accolade, or other formally or informally recognized positive attention. Additionally, it should be noted that the high achiever does not have to be the highest performing employee in the group/unit/company. The only necessary prerequisite for qualifying as a high achiever is the perception of the observer.

Similar to determining whether misfortune is deserved, the observers must decide if the target's achievement is deserved or undeserved with different reactions arising from that determination (Feather & Sherman, 2002). If the observer determines that the target is a high achiever due to internal factors and good decisions (i.e., high internal locus of control, high controllability), then it is less likely that the observer will experience Schadenfreude. However, if the observer assigns external factors such as luck or favoritism to the target's success, then the observer is more likely to feel Schadenfreude when observing a supervisor abuse that specific target (Cikara & Fiske, 2012; Feather & Nairn, 2005; Leach & Spears, 2008).

When determining whether someone is a high or low performer, an observer will estimate the target's cognitive ability, conscientiousness, and job experience; in turn, these three characteristics will influence attributions of locus of control, controllability, and stability (LePine & Van Dyne, 2001). If the observer judges the target to be a high performer due to an internal cause, then the observer will judge the abuse to have occurred due to an external circumstance. This will not result in Schadenfreude, rather, it will invoke empathy from the observer (LePine & Van Dyne, 2001). However, if the observer feels that the target is a high achiever due to external causes such as favoritism or luck, then the abuse will be judged to occur from an internal cause from the target such as incompetence or personal failure. If controllability is also high, then the observer should feel anger and possible Schadenfreude toward the target. Moreover, if the target's behavior is perceived as stable (i.e., something the target engages in repeatedly), then the likelihood of Schadenfreude further increases. For example, if an employee is considered a high achiever but is incompetent and chooses to repeatedly engage in negative behavior, then the observer should feel Schadenfreude if the target is mistreated by the supervisor.

Schadenfreude and Envy

Although envy is often seen as another side of Schadenfreude, the two emotions are clearly distinguishable because envy involves negative emotions while Schadenfreude is characterized by positive feelings (Brigham et al., 1997; Feather & Sherman, 2002; Heider, 1958; Smith et al., 1996). Envy is a negative emotion that occurs during social comparisons and includes feelings of discontent that often arise from an unfavorable comparison between the observer and the target (Ortony, Clore, & Collins, 1988; Schoeck, 1969; Smith, 1991). This perceived inferiority creates hostile envy that may be concealed due to external pressures (e.g., workplace culture, social repercussions; Feather & Sherman, 2002; Smith, Parrott, Ozer, & Moniz, 1994).

Due to its social nature, envy often results from perceived inferiority to a successful peer (Smith et al., 1996; Van Dijk et al., 2008); this inferiority can arise from one's own defeat or witnessing another's success. Similarity between an observer and a peer increases feelings of Schadenfreude because similar peers usually share a domain of interest with the observer that makes their misfortune more salient (Van Dijk, Ouwerkerk, Goslinga, Nieweg, & Gallucci, 2006). As such, one may derive Schadenfreude from witnessing a perceived superior experience misfortune if they believe the superior did not earn his or her advantageous position. In this case, envy occurs because the observer feels that their target's superiority was gained by something outside of the target's control (i.e., the target is superior not due to his/her own willingness, but by some other force).

When an observer witnesses a superior experiencing supervisor abuse, the observer must determine whether that abuse occurred due to the directed actions of the superior or if a possible alternate scenario was possible (e.g., no occurrence of abuse). That is, was the controllability of the abuse high or low? Research suggests that, if controllability is high (i.e., the abuse occurred due to something that was under the control of the superior), then Schadenfreude should be high because the observer possesses an antagonistic relationship with the superior and takes pleasure in the superior's misfortune (Feather, 2008). On the other hand, if controllability is low (i.e., the abuse happens due to an external circumstance that cannot be controlled) then Schadenfreude should be less likely to occur.

Schadenfreude and Personal Gain

When an individual seeks a certain outcome, its attainment is the primary driver of the subsequent emotional reaction. This is true even if the outcome is a result of someone else's loss (Smith et al., 2009). While most people would prefer not to observe another person's pain, that perspective can change if one stands to profit from it (Batson, 1991; Decety, Michalska, & Akitsuki, 2008; de Waal, 2008; Wispé, 1991). This may be especially true under competitive circumstances, such as a traditional work environment (Smith et al., 2009). As such, it should come as no surprise that Schadenfreude occurs when the misfortune of the target benefits the observer.

In addition to its dependency on external circumstances (i.e., a third party to cause the harm), Schadenfreude is promoted when the observer has something to personally gain (Feather, Boeckmann, & McKee, 2001; Smith et al., 2009). This can include the malicious pleasure of seeing a coworker get punished, vindication for a previous negative experience with the coworker, or the potential that a coworker's misfortune will lead to a personal windfall such as a promotion. In a zero-sum competitive scenario, this effect is likely exacerbated (Smith et al., 2009; Von Neumann & Morgenstern, 1944). A zero-sum scenario exists when one person's loss translates into an exactly proportionate gain for oneself (Von Neumann & Morgenstern, 1944). As such, the personal gain would most likely be more tangible, easier to measure, and have a more direct impact on the observer than in a non-zero-sum scenario. For example, a zero-sum scenario would occur if a person is fired and the observer is given the open position. On the other hand, if a person is disciplined but the observer is not rewarded, then a zero-sum scenario did not occur. In a zero-sum situation, part of the pleasure from winning is derived from another's loss (e.g., sports; Tauer & Harackiewicz, 2004).

As related to attribution theory, the potential for personal gain can be tied to the concept of stability. That is, one's expectations of personal gain will be impacted by the perceived stability of supervisor abuse. If supervisor abuse occurs frequently and that abuse consistently leads to negative consequences (e.g., reduced work hours, more difficult assignments), then it is possible that the observer will experience Schadenfreude from the knowledge that the target is experiencing a harsh penalty. Similarly, if work is shared between the observer and target, then the observer will more likely be assigned more desirable job tasks in lieu of the target's punishment. On the other hand, if the supervisor abuse does not consistently result in a certain consequence, then the observer's witness of abuse will not trigger a positive emotional response. Unpredictable consequences usually generate stress and anxiety in subjects, unlike predictable outcomes, which bolster an individual's confidence in the future (Feather, 2008). As such, as stability is higher, Schadenfreude should increase.

METHODOLOGICAL IMPLICATIONS

Empirical testing of Schadenfreude is a recent practice, with most studies focusing on the general emergence and measurement of the phenomenon through manipulations (e.g., Feather & Sherman, 2002; Feather, Wenzel, & McKee, 2013; Leach et al., 2003; Van Dijk et al., 2008). To the authors' knowledge, no study has directly examined Schadenfreude following observed supervisor abuse. However, Mitchell et al. (2014) conducted a field study that examined emotional reactions to abusive supervision where the observer's exclusion beliefs about the target affected subsequent emotions. They found that witnessing abusive supervision elicited different emotions depending on the observer's previous beliefs about the target and mention that the study of Schadenfreude would be an appropriate extension of their theoretical model.

In their article, Mitchell et al. (2014) tested the relationship between observed supervisor abuse, third-party emotional reactions (i.e., observer anger and observer contentment), and subsequent observer behaviors (i.e., supervisor directed deviance, coworker support, and coworker exclusion). They collected data at two time points (one month apart) through self-report surveys that were administered to employees across multiple industries through a convenience sampling method (Grant & Mayer, 2009; Greenbaum, Mawritz, & Eissa, 2012). Additionally, they integrated the critical incident technique that focused the study on specific actions; in this case, observed abusive supervision (Flanagan, 1954; Hershcovis, 2011; Korsgaard, Brodt, & Whitener, 2002).

As noted by Mitchel et al., the critical incident technique has been demonstrated as a valid method for measuring reactions to mistreatment (Bobocel, 2013; Korsgaard et al., 2002, Wang et al., 2013). This method prompted participants to recall and describe a recent time they had witnessed supervisor abuse before filling out surveys in order to aid in the accuracy of data collection (Lang, Kozak, Miller, Levin, & McLean, 1980; Robinson & Clore, 2001). The participants' description was utilized at the beginning of the Time 1 and Time 2 data collection during the study. Further, by asking participants to provide a description of supervisor abuse, the authors were able to screen whether the participants had in fact witnessed a legitimate case of mistreatment.

The Time 1 data collection included all demographics, controls, and variables of interest excluding observer behaviors. As such, Time 1 data included a description of the witnessed supervisor abuse, study-specific moderators, as well as self-report surveys of the emotional reactions stemming from it. The data gathered during Time 2 included a rating of the observer's behaviors (i.e., supervisor-directed deviance, coworker support, and coworker exclusion). By instituting a lag between the collection of emotions and behaviors, the authors allowed time for observer behaviors to manifest themselves following the witnessed supervisor abuse and emotional reactions. This type of longitudinal data collection provided an appropriate gap between the witnessing abusive supervision and the manifestation of a behavioral reaction. Additionally it was consistent with previous observing how perceptions influence behavior (e.g., Jensen, Patel, & Raver, 2014; Matthews, Wayne, & Ford, 2014; Rodell, 2013).

Studies seeking to build on the relationship between attribution styles, Schadenfreude and abusive supervision will face challenges, many of which are common to attribution research. Lord and Smith (1983) noted that it is often difficult to determine how individuals assign attributions. For example, an attribution can be made in an attempt to determine causality, to assess responsibility for a particular outcome, or to assess personal qualities of individuals involved with an event. In the case of observed supervisor mistreatment, an individual may go through all three of these paths. Further, an event may require high or low amounts of information processing depending on its complexity. As such, scholars will need to determine how assignments are prioritized when interpreting data as well as how much information processing is required.

A related problem concerns the self-report nature of most attribution data, which can prime attributional processes that would otherwise be unaddressed (Wong & Weiner, 1981). Abusive supervision, by its very nature, is an impactful event that often elicits strong reactions from others. As such, additional prompting from self-report surveys may lead to inflated reports from subjects. To alleviate the potential of biased data, Ericsson and Simon (1980) suggested that surveys ask for subjects to report the protocols they generated during the attribution process instead of only reporting the judgments reached. This would also help scholars identify the information processing component mentioned above as well as the prioritization of attribution assignments (e.g., for causality, assessment of responsibility, personal qualities).

Future research examining Schadenfreude should follow a method incorporating a longitudinal design similar to Mitchell et al. (2014). The attribution process takes time to unfold, oftentimes with a discrete gap between an emotional reaction and behaviors (Weiner, 1985). As such, a more unbiased dataset may be collected by allowing time for behaviors to manifest themselves (Mitchell & James, 2001). The goal of future research should be to accurately map how abusive supervision directly impacts Schadenfreude, collect data on emotional reactions to it, and introduce theoretically relevant moderators and mediators in order to further our understanding of reactions to abusive supervision.

Laboratory work has established a strong foundation for our understanding of Schadenfreude, particularly regarding the emotions that cause it, how it is elicited, and under what circumstances it may occur. Moving forward, future work should examine Schadenfreude in the workplace with theoretical models based on the knowledge gained from previous studies. Further, longitudinal field studies should be conducted in order to gather data for causal inferences regarding the role and place of Schadenfreude in the workplace.

Future research integrating an attribution theory approach should observe the attribution process in a natural context with the intent of documenting the attribution process, its effects on relationship quality, and the mediating effect of Schadenfreude on that process (Kelley & Michela, 1980). Collecting multilevel data on supervisor and subordinate attitudes and behaviors will shed additional light on both the supervisor abuse process and how it affects relationships and emotions within and between employees at multiple levels.

Despite its occurrence in the workplace, research on Schadenfreude has been mostly contained to experiments within the realm of social psychology. As such, there is both a need and room within the organizational science literature to explore this phenomenon. With recent empirical work indicating that Schadenfreude may motivate destructive work behaviors, it is important that scholars begin to unveil the events and processes by which Schadenfreude occurs (Mitchell et al., 2014). Scholars have much to learn as research continues.

CONCLUSION

We hope that our introduction of attribution theory to the study of Schadenfreude sheds some light on existing controversy within this area of research. Moving forward, empirical testing is required to verify our propositions and test our theoretical model. Our goal in this chapter was to extend our understanding of the understudied emotion of Schadenfreude in an organizational context.

Scholars exploring this phenomenon should focus on longitudinal research that examines the attribution process, emergence of negative emotions, and observer behavior. The absence of management literature studying Schadenfreude leaves a gap in our understanding of how supervisor abuse affects targets of abuse and, moreover, employees that witness supervisor abuse. Through the utilization of existing theory, management scholars can explore how observers regulate their emotions following witnessed abusive supervision, identify moderators that may impact engagement in abusive coworker behaviors, and utilize empirical work from other disciplines (e.g., social psychology, experimental psychology, sociology) to direct future testing.

In this chapter, we have drawn attention to the negative effects of Schadenfreude in light of abusive supervision. Perceptions of abusive supervision are tied to the traditional attribution process and integrated with known antecedents of Schadenfreude. Observing abusive supervision can trigger an attribution process that results in Schadenfreude and further impacts coworker relationships in ways that may not be measured by organizations.

REFERENCES

Amir, Y. (1969). Contact hypothesis in ethnic relations. *Psychological Bulletin, 71*, 319–342.

Amir, Y. (1976). The role of intergroup contact in change of prejudice and race relations. In P. Katz & D. A. Taylor (Eds.), *Towards the elimination of racism* (pp. 245–308). New York, NY: Pergamon Press.

Aryee, S., Chen, Z. X., Sun, L. Y., & Debrah, Y. A. (2007). Antecedents and outcomes of abusive supervision: Test of a trickle-down model. *Journal of Applied Psychology, 92*, 191–201.

Ashforth, B. E. (1997). Petty tyranny in organizations: A preliminary examination of antecedents and consequences. *Canadian Journal of Administrative Sciences, 14*, 126–140.

Ashforth, B. E., Harrison, S. H., & Corley, K. G. (2008). Identification in organizations: An examination of four fundamental questions. *Journal of Management, 34*(3), 325–374.

Ashforth, B. E., & Mael, F. (1989). Social identity theory and the organization. *Academy of Management Review, 14*(1), 20–39.

Batson, C. (1991). *The altruism question: Toward a social-psychological answer*. Hillsdale, NJ: Lawrence Erlbaum Associates, Inc.

Ben-Ze'ev, A. (2000). *The subtlety of emotions*. Cambridge, MA: MIT Press.

Bobocel, D. R. (2013). Coping with unfair events constructively and destructively: The effects of overall justice and self – other orientation. *Journal of Applied Psychology, 98*, 720–731. doi:10.1037/a0032857

Bond, M. H. (1988). Finding universal dimensions of individual variation in multicultural studies of values: The Rokeach and Chinese value surveys. *Journal of Personality and Social Psychology, 55*(6), 1009.

Brigham, N. L., Kelso, K. A., Jackson, M. A., & Smith, R. H. (1997). The roles of invidious comparisons and deservingness in sympathy and schadenfreude. *Basic and Applied Social Psychology, 19*, 363–380.

Burger, J. M. (1991). Changes in attributions over time: The ephemeral fundamental attribution error. *Social Cognition, 9*(2), 182–193.

Burger, J. M., & Pavelich, J. L. (1994). Attributions for presidential elections: The situational shift over time. *Basic and Applied Social Psychology, 15*(3), 359–371.

Cikara, M., & Fiske, S. T. (2012). Stereotypes and schadenfreude: Affective and physiological markers of pleasure at outgroup misfortunes. *Social Psychological and Personality Science, 3*(1), 63–71.

Cook, S. W. (1984). Cooperative interaction in multiethnic contexts. In N. Miller & M. B. Brewer (Eds.), *Groups in contact: The psychology of desegregation* (pp. 155–185). Orlando, FL: Academic Press.

Cortina, L. M., Magley, V. J., Williams, J. H., & Langhout, R. D. (2001). Incivility in the workplace: Incidence and impact. *Journal of Occupational Health Psychology*, *6*, 64–80.

Decety, J., Michalska, K. J., & Akitsuki, Y. (2008). Who caused the pain? An fMRI investigation of empathy and intentionality in children. *Neuropsychologia*, *46*, 2607–2614.

de Waal, F. B. M. (2008). Putting the altruism back in altruism: The evolution of empathy. *Annual Review of Psychology*, *59*, 279–300.

Douglas, S. C., & Martinko, M. J. (2001). Exploring the role of individual differences in the prediction of workplace aggression. *Journal of Applied Psychology*, *86*, 547–559.

Dutton, J. E., Roberts, L. M., & Bednar, J. (2010). Pathways for positive identity construction at work: Four types of positive identity and the building of social resources. *Academy of Management Review*, *35*(2), 265–293.

Ericsson, K. A., & Simon, H. A. (1980). Verbal reports as data. *Psychological Review*, *87*(3), 215.

Exline, J. J., & Lobel, M. (1999). The perils of outperformance: Sensitivity about being the target of a threatening upward comparison. *Psychological Bulletin*, *125*, 307–337.

Feather, N. T. (1993). Authoritarianism and attitudes toward high achievers. *Journal of Personality and Social Psychology*, *65*, 152–164.

Feather, N. T. (1994). Attitudes towards high achievers and reactions to their fall: Theory and research concerning tall poppies. *Advances in Experimental Social Psychology*, *26*, 1–73.

Feather, N. T. (1999). Judgments of deservingness: Studies in the psychology of justice and achievement. *Personality and Social Psychology Review*, *3*, 86–107.

Feather, N. T. (2008). Effects of observer's own status on reactions to a high achiever's failure: Deservingness, resentment, schadenfreude, and sympathy. *Australian Journal of Psychology*, *60*(1), 31–43.

Feather, N. T., Boeckmann, R. J., & McKee, I. R. (2001). Reactions to an offense in relation to authoritarianism, knowledge about risk, and freedom of action. *European Journal of Social Psychology*, *31*(2), 109–126.

Feather, N. T., & Nairn, K. (2005). Resentment, envy, schadenfreude, and sympathy: Effects of own and other's deserved or undeserved status. *Australian Journal of Psychology*, *57*(2), 87–102.

Feather, N. T., & Sherman, R. (2002). Envy, resentment, schadenfreude, and sympathy: Reactions to deserved and undeserved achievement and subsequent failure. *Personality and Social Psychology Bulletin*, *28*(7), 953–961.

Feather, N. T., Wenzel, M., & McKee, I. R. (2013). Integrating multiple perspectives on schadenfreude: The role of deservingness and emotions. *Motivation and Emotion*, *37*(3), 574–585.

Flanagan, J. C. (1954). The critical incident technique. *Psychological Bulletin*, *51*, 327–358. doi:10.1037/h0061470

Forgas, J. P. (1998). On being happy and mistaken: Mood effects on the fundamental attribution error. *Journal of Personality and Social Psychology*, *75*(2), 318.

Grant, A. M., & Mayer, D. M. (2009). Good soldiers and good actors: Prosocial and impression management motives as interactive predictors of affiliative citizenship behaviors. *Journal of Applied Psychology*, *94*, 900–912.

Greenbaum, R. L., Mawritz, M. B., & Eissa, G. (2012). Bottom-line mentality as an antecedent of social undermining and the moderating roles of core self-evaluations and conscientiousness. *Journal of Applied Psychology*, *97*, 343–359. doi:10.1037/a0025217

Harman, G. (1999). Moral philosophy meets social psychology: Virtue ethics and the fundamental attribution error. In *Proceedings of the Aristotelian society* (pp. 315–331), Aristotelian Society.

Harrington, H. J., & Miller, N. (1992). Research and theory in intergroup relations: Issues of consensus and controversy. In J. Lynch, C. Modgil, & S. Modgil (Eds.), *Cultural diversity and the schools* (Vol. 2, pp. 159–178). London: Falmer.

Harris, K. J., Harvey, P., Harris, R. B., & Cast, M. (2013). An investigation of abusive supervision, vicarious abusive supervision, and their joint impacts. *The Journal of Social Psychology*, *153*, 38–50. doi:10.1080/00224545.2012.703709

Harvey, J. H., Town, J. P., & Yarkin, K. L. (1981). How fundamental is "the fundamental attribution error"? *Journal of Personality and Social Psychology*, *40*(2), 346–349.

Harvey, P., Harris, K. J., Gillis, W. E., & Martinko, M. J. (2014). Abusive supervision and the entitled employee. *The Leadership Quarterly*, *25*(2), 204–217.

Heider, F. (1958). *The psychology of interpersonal relations*. New York, NY: Wiley.

Hershcovis, M. S. (2011). "Incivility, social undermining, bullying … oh my!": A call to reconcile constructs within workplace aggression research. *Journal of Organizational Behavior*, *32*, 499–519. doi:10.1002/job.689

Hewstone, M. (1989). *Causal attribution: From cognitive processes to collective beliefs*. Oxford: Blackwell.

Hewstone, M., Rubin, M., & Willis, H. (2002). Intergroup bias. *Annual review of psychology*, *53*(1), 575–604.

Hofmann, D. A., & Stetzer, A. (1998). The role of safety climate and communication in accident interpretation: Implications for learning from negative events. *Academy of Management Journal*, *41*(6), 644–657.

Hogg, M. A., & Terry, D. I. (2000). Social identity and self-categorization processes in organizational contexts. *Academy of Management Review*, *25*(1), 121–140.

Jackson, J. W. (1993). Contact theory of intergroup hostility: A review and evaluation of the theoretical and empirical literature. *International Journal of Group Tensions*, *23*, 43–65.

Jellison, J. M., & Green, J. (1981). A self-presentation approach to the fundamental attribution error: The norm of internality. *Journal of Personality and Social Psychology*, *40*(4), 643–649.

Jensen, J. M., Patel, P., & Raver, J. (2014). Is it better to be average? High and low performance as predictors of employee victimization. *Journal of Applied Psychology*, *99*, 296–309. doi:10.1037/a0034822

Kelley, H. H. (1967). Attribution theory in social psychology. In *Nebraska symposium on motivation*. Lincoln, NE: University of Nebraska Press.

Kelley, H. H. (1973). The processes of causal attribution. *American Psychologist*, *28*(2), 107–121.

Kelley, H. H., & Michela, J. L. (1980). Attribution theory and research. *Annual Review of Psychology*, *31*(1), 457–501.

Korsgaard, M. A., Brodt, S. E., & Whitener, E. M. (2002). Trust in the face of conflict: The role of managerial trustworthy behavior and organizational context. *Journal of Applied Psychology*, *87*, 312–319. doi:10.1037/0021-9010.87.2.312

Lang, P., Kozak, M., Miller, G., Levin, D., & McLean, A. (1980). Emotional imagery: Conceptual structure and pattern of somato-visceral response. *Psychophysiology*, *17*, 179–192. doi:10.1111/j.1469-8986.1980.tb00133.x

Lazarus, R. S., & Folkman, S. (1984). *Stress, appraisal, and coping*. New York, NY: Springer.

Leach, C. W., & Spears, R. (2008). "A vengefulness of the impotent": The pain of in-group inferiority and schadenfreude toward successful out-groups. *Journal of Personality and Social Psychology*, *95*(6), 1383.

Leach, C. W., Spears, R., Branscombe, N. R., & Doosje, B. (2003). Malicious pleasure: Schadenfreude at the suffering of another group. *Journal of Personality and Social Psychology*, *84*(5), 932–943.

LePine, J. A., & Van Dyne, L. (2001). Peer responses to low performers: An attributional model of helping in the context of groups. *Academy of Management Review*, *26*(1), 67–84.

Liu, J., Kwong Kwan, H., Wu, L. Z., & Wu, W. (2010). Abusive supervision and subordinate supervisor-directed deviance: The moderating role of traditional values and the mediating role of revenge cognitions. *Journal of Occupational and Organizational Psychology*, *83*, 835–856. doi:10.1348/096317909X485216

Lord, R. G., & Smith, J. E. (1983). Theoretical, information processing, and situational factors affecting attribution theory models of organizational behavior. *Academy of Management Review*, *8*(1), 50–60.

Martinko, M. J., Harvey, P., Brees, J. R., & Mackey, J. (2013). A review of abusive supervision research. *Journal of Organizational Behavior*, *34*(1), 120–137.

Martinko, M. J., Harvey, P., Sikora, D., & Douglas, S. C. (2011). Perceptions of abusive supervision: The role of subordinates' attribution styles. *The Leadership Quarterly*, *22*(4), 751–764.

Matthews, R. A., Wayne, J. H., & Ford, M. T. (2014). A work–family conflict/subjective well-being process model: A test of competing theories of longitudinal effects. *Journal of Applied Psychology*, *99*(6), 1173–1187.

Miles, J. A. (2012). *Management and organization theory*. San Francisco, CA: Jossey-Bass.

Miller, J. G. (1984). Culture and the development of everyday social explanation. *Journal of Personality and Social Psychology*, *46*, 961–978.

Miner, K., & Eischeid, A. (2012). Observing incivility toward coworkers and negative emotions: Do gender of the target and observer matter? *Sex Roles*, *66*(7–8), 492–505.

Miner-Rubino, K., & Cortina, L. M. (2004). Working in a context of hostility toward women: Implications for employees well-being. *Journal of Occupational Health Psychology*, *9*, 107–122.

Mitchell, M. S., Vogel, R. M., & Folger, R. (2012). Beyond the consequences to the victim: The impact of abusive supervision to third-party observers. *Handbook of unethical work behavior: Implications for well-being* (pp. 23–43). Armonk, NY: M.E. Sharpe.

Mitchell, M. S., Vogel, R. M., & Folger, R. (2014). Third parties' reactions to the abusive supervision of coworkers. *Journal of Applied Psychology*. Advance online publication. Retrieved from http://dx.doi.org/10.1037/apl0000002

Mitchell, T. R., & James, L. R. (2001). Building better theory: Time and the specification of when things happen. *Academy of Management Review*, *26*(4), 530–547.

Ortony, A., Clore, G. L., & Collins, A. (1988). *The cognitive structure of emotions*. New York, NY: Cambridge University Press.

Patchen, M. (1999). *Diversity and unity: Relations between racial and ethnic groups*. Chicago, IL: Nelson-Hall.

Pelham, B. W., & Hetts, J. J. (2001). Underworked and overpaid: Elevated entitlement in men's self-pay. *Journal of Experimental Social Psychology*, *37*(2), 93–103.

Pettigrew, T. F. (1971). *Racially separate or together?* New York, NY: McGraw-Hill.

Pettigrew, T. F. (1986). The contact hypothesis revisited. In H. Hewstone & R. Brown (Eds.), *Contact and conflict in intergroup encounters* (pp. 169–195). Oxford: Basil Blackwell.

Pettigrew, T. F. (1998). Intergroup contact theory. *Annual Review of Psychology*, *49*, 65–85.

Pettigrew, T. F., & Tropp, L. R. (2006). A meta-analytic test of intergroup contact theory. *Journal of Personality and Social Psychology*, *90*(5), 751.

Portmann, J. (2000). *When bad things happen to other people*. New York, NY: Routledge.

Robinson, M. D., & Clore, G. L. (2001). Simulation, scenarios, and emotional appraisal: Testing the convergence of real and imagined reactions to emotional stimuli. *Personality and Social Psychology Bulletin*, *27*, 1520–1532. doi:10.1177/01461672012711012

Rodell, J. B. (2013). Finding meaning through volunteering: Why do employees volunteer, and what does it mean for their jobs? *Academy of Management Journal*, *56*, 1274–1294. doi:10.5465/amj.2012.0611

Ross, L. (1977). The intuitive psychologist and his shortcomings: Distortions in the attribution process. *Advances in Experimental Social Psychology*, *10*, 173–220.

Rotter, J. B. (1966). Generalized expectancies for internal versus external control of reinforcement. *Psychological Monograph*, *80*, 1–28.

Rotundo, M., Nguyen, D. H., & Sackett, P. R. (2001). A meta-analytic review of gender differences in perceptions of sexual harassment. *Journal of Applied Psychology*, *86*(5), 914.

Schat, A. C. H., Desmarais, S., & Kelloway, E. K. (2006). *Exposure to workplace aggression from multiple sources: Validation of a measure and test of a model*. Unpublished manuscript. McMaster University, Hamilton, Canada.

Schaubroeck, J., & Lam, S. S. (2004). Comparing lots before and after: Promotion rejectees' invidious reactions to promotees. *Organizational Behavior and Human Decision Processes*, *94*(1), 33–47.

Schoeck, H. (1969). *Envy*. Boston, MA: Liberty Press.

Schwartz, S. H., & Bardi, A. (2001). Value hierarchies across cultures taking a similarities perspective. *Journal of Cross-Cultural Psychology*, *32*(3), 268–290.

Smith, R. H. (1991). Envy and the sense of injustice. In P. Salovey (Ed.), *The psychology of jealousy and envy* (pp. 79–99). New York, NY: Guilford Press.

Smith, R. H., Parrott, W. G., Ozer, D., & Moniz, A. (1994). Subjective injustice and inferiority as predictors of hostile and depressive feelings in envy. *Personality and Social Psychology Bulletin*, *20*, 705–711.

Smith, R. H., Powell, C. A., Combs, D. J., & Schurtz, D. R. (2009). Exploring the when and why of schadenfreude. *Social and Personality Psychology Compass*, *3*(4), 530–546.

Smith, R. H., Turner, T. J., Garonzik, R., Leach, C. W., Urch, V., & Weston, C. (1996). Envy and schadenfreude. *Personality and Social Psychology Bulletin*, *22*, 158–168.

Stets, J. E., & Burke, P. J. (2000). Identity theory and social identity theory. *Social Psychology Quarterly*, *63*, 224–237.

Tajfel, H., & Turner, J. C. (1985). The social identity theory of intergroup behavior. In S. Worchel & W. G. Austin (Eds.), *Psychology of intergroup relations* (2nd ed., pp. 7–24). Chicago, IL: Nelson-Hall.

Tauer, J. M., & Harackiewicz, J. M. (2004). The effects of cooperation and competition on intrinsic motivation and performance. *Journal of personality and social psychology, 86*(6), 849.

Tepper, B. J. (2000). Consequences of abusive supervision. *Academy of Management Journal, 43*(2), 178–190.

Tepper, B. J. (2007). Abusive supervision in work organizations: Review, synthesis, and research agenda. *Journal of Management, 33*(3), 261–289.

Tepper, B. J., Duffy, M. K., Henle, C. A., & Lambert, L. S. (2006). Procedural injustice, victim precipitation, and abusive supervision. *Personnel Psychology, 59*(1), 101–123.

Tepper, B. J., Henle, C. A., Lambert, L. S., Giacalone, R. A., & Duffy, M. K. (2008). Abusive supervision and subordinates' organization deviance. *Journal of Applied Psychology, 93*, 721–732. doi:10.1037/0021-9010.93.4.721

Tetlock, P. E. (1985). Accountability: A social check on the fundamental attribution error. *Social Psychology Quarterly, 48*, 227–236.

Thau, S., & Mitchell, M. S. (2010). Self-gain or self-regulation impairment? Tests of competing explanations of the supervisor abuse and employee deviance relationship through perceptions of distributive justice. *Journal of Applied Psychology, 95*, 1009–1031. doi:10.1037/a0020540

Truchot, D., Maure, G., & Patte, S. (2003). Do attributions change over time when the actor's behavior is hedonically relevant to the perceiver? *The Journal of Social Psychology, 143*(2), 202–208.

Turner, J. C. (1985). Social categorization and the self-concept: A social cognitive theory of group behavior. In E. J. Lawler (Ed.), *Advances in group processes* (Vol. 2, pp. 77–122). Greenwich, CT: JAI Press.

Van Dijk, W. W., Goslinga, S., & Ouwerkerk, J. W. (2008). Impact of responsibility for a misfortune on schadenfreude and sympathy: Further evidence. *Journal of Social Psychology, 148*, 631–636.

Van Dijk, W. W., Ouwerkerk, J. W., Goslinga, S., & Nieweg, M. (2005). Deservingness and schadenfreude. *Cognition and Emotion, 19*(6), 933–939.

Van Dijk, W. W., Ouwerkerk, J. W., Goslinga, S., Nieweg, M., & Gallucci, M. (2006). When people fall from grace: Reconsidering the role of envy in schadenfreude. *Emotion, 6*, 156–160.

Von Neumann, J., & Morgenstern, O. (1944). *Theory of games and economic behavior*. Princeton, NJ: Princeton University Press.

Waldron, V. (2009). Emotional tyranny at work. In P. Lutgen-Sandvik & B. D. Sypher (Eds.), *Destructive organizational communication: Processes, consequences, and constructive ways of organizing* (pp. 9–26). New York, NY: Routledge.

Wang, M., Liu, S., Liao, H., Gong, Y., Kammeyer-Mueller, J., & Shi, J. (2013). Can't get it out of my mind: Employee rumination after customer mistreatment and negative mood in the next morning. *Journal of Applied Psychology, 98*, 989–1004. doi:10.1037/a00333656

Weiner, B. (1985). An attributional theory of achievement motivation and motion. *Psychological Review, 92*(4), 548–573.

Weiner, B. (1986). *An attributional theory of motivation and emotion*. New York, NY: Springer.

Weiner, B. (2000). Attributional thoughts about consumer behavior. *Journal of Consumer Research, 27*(3), 382–387.

Weiss, H. M., & Cropanzano, R. (1996). Affective events theory: A theoretical discussion of the structure, causes, and consequences of affective experiences at work. In B. M. Staw & L. L. Cummings (Eds.), *Research in organizational behavior* (Vol. 18, pp. 1–74). Greenwich, CT: JAI.

West, M. A., & Altink, W. M. (1996). Innovation at work: Individual, group, organizational, and socio-historical perspectives. *European Journal of Work and Organizational Psychology*, *5*(1), 3–11.

Wheeler, A. R., Halbesleben, J. R., & Whitman, M. V. (2013). The interactive effects of abusive supervision and entitlement on emotional exhaustion and co-worker abuse. *Journal of Occupational and Organizational Psychology*, *86*(4), 477–496.

Wispé, L. (1991). *The psychology of sympathy*. New York, NY: Plenum Press.

Wong, P. T., & Weiner, B. (1981). When people ask "why" questions, and the heuristics of attributional search. *Journal of Personality and Social Psychology*, *40*(4), 650–663.

CONTEXTUAL FACTORS IN EMPLOYEE MISTREATMENT

Shani Pindek and Paul E. Spector

ABSTRACT

Contextual factors play a vital role in employee mistreatment. This chapter deals with the definition and scope of contextual factors, including a distinction between the objective environment and its idiosyncratic perception by employees. Several mechanisms are offered to explain the effects of context on mistreatment, including the stressor–strain framework, interaction with personal characteristics, and also mistreatment acting as a stressor. The framework suggested in this chapter uses levels of analysis, and proposes that the objective environment (group level variables) is perceived at the individual level, which consequently leads to both perpetrated and received mistreatment. Those same objective environment variables also have a direct effect on mistreatment, as well as a moderating role in the relationship between individually perceived context and mistreatment. Furthermore, there is some evidence that mistreatment acts as a contextual variable in and of itself, with perpetrators, victims, and bystanders perceiving mistreatment in their workplace and reporting higher levels of stressors and strains. Finally, we outline the need for more

Mistreatment in Organizations
Research in Occupational Stress and Well Being, Volume 13, 193–224

ISSN: 1479-3555/doi:10.1108/S1479-355520150000013007

longitudinal, multi-level studies to clearly discern the role of context in employee mistreatment.

Keywords: Context; environment; employee mistreatment; aggression; multi-level

This chapter is focused on contextual factors in organizations that might contribute to employee mistreatment. Whereas much of the literature on mistreatment has focused on the target's individual characteristics (e.g., personality) and response to mistreatment, it is important to understand the role of the work environment (e.g., Bowling, Camus, & Blackmore, 2015). Contextual or situational factors are aspects of the physical or psychosocial work environment that are perceived by organization members and that can be related to various outcomes (Hershcovis et al., 2007). These factors include the climate and norms in the organization or workgroup, as well as various job conditions and events, including stressors.

Employee mistreatment is defined here as intentional negative acts that are directed at an employee, and that cause him or her harm. We integrate both the actor and target perspective, combining existing literature on topics such as interpersonally directed counterproductive work behaviors (CWBI; behaviors that harm others in organizations) on the actor/perpetrator side, and perceived aggression or incivility on the target/victim side. The effects that mistreatment has on bystanders/observers are often studied together with the effects on victims, and Vartia (2001) has shown that bystanders, and not just victims, suffer from adverse effects as well. Similarly, observed hostility and unresponsiveness to sexual harassment by the organization can lead to decreased well-being and increased withdrawal when controlling for personal experiences of mistreatment for both men and women, indicating that these factors influence bystanders significantly (Miner-Rubino & Cortina, 2007). Therefore, effects on bystanders are also included in this chapter, despite the relative dearth of research concerning them.

There are several types of mistreatment including abusive supervision (Tepper, 2000), aggression (Schat & Kelloway, 2005), bullying (Rayner & Keashly, 2005), and incivility (Pearson, Andersson, & Porath, 2005). These various forms can be distinguished by factors such as the status differential between actor and target (higher, lower, or equal to the status of the victim), whether the mistreatment is direct or indirect (Aquino & Thau, 2009), if the actor is an organizational insider or outsider (e.g., customers mistreating customer service employees; Sliter, Pui, Sliter, & Jex, 2011), and the intensity and frequency of the mistreatment (Hershcovis, 2011). Another categorization differentiates between physical (including threats) and nonphysical (personal, psychological, or emotional) forms of behavior (e.g., Bartlett & Bartlett, 2011; Meglich-Sespico, Faley, & Knapp, 2007). Some studies indicate that predictors of mistreatment are differentially related to specific behaviors (e.g., Peterson, 2002). However, for the purpose of this chapter, we followed Aquino and Thau's (2009) approach, and set aside subcategories of mistreatment in favor of a broader view. One important argument in favor of this view is the great overlap between mistreatment constructs, which is apparent on both the actor and the target sides (Hershcovis, 2011).

Integrating the actor and target perspectives is appropriate because, as will be discussed in this chapter, the same employees are often both the actors and the targets of mistreatment, depending on the cross-section in time when data are collected. Furthermore, being an actor or a target is often related with the same contextual variables. For example, poor leadership and workplace injustice have both been studied as predictors of enacted mistreatment, and as outcomes of experienced mistreatment (Hershcovis & Reich, 2013).

This chapter begins with a definition of contextual factors and their meaning at different levels of analysis. Next we review several mechanisms through which context potentially affects mistreatment, and then we review the different contextual factors that have been studied with regard to mistreatment. We conclude by suggesting some directions for future research.

CONTEXT DEFINED

Context is concerned with the external work environment in which mistreatment occurs. A narrow view would only include the objective reality of the organization. The type of occupation and the size of the organization are examples. However, context is more commonly viewed as including psychosocial aspects of organizations that do not represent concrete objective reality. Rather they have some portion of objective reality (rather than being entirely objective), and therefore have some shared aspects among people (Frese & Zapf, 1988). For example, bureaucratic procedures that slow the work down are an objective reality, and they are perceived by all employees, possibly at different severity levels. Therefore, the shared aspects represent the objective existence of those bureaucratic procedures, while personal variables may influence their perceived level. In this chapter we adopt the broader view of context as having some portion of objective reality, albeit filtered through employee perception and interpretation. We look at contextual variables from a multi-level perspective in which their total variance can be partitioned into shared versus individual components. One major limitation of this literature is that most mistreatment studies have been conducted at the individual level, and we therefore know considerably more about the effects of individual perception than of the shared portions that better reflect objective features of the work environment.

More specifically, we can talk about three levels of context measurement:

(a) *Individually perceived contextual variables.* These variables, measured at the individual level, include individually perceived climate, leadership, and stressors, and their variance can be attributed partly to the work environment and partly to the person perceiving them.
(b) *Dual source.* If a coworker perceives the contextual variable similarly to the focal employee, and that variable as perceived by the coworker has an effect on the focal employee, it is more likely that the source of the variance is in the environment rather than in the idiosyncratic individual perception of it.
(c) *Aggregated variables.* When employees in a workgroup perceive a contextual variable similarly, it can be attributed with even greater certainty to the environment than to individual perceptions.

Tucker, Sinclair, and Thomas (2005) conducted a study on the relationships between several stressors and their outcomes, including well-being and strains, using a multi-level approach similar to the one we are suggesting here. They talked about shared stressors, which are aggregated individual data regarding organizational characteristics (as opposed to organizational characteristics that are inherently at the group level and cannot be disaggregated, such as group size). They suggested that shared stressors are a representation of "true" contextual factors, and that these factors have both a direct effect on individual level outcomes, and a moderating cross-level effect on the relationships between individual level stressors and outcomes. The same can be expected when we look at mistreatment variables.

One more issue to consider is the wording of the items used to measure contextual variables. If items are worded such that the focus is on the group level, they may invoke responses that represent the context to a greater extent than when the wording focuses on the individual level. For example, an item which is intended to tap individually perceived situational constraints (Spector & Jex, 1998) is worded "How often do you find it difficult or impossible to do your job because of poor equipment or supplies," but the same item could be worded differently in order to tap the group level, for example, "How often do members of your workgroup find it difficult or impossible to do their jobs because of poor equipment or supplies." Typically, perceived stressors are worded in a way that taps the individually perceived context, while climate variables are worded in a way that taps the group level.

Measures of climate typically have items that reflect a higher level than the individual, asking about policies and practices of the organization or workgroup. Such measures are often aggregated to the group level (i.e., Zohar, 2000), therefore representing the shared aspects of the perceived context that can be considered to reflect the objective environment or context. Objective context is, of course, perceived by members of the organization, and that perception can then lead to increased mistreatment (Frese & Zapf, 1988) through mechanisms that are described in the following section.

THE MECHANISMS THROUGH WHICH CONTEXTUAL FACTORS RELATE TO MISTREATMENT IN ORGANIZATIONS

Every case of mistreatment includes both an actor and target who are both exposed to the same organizational context, although as mentioned above, perceptions of contextual variables can be idiosyncratic. Because of the shared (objective) aspect of the organizational environment, it makes sense to consider context from the perspective of both actor and target simultaneously. This is different from research on personal characteristics, such as personality, because a personality characteristic of an actor that potentially leads to engaging in mistreatment (see Berry, Ones, & Sackett, 2007) might not be the same characteristic that potentially leads a target to be vulnerable to being mistreated by others (Aquino & Thau, 2009).

Based on meta-analytic evidence, we can say that contextual factors play a role in employees' mistreatment, probably no less than individual differences. Hershcovis et al. (2007) conducted a meta-analysis showing that mean correlations of interpersonal aggression at work correlated as strongly with situational as personal factors. For example, work conditions accounted for 10% of the variance in bullying in a Norwegian study across all the included organizations, and up to 24% of the variance within specific organizations/occupations, such as graphical workers (Einarsen, Raknes, & Matthiesen, 1994). The following sections expand on how contextual factors contribute to employee mistreatment.

The Stressor–Strain Framework

A commonly used theoretical framework for the relationship between the work environment and mistreatment is that actors respond to provocative conditions and events with negative emotions, and as a consequence lash out at others (Spector & Fox, 2005). These acts can be a form of retaliatory aggression (Skarlicki & Folger, 1997) or acts of revenge that are an attempt by the actor to restore justice to an unfair situation (Bies & Tripp, 2005). Restoring justice can be achieved by reducing inputs or engaging in CWB in order to readjust the input/output ratio (Cohen-Charash & Spector, 2001). Because it is a retaliatory behavior, target-specific responses are expected to be stronger and have been found to be so for several variables (Hershcovis et al., 2007). In their study, Taylor and Kluemper (2012) examined the process through which stressors (specifically, role ambiguity and role conflict) influence aggressive behavior, and found support for a mediator role for perceived workplace incivility, suggesting that milder forms of mistreatment tend to escalate into more severe forms. These researchers suggested a number of (non-mutually exclusive) explanations for the process, including a reciprocation process, where experienced incivility is reciprocated by aggressive behavior toward the same target, with some displacement of anger toward new targets occurring, thus expanding the phenomenon further. Explanations offered for the effects of role stressors on mistreatment included that stressors interfere with the understanding of guidelines for what is considered appropriate workplace behavior, and encourage employees to protect their self-interests and pursue their personal goals in a chaotic environment where performance goals may not be very clear. Alternatively, employees who are confused about their jobs may ask for clarifications or help, or they may complain about the situation, which may make them targets of incivility.

Mistreatment as a Stressor

Mistreatment can be conceptualized simply as another stressor, particularly for victims and bystanders. Bowling and Beehr (2006) showed that harassment was related to several negative outcomes after controlling for role conflict and role ambiguity. Furthermore, being harassed was related with exhibiting CWBs with a mean correlation of .30 in a meta-analysis (with some primary studies showing correlations as strong as .52; Glomb & Liao, 2003), indicating that targets tend to report being perpetrators as well, fitting with Aquino and Lamertz's (2004, p. 1025) conceptualization of how "people can become either a victim or a perpetrator in a relationship at various times." In the same vein, Hauge, Skogstad, and Einarsen (2011) suggested that contextual stressors create affective and behavioral reactions in employees which either enhance the probability that they will become the aggressors, or that they will become the targets of bullying. This fits with the idea that mistreatment acts as an additional stressor, which may lead victims to a strain response that includes negative emotions and behaviors. In a longitudinal study, one contextual factor (role conflict) was related with both being bullied and being the perpetrator of bullying 12 months later, while the reverse causation was not supported by the data (Balducci, Cecchin, & Fraccaroli, 2012).

When victims report the presence of high levels of stressors, these reports are indicative of the presence of ambient objective stressors that would be experienced by everyone in the workplace, including bystanders and perpetrators of harassment (Bowling & Beehr, 2006). As mentioned earlier, it is not just victims who are negatively affected but bystanders as well. Possible reasons include empathizing with the victim's suffering, attributing the mistreatment to an organizational characteristic (e.g., perceived injustice), or even a fear that they could too become victims. In that sense, mistreatment itself acts as an ambient stressor which is experienced by most employees in the original victim's workplace.

One special case of mistreatment as a stressor is abusive supervision, where supervisors exert physical and verbal violence/hostility and sexual harassment, though verbal hostility is the most common. It is typically conceptualized as displaced aggression, directed against convenient targets (subordinates) when retaliation against the source of the frustration is not feasible (Tepper, 2000, 2007). One main antecedent of abusive supervision is another contextual factor – organizational injustice (e.g., Aryee, Chen, Sun, & Debrah, 2007; Tepper, Duffy, Henle, & Lambert, 2006), and so again, contextual factors lead to mistreatment, which consequently acts as an ambient or contextual factor/stressor experienced by all workers, not just the abused subordinates.

Customer mistreatment (e.g., verbal aggression or incivility by customers) is another example of how mistreatment can be classified as a stressor, in that it has detrimental effects on the behavior and well-being of employees. For example, customer incivility is related to higher burnout (particularly emotional exhaustion), withdrawal behaviors such as tardiness and absenteeism, and lower customer service performance (Sliter, Jex, Wolford, & McInnerney, 2010; Sliter et al., 2011; Sliter, Sliter, & Jex, 2012). Customer mistreatment is discussed in detail later in the chapter.

To summarize, contextual factors may be the cause of mistreatment, in a stressor–strain framework, but mistreatment probably plays an additional role as a stressor in and of itself, increasing the likelihood of further mistreatment.

Interactions with Personal Characteristics

Another important path by which contextual factors might relate to mistreatment is through the interaction with personal characteristics. One example is the interaction effect found between gender and job stressors in predicting CWB. Specifically, Spector and Zhou (2013) found that men reported engaging in more CWBI than women, but only when organizational constraints were high. Another example is Zhou, Meier, and Spector (in press) who showed that personality traits (agreeableness and conscientiousness) moderated the positive relationship between the job stressors (interpersonal conflict and organizational constraints) and CWB, such that the relationships were stronger for individuals low on either of the personality measures. Similarly, trait locus of control moderated the relationship between the same stressors (interpersonal conflict and organizational constraints) and CWB, such that these relationships were stronger for employees with an external locus of control than for those with internal locus of control (Sprung & Jex, 2012). Finally, negative affectivity was shown to interact with ethical climate in predicting workplace deviance (Chen, Chen, & Liu, 2013). These studies suggest that contextual factors may be boosters for personality effects on workplace aggression (Hershcovis et al., 2007), as the effects of personal variables will be demonstrated to a greater extent when the situation becomes more stressful. The same interaction viewed differently can be interpreted such that the within-individual stressor–CWB relationships are dependent upon personality variables. For example, the daily relationships between perceived supervisor interpersonal injustice and CWBI (mediated by negative emotions) was moderated by negative affectivity (Yang & Diefendorff, 2009).

Interestingly, contextual factor also have a moderating effect on the negative consequences of workplace mistreatment. Zhou, Yan, Che, and Meier (in press) showed that incivility was more strongly related with negative emotions under conditions of high workload and high organizational constraints.

Contextual Factors Changing the Definition of Mistreatment

Contextual factors can also influence the very definition of mistreatment. Values and social norms of the workplace may act as filters for interpreting which behaviors are labeled as mistreatment and which are considered acceptable and are tolerated (see Cowie, Naylor, Rivers, Smith, & Pereira, 2002). For example, the same specific behavior can be perceived as "bullying" or alternatively, simply as "firm management," depending on the culture of the workplace.

Context at Different Level of Analysis

The level of analysis (individual, workgroup, or organization) is meaningful when studying mistreatment. Some variables are conceptualized at the group level (e.g., climate or leadership) but are often studied at the individual level. Contextual factors in general, are often meant to be representative of elements in the situation that all employees are exposed to, and therefore multi-level investigations would often be more appropriate in studying the role of contextual factors in employee mistreatment. While most mistreatment studies are done at the individual level, conceptual work suggests that there can be spillover from mistreatment in the individual level (or dyadic level, if one considers a perpetrator and a target) to the group or organization levels (Heames & Harvey, 2006). Empirical data suggests that aggression at the individual level is positively related to aggression at the workgroup level (Glomb & Liao, 2003; Robinson &

O'Leary-Kelly, 1998). We suggest that the group level affects the individual level, at least in part, through context, as the objective portion of context lies in the group level of analysis (Semmer, Zapf, & Greif, 1996).

WHICH CONTEXTUAL FACTORS RELATE TO MISTREATMENT IN ORGANIZATIONS?

Climate and other context variables (objective context, as is represented by level 2 variables) can foster higher levels of perceived stressors, which then lead to outcomes such as mistreatment, as well as moderate the relationship between those stressors (depicted in Fig. 1). Furthermore, since mistreatment that is apparent in the workplace acts as an additional stressor, causality likely runs in more than one direction.

The framework depicted in Fig. 1 refers to various contextual factors, which are described in detail in the next sections. Some contextual factors have received much attention, and their relationships with mistreatment

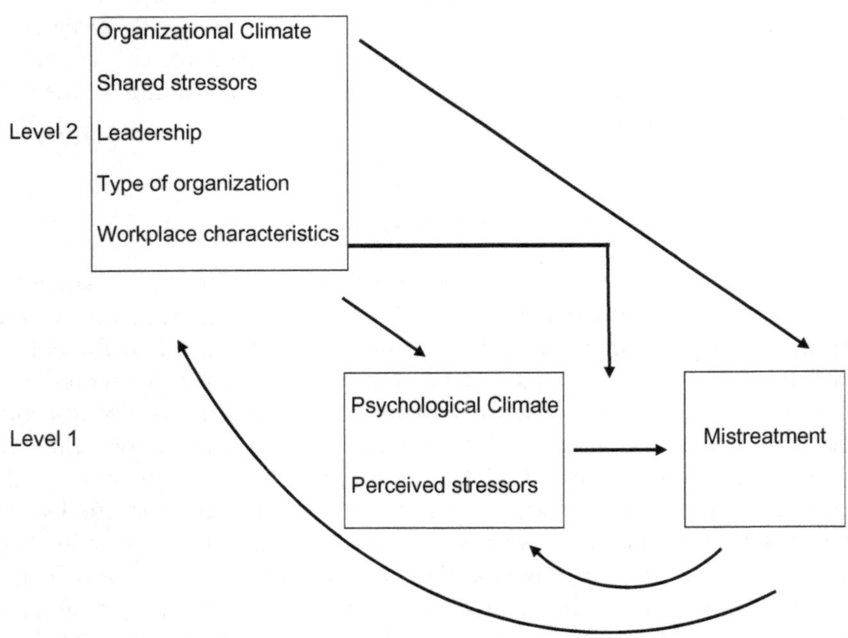

Fig. 1. A Suggested Framework for the Effects of Context on Mistreatment.

have been meta-analyzed, while other factors have received less attention. Many studies focused on differences in occupations – some occupations are characterized by more incidents of mistreatment than others.

Type of Organization and Occupation

The type of organization/occupation is an objective and clearly contextual factor, and different jobs potentially foster different manifestations of mistreatment. One notable example is customer service jobs that require interactions with customers, thus potentially exposing employees to customer mistreatment. A series of studies, most from Scandinavia, and many with large samples (greater than 1,000 employees), have addressed organizational and occupational differences. Mikkelsen and Einarsen (2001), for example, found that manufacturing company employees were exposed to more bullying than hospital employees. Being exposed to aggression from both colleagues and managers was more common in industry, transport, education, and less common in business services and financial institutions (Hubert & van Veldhoven, 2001). In a Norwegian study, a ranking between specific occupations revealed industrial workers receiving the highest prevalence rates of bullying and psychologists and university employees receiving the lowest; public company employees reported less bullying than those from private enterprises (Einarsen & Skogstad, 1996). However, in a later (smaller scale) study, no significant differences in bullying were observed between public and private sector employees (Salin, 2001). In addition to differences in prevalence, Einarsen et al. (1994) found that various contextual factors correlated with bullying, and that these relationships were different in magnitude among occupations.

While there are differences among occupations and work sectors in prevalence of receiving mistreatment there can be within occupation/sector differences as well. Aquino and Thau (2009) suggested that looking at broad occupations may leave room for many other contextual factors, for example, employees have a higher likelihood of being bullied or mistreated if their work requires that they interact frequently with one another rather than work independently, and this can vary within an occupation or an organization. If indeed the important contextual factors vary to a great extent within organizations, inconsistent results are expected when looking at broadly defined occupations, and a more promising research venue would be focusing on specific characteristics of the work environment. For example, bullying has been found to be higher when work is uninteresting and has low variability, challenge, and meaning, (Einarsen et al., 1994), as well as when the information flow is poor and the way to settle differences of opinion is authoritative rather than through discussions (Vartia, 1996). Another possible approach is to examine occupations using narrower definitions according to the work settings, thus creating more homogenous groups within occupations. An example for such an attempt can be found in the study of violence exposure in nurses, where various types of violence were differentially prevalent across settings. For example, a meta-analysis showed that over 80% of emergency department nurses but under 35% of geriatric department nurses had been exposed to nonphysical violence. There were also differences between nurses' exposure to violence in different world regions (Spector, Zhou, & Che, 2014). Another example can be found in a study of educators in Minnesota, where class size, school type and ages taught were related with physical and nonphysical violence (Wei et al., 2013).

More research (and replication of results) is needed in order to evaluate the usefulness and consistency of looking at differences in mistreatment between narrowly defined occupations. However, many studies have adopted the approach mentioned above, of studying characteristics (such as climate and stressors) of the work environment rather than occupations, and the remainder of this review is dedicated to those characteristics.

Norms

Social norms are the informal rules or conventions that groups adopt regarding how people ought to behave (Feldman, 1984). Norms are typically more "horizontal" than climate, as they are not resulting directly from the management's values and practices, but gleaned mostly from the actions of peers. Norms can be the result of climate, but they are not necessarily so. Incivility is often considered a violation of the social norms for mutual respect in interpersonal relationships (Andersson & Pearson, 1999), and uncivil behavior invites norms of individual self-interest and an erosion of cooperation (Pearson & Porath, 2005).

Norms of aggressive behavior potentially result in more individuals exhibiting aggressive behavior because if many members of the group are aggressive, it is likely that new group members would choose an aggressive role model, and subsequently behave in a more aggressive manner themselves. Moreover, nonaggressive members of the group would be less satisfied and have greater intentions to leave it (Robinson & O'Leary-Kelly, 1998).

Although norms can be specific to mistreatment behaviors, mistreatment can also arise in the enforcement of norms. For example, it has been shown that workgroups will often use physical and nonphysical mistreatment as a means of regulating adherence to production norms. Individuals who perform at levels that are above or below accepted levels can be subject to corrective mistreatment (Coch & French, 1948). This study also showed that the enforcement of norms, and hence the occurrence of mistreatment was affected by the contextual variable of group cohesion. Groups that are cohesive are more likely to enforce their norms.

Climate

Typically, climate is defined as the shared perceptions among employees with regard to the policies, procedures, and practices of their organization, with policies typically coming from the top leadership (Zohar, 2000). There are many types of organizational climates, some more relevant to the study of mistreatment than others. Organizational climates that are characterized by positive communication, and are uncompetitive (sometimes referred to as good *social climates*) are related to lower self-rated victimization rates (Agervold & Mikkelsen, 2004; Vartia, 1996). Bad social climates, however, are related with bullying and mobbing (Einarsen et al., 1994; Zapf, Knorz, & Kulla, 1996). Perceptions of a social climate, as measured at the individual level, are also related with group level observed workplace bullying, having an effect on observers/bystanders as well (Skogstad, Torsheim, Einarsen, & Hauge, 2011).

In addition to more general climates, some mistreatment-specific climates have been investigated. These climates are concerned with organizational policies and practices designed to reduce various forms of mistreatment. Studies have focused on psychosocial safety, violence prevention, incivility, and bullying climates. Each has been linked to various forms of mistreatment.

Psychosocial Safety Climate

Psychosocial safety climate concerns the shared perceptions of organizational policies, practices, and procedures regarding the protection of employees' psychological health and safety. A recent multi-level study has shown that psychosocial safety climate is related with workplace bullying and harassment (including sexual harassment, discrimination, and psychological humiliation) both at the organizational level and at the individual level. In addition, psychosocial safety climate moderated the relationship between bullying/harassment and psychosocial distress, emotional exhaustion, and engagement, such that a more positive climate buffered the negative effects of bullying/harassment. The hypothesized underlying process here is that psychosocial safety climate creates conditions that lead to fewer psychological injuries because employees' psychological health and safety is protected. For example, a poor psychosocial safety climate would allow for mistreatment to go unacknowledged, or even perpetrated from the top-down, thereby "institutionalizing" such behaviors. Conversely, when the psychosocial safety climate is strong, management would not tolerate mistreatment incidents (Law, Dollard, Tuckey, & Dormann, 2011).

Violence Prevention Climate

Originally developed in the healthcare industry, violence prevention climate concerns policies and practices that help prevent exposure of employees to both physical and nonphysical violence (Spector, Coulter, Stockwell, & Matz, 2007). A series of studies were conducted using the three-dimensional Violence Prevention Climate Scale (Kessler, Spector, Chang, & Parr, 2008), consisting of Policies and Procedures (formal rules and requirements), Practices and Response (behaviors concerning prevention of and response to violent incidents), and Pressure for Unsafe Practices (priority for productivity over violence safety). These studies showed that perceptions of violence prevention climate related to violence exposure using cross-sectional (Chang, Eatough, Spector, & Kessler, 2012) and longitudinal designs (Spector, Zhou, & Yang, 2013; Yang, Spector, Chang, Gallant-Roman, & Powell, 2012). Both longitudinal studies were able to provide evidence that climate leads to violence exposure, whereas experiencing violence did not affect perceptions of climate. More directly relevant to the idea of context is a multi-source study in which coworker reports of climate related to focal employee exposure to physical and nonphysical violence (Chang et al., 2012). Taken together these studies clearly show a link between climate and experience of mistreatment, with evidence that the direction of effects is from climate to violence and not the reverse.

Civility Climate

There have been several scales developed to assess civility climate, that is, climates that encourage employees to remain civil to one another. One such multidimensional scale was designed to assess policies and procedures that encourage civil behavior in the workplace (Ottinot, 2008). This scale has been used at all three measurement levels: Individual, dual source, and aggregated. Specifically, Ottinot found that this climate scale correlated with incivility with both employee and coworker reports of climate. Furthermore, not only did climate relate to individuals being the targets of incivility, but engaging in mistreatment of others as well. In a multi-level follow-up study of more than 2,000 teachers from more than 200 schools, Ottinot (2011) showed that civility climate assessed at the school level related to experiences of incivility and broader mistreatment. Yang, Caughlin, Gazica, Truxillo, and Spector (2014, May) located more than a dozen studies that used various civility climate scales that predicted incivility exposure (mean $r = -.36$).

Ethical Climate

Ethical climate refers to the shared perceptions of what is considered ethical behavior within the organization. Ethical behavior includes avoiding acts that might harm others, including various forms of mistreatment. Thus by encouraging employees to uphold ethical standards, organizations are also encouraging employees to avoid mistreating others. Not surprisingly, it has been shown that ethical climate relates to the ethical behavior of the employees, including aggression directed toward others or bullying (Bulutlar & Öz, 2009; Peterson, 2002).

Climate of Bullying

There have been a small number of studies that have investigated organizational tolerance of bullying as a form of climate. Hutchinson, Jackson, Wilkes, and Vickers (2008) developed a model of bullying that included several workplace contextual factors that fit under the category of climate, most prominently, tolerance and reward for bullying. Their measure of climate was significantly related to bullying experiences (Hutchinson, Wilkes, Jackson, & Vickers, 2010). Although not as fully developed as a bullying climate measure, Baillien, Neyens, and De Witte (2011) were able to show that their measure of anti-bullying policies was able to predict employee exposure to bullying.

Direction of Climate Effects

Although a number of studies have linked climate to mistreatment, except for the few longitudinal studies noted earlier that showed climate leads to mistreatment rather than the reverse (Spector et al., 2013; Yang et al., 2012), most studies have used cross-sectional designs. Thus, the direction of the association between climate and mistreatment cannot be determined from most studies. Although it makes intuitive sense that climate allowing for disrespectful behavior often encourages mistreatment by legitimizing it, those same behaviors over time, establish the informal rules and reinforce climate (Aquino & Lamertz, 2004). Alternatively, there is some evidence that bullying partially mediates the relationship between organizational climate and well-being of employees (Giorgi, 2010), and evidence that group level interactional justice climate mediates the relationship between group level environmental incivility and individual-level intention to quit (Griffin, 2010). It seems therefore, that bullying and climate are related in their prediction of well-being variables (across levels as well as at the individual level), likely through a mediation process, but since different studies place perpetrating mistreatment and perceived climate into different roles of predictor and mediator, it is hard to draw definite conclusions.

While almost all climate research focuses on the organizational climate, there is some evidence that the climate of the community in which the workplace is located geographically (the external environment of violence) is related with workplace aggression. When both external and justice climate were examined for their unique effects on aggression, only the external climate remained significant (Dietz, Robinson, Folger, Baron, & Schulz, 2003). Furthermore, there are broader cultural influences on mistreatment. Taking into account that not all commonly used measures in organizational research are invariant across cultures, Kernan, Watson, Chen, and Kim (2011) compared the United States and South Korea and found that some cultural values (achievement and benevolence, measured directly and not at the country level) moderated the effects of abusive supervision on workers' job-related attitudes. These relationships were stronger when achievement was high and when benevolence was high.

Leadership

The actions of leaders in the organizations are intimately related with the climate, as leaders transmit climate from higher to lower levels (Dragoni, 2005; Kozlowski & Doherty, 1989). Leaders carry out organizational policies, and employees judge the climate according to the actions of their leaders. Leaders' behaviors, therefore, can create conditions that facilitate or inhibit mistreatment among their subordinates. This could include being tolerant of mistreatment, or engaging in it (e.g., abusive supervision), and therefore being a negative role model.

Several types of leadership have been examined in the context of mistreatment. Einarsen et al. (1994) found that bullied employees reported being less satisfied with leadership in their organization. Furthermore, they experienced a more authoritarian and less employee-orientated management style, including insufficient information, receiving only negative feedback, or having serious conflict with their supervisor (Agervold & Mikkelsen, 2004). Employees who perceive their superiors to have a laissez-faire leadership style (i.e., an avoiding leadership style), also report higher levels of mistreatment. There is evidence that this relationship is mediated by role and social stressors. It seems that lack of proper leadership is reflected in unclear guidelines as to what is appropriate, both for the work role and for social behavior at work, which in turn influences employees' chances of being mistreated (Skogstad, Einarsen, Torsheim, Aasland, & Hetland, 2007). Moreover, poor leadership sometimes includes specific behaviors that target an employee (e.g., when a supervisor "puts me down in front of others") that could lead to more targeted retaliation, meaning employees becoming increasingly aggressive toward their supervisors (Hershcovis et al., 2007, p. 231). Often times leadership variables are measured at the individual level, but fair and supportive leadership is also related with lower observed bulling at the group (department) level (Hauge, Einarsen et al., 2011).

Workplace Characteristics

Organizational size and gender ratio favoring men are organizational characteristics that are related with higher prevalence of bullying and harassment (Einarsen & Skogstad, 1996). Gender ratios that favor men among customers also promote customer sexual harassment (Gettman & Gelfand, 2007). One study found that aggression perpetrated by men was much more common when the workplace was predominantly male, while aggression perpetrated by women was not related with the proportion of male/females in the sample. The explanation they offered was of a "culture of honor" between males, which dictates that insults and challenges have to be met with retaliatory aggression, and gender role theories, which allow for males but not females to express aggression openly (Kaukiainen et al., 2001). Culture of honor is typically used as context for studying norms of aggression in the southern (and western) parts of the United States and can be useful as a framework for understanding differences between the United States southern and northern norms regarding the perceived prevalence and desirability of aggressive behavior. For example, studies on culture of honor suggest that southern men are more likely to perceive violence as honorable and acceptable than their northern counterparts (Vandello, Cohen, & Ransom, 2008). While most culture of honor research was not done in the work context, it likely affects norms of aggressive behavior in different settings, including the organizational one. One study found that job applicants who had killed someone in an honor-related conflict were received better in southern companies than in northern ones (Cohen & Nisbett, 1997).

A study of over 200 organizational ethnographies (book-length organizational recordings of at least one year in the field) revealed that supervisory bullying was related with workplace characteristics such as the percent of minority employees, of female employees, lower pay, and job insecurity. In addition, organizational chaos (situations in which rationality and order are deficient) was predictive of bullying above and beyond these factors (Roscigno, Lopez, & Hodson, 2009).

It is hard to tell why diversity in the workplace is related with mistreatment. Findings are typically correlational: gender ratios and minority ratios are related with prevalence of mistreatment in some studies (e.g., Baillien et al., 2011), but not all. Causal explanations have been offered; for example, male-dominated work environments have been conceptualized as more sexual, leading to higher rates of sexual harassment, and people who seem to belong to minority groups are more likely to be "punished" when an opportunity arises according to principles of aversive racism (Grandey, Dickter, & Sin, 2004). However, alternative explanations are always possible. For example, it can be that men are responsible for most cases of sexual harassment, and so in organizations that employ more men, there are more potential perpetrators, and thus more potential aggressors.

Customer-Related Mistreatment

One unique source of mistreatment is *customer mistreatment*, which is in and of itself a workplace stressor that leads to negative outcomes (Sliter et al., 2010). While some of the contextual factors that are related with it have been covered above, there are some distinct contextual factors that are only relevant to occupations that involve extensive contact with clients or customers (or patients in healthcare settings). The type of service can involve contextual characteristics that can be relevant to mistreatment. For example, sexual harassment may be more prevalent in service roles where the environment is sexualized, such as restaurant servers who are required to wear revealing outfits. Furthermore, organizational policies such as

"The customer is always right," also referred to as high-pressure service climate, or management that denies customer misbehavior all promote putting up with customer abuse. These types of climates create a lack of accountability for the actions of customers, which they can discern. In such settings, where mistreatment can occur without consequences, it is more likely to occur (Gettman & Gelfand, 2007). Conversely, employees' sense of autonomy or control promotes feelings of empowerment in customer encounters, including aggressive ones, which buffers their perceived stress (Grandey et al., 2004). Similarly to high-pressure service climate, organizations characterized by a large power gap in favor of the customer puts customer representatives at more risk of mistreatment. This can happen when customer representatives are unskilled, young, or members of disadvantaged ethnic groups (as is often the case in some service jobs such as restaurant waiters and receptionists), or it can be a result of a commissions-based salary, which gives customers a great deal of power over employees (for review, see Yagil, 2008). Power gaps favoring customers are particularly relevant here, since harassment is often conceptualized as an outgrowth of power (Gettman & Gelfand, 2007).

In medical settings, employees interact with patients and patient family/friends. The context of many such encounters involves discomfort, emotional distress, and pain by patients that can contribute to mistreatment of healthcare workers. Beyond specific departments that were discussed earlier in this chapter, contextual factors such as procedures to check the patient's identity, prolonged waiting times and unavailability of a doctor, and even time passed since hospitalization all had effects on level of mistreatment (for review, see Hahn et al., 2008).

Virtual Harassment

Virtual harassment, or cyberbullying, is becoming increasingly prevalent with the proliferation of technological advancement in organizations and with individuals (e.g., the increasing prevalence of smart phones), and includes various forms of bullying: sexual harassment as well as other unwanted social exchanges. This is also evident by the increase of strategies/interventions to help organizations deal with cyber harassment (e.g., Piotrowski, 2012). Virtual harassment is influenced by some unique contextual factors. For example, non-sexual virtual harassment perpetrated by other employees is related with e-mail being required for the job, anonymity of the harasser (e.g., the harasser can create a fake e-mail account with a web-based e-mail company, and use a public computer) and media richness, which is the extent to which the medium, e-mail for example, is able to portray more than just words/text, and also emotions and contextual cues (Ford, 2013).

Workplace Stressors

Stressful work environments are associated with higher levels of victimization (Coyne, Smith-Lee Chong, Seigne, & Randall, 2003). Several specific stressors have received attention as factors related with mistreatment. Since almost all primary studies linking work stressors and mistreatment are typically cross-sectional, there is little direct evidence to indicate that stressors are the cause of mistreatment rather than the other way around, and, as mentioned earlier, mistreatment can be conceptualized as a stressor (Bowling & Beehr, 2006). Though most studies on workplace mistreatment used cross-sectional designs, there have been some studies that used temporal separation between the measurement of stressors and mistreatment. For example, one such study (Moreno-Jiménez, Rodríguez-Muñoz, Pastor, Sanz-Vergel, & Garrosa, 2009) showed relationships of two stressors – role conflict and workload, with workplace bullying that was measured a month later. Nevertheless, it is likely that, at least for some of the studied stressors, the process is bidirectional. One example is the "vicious cycle" portrayed in a recent five-wave study in which higher levels of stressors (organizational constraints) predicted subsequent increases in CWB, which subsequently predicted higher levels of experienced incivility as well as higher levels of the same initial stressor (Meier & Spector, 2013). Another relevant investigation was done by Coyne et al. (2003), who found that when bullying was both self and peer reported, bullying victims perceive the working environment to be more stressful (characterized more by negative aspects) than either the perpetrator or non-victims. Since this study was conducted on workgroups, which likely share the same work environment, it is likely that being a victim increases one's perception of the negative aspects of the working environment, as they are experiencing the additional stressor of mistreatment. However, experiencing high work strain is generally considered to have a negative impact on an employee's relationships with coworkers, and the social support they afford that employee (Marcelissen, Winnubst, Buunk, & de Wolff, 1988), which in turn relates to higher levels of mistreatment.

Agervold and Mikkelsen (2004) used a different approach to examine the direction of the relationship between the psychosocial work environment and bullying: after finding significant differences between bullied and non-bullied employees' in their ratings of various psychosocial factors (i.e., job control, management style, role clarity, social climate, social contact, and work centrality), and differences between departments with high, medium, or low levels of bullying, the ratings of the bullied employees were removed from the analysis, and the departments were compared again. With ratings from the bullied employees removed, departments only differed on rated job demands and management style. As a result, the authors called into question the importance of many work environment variables as causes of mistreatment. In a separate study of workgroups, organizational stress was more strongly related with being the target of aggression than of engaging in aggression (.40 and .26 respectively; Glomb & Liao, 2003), in line with the suggestion that mistreatment might be more of a stressor than it is a response to other work stressors. Both processes likely play a role in a negative mistreatment spiral.

Interpersonal Conflict

Interpersonal conflict between coworkers has a unique relevance to mistreatment, because mistreatment is conceptualized in a social context. Furthermore, when interpersonal conflict is concerned, it becomes harder to separate contextual stressor from mistreatment response, because the mistreatment that occurs many times fits the definition of social stressors such as interpersonal conflict, not only for the victim of mistreatment: "if social stressors occur in a department, almost everybody will be negatively affected after some time" (Zapf et al., 1996, p. 217). Interpersonal conflict can trigger a spiral of increasingly intensive expressions of aggression when employees reciprocate incivility they receive (a violation of the social norm of respect) by more severe behaviors they exhibit toward others (Andersson & Pearson, 1999; Hershcovis et al., 2007). Complimenting these findings, support from coworkers is related with lower levels of bullying and social isolation (Balducci, Fraccaroli, & Schaufeli, 2011). Mistreatment that taps social stressors, such as socially isolating someone or not sharing relevant information with him or her, makes it harder for that person to do his or her job and contributes to additional role stress (Hauge, Skogstad et al., 2011).

Organizational Justice

Early in the chapter, when discussing mistreatment as a stressor, we noted the case of abusive supervision, which is often facilitated by organizational injustice (Aryee et al., 2007; Tepper et al., 2006). In this section we discuss the direct effects of injustice on employees. In their meta-analysis, Berry et al. (2007) found that organizational justice (the perceived fairness of outcomes, procedures used to arrive at outcome, and interpersonal treatment of employees) was correlated with mistreatment (conceptualized as interpersonal deviance targeted toward individuals, e.g., violence, gossip, and theft from coworkers) at an absolute value of about .20 for most subcategories of organizational justice (with the exception of distributive justice, which had a lower correlation). These results were largely replicated by Colquitt et al. (2013). Previous meta-analyses (Bowling & Beehr, 2006; Cohen-Charash & Spector, 2001; Colquitt, Conlon, Wesson, Porter, & Ng, 2001) found stronger correlations, typically over .30, between organizational justice and deviant behaviors/harassment. While it is hard to determine the direction of effects, it is evident that in workplaces that are characterized by low levels of interactional/interpersonal/procedural justice, mistreatment abounds. Hershcovis et al. (2007) found similar results with injustice, but found that interpersonal conflict and situational constraints as the strongest situational predictors of interpersonal targeted aggression. Their framework focused on target specificity, and their results showed that poor leadership and interpersonal injustice were stronger predictors of supervisor-targeted aggression than of coworker-targeted aggression. Future use of scales that differentiate between targets of aggression may uncover other cases of target specificity of aggression as retaliation for situational factors.

Organizational justice also plays a moderating role in facilitating or inhibiting forgiveness/vengeance in response to unfair events. Specifically, perceived organizational justice both facilitated the constructive response of forgiveness in employees who have a strong other orientation, and suppressed the destructive response of revenge in employees who have a strong self-concern. In this study, vengeance included both reports of "getting even with the offender" and "wanting to see the offender hurt," so both enacted revenge and thoughts of revenge were included (Bobocel, 2013).

Control

Control over the job has been related with reports of bullying and mobbing in several studies (Einarsen et al., 1994; Zapf et al., 1996). In their meta-analysis, Bowling and Beehr (2006) found a significant relationship between autonomy (which is operationalized similarly to control) and harassment/bullying.

Organizational Constraints
Of all the work stressors included in Bowling and Beehr's (2006) meta-analysis, organizational constraints (also known as situational constrains, work constraints, or constraints on performance) had the strongest relationship with mistreatment, with an average correlation of .44. While organizational constraints where conceptualized as constraining performance, a recent meta-analysis (Pindek & Spector, 2014, unpublished) suggests that workers overcome these obstacles in terms of their levels of task performance, and instead "lash out" and engage in CWBs. The process has been described such that constraints interfere with employees' performance goals, and those employees consequently experience negative emotions such as frustration and act out in an aggressive manner.

Role Stressors
Several role stressors have also been linked to mistreatment, the most prominent ones being *role conflict* (Einarsen et al., 1994; Skogstad et al., 2007) and *role ambiguity* (Agervold & Mikkelsen, 2004). Role conflict, ambiguity, and *overload* were all related to harassment in a meta-analysis (Bowling & Beehr, 2006). Einarsen et al. (1994) suggested that stressors that can be attributed more easily to poor relationships will likely be more strongly related with various forms of mistreatment. Specifically, interpersonal conflict may more readily arise from role conflict than from role ambiguity. Interpersonal conflict is sometimes considered a form of mistreatment, or, alternatively, is a lush ground for bullying and harassment to occur. Furthermore, at the group level, role conflict was significantly related to bullying whereas role ambiguity was not. This held true for observing workplace bullying, and not only for being on the receiving end (Hauge, Einarsen et al., 2011; Skogstad et al., 2011).

Hauge, Skogstad et al. (2011) argued that role pressure can be manifested in behaviors that overlap with some forms of bullying behavior. These behaviors are repeatedly inflicted on an employee in order to signal them to comply with performance expectations, and are either perceived as functional and legitimate signals or as bullying. If the initial pressure toward performance change does not result in the expected changes, aggressors may increase the frequency and levels of those signals or even apply negative sanctions toward the target employee. Thus, Hauge, Skogstad et al. (2011) argued that role pressure and bullying would be intertwined, with role pressure increasing and overlapping more with bullying, which further increases the experienced role stress. However, their results only supported the effects of bullying on role stress, and not the effects of role stress on reported bullying. Nonetheless they maintained that when employees do not comply with role pressure, it may lead to increased role pressure, and that the mechanism involves certain forms of bullying behaviors. This, however, is not necessarily restricted to the same person who experienced the initial pressure. Other employees, who are experiencing high levels of work stress, may become aggressors by projecting their negative emotions onto a "scapegoat." Such an explanation points to a causal stressor–mistreatment relationship at the group level, while research findings indicate that at the individual level, there is also support for the causal mistreatment–stressor relationship (e.g., Hauge, Skogstad et al., 2011; Meier & Spector, 2013).

SUMMARY AND FUTURE DIRECTIONS

This chapter suggests a framework for the effects of contextual factors on both perpetrating and becoming the victim of mistreatment. We conceptualized contextual factors as having a shared aspect, which most likely represents an objective element in the workplace, and an individually perceived aspect. The perceived part can (but does not necessarily) mediate the effects of the objective part on mistreatment; the objective context can have a direct effect on mistreatment. In addition, objective context moderates the effects of individual level variables (both context and personality) on mistreatment. A high prevalence of mistreatment would, in turn, contribute to higher levels of stressors, and less conducive climates.

Though this framework somewhat resembles previously suggested models (e.g., Frese & Zapf, 1988), it highlights the usefulness of multi-level designs in separating the objective portion from the individually perceived portion. This will allow us to see more complicated relationships between context and mistreatment. Most mistreatment studies have been conducted at the individual level, and more research is needed to fill the gap. A multilevel approach would also help researchers to generalize their findings to observers/bystanders and not just the victims of mistreatment, establishing an even greater importance for the subject.

Furthermore, there is a dearth of multi-level longitudinal studies. Intervention studies may also be used to establish the direction of effects and to exhibit how changes made to the environment can affect levels of mistreatment. Intervention suggestions that have been made include, among other things, policies regarding cash-handling, physical separation between workers and customers, good lighting (Rai, 2002); fostering shared responsibility and positive group norms (Hutchinson, 2009), but very few intervention studies have used proper experimental designs that alter the environment and examine the effects on mistreatment.

The literature we have reviewed clearly shows a link between organizational context and mistreatment. As noted, the over-reliance on cross-sectional designs has limited our ability to draw conclusions about direction of effects. The over-reliance on individual-level employee self-reports has limited our ability to draw conclusions about the work environment independent of idiosyncratic perception. Nevertheless, existing evidence suggests that context is an important element in employee mistreatment from both an actor and target perspective. Continued research can help us better understand the role of the environment, the direction of effects, and the sorts of interventions that can be effective in reducing this important workplace hazard that can result in both physical and psychological harm to employees.

REFERENCES

Agervold, M., & Mikkelsen, E. G. (2004). Relationships between bullying, psychosocial work environment and individual stress reactions. *Work & Stress*, *18*(4), 336–351. doi:10.1080/02678370412331319794

Andersson, L. M., & Pearson, C. M. (1999). Tit for tat? The spiraling effect of incivility in the workplace. *Academy of Management Review*, *24*(3), 452–471. doi:10.5465/AMR.1999.2202131

Aquino, K., & Lamertz, K. (2004). A relational model of workplace victimization: Social roles and patterns of victimization in dyadic relationships. *Journal of Applied Psychology*, *89*(6), 1023–1034. doi:10.1037/0021-9010.89.6.1023

Aquino, K., & Thau, S. (2009). Workplace victimization: Aggression from the target's perspective. *Annual Review of Psychology*, *60*(1), 717–741. doi:10.1146/annurev.psych.60.110707.163703

Aryee, S., Chen, Z. X., Sun, L.-Y., & Debrah, Y. A. (2007). Antecedents and outcomes of abusive supervision: Test of a trickle-down model. *Journal of Applied Psychology*, *92*(1), 191–201. doi:10.1037/0021-9010.92.1.191

Baillien, E., Neyens, I., & De Witte, H. (2011). Organizational correlates of workplace bullying in small- and medium-sized enterprises. *International Small Business Journal*, *29*(6), 610–625. doi:10.1177/0266242610375774

Balducci, C., Cecchin, M., & Fraccaroli, F. (2012). The impact of role stressors on workplace bullying in both victims and perpetrators, controlling for personal vulnerability factors: A longitudinal analysis. *Work & Stress*, *26*(3), 195–212. doi:10.1080/02678373.2012.714543

Balducci, C., Fraccaroli, F., & Schaufeli, W. B. (2011). Workplace bullying and its relation with work characteristics, personality, and post-traumatic stress symptoms: An integrated model. *Anxiety, Stress, & Coping*, *24*(5), 499–513. doi:10.1080/10615806.2011.555533

Bartlett, J. E., & Bartlett, M. E. (2011). Workplace bullying: An integrative literature review. *Advances in Developing Human Resources*, *13*(1), 69–84. doi:10.1177/1523422311410651

Berry, C. M., Ones, D. S., & Sackett, P. R. (2007). Interpersonal deviance, organizational deviance, and their common correlates: A review and meta-analysis. *Journal of Applied Psychology*, *92*(2), 410–424. doi:10.1037/0021-9010.92.2.410

Bies, R. J., & Tripp, T. M. (2005). The study of revenge in the workplace: Conceptual, ideological, and empirical issues. In S. F. P. E. Spector (Ed.), *Counterproductive work behavior: Investigations of actors and targets* (pp. 65–81). Washington, DC: American Psychological Association.

Bobocel, D. R. (2013). Coping with unfair events constructively or destructively: The effects of overall justice and self–other orientation. *Journal of Applied Psychology*, *98*(5), 720–731. doi:10.1037/a0032857

Bowling, N. A., & Beehr, T. A. (2006). Workplace harassment from the victim's perspective: A theoretical model and meta-analysis. *Journal of Applied Psychology*, *91*(5), 998–1012. doi:10.1037/0021-9010.91.5.998

Bowling, N. A., Camus, K. A., & Blackmore, C. E. (2015). Conceptualizing and measuring workplace abuse: Implications for the study of abuse's predictors and consequences. In P. L. Perrewé, C. C. Rosen & J. R. B. Halbesleben (Eds.), *Mistreatment in organizations* (Vol. 13). Research in Occupational Stress and Well Being. Bingley, UK: Emerald Group Publishing Limited.

Bulutlar, F., & Öz, E. (2009). The effects of ethical climates on bullying behaviour in the workplace. *Journal of Business Ethics*, *86*(3), 273–295. doi:10.1007/s10551-008-9847-4

Chang, C.-H., Eatough, E. M., Spector, P. E., & Kessler, S. R. (2012). Violence-prevention climate, exposure to violence and aggression, and prevention behavior: A mediation model. *Journal of Organizational Behavior*, *33*(5), 657–677. Retrieved from http://dx.doi.org/10.1002/job.776

Chen, C.-C., Chen, M. Y.-C., & Liu, Y.-C. (2013). Negative affectivity and workplace deviance: The moderating role of ethical climate. *The International Journal of Human Resource Management*, *24*(15), 2894–2910. doi:10.1080/09585192.2012.753550

Coch, L., & French, J. R. (1948). Overcoming resistance to change. *Human Relations*, *1*, 512–532. Retrieved from http://dx.doi.org/10.1177/001872674800100408

Cohen, D., & Nisbett, R. E. (1997). Field experiments examining the culture of honor: The role of institutions in perpetuating norms about violence. *Personality and Social Psychology Bulletin*, *23*, 1188–1199. doi:10.1177/01461672972311006

Cohen-Charash, Y., & Spector, P. E. (2001). The role of justice in organizations: A meta-analysis. *Organizational Behavior and Human Decision Processes*, *86*(2), 278–321. doi:10.1006/obhd.2001.2958

Colquitt, J. A., Conlon, D. E., Wesson, M. J., Porter, C. O., & Ng, K. Y. (2001). Justice at the millennium: A meta-analytic review of 25 years of organizational justice research. *Journal of Applied Psychology*, *86*(3), 425–445. doi:10.1037/0021-9010.86.3.425

Colquitt, J. A., Scott, B. A., Rodell, J. B., Long, D. M., Zapata, C. P., Conlon, D. E., & Wesson, M. J. (2013). Justice at the millennium, a decade later: A meta-analytic test of social exchange and affect-based perspectives. *Journal of Applied Psychology*, *98*(2), 199–236. doi:10.1037/a0031757

Cowie, H., Naylor, P., Rivers, I., Smith, P. K., & Pereira, B. (2002). Measuring workplace bullying. *Aggression and Violent Behavior*, *7*(1), 33–51. doi:10.1016/S1359-1789(00)00034-3

Coyne, I., Smith-Lee Chong, P., Seigne, E., & Randall, P. (2003). Self and peer nominations of bullying: An analysis of incident rates, individual differences, and perceptions of the working environment. *European Journal of Work and Organizational Psychology*, *12*(3), 209–228. doi:10.1080/13594320344000101

Dietz, J., Robinson, S. L., Folger, R., Baron, R. A., & Schulz, M. (2003). The impact of community violence and an organization's procedural justice climate on workplace aggression. *Academy of Management Journal*, *46*(3), 317–326. doi:10.2307/30040625

Dragoni, L. (2005). Understanding the emergence of state goal orientation in organizational work groups: The role of leadership and multilevel climate perceptions. *Journal of Applied Psychology*, *90*(6), 1084–1095. doi:10.1037/0021-9010.90.6.1084

Einarsen, S., Raknes, B. r. I., & Matthiesen, S. B. (1994). Bullying and harassment at work and their relationships to work environment quality: An exploratory study. *European Work and Organizational Psychologist*, *4*(4), 381–401. doi:10.1080/13594329408410497

Einarsen, S., & Skogstad, A. (1996). Bullying at work: Epidemiological findings in public and private organizations. *European Journal of Work and Organizational Psychology*, *5*(2), 185–201. doi:10.1080/13594329608414854

Feldman, D. C. (1984). The development and enforcement of group norms. *Academy of Management Review*, *9*(1), 47–53. doi:10.5465/amr.1984.4277934

Ford, D. P. (2013). Virtual harassment: Media characteristics' role in psychological health. *Journal of Managerial Psychology*, *28*(4), 408–428. doi:10.1108/JMP-12-2012-0398

Frese, M., & Zapf, D. (1988). Methodological issues in the study of work stress: Objective vs subjective measurement of work stress and the question of longitudinal studies. In C. L. Cooper & R. Payne (Eds.), *Causes, coping and consequences of stress at work* (pp. 375–411). Chichester: John Wiley & Sons.

Gettman, H. J., & Gelfand, M. J. (2007). When the customer shouldn't be king: Antecedents and consequences of sexual harassment by clients and customers. *Journal of Applied Psychology*, *92*(3), 757–770.

Giorgi, G. (2010). Workplace bullying partially mediates the climate-health relationship. *Journal of Managerial Psychology*, *25*(7), 727–740. doi:10.1108/02683941011075274

Glomb, T. M., & Liao, H. (2003). Interpersonal aggression in work groups: Social influence, reciprocal, and individual effects. *Academy of Management Journal*, *46*(4), 486–496. doi:10.2307/30040640

Grandey, A. A., Dickter, D. N., & Sin, H.-P. (2004). The customer is not always right: Customer aggression and emotion regulation of service employees. *Journal of Organizational Behavior*, *25*(3), 397–418. doi:10.1002/job.252

Griffin, B. (2010). Multilevel relationships between organizational-level incivility, justice and intention to stay. *Work & Stress*, *24*(4), 309–323. doi:10.1080/02678373.2010.531186

Hahn, S., Zeller, A., Needham, I., Kok, G., Dassen, T., & Halfens, R. J. G. (2008). Patient and visitor violence in general hospitals: A systematic review of the literature. *Aggression and Violent Behavior*, *13*(6), 431–441. Retrieved from http://dx.doi.org/10.1016/j.avb.2008.07.001

Hauge, L. J., Einarsen, S., Knardahl, S., Lau, B., Notelaers, G., & Skogstad, A. (2011). Leadership and role stressors as departmental level predictors of workplace bullying. *International Journal of Stress Management*, *18*(4), 305–323. doi:10.1037/a0025396

Hauge, L. J., Skogstad, A., & Einarsen, S. (2011). Role stressors and exposure to workplace bullying: Causes or consequences of what and why? *European Journal of Work and Organizational Psychology*, *20*(5), 610–630. doi:10.1080/1359432X.2010.482264

Heames, J., & Harvey, M. (2006). Workplace bullying: A cross-level assessment. *Management Decision*, *44*(9), 1214–1230. doi:10.1108/00251740610707695

Hershcovis, M. S. (2011). "Incivility, social undermining, bullying … oh my!": A call to reconcile constructs within workplace aggression research. *Journal of Organizational Behavior*, *32*(3), 499–519. doi:10.1002/job.689

Hershcovis, M. S., & Reich, T. C. (2013). Integrating workplace aggression research: Relational, contextual, and method considerations. *Journal of Organizational Behavior*, *34*(S1), S26–S42. doi:10.1002/job.1886

Hershcovis, M. S., Turner, N., Barling, J., Arnold, K. A., Dupré, K. E., Inness, M., … Sivanathan, N. (2007). Predicting workplace aggression: A meta-analysis. *Journal of Applied Psychology*, *92*(1), 228–238. doi:10.1037/0021-9010.92.1.228

Hubert, A. B., & van Veldhoven, M. (2001). Risk sectors for undesirable behaviour and mobbing. *European Journal of Work and Organizational Psychology*, *10*(4), 415–424. doi:10.1080/13594320143000799

Hutchinson, M. (2009). Restorative approaches to workplace bullying: Educating nurses towards shared responsibility. *Contemporary Nurse*, *32*(1–2), 147–155. doi:10.5172/conu.32.1-2.147

Hutchinson, M., Jackson, D., Wilkes, L., & Vickers, M. H. (2008). A new model of bullying in the nursing workplace: Organizational characteristics as critical antecedents. *Advances in Nursing Science Violence, Injury, and Human Safety April/June*, *31*(2), E60–E71.

Hutchinson, M., Wilkes, L., Jackson, D., & Vickers, M. H. (2010). Integrating individual, work group and organizational factors: Testing a multidimensional model of bullying in the nursing workplace. *Journal of Nursing Management*, *18*(2), 173–181. doi:10.1111/j.1365-2834.2009.01035.x

Kaukiainen, A., Salmivalli, C., Björkqvist, K., Österman, K., Lahtinen, A., Kostamo, A., & Lagerspetz, K. (2001). Overt and covert aggression in work settings in relation to the subjective well-being of employees. *Aggressive Behavior*, *27*(5), 360–371. doi:10.1002/ab.1021

Kernan, M. C., Watson, S., Chen, F. F., & Kim, T. G. (2011). How cultural values affect the impact of abusive supervision on worker attitudes. *Cross Cultural Management: An International Journal*, *18*(4), 464–484. doi:10.1108/13527601111179528

Kessler, S. R., Spector, P. E., Chang, C.-H., & Parr, A. D. (2008). Organizational violence and aggression: Development of the three-factor violence climate survey. *Work & Stress*, *22*(2), 108–124. doi:10.1080/02678370802187926

Kozlowski, S. W., & Doherty, M. L. (1989). Integration of climate and leadership: Examination of a neglected issue. *Journal of Applied Psychology*, *74*(4), 546–553. doi:10.1037/0021-9010.74.4.546

Law, R., Dollard, M. F., Tuckey, M. R., & Dormann, C. (2011). Psychosocial safety climate as a lead indicator of workplace bullying and harassment, job resources, psychological health and employee engagement. *Accident Analysis & Prevention*, *43*(5), 1782–1793. doi:10.1016/j.aap.2011.04.010

Marcelissen, F. H. G., Winnubst, J. A. M., Buunk, B., & de Wolff, C. J. (1988). Social support and occupational stress: A causal analysis. *Social Science & Medicine*, *26*(3), 365–373. doi:10.1016/0277-9536(88)90402-9

Meglich-Sespico, P., Faley, R., & Knapp, D. (2007). Relief and redress for targets of workplace bullying. *Employee Responsibilities and Rights Journal, 19*(1), 31–43. doi:10.1007/s10672-006-9030-y

Meier, L. L., & Spector, P. E. (2013). Reciprocal effects of work stressors and counterproductive work behavior: A five-wave longitudinal study. *Journal of Applied Psychology, 98*(3), 529–539. doi:10.1037/a0031732

Mikkelsen, E. G., & Einarsen, S. (2001). Bullying in Danish work-life: Prevalence and health correlates. *European Journal of Work and Organizational Psychology, 10*(4), 393–413. doi:10.1080/13594320143000816

Miner-Rubino, K., & Cortina, L. M. (2007). Beyond targets: Consequences of vicarious exposure to misogyny at work. *Journal of Applied Psychology, 92*(5), 1254–1269. doi:10.1037/0021-9010.92.5.1254

Moreno-Jiménez, B., Rodríguez-Muñoz, A., Pastor, J. C., Sanz-Vergel, A. I., & Garrosa, E. (2009). The moderating effects of psychological detachment and thoughts of revenge in workplace bullying. *Personality and Individual Differences, 46*(3), 359–364. doi:10.1016/j.paid.2008.10.031

Ottinot, R. C. (2008). *The development and validation of the perceived workplace civility climate scale*. Master's thesis, University of South Florida, Tampa. Retrieved from http://scholarcommons.usf.edu/etd/439/

Ottinot, R. C. (2011). A multi-level study investigating the impact of workplace civility climate on incivility and employee well-being. *Dissertation Abstracts International: Section B: The Sciences and Engineering, 72*(2-B), 1149.

Pearson, C. M., Andersson, L. M., & Porath, C. L. (2005). Workplace incivility. In S. Fox & P. E. Spector (Eds.), *Counterproductive work behavior: Investigations of actors and targets* (pp. 177–200). Washington, DC: American Psychological Association.

Pearson, C. M., & Porath, C. L. (2005). On the nature, consequences and remedies of workplace incivility: No time for "Nice"? Think again. *The Academy of Management Executive (1993–2005), 19*(1), 7–18. doi:10.2307/4166149

Peterson, D. K. (2002). Deviant workplace behavior and the organization's ethical climate. *Journal of Business and Psychology, 17*(1), 47–61. doi:10.1023/A:1016296116093

Pindek, S., & Spector, P. E. (2014). *Organizational constraints: A meta-analysis of a major stressor*. Unpublished, University of South Florida.

Piotrowski, C. (2012). From workplace bullying to cyberbullying: The enigma of e-harassment in modern organizations. *Organization Development Journal, 30*(4), 44–53.

Rai, S. (2002). Preventing workplace aggression and violence – A role for occupational therapy. *Work: A Journal of Prevention, Assessment and Rehabilitation, 18*(1), 15–22.

Rayner, C., & Keashly, L. (2005). Bullying at work: A perspective from Britain and North America. In S. Fox & P. E. Spector (Eds.), *Counterproductive work behavior: Investigations of actors and targets*. (pp. 271–296). Washington, DC: American Psychological Association.

Robinson, S. L., & O'Leary-Kelly, A. M. (1998). Monkey see, monkey do: The influence of work groups on the antisocial behavior of employees. *Academy of Management Journal, 41*(6), 658–672. doi:10.2307/256963

Roscigno, V. J., Lopez, S. H., & Hodson, R. (2009). Supervisory bullying, status inequalities and organizational context. *Social Forces, 87*(3), 1561–1589. doi:10.1353/sof.0.0178

Salin, D. (2001). Prevalence and forms of bullying among business professionals: A comparison of two different strategies for measuring bullying. *European Journal of Work and Organizational Psychology*, *10*(4), 425–441. doi:10.1080/13594320143000771

Schat, A. C. H., & Kelloway, E. K. (2005). Workplace aggression. In J. Barling, E. K. Kelloway, & M. R. Frone (Eds.), *Handbook of work stress* (pp. 189–218). Thousand Oaks, CA: Sage.

Semmer, N., Zapf, D., & Greif, S. (1996). 'Shared job strain': A new approach for assessing the validity of job stress measurements. *Journal of occupational and organizational psychology*, *69*(3), 293–310. doi:10.1111/j.2044-8325.1996.tb00616.x

Skarlicki, D. P., & Folger, R. (1997). Retaliation in the workplace: The roles of distributive, procedural, and interactional justice. *Journal of Applied Psychology*, *82*(3), 434–443.

Skogstad, A., Einarsen, S., Torsheim, T., Aasland, M. S., & Hetland, H. (2007). The destructiveness of laissez-faire leadership behavior. *Journal of Occupational Health Psychology*, *12*(1), 80–92. doi:10.1037/1076-8998.12.1.80

Skogstad, A., Torsheim, T., Einarsen, S., & Hauge, L. J. (2011). Testing the work environment hypothesis of bullying on a group level of analysis: Psychosocial factors as precursors of observed workplace bullying. *Applied Psychology: An International Review*, *60*(3), 475–495. doi:10.1111/j.1464-0597.2011.00444.x

Sliter, M. T., Jex, S., Wolford, K., & McInnerney, J. (2010). How rude! Emotional labor as a mediator between customer incivility and employee outcomes. *Journal of Occupational Health Psychology*, *15*(4), 468–481. doi:10.1037/a0020723

Sliter, M. T., Pui, S. Y., Sliter, K. A., & Jex, S. M. (2011). The differential effects of interpersonal conflict from customers and coworkers: Trait anger as a moderator. *Journal of Occupational Health Psychology*, *16*(4), 424–440. doi:10.1037/a0023874

Sliter, M. T., Sliter, K. A., & Jex, S. (2012). The employee as a punching bag: The effect of multiple sources of incivility on employee withdrawal behavior and sales performance. *Journal of Organizational Behavior*, *33*(1), 121–139. doi:10.1002/job.767

Spector, P. E., Coulter, M. L., Stockwell, H. G., & Matz, M. W. (2007). Perceived violence climate: A new construct and its relationship to workplace physical violence and verbal aggression, and their potential consequences. *Work & Stress*, *21*(2), 117–130. doi:10.1080/02678370701410007

Spector, P. E., & Fox, S. (2005). The stressor-emotion model of counterproductive work behavior. In S. Fox & P. E. Spector (Eds.), *Counterproductive work behavior: Investigations of actors and targets* (pp. 151–174). Washington, DC: American Psychological Association.

Spector, P. E., & Jex, S. M. (1998). Development of four self-report measures of job stressors and strain: Interpersonal conflict at work scale, organizational constraints scale, quantitative workload inventory, and physical symptoms inventory. *Journal of Occupational Health Psychology*, *3*(4), 356–367. doi:10.1037/1076-8998.3.4.356

Spector, P. E., & Zhou, Z. E. (2013). The moderating role of gender in relationships of stressors and personality with counterproductive work behavior. *Journal of Business and Psychology*, 1–13. doi:10.1007/s10869-013-9307-8

Spector, P. E., Zhou, Z. E., & Che, X. X. (2014). Nurse exposure to physical and nonphysical violence, bullying, and sexual harassment: A quantitative review. *International Journal of Nursing Studies*, *51*(1), 72–84. Retrieved from http://dx.doi.org/10.1016/j.ijnurstu.2013.01.010

Spector, P. E., Zhou, Z. E., & Yang, L.-Q. (2013). A longitudinal study of the link between climate and workplace violence. Paper presented at the Southern Management Association, New Orleans.

Sprung, J. M., & Jex, S. M. (2012). Work locus of control as a moderator of the relationship between work stressors and counterproductive work behavior. *International Journal of Stress Management, 19*(4), 272–291. doi:10.1037/a0030320

Taylor, S. G., & Kluemper, D. H. (2012). Linking perceptions of role stress and incivility to workplace aggression: The moderating role of personality. *Journal of Occupational Health Psychology, 17*(3), 316–329. doi:10.1037/a0028211

Tepper, B. J. (2000). Consequences of abusive supervision. *Academy of Management Journal, 43*(2), 178–190. Retrieved from http://dx.doi.org/10.2307/1556375

Tepper, B. J. (2007). Abusive supervision in work organizations: Review, synthesis, and research agenda. *Journal of Management, 33*(3), 261–289. doi:10.1177/0149206307300812

Tepper, B. J., Duffy, M. K., Henle, C. A., & Lambert, L. S. (2006). Procedural injustice, victim precipitation, and abusive supervision. *Personnel Psychology, 59*(1), 101–123. doi:10.1111/j.1744-6570.2006.00725.x

Tucker, J. S., Sinclair, R. R., & Thomas, J. L. (2005). The multilevel effects of occupational stressors on soldiers' well-being, organizational attachment, and readiness. *Journal of Occupational Health Psychology, 10*(3), 276–299. doi:10.1037/1076-8998.10.3.276

Vandello, J. A., Cohen, D., & Ransom, S. (2008). U.S. Southern and Northern differences in perceptions of norms about aggression: Mechanisms for the perpetuation of a culture of honor. *Journal of Cross-Cultural Psychology, 39*(2), 162–177. doi:10.1177/0022022107313862

Vartia, M. (1996). The sources of bullying–psychological work environment and organizational climate. *European Journal of Work and Organizational Psychology, 5*(2), 203–214. doi:10.1080/13594329608414855

Vartia, M. (2001). Consequences of workplace bullying with respect to the well-being of its targets and the observers of bullying. *Scandinavian Journal of Work, Environment & Health, 27*(1), 63–69. doi:10.5271/sjweh.588

Wei, C., Gerberich, S. G., Alexander, B. H., Ryan, A. D., Nachreiner, N. M., & Mongin, S. J. (2013). Work-related violence against educators in Minnesota: Rates and risks based on hours exposed. *Journal of Safety Research, 44*, 73–85. doi:10.1016/j.jsr.2012.12.005

Yagil, D. (2008). When the customer is wrong: A review of research on aggression and sexual harassment in service encounters. *Aggression and Violent Behavior, 13*(2), 141–152. doi:10.1016/j.avb.2008.03.002

Yang, J., & Diefendorff, J. M. (2009). The relations of daily counterproductive workplace behavior with emotions, situational antecedents, and personality moderators: A diary study in Hong Kong. *Personnel Psychology, 62*(2), 259–295. doi:10.1111/j.1744-6570.2009.01138.x

Yang, L.-Q., Caughlin, D. E., Gazica, M. W., Truxillo, D. M., & Spector, P. E. (2014, May). Workplace mistreatment climate and potential taarget outcomes: A meta-analysis. Paper presented at the Society for Industrial and Organizational Psychology, Honolulu, Hawaii.

Yang, L.-Q., Spector, P. E., Chang, C.-H., Gallant-Roman, M., & Powell, J. (2012). Psychosocial precursors and physical consequences of workplace violence towards nurses: A longitudinal examination with naturally occurring groups in hospital settings.

International Journal of Nursing Studies, *49*(9), 1091–1102. Retrieved from http://dx.doi.org/10.1016/j.ijnurstu.2012.03.006

Zapf, D., Knorz, C., & Kulla, M. (1996). On the relationship between mobbing factors, and job content, social work environment, and health outcomes. *European Journal of Work and Organizational Psychology*, *5*(2), 215–237. doi:10.1080/13594329608414856

Zhou, Z. E., Meier, L. L., & Spector, P. E. (in press). The role of personality and job stressors in predicting counterproductive work behavior: A three-way interaction. *International Journal of Selection and Assessment*.

Zhou, Z. E., Yan, Y., Che, X. X., & Meier, L. L. (in press). Effect of workplace incivility on end-of-work negative affect: Examining individual and organizational moderators in a daily diary study. *Journal of Occupational Health Psychology*.

Zohar, D. (2000). A group-level model of safety climate: Testing the effect of group climate on microaccidents in manufacturing jobs. *Journal of Applied Psychology*, *85*(4), 587–596. doi:10.1037/0021-9010.85.4.587

CONCEPTUALIZING AND MEASURING WORKPLACE ABUSE: IMPLICATIONS FOR THE STUDY OF ABUSE'S PREDICTORS AND CONSEQUENCES

Nathan A. Bowling, Kelly A. Camus and Caitlin E. Blackmore

ABSTRACT

Workplace abuse, interpersonal mistreatment that occurs within the victim's work environment, has attracted considerable attention in recent years. In this chapter, we argue that problems with the conceptualization and measurement of workplace abuse have thwarted scientific progress. We identify two needs that we believe are especially pressing: (a) the need to consider the construct breadth of workplace abuse scales and (b) the need to test whether the measures of various types of workplace abuse effectively capture the unique qualities of the constructs they purport to assess. To guide our discussion of these issues, we conducted a review of the item content of several workplace abuse measures. We offer suggestions for addressing these and other conceptualization and

Mistreatment in Organizations
Research in Occupational Stress and Well Being, Volume 13, 225–263

ISSN: 1479-3555/doi:10.1108/S1479-355520150000013008

measurement issues, and we discuss the possible implications of these issues on the study of the hypothesized predictors and consequences of workplace abuse.

Keywords: Workplace abuse; workplace aggression; workplace mistreatment; workplace deviance; counterproductive work behavior

Workplace abuse – negative interpersonal treatment that one experiences within the context of the work environment – is harmful to the well-being of both victims and their employers (Aquino & Thau, 2009; Bowling & Beehr, 2006; Fox & Spector, 2005). Given its practical and theoretical relevance, it is of little surprise that a growing body of research, much of which has been published since 2000, has examined workplace abuse (see Neall & Tuckey, 2014). In this chapter, we first provide a definition of the term "workplace abuse" and we review research on the hypothesized predictors and consequences of workplace abuse. We then identify problems with how workplace abuse has been conceptualized and measured, with particular emphasis on the implications those problems have for the study of workplace abuse's predictors and consequences. To guide this discussion, we conducted a review of the item content of several workplace abuse measures.

DEFINING "WORKPLACE ABUSE"

In this chapter, we conceptualize "workplace abuse" as an inclusive construct. It includes both physical and non-physical mistreatment, both active and passive mistreatment, and it includes mistreatment perpetrated by various people encountered within the workplace – the victim's supervisors, coworkers, subordinates, and customers, for instance. Several researchers have previously used umbrella terms to encompass various forms of workplace abuse. Hershcovis (2011), for instance, referred to "workplace aggression"; Bowling and Beehr (2006) referred to "workplace harassment"; Cortina and Marchiondo (2012) referred to "interpersonal mistreatment"; and Aquino and Thau (2009) referred to "workplace victimization."

We regard each of these umbrella terms as identical to what we refer to as "workplace abuse."

Most studies, however, have not assessed broad conceptualizations of workplace abuse. Instead, several ostensibly distinct – and more specific – forms of abusive work behavior appear in the literature: "abusive supervision" (Tepper, 2000), "bullying" (Einarsen, 2000), "incivility" (Andersson & Pearson, 1999), "interpersonal conflict" (Spector & Jex, 1998), "interpersonal deviance" (Bennett & Robinson, 2000), "mobbing" (Leymann, 1996), "petty tyranny" (Ashforth, 1994), "social undermining" (Duffy, Ganster, & Pagon, 2002), and "violence" (Rogers & Kelloway, 1997). Our use of umbrella terminology, however, is not intended to imply that all forms of abuse are interchangeable. Instead, we use the term "workplace abuse" in much the same way organizational researchers have used the term "job attitudes." Specific job attitudes (e.g., job satisfaction and organizational commitment) are related, yet conceptually and empirically distinct from each other (Mathieu & Farr, 1991). We suspect that the same is true of specific forms of workplace abuse – that they are distinct from each other – and thus we use the term "workplace abuse" to refer to a general research topic rather than to a particular variable.

Before continuing further, we acknowledge two complementary perspectives found within the workplace abuse literature: *the perpetrator's perspective* and *the victim's perspective* (see Cortina & Marchiondo, 2012; Fox & Spector, 2005; Hershcovis, 2011). Researchers taking the perpetrator's perspective assess the extent to which research participants have *engaged* in abusive behavior, whereas researchers taking the victim's perspective assess the extent to which research participants have been the *targets* of abusive behavior. This chapter considers both perspectives.

HYPOTHESIZED PREDICTORS OF WORKPLACE ABUSE

A large body of research has examined the potential predictors of workplace abuse (see Aquino & Thau, 2009; Bowling & Beehr, 2006; Neall & Tuckey, 2014). These predictors can be organized into three general categories: (a) characteristics of the work environment, (b) characteristics of perpetrators, and (c) characteristics of victims. We discuss each of these predictor categories below.

Characteristics of the Work Environment

Workers who report being the victims of abuse tend to also describe their work environments as having other negative qualities (Bowling & Beehr, 2006; Einarsen, Raknes & Matthiesen, 1994; Reknes, Einarsen, Knardahl, & Lau, 2014). A meta-analysis by Bowling and Beehr (2006), for instance, found that workers who reported being the victims of abuse generally reported high levels of role ambiguity (ρ = .30), role conflict (ρ = .44), role overload (ρ = .28), and organizational constraints (ρ = .53), as well as low levels of job autonomy (ρ = −.25).

Several explanations exist for these relationships. First, researchers have suggested that negative features in one's work environment can *cause* one to experience workplace abuse (Einarsen et al., 1994; Leymann, 1996; Reknes et al., 2014). Exposure to work stressors (e.g., role ambiguity and role conflict), for instance, may cause workers to engage in behaviors that provoke subsequent abuse. Alternatively, exposure to work stressors may influence the likelihood that one will become an abuse perpetrator (Balducci, Cecchin, & Fraccaroli, 2012). Work stressors, for example, may produce negative emotions, which in turn may cause one to engage in abusive behavior (Fox, Spector, & Miles, 2001; Spector & Fox, 2002, 2005).

Another possibility is that negative environmental features correlate with workplace abuse because they share one or more common causes. Target personality traits – particularly neuroticism (Costa & McCrae, 1992; Goldberg, 1990) – are a possible source of spurious work stressor–workplace abuse relationships. That is, target personality may influence the extent to which one is predisposed to experiencing workplace abuse and is predisposed to experiencing other work stressors (see Spector, Zapf, Chen, & Frese, 2000). Controlling for relevant personality traits may thus cause the observed relationship between workplace abuse and other work stressors to significantly weaken.

Finally, relationships between work stressors and workplace abuse may in some instances be attributed to the fact that particular forms of workplace abuse share conceptual similarity with particular work stressors. Having a heavy workload, for example, may have conceptual overlap with abuse perpetrated by one's supervisor – particularly if one's supervisor assigns unreasonable workloads in a deliberate attempt to harm his or her subordinates (see Bowling & Kirkendall, 2012). The presence of conceptual similarity would undoubtedly produce inflated relationships between some forms of workplace abuse and some work stressors.

Characteristics of Perpetrators

Research addressing the perpetrator's perspective has found that personality traits predict the extent to which workers engage in workplace abuse (Berry, Ones, & Sackett, 2007; Hershcovis et al., 2007). This research is typically conducted using the labels "counterproductive work behavior" (CWB; see Spector et al., 2006) or "workplace deviance" (see Bennett & Robinson, 2000). That literature has distinguished between counterproductive work behaviors intended to harm other *people* (CWB-Ps) and counterproductive work behaviors intended to harm the perpetrator's *organization* (CWB-Os). Because only the former refers to abusive behavior targeting people, we focus the current discussion on CWB-Ps.

Three traits from the Five Factor Model (FFM; Costa & McCrae, 1992; Goldberg, 1990) are consistently related to the extent to which one engages in CWB-Ps: agreeableness, neuroticism, and conscientiousness (Berry et al., 2007). Agreeableness – the extent to which a person is generally kind, considerate, and cooperative – is antithetical to engagement in workplace abuse. As a result, researchers have hypothesized a negative relationship between agreeableness and the extent to which a worker engages in abusive behavior. Consistent with this prediction, a meta-analysis by Berry et al. found a mean corrected correlation of −.46 between agreeableness and CWB-Ps.

Neuroticism, which is the extent to which a person habitually experiences negative emotions (e.g., anger, anxiety, and frustration), is expected to be positively related to the extent to which one engages in workplace abuse. This is because the state emotions that result from high neuroticism – particularly negative emotions experienced while at work – are thought to be an immediate cause of engagement in workplace abuse (Spector & Fox, 2002, 2005). Indeed, Berry et al. (2007) reported a positive correlation between neuroticism and CWB-Ps ($\rho = .24$).

Conscientiousness, which is the extent to which a person is generally hardworking, self-disciplined, and dutiful, is expected to be negatively related to the extent to which one engages in workplace abuse. People who are high in conscientiousness, in other words, are likely to have sufficient self-discipline to avoid the temptation to engage in workplace abuse, and they are likely to closely follow formal and informal rules prohibiting abusive behavior. Consistent with this theorizing, Berry et al. (2007) found a negative correlation between conscientiousness and CWB-Ps ($\rho = -.23$).

Characteristics of Victims

Several distinct pieces of evidence suggest that personal characteristics influence the likelihood that a given worker will become the victim of abuse. Research, for instance, has found that the extent to which a worker is abused is stable across time (Bowling, Beehr, Bennett, & Watson, 2010), that the extent to which workers are abused by coworkers is positively related to the extent to which they are abused by supervisors (Duffy et al., 2002; Frone, 2000), and that abuse experienced within one's personal life – such as mistreatment perpetrated by family members and friends – predicts workplace abuse (Skjorshammer & Hofoss, 1999). Such findings suggest that one or more enduring personal characteristics predispose some workers to be the targets of abusive behavior.

Furthermore, some studies have linked specific personality traits to exposure to workplace abuse. Milam, Spitzmueller, and Penney (2009), for instance, found that agreeableness was negatively related and that neuroticism was positively related to the extent to which one was the victim of workplace abuse. Furthermore, a two-wave study by Bowling et al. (2010) found that both trait positive affectivity and trait negative affectivity predicted subsequent levels of workplace abuse experienced over a year later.

There are several possible mechanisms linking target personality to workplace abuse (see Bowling et al., 2010; Milam et al., 2009; Spector et al., 2000). First, some personality traits – particularly target neuroticism – may contribute to *perceptions* of abuse that are independent of the effects of objective abuse levels. Target personality, in other words, could influence whether one interprets any given social situation as being abusive. Second, personality may directly influence objective workplace abuse levels via a *stressor–creation* mechanism. That is, personality could predispose some people to behave in ways that cause themselves to become abuse victims. A worker who is low in agreeableness, for instance, may engage in provocative behaviors that incite abuse from supervisors or coworkers. To directly test both perceptual and stressor–creation mechanisms, future research should include separate measures of objective abuse and perceived abuse.

HYPOTHESIZED CONSEQUENCES OF WORKPLACE ABUSE

Much of the research on workplace abuse has focused on its undesirable consequences – primarily its negative relationships with various indicators of victim well-being and victim job effectiveness (Aquino & Thau, 2009; Bowling & Beehr, 2006; Tepper, 2007). The current section begins with a review of research linking workplace abuse to victim psychological and physical well-being, with particular attention given to the theoretical mechanisms underlying such relationships. We then review research on the relationships between workplace abuse and three indicators of victim's job effectiveness: in-role job performance (Williams & Anderson, 1991), workplace deviance (Bennett & Robinson, 2000), and withdrawal behaviors (Hanisch, & Hulin, 1991).

The Relationship between Workplace Abuse and Victim Well-Being

Research has consistently found that workplace abuse is related to various indicators of victim well-being (Aquino & Thau, 2009; Bowling & Beehr, 2006; Hershcovis & Barling, 2010). The Bowling and Beehr (2006) meta-analysis, for instance, found that workplace abuse was positively related to anxiety ($\rho = .31$), depression ($\rho = .34$), burnout ($\rho = .39$), frustration ($\rho = .40$), and physical symptoms ($\rho = .31$), and negatively related to job satisfaction ($\rho = -.39$), life satisfaction ($\rho = -.21$), and self-esteem ($\rho = -.21$).

Surprisingly few studies, however, have examined the theoretical processes underlying these relationships (Tuckey & Neall, 2014). We suspect that the mechanisms linking workplace abuse to victim well-being are similar for various forms of abuse and that they mirror the mechanisms by which *any stressful condition* – including non-work stressors – influences a person's well-being. Although a detailed discussion is beyond the scope of this chapter, the mechanisms described by conservation of resources (COR) theory (Hobfoll, 1989, 1998, 2001) and self-determination theory (Deci & Ryan, 1985; Ryan, & Deci, 2000) may underlie the relationships between workplace abuse and victim well-being.

The Relationship between Workplace Abuse and Victim Job Effectiveness

In addition to negatively affecting victim well-being, workplace abuse might also cause victims to engage in behaviors that undermine their own job effectiveness. Workplace abuse, therefore, may have implications for organizational functioning. In the following subsections, we consider the potential effects of workplace abuse on three categories of victim behaviors that are directly relevant to organizational functioning: (a) in-role job performance, (b) workplace deviance, and (c) withdrawal behaviors.

Workplace Abuse and Victim's In-Role Job Performance

Workplace abuse's relationships with in-role job performance – the extent to which a worker effectively performs his or her official job duties (Williams & Anderson, 1991) – is likely complex. On one hand, some theories suggest that workplace abuse is detrimental to victims' job performance (Hershcovis & Barling, 2010). Workplace abuse, for instance, may be classified as a hindrance stressor (see LePine, LePine, & Jackson, 2004) or as an organizational constraint (see Spector & Jex, 1998), thereby implying that abuse has negative effects on victim's job performance. Having to cope with workplace abuse may also consume the psychological resources needed for the successful execution of one's job tasks (see COR Theory; Hobfoll, 1989, 1998, 2001). Alternatively, workplace abuse might result in an immediate *increase* in performance (perhaps at the expense of long-term performance levels). A victim of abusive supervision, for instance, may respond to an abuse episode by immediately – and perhaps temporarily – increasing his or her job performance. On the other hand, a causal path may instead run from in-role performance to workplace abuse. Exceptionally good performers and exceptionally bad performers, for instance, might become victims of abuse because they "stand-out" from their coworkers (Zapf, 1999). Given these conflicting possibilities, it is of little surprise that research has found a weak negative relationship between workplace abuse and in-role job performance (see Bowling & Beehr, 2006; Hershcovis & Barling, 2010; Spector & Jex, 1998).

Workplace Abuse and Victim's Workplace Deviance

Victims of workplace abuse often engage in deviant behaviors that harm other people (e.g., supervisors, coworkers, or customers) or harm the organization as a whole (Bowling & Beehr, 2006; Chen & Spector, 1992; Fox et al., 2001). The Bowling and Beehr (2006) meta-analysis, for example, found a mean corrected correlation of .37 between workplace abuse and victim-perpetrated deviance.

Because most research on the abuse–deviance relationship has used cross-section designs, however, the causal nature of workplace abuse–victim deviance relationships is unclear. On one hand, several theoretical mechanisms suggest a causal path from abuse exposure to victim deviance. The norm of reciprocity (see Gouldner, 1960), for instance, suggests that abuse victims may engage in workplace deviance as a means of "evening the score" with the perpetrator. A second possibility is that abuse influences victim-perpetrated deviance via effects on victims' emotions (Fox et al., 2001; Spector & Fox, 2002, 2005). Abuse victims, in other words, may engage in workplace deviance as a means of coping with the immediate negative emotional responses that follow their exposure to abuse (see Krischer, Penney, & Hunter, 2010). On the other hand, there is also a conceptual basis for a causal path from target-perpetrated deviance to workplace abuse. Again, the norm of reciprocity (see Gouldner, 1960) suggests that those who engage in workplace deviance are likely to face subsequent workplace abuse perpetrated by people affected by the initial instances of deviance.

Workplace Abuse and Victim's Withdrawal Behaviors
Withdrawal behaviors, which include absenteeism and turnover, are used by employees to distance themselves from unpleasant working conditions (Hanisch, & Hulin, 1991). Some definitions of workplace abuse explicitly note that victims are motivated to avoid abusive behavior (e.g., Hershcovis, & Reich, 2013; Neuman & Baron, 2005). Workplace abuse victims, therefore, may engage in withdrawal as a means of avoiding contact with abuse perpetrators, suggesting a causal path from abuse to withdrawal. Alternatively, we predict that those who engage in excessive withdrawal behavior may become subsequent targets of abuse. Workers who are chronically absent, for instance, might find themselves victims of abusive behavior perpetrated by coworkers who have been inconvenienced by the abuse victims' frequent absences. Despite this theorizing, research has generally found modest positive relationships between workplace abuse and victim withdrawal behaviors (see Bowling & Beehr, 2006; Chen & Spector, 1992; Spector & Jex, 1998).

In the above sections we reviewed research on the hypothesized predictors and consequences of workplace abuse. We now consider problems with how workplace abuse has been conceptualized and measured, giving particular attention to the implications of those problems to the study of workplace abuse's predictors and consequences.

PROBLEMS CONCEPTUALIZING AND MEASURING WORKPLACE ABUSE

As with any phenomenon of scientific interest, workplace abuse can be effectively studied only to the extent that clear construct definitions exist and that valid measures of those constructs are available. Unfortunately, the workplace abuse literature has been plagued by conceptualization and measurement problems (see Hershcovis, 2011; Shapiro, Duffy, Kim, Lean, & O'Leary-Kelly, 2008; Tepper & Henle, 2011). In the current section, we review two conceptualization/measurement issues that we believe are especially pressing: (a) the need to consider the construct breadth of workplace abuse scales and (b) the need to examine whether the scales used to measure various types of workplace abuse effectively capture the unique qualities of the constructs they purport to assess. To aid our discussion of these two issues, we conducted a review of the item content of several workplace abuse scales. This allowed us to explore the breadth of various workplace abuse measures and it also allowed us to assess conceptual similarities and differences between measures.

Review of the Item Content of Workplace Abuse Measures

This chapter's first author evaluated items from 15 commonly used workplace abuse scales (for a list of these scales, see Table 1). He sorted the 305 items from these scales into 16 themes and 25 subthemes, which are

Table 1. Workplace Abuse Measures Included in Review of Item Content.

Measure	Construct Name Used by Scale Authors	Perspective
Aquino et al. (1999)	Victimization	Victim
Bennett and Robinson (2000)	Deviance	Perpetrator
Blau and Andersson (2005)	Incivility	Perpetrator
Cortina et al. (2001)	Incivility	Victim
Duffy et al. (2002)	Social undermining	Victim
Einarsen et al. (2009)	Bullying	Victim
Glomb (2010)	Aggression	Victim and perpetrator
Martin and Hine (2005)	Incivility	Victim
Neuman and Keashly (2004)	Aggression	Victim
Rogers and Kelloway (1997)	Violence	Victim
Rospenda and Richman (2004)	Generalized workplace harassment	Victim
Spector et al. (2006)	Counterproductive work behavior directed at people	Perpetrator
Spector and Jex (1998)	Interpersonal conflict	Primarily victim
Tepper (2000)	Abusive supervision	Victim
Zapf et al. (1996)[a]	Bullying	Victim

[a]Revised version of Leymann (1990).

described in the appendix.[1] Table 2 shows which themes/subthemes are represented within each of the 15 workplace abuse scales.

The examination of the workplace abuse measures' item content revealed several interesting patterns. First, there is considerable overlap in item content across different workplace abuse measures. Twelve of the 15 measures used in the review, for instance, included items that assess *Social Isolation*. In some cases, different measures included nearly identical items. For example, eight scales – Aquino, Grover, Bradfield, and Allen (1999), Bennett and Robinson (2000), Blau and Andersson (2005), Glomb (2010), the Zapf, Knorz, and Kulla (1996) version of Leymann's (1990) scale, Neuman and Keashly (2004), Rogers and Kelloway (1997), and Rospenda and Richman (2004) – include items that specifically reference either "swearing" or "cursing." This suggests that workplace abuse measures often share conceptual similarities.

Second, the review found that some measures have heterogeneous item content, whereas others have homogeneous item content (see Table 2). As we discuss below in the section on the hypothesized consequences of workplace abuse, we do not categorically recommend either type of measure over the other. Instead, heterogeneous measures may be more useful for some purposes, and homogeneous measures may be more useful for other purposes.

Finally, some measures include *Omnibus Abuse* content. The Spector and Jex (1998) scale, for example, includes the item "How often do other people do nasty things to you at work?"; the Tepper (2000) scale includes the item "My boss is rude to me"; and the Duffy et al. (2002) scale includes the item "How often has the coworker closest to you intentionally hurt your feelings?" These items are inclusive and as such could be endorsed by victims after being targeted by any number of specific forms of abusive behavior. Being punched, sworn at, ignored, or having one's personal property vandalized each represent "nasty" or "rude" behaviors and each may hurt the target's feelings. As we discuss in subsequent sections, *Omnibus Abuse* may have predictors and consequences that differ from those of more specific forms of abuse.

In sum, our review of the item content of widely used workplace abuse measures revealed many interesting patterns. As a means of building on our informal item review, we encourage researchers to use factor analyses to more formally examine the relationships between various workplace abuse measures. We believe that such work is likely to find that the structure of workplace abuse is better described by the *themes* that we observed in our examination of item content (i.e., the columns in Table 2) than by

Table 2. Summary of Themes Represented within Each Workplace Abuse Measure.

	Omnibus Abuse	General Verbal Abuse	Personal Verbal Abuse	Work-Specific Verbal Abuse	Demographic-Specific Verbal Abuse	Swearing	Yelling	Doubting Competence	Blaming	Social Isolation	Social Manipulation	Failing to Protect from Harm	Lying
Aquino et al. (1999)					X	X				X	X		
Bennett and Robinson (2000)	X	X			X	X					X		
Blau and Andersson (2005)	X	X			X	X		X		X	X		
Cortina et al. (2001)		X						X		X			
Duffy et al. (2002)	X	X	X	X						X	X	X	X
Einarsen et al. (2009)		X	X	X			X			X	X		
Glomb (2010)		X				X	X			X	X	X	
Martin and Hine (2005)		X					X			X	X		
Neuman and Keashly (2004)	X	X	X	X	X	X	X		X	X	X	X	X
Rogers and Kelloway (1997)						X							
Rospenda and Richman (2004)		X	X	X		X	X	X	X	X	X		
Spector et al. (2006)	X	X	X	X					X	X	X		
Spector and Jex (1998)	X	X					X						
Tepper (2000)	X	X		X					X	X	X		X
Zapf et al. (1996)		X	X	X	X	X	X	X		X	X		

	Manipulation of Work Tasks	Supervisor-Specific Abuse	General Obstructionism	Restricted Communication	Withheld Credit	Invasion of Privacy	Unwanted Jokes	Aggressive Gestures	Harming Property/ Theft	Sexual Aggression	Threats of Physical Violence	Actual Physical Violence
Aquino et al. (1999)			X					X	X		X	X
Bennett and Robinson (2000)							X					
Blau and Andersson (2005)						X	X					
Cortina et al. (2001)						X						
Duffy et al. (2002)			X									
Einarsen et al. (2009)	X	X	X				X				X	X
Glomb (2010)			X	X				X	X			X
Martin and Hine (2005)			X	X		X		X	X			
Neuman and Keashly (2004)	X	X	X	X	X	X	X	X	X	X	X	X
Rogers and Kelloway (1997)									X		X	X
Rospenda and Richman (2004)	X	X		X	X	X		X				X
Spector et al. (2006)			X			X	X	X	X		X	X
Spector and Jex (1998)												
Tepper (2000)		X			X	X						
Zapf et al. (1996)	X	X		X				X		X	X	X

the *measures* that we used to identify those themes (i.e., the rows in Table 2; note that Tepper and Henle [2011] similarly endorsed a "behavior-specific approach" to measuring workplace abuse and Hershcovis and Reich [2013] suggested using abuse measures with homogeneous item content).

The Construct Breadth of Workplace Abuse Measures

As shown in our review of the item content, the construct breadth of workplace abuse varies across measures (see Table 2). Some scales, for instance, assess relatively broad conceptualizations of workplace abuse. Duffy et al. (2002), for example, assesses social undermining, which is workplace abuse that damages the victim's interpersonal relationships, reputation, and work-related effectiveness. Given the heterogeneity of their social undermining items (sample items include "Spread rumors about you"; "Gave you the silent treatment"; "Did not give as much help as they promised"), the Duffy et al. measure represents a relatively broad conceptualization of workplace abuse. Other researchers, however, have examined relatively narrow conceptualizations of workplace abuse. Ferris, Brown, Berry, and Lian (2008), for example, focused on workplace ostracism – a narrow form of workplace abuse in which the victim is socially excluded, rejected, or ignored.

The breadth of workplace abuse measures has important implications. Combining heterogeneous behaviors into a single scale is often conceptually and empirically justified. Bennett and Robinson (2000), for instance, suggest that perpetrators have a repertoire of abusive behaviors at their disposal. Although different forms of abusive behavior are conceptually distinct – yelling at someone, for instance, is not identical to ignoring them – they are often functionally equivalent: They each serve the purpose of harming the target. This shared function causes conceptually distinct forms of abuse to be positively related to one another (see Einarsen et al., 2009; Martin & Hine, 2005; Zapf et al., 1996).

Combining conceptually distinct behaviors into a broad abuse scale may provide several advantages. This practice, for instance, increases the breadth of an abuse measure and may thus increase the strength of the relationship between workplace abuse and broadly measured predictor and criterion variables (see Fishbein & Ajzen, 1975; Ones & Viswesvaran, 1996; Tepper & Henle, 2011).[2] Furthermore, combining heterogeneous items into an overall scale may help to avoid range restriction that could occur when researchers confine their measures to a single type of abuse (see Spector et al., 2006).

Reliance on broad abuse measures, however, may cause researchers to overlook the distinct nature of specific forms of abuse. Indeed, recent research – such as that examining workplace ostracism (Ferris et al., 2008) – has shown benefits to measuring more narrow forms of abusive behavior. As a result, broad abuse measures may be preferred in some contexts, whereas narrow abuse measures may be preferred in other contexts.

Capturing the Unique Qualities of Various Forms of Workplace Abuse

In addition to the need for added attention to the breadth of workplace abuse scales, there is a pressing need for research that examines the construct validity of workplace abuse measures. In many cases, the measures used to assess a given form of workplace abuse do not appear to faithfully capture the attributes that distinguish that form of abuse from other forms of abuse (see Tepper & Henle, 2011). Although the definition of incivility (Andersson & Pearson, 1999; Cortina, Magley, Williams, & Langhout, 2001), for example, distinguishes it from other forms of workplace abuse – only incivility is confined to low-intensity abuse that has ambiguous intent – the three incivility measures that we reviewed (i.e., Blau & Andersson, 2005; Cortina et al., 2001; Martin & Hine, 2005) include largely the same item content as is found in scales used to assess other ostensibly distinct forms of workplace abuse (see Table 2).

Fortunately, there are ways to improve the construct validity of workplace abuse measures. First, researchers should take pains to develop scales that reflect the unique qualities of the type of workplace abuse that they are attempting to measure. Consider, for example, the hypothetical development of a new measure of *Lying* – a form of workplace abuse in which the perpetrator breaks promises that he or she has made or gives incorrect information to the victim (see the appendix). In developing such a scale, the researcher should ask subject matter experts (SMEs) to judge the extent to which each item included in an initial item pool represents deceitful behavior. Only those items that SMEs judge as being deceitful should be retained.

Furthermore, the researcher should develop a nomological network that identifies external variables that are hypothesized to yield relationships with *Lying* that are different from their relationships with other forms of workplace abuse. Several commonly studied external variables (e.g., anxiety, physical symptoms, and job satisfaction) are likely to be of limited value because they are conceptually related to most – or perhaps all – forms of workplace abuse. Instead, researchers should include external variables that are likely to yield distinct relationships with *Lying*. *Lying* involves the transmission of misinformation; therefore the presence of victim misconceptions about job tasks might be useful as an external variable.

Hershcovis (2011) suggested an additional means of improving the measurement of workplace abuse. Rather than measure the distinguishing features of a particular form of workplace abuse within the abuse measure, she suggested measuring these features as *separate* constructs, which could be used as moderator variables. Instead of using a social undermining scale to assess the degree to which one is exposed to abusive behavior that harms his or her reputation (see Duffy et al., 2002), for example, one could assess exposure to abusive behavior and harm to reputation as two separate constructs. Based on a reading of the social undermining literature, one might predict that workplace abuse has particularly strong negative effects when it is accompanied by harm to the victim's reputation.

Additional Considerations for the Measurement of Workplace Abuse

We believe that the two issues that we raised above – the need for an increased focus on the construct breadth of workplace abuse measures and the need for workplace abuse measures that accurately reflect the unique qualities of the type of abuse they were designed to measure – should be addressed immediately. Scientific progress regarding the substantive relationships between workplace abuse and its hypothesized predictors and consequences rests on the resolution of these issues.

Placing these issues aside for now, we present additional observations about the conceptualization and measurement of workplace abuse. Specifically, we discuss the nature of the perpetrator–victim relationship, the distinction between subjective and objective measures of abuse, the timeframe referenced in abuse measures, and the need for multiple measures of each form of abuse.

The Nature of the Perpetrator–Victim Relationship

The nature of the perpetrator–victim relationship is explicitly acknowledged within some conceptualizations of workplace abuse (see Hershcovis & Barling, 2010). Researchers, for instance, have examined supervisor-to-subordinate abuse (Ashforth, 1994; Tepper, 2000), peer-to-peer abuse

(Duffy et al., 2002; Frone, 2000), and customer-to-employee abuse (Grandey, Dickter, & Sin, 2004). Most conceptualizations of workplace abuse, however, do not specify the relationship between perpetrator and victim (see Hershcovis, & Reich, 2013; Neall & Tuckey, 2014). The original version of the Interpersonal Conflict at Work Scale (Spector & Jex, 1998), for instance, does not identify the perpetrator's relationship with the questionnaire respondent; instead, the scale simply asks if "others at work" have engaged in abusive behavior.

Because the predictors and consequences of workplace abuse are likely to depend on the source of the abuse (Frone, 2000; Hershcovis & Barling, 2010), there are benefits to specifying the nature of the perpetrator–victim relationship. We will return to the nature of the perpetrator–victim relationship in a later section on the hypothesized consequences of workplace abuse.

The Distinction between Subjective and Objective Measures of Workplace Abuse

Nearly all studies have used victim self-reports to assess workplace abuse (see Neall & Tuckey, 2014). As a result, little is known about the extent to which victim self-reports reflect objectively verifiable instances of abuse. Indeed, self-report abuse measures may instead reflect the idiosyncratic characteristics of respondents. In other words, differences might exist across workers in how intense or how frequent a given behavior must be before they perceive it as "abusive."

To address this problem, researchers could use one of several approaches to assess objective exposure to workplace abuse. First, single-organization studies could adopt a peer-nomination approach in which workers are asked to name victims and perpetrators within their workgroups. This approach helps avoid the potential biases inherent to self-report measures, and it could also be used to examine social patterns of workplace abuse. Only a few studies, however, have used the peer-nomination approach to assess workplace abuse (e.g., Coyne, Chong, Seigne, & Randall, 2003; Coyne, Craig, & Chong, 2004).

Second, researchers could create self-report abuse measures that consist of objectively verifiable items (see Hershcovis, & Reich, 2013). Spector and Fox (2003) used such an approach to develop a relatively objective self-report measure of job autonomy. They found that their *Factual Autonomy Scale* (a sample item is "In your present job, how often do you have to ask permission to take a lunch/meal break?") had superior construct validity to that of a subjective measure of workplace autonomy (a sample subjective item is "How much autonomy is there in your job?"; Hackman & Oldham, 1975). A similar approach could be used to create objective workplace abuse measures. Indeed, existing self-report workplace abuse measures do seem to vary in the objectivity of their item content. The Rogers and Kelloway (1997) item "Have you been threatened with a weapon while at work?" for example, is more objective than the Spector and Jex (1998) item "How often do other people do nasty things to you at work?" It is likely that the convergent validity between victim-reports, perpetrator-reports, and witness-reports would be greater when objective rather than subjective items are used to assess workplace abuse.

Finally, it may also be possible to use research participants' job titles to infer the objective *potential* for exposure to workplace abuse. A similar imputation method has been used to assess various work stressors (see Ganster, 2008). The Occupational Information Network (O*NET; Peterson et al., 2001), an on-line job analysis tool sponsored by the U.S. Department of Labor/Employment and Training Administration, might prove particularly useful as a means of assessing the objective potential for exposure to workplace abuse. O*NET includes several dimensions representing various employee requirements, job tasks, and environmental conditions for several hundred job titles. These dimensions, in other words, reflect the nature of work at the *occupational* level-of-analysis. As such, O*NET introduces the obvious limitation of assuming that two people with identical job titles necessarily perform identical job tasks and work in identical environments. Despite this limitation, two O*NET items might be particularly useful for objectively measuring the potential for exposure to workplace abuse: "Deal with unpleasant or angry people" and "Deal with physically aggressive people." Other O*NET items that reflect the degree of social interaction at work (e.g., "Performing for or working directly with the public") might also be useful for assessing the potential for workplace abuse. As we discuss below in the sections on the hypothesized predictors and consequences of workplace abuse, the inclusion of separate measures of objective abuse and subjective abuse provides the possibility for several interesting theoretical developments.

The Timeframe Referenced in Workplace Abuse Measures

Workplace abuse measures vary in the timeframe in which participants are asked to consider when reporting abusive experiences (see Hershcovis, & Reich, 2013; Neall & Tuckey, 2014). The Duffy et al. (2002) social undermining scales, for example, asks participants about behaviors experienced during the *last month*, whereas the Rogers and Kelloway (1997) violence scale asks participants about behaviors experienced during the *last year*. Still other measures – such as Tepper's (2000) abusive supervision scale – do not specify a timeframe. We predict that various timeframes offer complementary advantages and disadvantages. Short timeframes, for instance, help avoid problems caused by participant forgetting; however, they may provide insufficient time for participants to experience abusive behavior and thus result in range restriction. Long timeframes, however, may provide sufficient time for participants to experience abusive behavior, but they may be affected by participant forgetting. We thus encourage research that examines the validity of self-reported workplace abuse measures for participants randomly assigned to different timeframes. Such research could examine the effects of timeframe manipulations on the convergence between self-reported abuse and other-reported abuse (e.g., coworker reports of *participants*' abuse experiences). Researchers are likely to find that the ideal timeframe – the timeframe that yields the highest convergent validity – depends on the intensity of the abusive behavior. Short timeframes, for example, might be ideal for low-intensity abuse, because such behavior is generally frequent, but unmemorable; long timeframes, however, might be ideal for high-intensity abuse, because such abuse is generally infrequent, but memorable.

The Need for Multiple Measures of Each Form of Workplace Abuse

Ideally, multiple measures would exist for any given form of workplace abuse. This is important because the use of multiple measures contributes to understanding of phenomena at the *construct level*. As an illustration, consider the fact that several job satisfaction scales exist – the Job Descriptive Index (JDI; Smith, Kendall, & Hulin, 1969), the Minnesota Satisfaction Questionnaire (MSQ; Weiss, Dawis, England, & Lofquist, 1967), and the Job Satisfaction Survey (JSS; Spector, 1985), for example, have each been used in many studies. Because the job satisfaction literature is not dominated by a single measure, researchers have been able to gain a better understanding of the job satisfaction *construct*. If researchers had instead used only one scale to assess job satisfaction, then one could argue that the job satisfaction literature has taught us more about the construct validity of that particular scale and less about the nature of job satisfaction.

Unfortunately, the measurement of any given form of abuse has generally been dominated by a single measure. Nearly all studies of abusive supervision, for instance, use the Tepper (2000) scale; nearly all studies of social undermining use the Duffy et al. (2002) scale; and nearly all studies of interpersonal conflict use the Spector and Jex (1998) scale. In other words, the type of abuse that researchers have attempted to assess is often confounded with the particular measure that is used. As a result, researchers may know more about the construct validity of particular measures than about the causes and consequences of a particular type of abuse. It would thus aid scientific progress if multiple measures were available for any given form of workplace abuse. We particularly encourage the development of multiple measures of the individual themes described in the appendix.

The previous sections address several issues relating to the conceptualization and measurement of workplace abuse. In the remainder of this chapter, we discuss future research on the predictors and consequences of workplace abuse.

Future Research on the Predictors of Workplace Abuse

The measurement issues that we discussed above have implications for future research on the predictors of workplace abuse. Two of those issues – the differing item content of various workplace abuse measures and the distinction between subjective and objective workplace abuse measures – are the focus of the following subsections.

The Item Content Workplace Abuse Measures

Different forms of workplace abuse are likely to have different predictors. Such differential relationships may result from differences in the distinct behavioral qualities of various forms of workplace abuse. For example, some forms of workplace abuse – *Obstructionism*, *Social Manipulation*, and *Swearing* – involve the effortful actions of perpetrators. These active forms of workplace abuse are likely to have predictors that differ from those of more passive forms of workplace abuse, such as *Failing to Protect from Harm*, *Social Isolation*, and *Withheld Credit*. We predict, for example, that trait anger (Spielberger, Jacobs, Russell, & Crane, 1983) is more likely to predict engagement in active abuse than engagement in passive abuse.

Differential predictor–abuse relationships could also result from differences in *who* engages in particular forms of workplace abuse. Whereas most of the types of workplace abuse described in the appendix are likely to be perpetrated by the victim's supervisors or coworkers, for example, *Physical Violence* is different in that it is in most cases perpetrated by organizational outsiders, such as customers, clients, or patients (Barling,

Dupré, & Kelloway, 2009). As a result, we suspect that unlike other forms of workplace abuse, the degree to which one is exposed to *Physical Violence* is primarily a function of the extent to which one's job tasks bring him or her into contact with organizational outsiders.

In sum, more theoretical development is needed to identify the unique predictors of various forms of abusive behavior. Such efforts would have important practical implications because they could show that different types of interventions may be needed to combat different types of workplace abuse.

The Distinction between Subjective and Objective Measures of Workplace Abuse

As we suggested earlier, workplace abuse measures vary in the degree to which they assess subjective versus objective content. Whereas *Omnibus Abuse* items (see the appendix), for instance, assess subjective abuse, other types of abuse items assess more objective forms of abuse. We predict that victim personality traits will have a particularly strong relationship with subjective abuse measures. This is because subjective abuse measures – relative to objective abuse measures – are more open to interpretation and hence more likely to be influenced by victim personality.

Future Research on the Consequences of Workplace Abuse

In the previous section, we discussed future research on the hypothesized predictors of workplace abuse. We now consider how future research on the consequences of workplace abuse could be informed by four of the conceptualization and measurement issues we discussed earlier: (a) the differing item content of various workplace abuse measures, (b) the construct breadth of abuse measures, (c) the nature of the perpetrator–victim relationship, and (d) the distinction between subjective and objective measures of workplace abuse.

The Item Content Workplace Abuse Measures

Various forms of workplace abuse are likely to yield differential relationships with the hypothesized outcomes of abuse. Some forms of abuse may consistently produce relatively stronger (or weaker) relationships with most outcome variables. One may expect, for example, that *Workplace Violence* – because of its relatively high intensity – will generally yield stronger relationships with outcome variables than will less serious forms of workplace abuse, such as *Harming Property/Theft*. In other instances, a given form of workplace abuse may yield particularly strong relationships with some outcomes but not with others. *General obstructionism*, for example, may have a particularly strong negative relationship with victims' in-role job performance, whereas *Social Manipulation* may have a particularly strong negative relationship with victims' popularity among their coworkers. We encourage researchers to give further attention to developing models linking particular forms of workplace abuse to particular outcomes.

The Construct Breadth of Workplace Abuse Measures

Researchers working in various domains – particularly personality assessment (Ones & Viswesvaran, 1996) and attitude assessment (Fishbein & Ajzen, 1975) – have articulated the importance of variable breadth. Generally speaking, broad predictor variables are expected to yield especially strong relationships with broad criterion variables; narrow predictor variables are expected to yield especially strong relationships with narrow criterion variables (for an alternative perspective, see O'Neill & Paunonen, 2013). We thus encourage workplace abuse researchers to consider the breadth of the measures that they use in their research. As shown in Table 2, some workplace abuse scales may assess broad content (e.g., the Neuman & Keashly, 2004 scale), whereas others may assess narrow content (e.g., the Rogers & Kelloway, 1997 scale). Workplace abuse may yield its strongest relationships when abuse measures and criterion measures share a similar level of breadth (see Tepper & Henle, 2011).

The Nature of the Perpetrator–Victim Relationship

The effects of workplace abuse may vary depending on the nature of the perpetrator–victim relationship. Some researchers, for example, have suggested that workplace abuse perpetrated by one's supervisor may have stronger effects on victim well-being than does workplace abuse perpetrated by one's peers (Hershcovis & Barling, 2010). In other words, the power imbalance inherent within supervisor–subordinate relationships may cause supervisor-perpetrated abuse to be particularly harmful to victims. Consistent with this prediction, a meta-analysis by Hershcovis and Barling (2010) found that when compared with coworker-perpetrated abuse, supervisor-perpetrated abuse yielded relatively stronger relationships with victim job attitudes and behaviors. Frone (2000), however, found that supervisor-perpetrated abuse yielded relatively strong relationships with work-specific outcomes (i.e., job satisfaction, organizational commitment, and turnover intention), but that coworker-perpetrated abuse yielded relatively strong relationships with non-work outcomes (i.e., depression, self-esteem, and physical health symptoms). We encourage additional research on the role that perpetrator–victim relationships play in determining the effects of workplace abuse. Such research could examine whether the effects of various forms of abuse described in the appendix depend on the nature of the perpetrator–victim relationship.

The Distinction between Subjective and Objective Measures of Workplace Abuse

Subjective abuse measures and objective abuse measures may yield distinct relationships with outcome variables. We expect, for example, that subjective abuse measures would yield particularly strong relationships with victim well-being. This prediction is based on the Transactional Model of Stress (Lazarus, 1999; Lazarus & Folkman, 1984; Perrewé & Zellars, 1999), which suggests that perceived stressors directly influence one's well-being, whereas objective stressors have indirect effects that are mediated via perceived stressors. Objective abuse measures, however, may sometimes have effects on outcome variables that are independent of victim perceptions. The objective presence of *Obstructionism*, for instance, may undermine a victim's in-role job performance, even if that victim is unaware that abuse has occurred.

SUMMARY

This chapter provides a critical review of the workplace abuse literature. We began by defining workplace abuse and we summarized research on workplace abuse's hypothesized predictors and consequences. We then presented a review of issues relating to the conceptualization and measurement of workplace abuse. Finally, we consider the relevance of these issues to the study of the hypothesized predictors and consequences of workplace abuse.

NOTES

1. Not surprisingly, some of these themes overlap with subdimensions of workplace abuse described in previous studies (see Einarsen, Hoel, & Notelaers, 2009; Martin & Hine, 2005; Rospenda & Richman, 2004). In their examination of the factor structure of the Uncivil Workplace Behavior Questionnaire – a measure of workplace incivility – Martin and Hine (2005) observed four factors: *Hostility*,

Privacy Invasion, *Exclusionary Behavior*, and *Gossiping*. These factors are similar to the themes we labeled *Yelling*, *Invasion of Privacy*, *Social Isolation*, and *Social Manipulation*, respectively.

2. Some researchers, however, have challenged the notion that broad predictors necessarily predict broad criteria and that narrow predictors necessarily predict narrow criteria (for one such example from the personality assessment literature, see O'Neill & Paunonen, 2013).

REFERENCES

Andersson, L. M., & Pearson, C. M. (1999). Tit for tat? The spiraling effect of incivility in the workplace. *The Academy of Management Review*, *24*, 452–471.

Aquino, K., Grover, S. L., Bradfield, M., & Allen, D. G. (1999). The effects of negative affectivity, hierarchical status, and self-determination on workplace victimization. *Academy of Management Journal*, *42*, 260–272.

Aquino, K., & Thau, S. (2009). Workplace victimization: Aggression from the target's perspective. *Annual Review of Psychology*, *60*, 717–741.

Ashforth, B. E. (1994). Petty tyranny in organizations. *Human Relations*, *47*, 755–778.

Balducci, C., Cecchin, M., & Fraccaroli, F. (2012). The impact of role stressors on workplace bullying in both victims and perpetrators, controlling for personal vulnerability factors: A longitudinal analysis. *Work and Stress*, *26*, 195–212.

Barling, J., Dupré, K. E., & Kelloway, E. K. (2009). Predicting workplace aggression and violence. *Annual Review of Psychology*, *60*, 671–692.

Bennett, R. J., & Robinson, S. L. (2000). Development of a measure of workplace deviance. *Journal of Applied Psychology*, *85*, 349–360.

Berry, C. M., Ones, D. S., & Sackett, P. R. (2007). Interpersonal deviance, organizational deviance, and their common correlates: A review and meta-analysis. *Journal of Applied Psychology*, *92*, 410–424.

Blau, G., & Andersson, L. (2005). Testing a measure of instigated workplace incivility. *Journal of Occupational and Organizational Psychology*, *78*, 595–614.

Bowling, N. A., & Beehr, T. A. (2006). Workplace harassment from the victim's perspective: A theoretical model and meta-analysis. *Journal of Applied Psychology*, *91*, 998–1012.

Bowling, N. A., Beehr, T. A., Bennett, M. M., & Watson, C. P. (2010). Target personality and workplace victimization: A prospective analysis. *Work & Stress*, *24*, 140–158.

Bowling, N. A., & Kirkendall, C. (2012). Workload: A review of potential causes, consequences, and interventions. In J. Houdmont, S. Leka, & R. Sinclair (Eds.), *Contemporary occupational health psychology: Global perspectives on research and practice* (Vol. 2, pp. 221–238). Chichester: Wiley-Blackwell.

Chen, P. Y., & Spector, P. E. (1992). Relationship of work stressors with aggression, withdrawal, theft and substance use: An exploratory study. *Journal of Occupational and Organizational Psychology*, *65*, 177–184.

Cortina, L. M., Magley, V. J., Williams, J. H., & Langhout, R. D. (2001). Incivility in the workplace: Incidence and impact. *Journal of Occupational Health Psychology*, *6*, 64–80.

Cortina, L. M., & Marchiondo, L. (2012). Measurement of interpersonal mistreatment in organizations. In R. Sinclair, M. Wang, & L. Tetrick (Eds.), *Research methods in occupational health psychology: State of the art in measurement, design, and data analysis* (pp. 91–106). New York, NY: Routledge.

Costa, P. T., Jr., & McCrae, R. R. (1992). *Revised NEO Personality Inventory (NEO PI R) and NEO Five Factor Inventory (NEO-FFI) professional manual.* Odessa, FL: Psychological Assessment Resources, Inc.

Coyne, I., Chong, P. S. L., Seigne, E., & Randall, P. (2003). Self and peer nominations of bullying: An analysis of incident rates, individual differences, and perceptions of the working environment. *European Journal of Work and Organizational Psychology, 12*, 209–228.

Coyne, I., Craig, J., & Chong, P. S. L. (2004). Workplace bullying in a group context. *British Journal of Guidance & Counselling, 32*, 301–317.

Deci, E. L., & Ryan, R. M. (1985). *Intrinsic motivation and self-determination in human behavior.* New York, NY: Plenum Press.

Duffy, M. K., Ganster, D. C., & Pagon, M. (2002). Social undermining in the workplace. *Academy of Management Journal, 45*, 331–351.

Einarsen, S. (2000). Harassment and bullying at work: A review of the Scandinavian approach. *Aggression and Violent Behavior: A Review Journal, 5*, 371–401.

Einarsen, S., Hoel, H., & Notelaers, G. (2009). Measuring exposure to bullying and harassment at work: Validity, factor structure and psychometric properties of the Negative Acts Questionnaire-Revised. *Work & Stress, 23*, 24–44.

Einarsen, S., Raknes, B. I., & Matthiesen, S. (1994). Bullying and harassment at work and their relationships to work environment quality: An exploratory study. *European Journal of Work and Organizational Psychology, 4*, 381–401.

Ferris, D. L., Brown, D. J., Berry, J. W., & Lian, H. (2008). The development and validation of the workplace ostracism scale. *Journal of Applied Psychology, 93*, 1348–1366.

Fishbein, M., & Ajzen, I. (1975). *Belief, attitude, intention, and behavior: An introduction to* theory and research. Reading, MA: Addison-Wesley.

Fox, S., & Spector, P. E. (2005). *Counterproductive workplace behavior: Investigations of actors and targets.* Washington, DC: American Psychological Association.

Fox, S., Spector, P. E., & Miles, D. (2001). Counterproductive work behavior (CWB) in response to job stressors and organizational justice: Some mediator and moderator tests for autonomy and emotions. *Journal of Vocational Behavior, 59*, 291–309.

Frone, M. R. (2000). Interpersonal conflict at work and psychological outcomes: Testing a model among young workers. *Journal of Occupational Health Psychology, 5*, 246–255.

Ganster, D. C. (2008). Measurement challenges for studying work-related stressors and strains. *Human Resource Management Review, 18*, 259–270.

Glomb, T. M. (2010). Predicting workplace aggression: Reciprocal aggression, organizational, and individual antecedents. *International Journal of Organization Theory and Behavior, 13*, 249–291.

Goldberg, L. R. (1990). An alternative "description of personality": The Big-Five factor structure. *Journal of Personality and Social Psychology, 59*, 1216–1229.

Gouldner, A. W. (1960). The norm of reciprocity: A preliminary statement. *American Sociological Review, 25*, 161–178.

Grandey, A. A., Dickter, D. N., & Sin, H. P. (2004). The customer is not always right: Customer aggression and emotion regulation of service employees. *Journal of Organizational Behavior, 25*, 397–418.

Hackman, J. R., & Oldham, G. R. (1975). Development of the job diagnostic survey. *Journal of Applied Psychology*, *60*, 159–170.

Hanisch, K. A., & Hulin, C. L. (1991). General attitudes and organizational withdrawal: An evaluation of a causal model. *Journal of Vocational Behavior*, *39*, 110–128.

Hershcovis, M. S. (2011). "Incivility, social undermining, bullying ... oh my!": A call to reconcile constructs within workplace aggression research. *Journal of Organizational Behavior*, *32*, 499–519.

Hershcovis, M. S., & Barling, J. (2010). Towards a multi-foci approach to workplace aggression: A meta-analytic review of outcomes from different perpetrators. *Journal of Organizational Behavior*, *31*, 24–44.

Hershcovis, M. S., & Reich, T. C. (2013). Integrating workplace aggression research: Relational, contextual, and method considerations. *Journal of Organizational Behavior*, *34*, S26–S42.

Hershcovis, M. S., Turner, N., Barling, J., Arnold, K. A., Dupré, K. E., Inness, M., ... Sivanathan, N. (2007). Predicting workplace aggression: A meta-analysis. *Journal of Applied Psychology*, *92*, 228–238.

Hobfoll, S. E. (1989). Conservation of resources: A new attempt at conceptualizing stress. *American Psychologist*, *44*, 513–524.

Hobfoll, S. E. (1998). *Stress, culture, and community: The psychology and philosophy of stress*. New York, NY: Plenum Press.

Hobfoll, S. E. (2001). The influence of culture, community, and the nested-self in the stress process: Advancing conservation of resources theory. *Applied Psychology: An International Review*, *50*, 337–421.

Krischer, M. M., Penney, L. M., & Hunter, E. M. (2010). Can counterproductive work behaviors be productive? CWB as emotion-focused coping. *Journal of Occupational Health Psychology*, *15*, 154–166.

Lazarus, R. S. (1999). *Stress and emotion: A new synthesis*. New York, NY: Springer Publishing Company.

Lazarus, R. S., & Folkman, S. (1984). *Stress, appraisal, and coping*. New York, NY: Springer Publishing Company.

LePine, J. A., LePine, M. A., & Jackson, C. L. (2004). Challenge and hindrance stress: Relationships with exhaustion, motivation to learn, and learning performance. *Journal of Applied Psychology*, *89*, 883–891.

Leymann, H. (1990). Mobbing and psychological terror at workplaces. *Violence and Victims*, *5*, 119–126.

Leymann, H. (1996). The content and development of mobbing at work. *European Journal of Work and Organizational Psychology*, *5*, 165–184.

Martin, R. J., & Hine, D. W. (2005). Development and validation of the uncivil workplace behavior questionnaire. *Journal of Occupational Health Psychology*, *10*, 477–490.

Mathieu, J. E., & Farr, J. L. (1991). Further evidence for the discriminant validity of measures of organizational commitment, job involvement, and job satisfaction. *Journal of Applied Psychology*, *76*, 127–133.

Milam, A. C., Spitzmueller, C., & Penney, L. M. (2009). Investigating individual differences among targets of workplace incivility. *Journal of Occupational Health Psychology*, *14*, 58–69.

Neall, A. M., & Tuckey, M. R. (2014). A methodological review of research on the antecedents and consequences of workplace harassment. *Journal of Occupational and Organizational Psychology*, *87*, 225–257.

Neuman, J. H., & Baron, R. A. (2005). Aggression in the workplace: A social-psychological perspective. In S. Fox & P. E. Spector (Eds.), *Counterproductive work behavior: Investigations of actors and targets* (pp. 13–40). Washington, DC: American Psychological Association.

Neuman, J. H., & Keashly, L. (2004, April 4). Development of the workplace aggression research questionnaire (WAR-Q): Preliminary data from the workplace stress and aggression project. In R. J. Bennett & C. D. Crossley (Charis), *Theoretical advancements in the study of anti-social behavior at work*. Symposium conducted at the meeting of the Society for Industrial and Organizational Psychology, Chicago, IL.

O'Neill, T. A., & Paunonen, S. V. (2013). Breadth in personality assessment: Implications for the understanding and prediction of work behavior. In N. Christiansen & R. P. Tett (Eds.), *Handbook of personality at work* (pp. 299–332). New York, NY: Routledge.

Ones, D. S., & Viswesvaran, C. (1996). Bandwidth-fidelity dilemma in personality measurement for personnel selection. *Journal of Organizational Behavior*, *17*, 609–626.

Perrewé, P. L., & Zellars, K. L. (1999). An examination of attributions and emotions in the transactional approach to the organizational stress process. *Journal of Organizational Behavior*, *20*, 739–752.

Peterson, N. G., Mumford, M. D., Borman, W. C., Jeanneret, P. R., Fleishman, E. A., Levin, K. Y., ... Dye, D. M. (2001). Understanding work using the occupational information network (O*NET): Implications for practice and research. *Personnel Psychology*, *54*, 451–492.

Reknes, I., Einarsen, S., Knardahl, S., & Lau, B. (2014). The prospective relationship between role stressors and new cases of self-reported workplace bullying. *Scandinavian Journal of Psychology*, *55*, 45–52.

Rogers, K. A., & Kelloway, E. K. (1997). Violence at work: Personal and organizational outcomes. *Journal of Occupational Health Psychology*, *2*, 63–71.

Rospenda, K. M., & Richman, J. A. (2004). The factor structure of generalized workplace harassment. *Violence and Victims*, *19*, 221–238.

Ryan, R. M., & Deci, E. L. (2000). Self-determination theory and the facilitation of intrinsic motivation, social development, and well-being. *American Psychologist*, *55*, 68–78.

Shapiro, D. L., Duffy, M. K., Kim, T. Y., Lean, E. R., & O'Leary-Kelly, A. (2008). "Rude," "uncivil," or "disrespectful" treatment in the workplace: What's in a name? In S. Gilliland, D. Steiner, & D. Skarlicki (Eds.), *Justice, morality, and social responsibility: Research in social issues in management* (Vol. 7, pp. 201–226). Charlotte, NC: Information Age Publishing, Inc.

Skjorshammer, M., & Hofoss, D. (1999). Physician in conflict: A survey study of individual and work-related characteristics. *Scandinavian Journal of Caring Science*, *13*, 211–216.

Smith, P. C., Kendall, L. M., & Hulin, C. L. (1969). *Measurement of satisfaction in work and retirement*. Chicago, IL: Rand McNally.

Spector, P. E. (1985). Measurement of human service staff satisfaction: Development of the job satisfaction survey. *American Journal of Community Psychology*, *13*, 693–713.

Spector, P. E., & Fox, S. (2002). An emotion-centered model of voluntary work behavior: Some parallels between counterproductive work behavior and organizational citizenship behavior. *Human Resources Management Review*, *12*, 269–292.

Spector, P. E., & Fox, S. (2003). Reducing subjectivity in the assessment of the job environment: Development of the factual autonomy scale (FAS). *Journal of Organizational Behavior*, *24*, 417–432.

Spector, P. E., & Fox, S. (2005). The stressor-emotion model of counterproductive work behavior. In S. Fox & P. E. Spector (Eds.), *Counterproductive work behavior: Investigations of actors and targets* (pp. 151–174). Washington, DC: American Psychological Association.

Spector, P. E., Fox, S., Penney, L. M., Bruursema, K., Goh, A., & Kessler, S. (2006). The dimensionality of counterproductivity: Are all counterproductive behaviors created equal? *Journal of Vocational Behavior*, *68*, 446–460.

Spector, P. E., & Jex, S. M. (1998). Development of four self-report measures of job stressors and strain: Interpersonal conflict at work scale, organizational constraints scale, quantitative workload inventory, and physical symptoms inventory. *Journal of Occupational Health Psychology*, *3*, 356–367.

Spector, P. E., Zapf, D., Chen, P. Y., & Frese, M. (2000). Why negative affectivity should not be controlled in job stress research: Don't throw out the baby with the bath water. *Journal of Organizational Behavior*, *21*, 79–95.

Spielberger, C. D., Jacobs, G., Russell, S., & Crane, R. S. (1983). Assessment of anger: The state-trait anger scale. In J. N. Butcher & C. D. Spielberger (Eds.), *Advances in personality assessment* (Vol. 2, pp. 161–189). Hillsdale, NJ: Lawrence Erlbaum Associates Publishers.

Tepper, B. J. (2000). Consequences of abusive supervision. *Academy of Management Journal*, *43*, 178–190.

Tepper, B. J. (2007). Abusive supervision in work organizations: Review, synthesis, and research agenda. *Journal of Management*, *33*, 261–289.

Tepper, B. J., & Henle, C. A. (2011). A case for recognizing distinctions among constructs that capture interpersonal mistreatment in work organizations. *Journal of Organizational Behavior*, *32*, 487–498.

Tuckey, M. R., & Neall, A. M. (2014). Workplace bullying erodes job and personal resources: Between- and within-person perspectives. *Journal of Occupational Health Psychology*, *19*, 413–424.

Weiss, D. J., Dawis, R. V., England, G. W., & Lofquist, L. H. (1967). *Manual for the Minnesota Satisfaction Questionnaire*. Minneapolis, MN: University of Minnesota.

Williams, L. J., & Anderson, S. E. (1991). Job satisfaction and organizational commitment as predictors of organizational citizenship and in-role behaviors. *Journal of Management*, *17*, 601–617.

Zapf, D. (1999). Organizational, work group related and personal causes of mobbing/bullying at work. *International Journal of Manpower*, *20*, 70–85.

Zapf, D., Knorz, C., & Kulla, M. (1996). On the relationship between mobbing factors, and job content, social work environment, and health outcomes. *European Journal of Work and Organizational Psychology*, *5*, 215–237.

APPENDIX

Workplace Abuse Items Organized by Themes

Omnibus Abuse (All-encompassing abuse items with ambiguous content.)

1. Hurt your feelings? (Duffy et al., 2002)
2. Made you feel incompetent? (Duffy et al., 2002)
3. How often are people rude to you at work? (Spector & Jex, 1998)
4. How often do other people do nasty things to you at work? (Spector & Jex, 1998)
5. Is rude to me (Tepper, 2000)
6. Been treated in a rude and/or disrespectful manner (Neuman & Keashly, 2004)
7. Acted rudely toward someone at work (Bennett & Robinson, 2000)
8. Been nasty or rude to a client or customer (Spector et al., 2006)
9. Acted rudely towards someone at work (Blau & Andersson, 2005)

Verbal Abuse

General Verbal Abuse Subtheme (All-encompassing verbal abuse items with ambiguous content.)

1. Put you down when you questioned work procedures? (Duffy et al., 2002)
2. Insulted you? (Duffy et al., 2002)
3. Belittled you or your ideas? (Duffy et al., 2002)
4. Talked down to you? (Duffy et al., 2002)
5. How often do you get into arguments with others at work? (Spector & Jex, 1998)
6. Put you down or was condescending to you? (Cortina et al., 2001)
7. Made demeaning or derogatory remarks about you? (Cortina et al., 2001)
8. Addressed you in unprofessional terms, either publicly or privately? (Cortina et al., 2001)
9. Ridicules me (Tepper, 2000)
10. Tells me my thoughts or feelings are stupid (Tepper, 2000)
11. Tells me I'm incompetent (Tepper, 2000)
12. Being the subject of excessive teasing and sarcasm (Einarsen et al., 2009)
13. Talked down to you (e.g., treated you like a child or as inferior to them)? (Rospenda & Richman, 2004)
14. Made snide remarks about you (Martin & Hine, 2005)
15. Insulting, criticizing you (including sarcasm) (Glomb, 2010)
16. Getting "in your face" (Glomb, 2010)
17. Been subjected to derogatory name calling (Neuman & Keashly, 2004)
18. Telephone terror (Zapf et al., 1996)
19. Made fun of someone at work (Bennett & Robinson, 2000)
20. Said something hurtful to someone at work (Bennett & Robinson, 2000)
21. Started an argument with someone at work (Spector et al., 2006)
22. Verbally abused someone at work (Spector et al., 2006)
23. Threatened someone at work, but not physically (Spector et al., 2006)

Appendix. (*Continued*)

24. Said something obscene to someone at work to make them feel bad (Spector et al., 2006)
25. Insulted or made fun of someone at work (Spector et al., 2006)
26. Put you down or was condescending to you in some way (Blau & Andersson, 2005)
27. Made demeaning, rude or derogatory remarks about you (Blau & Andersson, 2005)
28. Addressed you in unprofessional terms, either privately or publicly (Blau & Andersson, 2005)
29. Put down others or were condescending to them in some way (Blau & Andersson, 2005)
30. Made demeaning, rude or derogatory remarks about someone (Blau & Andersson, 2005)
31. Addressed someone in unprofessional terms either privately or publicly (Blau & Andersson, 2005)
32. Made fun of someone at work (Blau & Andersson, 2005)
33. Said something hurtful to someone at work (Blau & Andersson, 2005)

Personal Verbal Abuse Subtheme (Perpetrator makes fun of victim's personal life or criticizes victim's personal characteristics [e.g., personality, physical appearance].)

1. Let you know they did not like you or something about you? (Duffy et al., 2002)
2. Having insulting or offensive remarks made about your person, attitudes or your private life (Einarsen et al., 2009)
3. Made negative comments to you about your personality? (Rospenda & Richman, 2004)
4. Made negative comments to you about your appearance? (Rospenda & Richman, 2004)
5. Been subjected to negative comments about your intelligence or competence (Neuman & Keashly, 2004)
6. Been criticized for non-work (personal) life and activities (Neuman & Keashly, 2004)
7. Permanently criticizing a person's private life (Zapf et al., 1996)
8. Making fun of a person's private life (Zapf et al., 1996)
9. Made fun of someone's personal life (Spector et al., 2006)

Work-Specific Verbal Abuse Subtheme (Perpetrator reminds victim of his or her past work mistakes or criticizes victim's job performance.)

1. Criticized the way you handled things on the job in a way that was not helpful? (Duffy et al., 2002)
2. Reminds me of my past mistakes and failures (Tepper, 2000)
3. Being humiliated or ridiculed in connection with your work (Einarsen et al., 2009)
4. Repeated reminders of your errors or mistakes (Einarsen et al., 2009)
5. Persistent criticism of your errors or mistakes (Einarsen et al., 2009)
6. Made negative comments to you about your intelligence, competence, or productivity? (Rospenda & Richman, 2004)
7. Been subjected to excessively harsh criticism about your work (Neuman & Keashly, 2004)
8. Permanently criticizing a person's work (Zapf et al., 1996)
9. Insulted someone about their job performance (Spector et al., 2006)

Demographic-Specific Verbal Abuse Subtheme (Verbal abuse that makes reference to the victim's race, ethnicity, religion, sexual orientation, nationality, disability, or political beliefs.)

Appendix. (*Continued*)

1. Made an ethnic, racial, religious or offensive slur towards you (Aquino et al., 1999)
2. Been subjected to negative comments about your religious beliefs (Neuman & Keashly, 2004)
3. Been subjected to negative comments about a disability (Neuman & Keashly, 2004)
4. Been subjected to negative comments about your sexual orientation (Neuman & Keashly, 2004)
5. Been subjected to racist remarks (Neuman & Keashly, 2004)
6. Been subjected to ethnic or racial jokes or slurs (Neuman & Keashly, 2004)
7. Making fun of a person's handicap (Zapf et al., 1996)
8. Attacking a person's political attitudes (Zapf et al., 1996)
9. Attacking a person's religious attitudes (Zapf et al., 1996)
10. Making fun of a person's nationality (Zapf et al., 1996)
11. Made an ethnic, religious, or racial remark at work (Bennett & Robinson, 2000)
12. Made an ethnic, religious or racial remark or joke at work (Blau & Andersson, 2005)

Swearing Subtheme (Perpetrator swears directly at victim.)

1. Have you been sworn at while you've been at work? (Rogers & Kelloway, 1997)
2. Cursed at you (Aquino et al., 1999)
3. Swore at you? (Rospenda & Richman, 2004)
4. Swearing directed at you (Glomb, 2010)
5. Been sworn at in a hostile manner (Neuman & Keashly, 2004)
6. Cursed at someone at work (Bennett & Robinson, 2000)
7. Cursed at someone at work (Blau & Andersson, 2005)

Yelling Subtheme (Perpetrator yells or uses an aggressive tone when speaking to victim.)

1. How often do other people yell at you at work? (Spector & Jex, 1998)
2. Being shouted at or being the target of spontaneous anger (Einarsen et al., 2009)
3. Yelled or screamed at you? (Rospenda & Richman, 2004)
4. Raised their voice while speaking to you (Martin & Hine, 2005)
5. Used an inappropriate tone when speaking to you (Martin & Hine, 2005)
6. Spoke to you in an aggressive tone of voice (Martin & Hine, 2005)
7. Using an angry tone of voice (Glomb, 2010)
8. Yelling or raising one's voice (Glomb, 2010)
9. Been yelled at or shouted at in a hostile manner (Neuman & Keashly, 2004)
10. Shouting at or cursing loudly at a person (Zapf et al., 1996)

Doubted Competence Subtheme (Perpetrator expresses doubt in victim's judgment or competence.)

1. Doubted your judgment on a matter over which you have responsibility? (Cortina et al., 2001)
2. Expected less of you than others in your position? (Rospenda & Richman, 2004)

Appendix. (*Continued*)

3. Questioning a person's decisions (Zapf et al., 1996)
4. Doubted your judgment in a matter over which you have responsibility (Blau & Andersson, 2005)
5. Doubted someone's judgment in a matter over which they have responsibility (Blau & Andersson, 2005)

Blaming Subtheme (Perpetrator blames victim for another person's work mistakes or accuses victim of intentionally making an error at work.)

1. Blames me to save himself/herself embarrassment (Tepper, 2000)
2. Blamed you personally for things that other people did, or that weren't your fault? (Rospenda & Richman, 2004)
3. Been blamed for other peoples' mistakes (Neuman & Keashly, 2004)
4. Been accused of deliberately making an error (Neuman & Keashly, 2004)
5. Blamed someone at work for error you made (Spector et al., 2006)

Social Isolation (Victim is excluded from social interaction or is ignored.)

1. Gave you the silent treatment? (Duffy et al., 2002)
2. Paid little attention to your statement or showed little interest in your opinion? (Cortina et al., 2001)
3. Ignored or excluded you from professional camaraderie? (Cortina et al., 2001)
4. Gives me the silent treatment (Tepper, 2000)
5. Having your opinions ignored (Einarsen et al., 2009)
6. Being ignored or excluded (Einarsen et al., 2009)
7. Being ignored or facing a hostile reaction when you approach (Einarsen et al., 2009)
8. Refused to talk to you (Aquino et al., 1999)
9. Ignored you or your work contributions? (Rospenda & Richman, 2004)
10. Excluded you from important work activities or meetings? (Rospenda & Richman, 2004)
11. Did not consult you in reference to a decision you should have been involved in (Martin & Hine, 2005)
12. Avoided consulting you when they would normally be expected to do so (Martin & Hine, 2005)
13. Avoiding you (Glomb, 2010)
14. Been excluded from work-related social gatherings (Neuman & Keashly, 2004)
15. Had others storm out of the work area when you entered (Neuman & Keashly, 2004)
16. Been given the "silent treatment" (Neuman & Keashly, 2004)
17. One does not talk to the person concerned (Zapf et al., 1996)
18. Refusal to be talked to (Zapf et al., 1996)
19. Being treated like air (Zapf et al., 1996)
20. Ignored someone at work (Spector et al., 2006)
21. Paid little attention to a statement you made or showed little interest in their opinion (Blau & Andersson, 2005)
22. Ignored or excluded you from professional camaraderie (e.g. social conversation) (Blau & Andersson, 2005)

Appendix. *(Continued)*

23. Paid little attention to a statement made by someone or showed little interest in their opinion (Blau & Andersson, 2005)
24. Ignored or excluded someone from professional camaraderie (e.g. social conversation) (Blau & Andersson, 2005)

Social Manipulation (Behavior intended to damage victim's interpersonal relationships within the workplace.)

1. Talked bad about you behind your back? (Duffy et al., 2002)
2. Spread rumors about you? (Duffy et al., 2002)
3. Puts me down in front of others (Tepper, 2000)
4. Makes negative comments about me to others (Tepper, 2000)
5. Spreading of gossip and rumours about you (Einarsen et al., 2009)
6. Having allegations made against you (Einarsen et al., 2009)
7. Said bad things about you to your coworkers (Aquino et al., 1999)
8. Did something to make you look bad (Aquino et al., 1999)
9. Lied to get you in trouble (Aquino et al., 1999)
10. Embarrassed you in front of other employees (Aquino et al., 1999)
11. Gossiped about you and/or spread rumors about you behind your back? (Rospenda & Richman, 2004)
12. Labeled you a "troublemaker" if you expressed a difference of opinion? (Rospenda & Richman, 2004)
13. Humiliated or belittled you in front of others? (Rospenda & Richman, 2004)
14. Turned others in your work environment against you? (Rospenda & Richman, 2004)
15. Talked about you behind your back (Martin & Hine, 2005)
16. Gossiped behind your back (Martin & Hine, 2005)
17. Making you look bad (Glomb, 2010)
18. Spreading rumors (Glomb, 2010)
19. Belittling your opinions in front of other people (Glomb, 2010)
20. Been the target of rumors or gossip (Neuman & Keashly, 2004)
21. Had attempts made to turn other employees against you (Neuman & Keashly, 2004)
22. Making a person look stupid (Zapf et al., 1996)
23. Been reprimanded or "put down" in front of others (Neuman & Keashly, 2004)
24. Saying nasty things about a person behind his/her back (Zapf et al., 1996)
25. Spreading rumors (Zapf et al., 1996)
26. Publicly embarrassed someone at work (Bennett & Robinson, 2000)
27. Started or continued a damaging or harmful rumor at work (Spector et al., 2006)
28. Did something to make someone at work look bad (Spector et al., 2006)
29. Publicly embarrassed someone at work (Blau & Andersson, 2005)

Failing to Protect from Harm (Perpetrator fails to defend victim from verbal abuse or physical danger.)

1. Did not defend you when people spoke poorly of you? (Duffy et al., 2002)
2. Failing to correct false information about you (Glomb, 2010)
3. Had others fail to take action to protect you from harm (Neuman & Keashly, 2004)

Appendix. (*Continued*)

4. Had others fail to deny false rumors about you (Neuman & Keashly, 2004)
5. Had others fail to warn you about impending dangers (Neuman & Keashly, 2004)
6. Had co-workers fail to defend your plans or ideas to others (Neuman & Keashly, 2004)

Lying (Perpetrator breaks promises or gives incorrect information to the victim.)

1. Did not give as much help as they promised? (Duffy et al., 2002)
2. Gave you incorrect or misleading information about the job? (Duffy et al., 2002)
3. Breaks promises he/she makes (Tepper, 2000)
4. Lies to me (Tepper, 2000)
5. Been lied to (Neuman & Keashly, 2004)

Manipulation of Work Tasks (Perpetrator changes victim's work tasks or workload in an undesirable way.)

1. Being ordered to do work below your level of competence (Einarsen et al., 2009)
2. Being given tasks with unreasonable deadlines (Einarsen et al., 2009)
3. Excessive monitoring of your work (Einarsen et al., 2009)
4. Being exposed to an unmanageable workload (Einarsen et al., 2009)
5. Having key areas of responsibility removed or replaced with more trivial or unpleasant tasks (Einarsen et al., 2009)
6. Asked you to do work which really wasn't part of your job? (Rospenda & Richman, 2004)
7. Been given unreasonable workloads or deadlines—more than others (Neuman & Keashly, 2004)
8. Forcing someone to carry out tasks affecting his or her self-consciousness (Zapf et al., 1996)
9. Refusal to assign any tasks to the person concerned (Zapf et al., 1996)
10. Removing a person from all occupations so that even the person concerned is at a loss for what to do next (Zapf et al., 1996)
11. Assigning senseless tasks to the person concerned (Zapf et al., 1996)
12. Assigning the person concerned tasks far below his/her skills (Zapf et al., 1996)
13. Assigning degrading tasks to the person concerned (Zapf et al., 1996)

Supervisor-Specific Abuse (Heterogeneous set of abusive behaviors that are facilitated by the supervisor's role.)

1. Does not allow me to interact with my coworkers (Tepper, 2000)
2. Pressure not to claim something to which by right you are entitled (e.g. sick leave, holiday entitlement, travel expenses) (Einarsen et al., 2009)
3. Treated you or evaluated you as though you were less good at your work than you really are? (Rospenda & Richman, 2004)
4. Treated you unfairly compared to others in your some position (e.g., in terms of tasks or assignments, salary, promotions, resources, reprimands)? (Rospenda & Richman, 2004)
5. Been given little or no feedback about your performance (Neuman & Keashly, 2004)
6. Been denied a raise or promotion without being given a valid reason (Neuman & Keashly, 2004)

Appendix. (*Continued*)

7. Moving a person to a room far from his/her colleagues (Zapf et al., 1996)
8. Forbidding his/her colleagues to talk to the person concerned (Zapf et al., 1996)
9. Judging a person's job performance wrongly or in an offending manner (Zapf et al., 1996)

Obstructionism

General Obstructionism Subtheme (Perpetrator creates conditions that inhibit the victim's job performance.)

1. Undermined your effort to be successful on the job? (Duffy et al., 2002)
2. Delayed work to make you look bad or slow you down? (Duffy et al., 2002)
3. Someone withholding information which affects your performance (Einarsen et al., 2009)
4. Sabotaged your work (Aquino et al., 1999)
5. Gave unreasonably short notice when canceling or scheduling events you were required to be present for (Martin & Hine, 2005)
6. Failed to inform you of a meeting you should have been informed about (Martin & Hine, 2005)
7. Was excessively slow in returning your phone messages or e-mails without good reason for the delay (Martin & Hine, 2005)
8. Intentionally failed to pass on information which you should have been made aware of (Martin & Hine, 2005)
9. Were unreasonably slow in seeing to matters on which you were reliant on them for, without good reason (Martin & Hine, 2005)
10. Sabotaging your work (Glomb, 2010)
11. Withholding information from you (Glomb, 2010)
12. Withholding resources (e.g., supplies, equipment) needed to do job (Glomb, 2010)
13. Had others consistently arrive late for meetings that you called (Neuman & Keashly, 2004)
14. Had others refuse your requests for assistance (Neuman & Keashly, 2004)
15. Had others delay action on matters that were important to you (Neuman & Keashly, 2004)
16. Had others consistently fail to return your telephone calls and/or respond to your memos or e-mail (Neuman & Keashly, 2004)
17. Had someone interfere with your work activities (Neuman & Keashly, 2004)
18. Had others fail to give you information that you really needed (Neuman & Keashly, 2004)
19. Had others destroy or needlessly take resources that you needed to do your job (Neuman & Keashly, 2004)
20. Refused to help someone at work (Spector et al., 2006)
21. Withheld needed information from someone at work (Spector et al., 2006)
22. Purposely interfered with someone at work doing his/her job (Spector et al., 2006)
23. Hid something so someone at work couldn't find it (Spector et al., 2006)
24. Avoided returning a phone call to someone you should at work (Spector et al., 2006)

Restricting Communication Subtheme (Perpetrator prevents victim from speaking.)

1. Prevented you from expressing yourself by interrupting you? (Rospenda & Richman, 2004)
2. Interrupted you while you were speaking on the telephone (Martin & Hine, 2005)
3. Interrupting or "cutting you off" while speaking (Glomb, 2010)

Appendix. *(Continued)*

4. Been prevented from expressing yourself (e.g., interrupted when speaking) (Neuman & Keashly, 2004)
5. The supervisor restricts a person's possibilities to speak (Zapf et al., 1996)
6. Colleagues restrict the person's possibilities to speak (Zapf et al., 1996)

Withheld Credit (Perpetrator ignores victim's work contributions or takes credit for victim's contributions.)

1. Doesn't give me credit for jobs requiring a lot of effort (Tepper, 2000)
2. Took credit for your work or ideas? (Rospenda & Richman, 2004)
3. Not been given the praise for which you felt entitled (Neuman & Keashly, 2004)
4. Had your contributions ignored by others (Neuman & Keashly, 2004)
5. Had someone else take credit for your work or ideas (Neuman & Keashly, 2004)

Invasion of Privacy (Perpetrator shares victim's personal information or engages in unwanted involvement in victim's personal life.)

1. Made unwanted attempts to draw you into a discussion of personal matters? (Cortina et al., 2001)
2. Invades my privacy (Tepper, 2000)
3. Tried to control your non-work related time or activities? (Rospenda & Richman, 2004)
4. Read communications addressed to you, such as e-mails or faxes (Martin & Hine, 2005)
5. Opened your desk drawers without prior permission (Martin & Hine, 2005)
6. Publicly discussed your confidential personal information (Martin & Hine, 2005)
7. Been subjected to threats to reveal private or embarrassing information about you to others (Neuman & Keashly, 2004)
8. Been told how to spend your personal time when not at work (Neuman & Keashly, 2004)
9. Looked at someone at work's private mail/property without permission (Spector et al., 2006)
10. Made unwanted attempts to draw you into a discussion of personal matters (Blau & Andersson, 2005)
11. Made unwanted attempts to draw someone into a discussion of personal matters (Blau & Andersson, 2005)

Unwanted Jokes (Perpetrator plays mean prank on victim.)

1. Practical jokes carried out by people you don't get along with (Einarsen et al., 2009)
2. Been subjected to mean pranks (Neuman & Keashly, 2004)
3. Played a mean prank on someone at work (Bennett & Robinson, 2000)
4. Played a mean prank to embarrass someone at work (Spector et al., 2006)
5. Played a mean prank on someone at work (Blau & Andersson, 2005)

Aggressive Gestures (Perpetrator engages in aggressive facial expression or aggressive gestures.)

1. Made an obscene comment or gesture in front of you (Aquino et al., 1999)
2. Made hostile or offensive gestures at you? (Rospenda & Richman, 2004)

Appendix. (*Continued*)

3. Rolled their eyes at you (Martin & Hine, 2005)
4. Making angry gestures (e.g., pound fist, roll eyes) (Glomb, 2010)
5. Using hostile body language (Glomb, 2010)
6. Been glared at in a hostile manner (Neuman & Keashly, 2004)
7. Been subjected to obscene or hostile gestures (Neuman & Keashly, 2004)
8. Refusal to communicate with the person concerned by means of slighting glances and gestures (Zapf et al., 1996)
9. Imitating a person's gait, voice, or gestures to make him/her look stupid (Zapf et al., 1996)
10. Made an obscene gesture (the finger) to someone at work (Spector et al., 2006)

Harming Property/Theft (Abusive behavior directed at victim's property.)

1. Has your personal property been damaged while you've been at work? (Rogers & Kelloway, 1997)
2. Have you been threatened with property damage while at work? (Rogers & Kelloway, 1997)
3. Stole your possessions (Aquino et al., 1999)
4. Took stationery from your desk without later returning it (Martin & Hine, 2005)
5. Took items from your desk without prior permission (Martin & Hine, 2005)
6. Damaging property (Glomb, 2010)
7. Had your personal property defaced, damaged, or stolen (Neuman & Keashly, 2004)
8. Destroyed property belonging to someone at work (Spector et al., 2006)

Sexual Aggression (Perpetrator engages in verbal or physical abuse with sexualized content.)

1. Been subjected to unwanted attempts to touch, fondle, kiss, or grab you (Neuman & Keashly, 2004)
2. Been subjected to unwanted terms of endearment (Neuman & Keashly, 2004)
3. Been subjected to suggestive and/or offensive stories (Neuman & Keashly, 2004)
4. Been subjected to sexist remarks (Neuman & Keashly, 2004)
5. Been raped or sexually assaulted (Neuman & Keashly, 2004)
6. Sexual approaches and sexual offers (Zapf et al., 1996)
7. Sexual violence (Zapf et al., 1996)

Workplace Violence
Threats of Physical Violence Subtheme (Perpetrator threatens victim with physical harm.)

1. Threats of violence or physical abuse or actual abuse (Einarsen et al., 2009)
2. Have you been threatened with physical violence while at work? (Rogers & Kelloway, 1997)
3. Have you been threatened with a weapon while at work? (Rogers & Kelloway, 1997)
4. Threatened you with physical harm (Aquino et al., 1999)
5. Been threatened with physical harm (Neuman & Keashly, 2004)
6. Threat of physical violence (Zapf et al., 1996)
7. Threatened someone at work with violence (Spector et al., 2006)

Appendix. (*Continued*)

Actual Physical Violence Subtheme (Perpetrator engages in some form of physical abuse, such as hitting, throwing objects, or spitting.)

1. Intimidating behaviours such as finger-pointing, invasion of personal space, shoving, blocking your way (Einarsen et al., 2009)
2. Have you had objects thrown at you while you've been at work? (Rogers & Kelloway, 1997)
3. Have you been hit, kicked, grabbed, shoved, or pushed by anyone while you've been at work? (Rogers & Kelloway, 1997)
4. Have you been spat on or bitten by anyone while you've been at work? (Rogers & Kelloway, 1997)
5. Threw something at you when angry (Aquino et al., 1999)
6. Pushed or punched you (Aquino et al., 1999)
7. Pushed you or grabbed you? (Rospenda & Richman, 2004)
8. Threw something at you? (Rospenda & Richman, 2004)
9. Hit you physically? (Rospenda & Richman, 2004)
10. Physically assaulting you (Glomb, 2010)
11. Been kicked, bitten, or spat on (Neuman & Keashly, 2004)
12. Had someone hit you with an object (Neuman & Keashly, 2004)
13. Been pushed, shoved, thrown, or bumped into with unnecessary force (Neuman & Keashly, 2004)
14. Been assaulted with a weapon or other dangerous object (Neuman & Keashly, 2004)
15. Minor use of violence (Zapf et al., 1996)
16. Physical maltreatment (Zapf et al., 1996)
17. Hit or pushed someone at work (Spector et al., 2006)

Items that Could Not be Placed into any of the Above Themes

1. Competed with you for status and recognition? (Duffy et al., 2002)
2. Expresses anger at me when he/she is mad for another reason (Tepper, 2000)
3. Hints or signals from others that you should quit your job (Einarsen et al., 2009)
4. Endangered you with their reckless behavior (Aquino et al., 1999)
5. Pressured you to change your beliefs or opinions at work? (Rospenda & Richman, 2004)
6. Offered you a subtle or obvious bribe to do something that you did not agree with? (Rospenda & Richman, 2004)
7. Told you insulting jokes? (Rospenda & Richman, 2004)
8. Left notes, signs, or other materials which were meant to embarrass you? (Rospenda & Richman, 2004)
9. Threatened that they would "get back at you" if you resisted doing something that you thought was wrong, or if you challenged things about the workplace? (Rospenda & Richman, 2004)
10. Making threats (Glomb, 2010)
11. Whistle-blowing or telling supervisors about negative behavior (Glomb, 2010)
12. Been subjected to threats and/or harassment for "blowing the whistle" about activities at work (Neuman & Keashly, 2004)
13. Had signs or notes left that embarrassed you (Neuman & Keashly, 2004)

Appendix. (*Continued*)

14. Shown little empathy/sympathy when you were having a tough time (Neuman & Keashly, 2004)
15. Been subjected to temper tantrums when disagreeing with someone (Neuman & Keashly, 2004)
16. Had someone flaunt his/her status or treat you in a condescending manner (Neuman & Keashly, 2004)
17. Refusal to communicate with the person concerned by means of dropping hints without speaking out directly (Zapf et al., 1996)
18. Suspecting a person to be psychologically disturbed (Zapf et al., 1996)
19. Forced psychiatric treatment (Zapf et al., 1996)
20. Verbal threats (Zapf et al., 1996)

ABOUT THE AUTHORS

Maureen L. Ambrose is the Gordon J. Barnett Professor of Business Ethics in the College of Business at the University of Central Florida. She received her Ph.D. in 1986 from the University of Illinois at Urbana-Champaign. Her research interests include organizational fairness, ethics, and workplace deviance. Her work has appeared in the *Academy of Management Journal, Academy of Management Review*, *Journal of Applied Psychology*, *Journal of Management*, *Organizational Behavior and Human Decision Processes* and *Administrative Sciences Quarterly*. She is Fellow of the Academy of Management, the Society of Industrial and Organizational Psychology, and the Association for Psychological Science.

Caitlin E. Blackmore is currently a Ph.D. student at Wright State University, where she obtained her M.S. in Industrial/Organizational Psychology in 2014. She earned a bachelor's degree from Texas State University. Her research interests include personality measurement, counterproductive work behavior, and occupational stress.

Nathan A. Bowling is a Professor of Psychology and I/O Area Leader in the Psychology Ph.D. Program at Wright State University. He earned a Ph.D. in industrial/organizational psychology in 2005 from Central Michigan University. Nathan has published over 50 peer-refereed articles and book chapters. His research, which focuses on such topics as counterproductive work behavior, job satisfaction, and occupational stress, has appeared in the *Journal of Applied Psychology*, the *Journal of Occupational Health Psychology*, and the *Journal of Occupational and Organizational Psychology*. Nathan currently serves as an Associate Editor for *Work & Stress*.

Kelly A. Camus is currently an industrial and organizational psychology Ph.D. student at Wright State University. She graduated in 2011 with a B.A. in Psychology and French from Washington and Lee University. Her research interests include careless responding, workplace aggression, and personality.

Chu-Hsiang (Daisy) Chang is an associate professor at the Department of Psychology of Michigan State University. She received her Ph.D. in industrial and organizational psychology from the University of Akron. Her research interests focus on occupational health and safety, leadership, and motivation. Specifically, she studies issues related to occupational stress, workplace violence, and how employee motivation and organizational leadership intersect with issues concerning employee health and well-being. Her work has been published in *Academy of Management Review*, *Academy of Management Journal*, *Journal of Applied Psychology*, *Journal of Organizational Behavior*, *Organizational Behavior and Human Decision Processes*, *Psychological Bulletin*, and *Work & Stress*.

Aurora J. Dixon is a Ph.D. student and holds a University Distinguished Fellowship in the Organizational Psychology Department at Michigan State University. She entered the program at Michigan State in 2013 after receiving her Bachelor's of Science from The Georgia Institute of Technology. As an undergraduate student, she did research on individual differences, self-regulation, and motivation over the course of three years in the Knowledge and Skill Lab at Georgia Tech. Her current research interests include team dynamics and processes, as well as the fit between individuals and their organizations, with a specific focus on person-group fit.

Michelle K. Duffy is the Board of Overseers Professor of Work and Organizations in the Carlson School of Management. She has a Ph.D. in Organizational Behavior and Human Resource Management from the University of Arkansas and a Master's in Psychology from Xavier University. Her research focuses on: (1) the ways in which employee emotions and affect influences organizational outcomes, (2) the antecedents and consequences of antisocial behavior at work, and (3) the role of mindfulness in organizational life. Her current projects include a focus on employee envy, affective balance, resume fraud and mindfulness. She is an Associate Editor for the *Journal of Applied Psychology* and the *Journal of Management* and her work has been published in journals such as the *Journal of Applied Psychology*, the *Academy of Management Journal*, *Organizational Behavior and Human Decision Processes*, and *Personnel Psychology*. She received the Herbie Award for Excellence in Teaching in 2007 and the Carlson School of Management Award for Service in 2011. She became a SIOP and APA Fellow in 2012.

Stephanie Gumuchian is a research assistant working with Dr. Brett D. Thombs at the Lady Davis Institute for Medical Research of the Jewish

General Hospital in Montreal, Quebec. She is currently pursuing a Master's Degree in Psychiatry at McGill University. Her research focuses on examining the effectiveness of support groups for patients with scleroderma. Stephanie completed her BSc Honours in Psychology degree at Acadia University, where she was awarded a Deans' List Scholarship, Honours Summer Research Award, and the Dean's List and University Scholar awards for her academic achievements. Her undergraduate thesis, conducted under the supervision of Dr. Michael P. Leiter, examined the moderating effects of resilience on six areas of worklife and the development of burnout among a population of healthcare employees.

Jonathon R. B. Halbesleben, Ph.D., is the HealthSouth Chair of Health Care Management in the Department of Management at the University of Alabama. He received his Ph.D. in industrial/organizational psychology from the University of Oklahoma. His research concerning employee well-being and relationships in and out of the workplace has been published in such journals as the *Journal of Applied Psychology, Journal of Management, Journal of Organizational Behavior, Journal of Occupational Health Psychology*, and *Leadership Quarterly*, among others. He is the editor of the *Journal of Occupational and Organizational Psychology* and co-editor of *Research in Occupational Stress and Well-Being* and *Research in Personnel and Human Resources.*

Ronald L. Hess Jr is an Associate Professor of Marketing at the Mason School of Business at the College of William & Mary. He received his Ph. D. in marketing from Virginia Tech in 1999. His research interests are in the areas of customer responses to service failures, organizational recovery strategies, customer satisfaction, fairness, and relationships. He has published his research in *Organizational Behavior and Human Decision Processes, Journal of Retailing, Journal of the Academy of Marketing Science, Journal of Service Marketing, Marketing Letters,* and *International Journal of Retail & Distribution Management.*

Russell E. Johnson is an Associate Professor of Management in the Broad College of Business at Michigan State University. He received his Ph.D. in industrial and organizational psychology from the University of Akron in 2006. Dr. Johnson's research explores affective and cognitive mechanisms that underlie organizational behavior. His research has appeared in *Academy of Management Journal, Academy of Management Review, Journal of Applied Psychology*, and *Psychological Bulletin*, and has been cited in media outlets such as *Forbes, Psychology Today, TIME*, and *The*

Wall Street Journal. In 2013, he received the Distinguished Early Career Contributions Award for Science from the Society for Industrial and Organizational Psychology.

Jaclyn Koopmann is a Ph.D. Candidate in the Department of Management at the Warrington College of Business Administration at University of Florida. She earned her M.S. in Human Resource Management from Texas A&M University. Her research interests include team interpersonal processes and states, self-regulation, and workgroup socialization.

Michael P. Leiter, Ph.D. (Oregon) holds the Canada Research Chair in Occupational Health and Wellbeing at Acadia University where he is Professor of Psychology. At Acadia he directs the Centre for Organizational Research & Development (COR&D: http://cord.acadiau.ca) that applies high quality research methods to address organizational challenges. His research focuses on the psychological connections of people with their work: how people find meaning in their work and the crises that occur when connections with work go badly. He provides consulting services and maintains a blog www.workengagement.com where he focuses on interventions to improve the quality of worklife.

Matthew R. Leon is a doctoral student in the Department of Management at the Culverhouse College of Commerce at the University of Alabama. He received his Master's degree in Industrial/Organizational Psychology from the University of West Florida. His current research interests focus on employee well-being, adverse impacts of coworkers and workplace policies, and performance under stress. Before entering the University of Alabama's business administration doctoral program, Leon worked as a civilian research scientist for the Naval Aerospace Medical Research Laboratory and Naval Medicine Operational Training Center, with research focused on psychological and physiological resilience during combat as well as selection of Navy pilots.

Yihao Liu is a Ph.D. candidate in the Department of Management at the Warrington College of Business Administration at University of Florida. He earned his B.S. in Psychology from Peking University in China. His research has been focused on self-regulation and maladaptive behaviors, newcomer socialization and adjustment, and work teams.

Emily Peck is a Clinical Psychology graduate student at Acadia University working with Dr. Michael P. Leiter at the Centre for Organizational Research and Development in Nova Scotia, Canada. Emily completed her

First-Class Honours degree in Psychology from Brock University, where she won the Distinguished Graduating Student Award and the Queen Elizabeth II Scholarship. Emily's undergraduate thesis, which explored subjective life satisfaction trajectories among clinically depressed and anxious individuals, was recently published in the *Journal of Clinical Psychological Science*. While at Acadia University, Emily has received funding from the Nova Scotia Health Research Foundation for her Master's thesis. Emily's current research explores patterns of workplace mistreatment and burnout between and within days, using daily diary studies. In addition to research activities at the COR&D, Emily is also pursuing clinical training at Annapolis Valley Health Association in Nova Scotia.

Shani Pindek, Ph.D., is currently a visiting scholar at the University of South Florida. Her research interests include stress and other occupational health psychology topics, counterproductive work behavior and organizational climate. Dr. Pindek received her Ph.D. from Bar-Ilan University (Israel), and the topic of her dissertation was on organizational citizenship behaviors.

Kristin L. Scott is an Associate Professor at Clemson University and teaches courses in the areas of business management with an emphasis on human resources management (e.g., Fundamentals of HR, Advanced HR Topics). Her current research interests focus on workplace exclusion and dysfunctional organizational behavior, employee rewards and motivation, and occupational stress. Her articles have been published in the *Journal of Applied Psychology*, *Academy of Management Journal*, *Organizational Behavior and Human Decision Processes*, *Journal of Organizational Behavior*, *Journal of Management Studies* and *Research in Occupational Stress and Well-Being*. She received Clemson's College of Business and Behavioral Science Emerging Scholar Research Excellence Award (2012–2013).

Yifan Song is a Ph.D. student in the Department of Management at the Warrington College of Business Administration at University of Florida. She holds a B.S. in Psychology from Peking University in China. Her current research interests include newcomer adjustment, customer mistreatment, work motivation, and quantitative research methods.

Paul E. Spector is a distinguished professor of industrial/organizational (I/O) psychology and I/O doctoral program director at the University of South Florida. He is also director of the NIOSH funded Sunshine Education and Research Center's Occupational Health Psychology doctoral program. He is the Associate Editor for Point/Counterpoint for *Journal of Organizational Behavior*, Associate Editor for *Work & Stress*, and is on the editorial boards of *Journal of Applied Psychology* and *Human Resources Management Review*. He has research interests in both content and research methodology. His content research concerns occupational health and safety, including injuries, stress and workplace violence. His methodology interests involve the connections among measurement, statistics, and inference. He was noted as one of the most impactful management scholars in Aguinis, H., Suarez-González, I., Lannelongue, G., & Joo, H. (2012). Scholarly impact revisited. *Academy of Management Perspectives*, *26*, 105–132.

Regina Taylor is an Assistant Professor at Creighton University. She received her Ph.D. in 2015 from the University of Central Florida. Her research interests include ethics, workplace deviance and organizational fairness. Her work has appeared in the *Journal of Business Ethics* and *Human Relations*.

Mo Wang is a tenured Professor at the Warrington College of Business Administration at University of Florida. He is also the Director of Human Resource Research Center at University of Florida. He specializes in research areas of retirement and older worker employment, expatriate and newcomer adjustment, occupational health psychology, leadership and team processes, and advanced quantitative methodologies. He has received numerous awards for his research, and his research has been reported in the popular media, including the *NPR*, *BBC*, *Wall Street Journal*, and *New York Times*. Dr. Wang currently serves as the Editor for *Work, Aging, and Retirement* and an Associate Editor for *Journal of Applied Psychology*.